Race

BLACKWELL READINGS IN CONTINENTAL PHILOSOPHY

Series Editor: Simon Critchley, University of Essex

Each volume in this superb new series provides a detailed introduction to and overview of a central philosophical topic in the Continental tradition. In contrast to the author-based model that has hitherto dominated the reception of the Continental philosophical tradition in the English-speaking world, this series presents the central issues of that tradition, topics that should be of interest to anyone concerned with philosophy. Cutting across the stagnant ideological boundaries that mark the analytic/Continental divide, the series will initiate discussions that reflect the growing dissatisfaction with the organization of the English-speaking philosophical world. Edited by a distinguished international forum of philosophers, each volume provides a critical overview of a distinct topic in Continental philosophy through a mix of both classic and newly commissioned essays from both philosophical traditions.

The Body: Classic and Contemporary Readings
Edited and introduced by Donn Welton

Race
Edited by Robert Bernasconi

Forthcoming

The Religious
Edited by John Caputo

Race

Edited by

Robert Bernasconi

First published 2001

2 4 6 8 10 9 7 5 3 1

Blackwell Publishers Inc.
350 Main Street
Malden, Massachusetts 02148
USA

Blackwell Publishers Ltd
108 Cowley Road
Oxford OX4 1JF
UK

Library of Congress Cataloging-in-Publication Data

Race / edited by Robert Bernasconi
p.cm.—(Blackwell readings in Continental philosophy)
Includes bibliographical references and index.
ISBN 0-631-20782-1 (alk.paper)—ISBN 0-631-20783-X (pb : alk.paper)
1. Race. I. Bernasconi, Robert. II. Series
HT1521.R233 2001
305.8—dc21 00-034326

British Library Cataloging in Publication Data
A CIP catalogue record for this book is available from the British Library.

Typeset in Bembo on 10.5/12.5 pt
by Kolam Information Services Pvt. Ltd., Pondicherry, India.
Printed in Great Britain by Biddles Ltd, Guildford, Surrey

This book is printed on acid-free paper.

CONTENTS

ACKNOWLEDGMENTS

The editor and publishers gratefully acknowledge the following for permission to reprint copyright material:

Alcoff, Linda Martín, "Toward a Phenomenology of Racial Embodiment."

Bernasconi, Robert, "Who Invented the Concept of Race?" A revised and expanded version of a paper previously available only in *Defter*, 38, (1998) in a Turkish translation by Tendu Meriç.

Bernasconi, Robert, "The Invisibility of Racial Minorities in the Public Realm of Appearances." Reprinted from *Phenomenology of the Political*, eds. Kevin Thompson and Lester Embree, by permission of Kluwer Academic Publishers.

Butler, Judith, "Conversational Break: A Reply to Robert Gooding-Williams."

Du Bois, W. E. Burghardt, *The Conservation of Races*. The American Negro Academy, Occasional Papers, no. 2. Washington, DC, 1897.

Dumont, Louis, "Class, Racism and 'Stratification'." From Louis Dumont, *Homo Hierarchicus: The Caste System and Its Implications. Complete Revised English Edition*, translated by Mark Sainsbury, Louis Dumont, and Basia Gulati, 1980, pp. 247–66. Reprinted by permission of the publisher, the University of Chicago Press.

Fanon, Frantz, "The Lived Experience of the Black." Translated by Valentine Moulard from Frantz Fanon, "L'expérience vécue du Noir," *Esprit*, 19, (179), May 1951, pp. 657–79 by permission of *Esprit*.

Gooding-Williams, Robert, "Race, Multiculturalism and Democracy."

Kant, Immanuel, "On the Use of Teleological Principles in Philosophy." Newly translated by Jon Mark Mikkelsen.

Lott, Tommy, "Du Bois's Anthropological Notion of Race."

Nardal, Paulette, "The Awakening of Race Consciousness." Annotated re-translation by T. Denean Sharpley-Whiting from "Eveil de la Conscience de Race," *La Revue du Monde Noir*, 6, 1932, pp. 25–31.

Sartre, Jean-Paul, "Black Orpheus." Reprinted from *The Massachusetts Review*, © 1965 The Massachusetts Review, Inc. Translated by John MacCombie with permission for minor revisions and additional endnotes by Robert Bernasconi.

Senghor, Léopold, "Negritude and Modernity or Negritude as a Humanism for the Twentieth Century." From *Liberté t. III. Négritude et civilisation de l'universel* by Léopold Sédar Senghor. © Editions du Seuil, 1977. Used by permission. Newly translated by Valentine Moulard.

Visweswaran, Kamala, "Is there a Structuralist Analysis of Racism?"

The publishers apologize for any errors or omissions in the above list, and would be grateful to be notified of any corrections that should be incorporated in the next edition or reprint of this book.

The editor would like to express his thanks to Stacy Keltner and Christine Harris for their invaluable assistance preparing the volume.

INTRODUCTION

To date, the philosophical discussion of race in the English-speaking world has been largely dominated by Anglo-American philosophy. Nothing shows this better than the continuing concentration on Anthony Appiah's questioning of the reality of race: "The truth is that there are no races: there is nothing in the world that can do all we ask 'race' to do for us."[1] Even though not all the participants in this debate can be described as Anglo-American philosophers, the agenda was set by Appiah's philosophical naturalism. His argument was, if the hard sciences have no place for race, then that should be the end of the matter. However, under pressure from his critics, Appiah was forced to concede that to combat racism something like a notion of race had to be retained.[2] Many philosophers, determined to interrogate the concept of race and its continuing effects, have come to recognize that a broader approach is made possible by drawing on the resources offered not only by biology, but also, for example, by history, literature, anthropology and sociology. This broader approach has long been practiced by certain philosophers within the traditions of existential phenomenology, structuralism, and post-structuralism. The aim of the present anthology is to make some of those resources more readily available. Classic texts have been coupled with original essays offering commentary and discussion of those texts so as to make the volume particularly suitable for class use. Some readers may find it helps to read the second text of each pair first.

The volume begins with an excursion into the history of the scientific concept of race. In my essay, "Who Invented the Concept of Race?", I rehearse some of the decisive moments in the history of the concept in the eighteenth century. The idea that the scientific concept of race had an inventor may be artificial, but it helps to concentrate the mind. According to Deleuze and Guattari, philosophy is about the continuous creation of concepts.[3] They also said that concepts are signed.[4] One way of understanding my essay would be to say that I argue that the creation of the concept of race can serve as a prime example of what they meant and that the concept of race bears Kant's signature. Even though the word "race" had been in circulation for almost a century as a way of organizing human beings into a few groups on the basis primarily of their visible characteristics, it was not until 1775 that Kant became the first to define it clearly[5] In this essay I also try to identify the problems to which Kant thought "race" in his sense was a solution. In brief, Kant wanted to be able to account for permanent hereditary characteristics, particularly skin color, without having recourse to polygenesis.

The authority which science lent to the concept of race was an invaluable resource for racism, but more significant was the racism that science incorporated and developed. Both are evident in Kant's 1788 essay "On the Use of Teleological Principles in Philosophy." It is printed here because, in spite of its initial difficulty, it provides an excellent introduction to some of the theoretical issues raised by the concept of race in its Kantian formulation.[6] It is in this essay that it is most apparent that an interest in race is not a diversion for Kant, but goes to the heart of the issue in which the critical project culminate: the unification of mechanism and teleology. "On the Use of Teleological Principles in Philosophy" opens the way to the discussion of teleological judgment in the *Critique of Judgment.* Much of the current philosophical discussion of the concept of race is hampered by the fact that the history of race theory is not better known.

The debate about the reality of race opened by Appiah began with his critical reading of Du Bois's "The Conservation of Races." The subsequent controversy has largely continued to focus on a few sentences from that essay where Du Bois defines race as follows:

> It is a vast family of human beings, generally of common blood and language, always of common history, traditions and involuntarily striving together for the accomplishment of certain more or less vividly conceived ideals of life.

Appiah took apart the definition clause by clause. Nevertheless, there is so much more to Du Bois's essay than the definition itself, which may not have been of particular significance to him anyway. Although some participants in the debate make claims about what was and was not widely thought about race in 1897 when Du Bois wrote his essay, there is still a great deal of historical work to be done to restore Du Bois's definition of race to its context. In addition to the scientific writers of the day, like Huxley and Ratzel, whom Du Bois mentions, Social Darwinism was clearly of crucial importance to Du Bois. Du Bois was not opposed to Social Darwinism, but was critical of its misuse. Du Bois was also concerned to respond to Frederick Douglass's arguments in favor of the early assimilation of Blacks into the larger American population. In addition, Du Bois's essay must be seen in relation to the philosophical writings on race of Hegel, Herder, and Trietschke, with their sweeping arguments about the role a people or race has in history. In "The Conservation of Races" Du Bois is more concerned to engage that debate than the question of the reality of race. Du Bois had found the proper answer to Kant and Hegel. If, as Kant and Hegel believed, Africans had not made a major contribution to history, then, so Du Bois seems to argue, on their own principles, this should be taken as evidence that the future belonged to Africans. Otherwise one would be obliged to question the foresight of that providence on which Kant and, in his own terms, Hegel relied for establishing the place of race in history at all. It was a brilliant internal refutation.

Tommy Lott has been at the forefront of philosophers trying to offer a broader reading of Du Bois's essay, one that places "The Conservation of Races" in the context of Du Bois's thought as a whole.[7] In his essay for this volume, Lott draws on his extensive study of Du Bois's anthropological writings to offer a more rounded account of Du Bois's concept of race than that which is found throughout most of the secondary literature. Future studies of Du Bois will be ill-advised to ignore the more complete picture of Du Bois that emerges from Lott's essay. Lott argues that Du Bois used racial categories to establish a Black presence in history for largely pragmatic reasons, in spite of his own skepticism toward the scientific concept of race. Furthermore, Lott has put the question of racial intermingling at the very center of Du Bois's concern, and he has shown how Du Bois saw the contemporary science of race as an effect of racism. The fact of the matter is that it is not so much the reality of race as racial purity that has been at the center of discussions of race over the last two hundred years. One fails to see how race has functioned as an instrument of power if one sees it only in terms of classification. It is important to see the way that the taboo against race mixing, which is reflected, particularly in the United States, in the association of Whiteness with racial purity, is part of the logic of the concept of race that needs to be deconstructed.

The next six essays in the volume are all related in one way or another to the negritude movement and the responses it provoked. Strongly indebted to the Harlem Renaissance, the negritude movement arose in France in the 1930s among Blacks who realized that whether they came from Africa or the Caribbean, the White racist gaze brought them together. T. Denean Sharpley-Whiting is currently writing a book on the women of the negritude movement and her essay on Paulette Nardal in this volume belongs to that research. Sharpley-Whiting sketches the early history of the negritude movement and illustrates its powerful mode of expression. The decisive contribution of her ground-breaking research has been to highlight the importance of women writers who, until now, have been largely ignored. Sharpley-Whiting argues that Black women like Paulette Nardal, who were objectified through the gaze not only as Black, but also as women, were particularly well-placed to understand the operation of racism in daily life. On this basis of their experiences they recognized the need to develop race-consciousness as a way to combat racism.

Sartre's "Black Orpheus" has been recognized as an important moment in the theoretical elaboration of negritude from the time of its first publication in 1948. Sartre had been asked at short notice to write the Preface to an anthology of poems by Black writers edited by Léopold Senghor. The result, "Black Orpheus," was a major essay in its own right. Translated into English at least three different times, the best of these translations has been reprinted here with some minor revisions only where Sartre's philosophical terminology had not been accurately reflected. In addition the authors of the various poems quoted by Sartre have been identified in the notes. When the essay was originally published as a preface, the poems were, of course, readily available in the same volume. Although Sartre made no effort to specify the authors of the various quotations, when he published extracts from the essay in *Les Temps modernes* or republished the whole piece in the third volume of *Situations*, it seems only just that the authors of these wonderful poems be acknowledged by name.

"Black Orpheus" has often been severely criticized from various angles. Some critics focused on his legitimation of an "anti-racist racism," although the idea, widely regarded as scandalous at the time, seems more familiar now. Indeed, one can think of some affirmative action programs in these terms. The most powerful criticism is that to be found in Fanon's essay "The Lived Experience of the Black." Fanon objected to the way Sartre located negritude within a dialectic. Negritude was the negative movement of this dialectic. It was the response to anti-Black racism. Nevertheless, it was Blacks, not Whites, who were asked to renounce race pride in favor of universalism. Fanon's objection was carefully phrased. He did not specifically deny the dialectic. He merely said, "I needed not to know." This same dialectic can be found in Senghor, Martin Luther King, Steve Biko, and perhaps even Du Bois, judging from the second article of the creed of the Negro Academy as formulated in "The Conservation of Races."

Sartre had no more ambiguous reader than Senghor himself who, at times, welcomed "Black Orpheus" and, at other times, complained about it. In the essay printed here, "Negritude and Modernity," Senghor responds positively to Sartre's formulation "anti-racist racism" as a way of describing the negritude movement. This essay is translated here in an effort to correct some of the current misconceptions about Senghor's philosophy. Although his poetry is readily available in English translation, most of his philosophical essays are not. This is surprising given the current interest in African philosophy and is perhaps best explained by the fact that the idea of negritude is currently out of favor.

The critics of the negritude movement have found much to question in Senghor's characterizations of Blacks as emotional, but it is remarkable how little attention has been given to Senghor's advocacy of cultural miscegenation. There is a widespread misconception that the negritude movement was committed to developing a conceptuality that would be free from Western influence. Nothing could be further from the truth and this essay shows why. Senghor has acknowledged that, in his first formulations of negritude in the 1930s, he was too readily influenced by Gobineau and the other discourses on race being expressed in Europe at that time. But in promoting both cultural and biological miscegenation, Senghor clearly broke free from those discourses. Senghor's essay is important not only for what it says about African philosophy, but also, and perhaps above all, for the light it sheds on his idea of a universal humanism quite different from Western humanism.

I have already mentioned Fanon's "The Lived Experience of the Black" for its critique of negritude. This essay, published in *Esprit* in 1951, is here translated for the first time. Although the essay was republished with only relatively minor changes as chapter 5 of *Black Skin, White Masks*, the English translator of that book was more concerned with readability than philosophical nuance. This is already shown in the fact that the title," L'expérience vécue du Noir," was translated as "The Fact of Blackness." Valentine Moulard's translation published here for the first time allows the philosophical nuances of Fanon's essay to emerge. When Fanon republished this essay in *Black Skin, White Masks*, he presented it as a "phenomenological description."[8] It is certainly that, but by its integration of poetry and psychoanalysis, and by its creative use of language, "The Lived Experience of the Black" is one of the most innovative exercises in existential phenomenology to date. Perhaps only Merleau-Ponty came close to accomplishing anything of similar sophistication and creativity.

According to Simone de Beauvoir, Fanon heard Merleau-Ponty lecture in Lyons.[9] So far as I am aware, it is not known how often Fanon attended his lectures or which lecture courses he heard, but Fanon had the opportunity to hear Merleau-Ponty's courses *Soul and Body according to Malbranche, Maine de Biran, and Bergson* and *Language and Communication.*[10] Jeremy Wheate persuasively presents the internal evidence for reading Fanon not only as a student of Merleau-Ponty, but also an important critic. Wheate argues that Fanon's attempt to understand interracial relations and racialized bodies requires a revision at very least of Merleau-Ponty's approach to agency, freedom, and history.

The present anthology is predominantly concerned with race as conceived in terms of Blacks and Whites. A study of the European and North American concept of race will inevitably highlight the image of Blacks among Whites, because it was with reference to Blacks specifically that European scientists and philosophers, like Kant, found it necessary to develop this concept. That is to say, it was primarily with reference to Blacks that Whites found themselves speculating about polygenesis, natural inequality and the permanence of racial characteristics. However, the work of Louis Dumont introduces a broader perspective and, by taking up the notion of caste, explores the possibility of a comparative approach.

Kamala Visweswaran establishes the proper context for rereading Dumont's essay not only by recalling the sources on which he drew and assessing the strengths and limitations of his comparative, Structuralist, approach, but also the argument of Dumont's subsequent and highly debated classic *Homo Hierarchicus*. Visweswaran also shows how Dumont revived Myrdal's attempt to draw a connection between egalitarianism and racism. Even though she exposes problems with the historical basis of the argument that Dumont employs to describe how racism succeeded slavery in the USA, Visweswaran demonstrates the necessity of taking seriously this question of the possible complicity between egalitarianism and racism. Although many philosophers are content simply to dismiss the question, reading Kant's essay "On the Use of Teleological Principles of Philosophy" renders it all the more pressing.

With Robert Gooding-William's paper, "Race, Multiculturalism and Democracy," the anthology returns to the question of racial identities in the USA. Although African-American identity is his main focus, he also explores other examples. Within a wide-ranging essay that provides a valuable introduction to some of the recent debates in this area, Gooding-Williams defends the approach associated with the politics of recognition.

Judith Butler's response to Robert Gooding-Williams's at Pacific A.P.A. in March 1997 was an important moment in the continuing dialogue between race theory and feminism. Although Butler does not discuss feminism specifically, it is clear that her insights into identity and identification arise out of her engagement with gender issues. As the example of Paulette Nardal has already shown, what we call "race" and "gender" do not – or should not – represent two separate fields. Race and gender cut across each other in ways that make it impossible for us to suppose we have an adequate analysis of one, if the other term has been ignored. The same must be said of "class" too, discussion of which is represented in this anthology by the contributions of Sartre and Dumont.

With Linda Alcoff's essay, the volume returns to the task of correcting the tendency of most discussions of race to focus on the Black–White polarity, but with questions of identity and identification still very much at the center. Linda Alcoff provides an excellent example of the use of biography and autobiography in the counter discourse against racism. After distinguishing various approaches to race, she opts for contextualism and in this paper develops it in what she calls its subjectivist form. Particularly instructive is the way she succeeds in employing the insights of existential phenomenology, especially Merleau-Ponty, for this purpose. I decided, somewhat as an afterthought, to include my own piece "The Invisibility of Racial Minorities in the Public Realm of Appearances" because it seemed to complement nicely Alcoff's essay. Like Alcoff, I use the resources of phenomenology. My concern is to show how the much discussed invisibility of Blacks and other racial minorities is sustained by White invisibility, in the sense that Whites often fail to think of themselves as raced, at the very same time that they see "non-Whites" as racialized. This brings us back to the issue of the gaze that is discussed in many of the essays in the volume, most notably those by Nardal, Sartre, and Fanon. That the gaze that sees race so readily sustains racism is one of the lessons phenomenology has to teach. The gaze is an instrument of objectification, as Sartre eloquently showed already in *Being and Nothingness*. But it is important to know how racism operates, particularly in an environment where the lack of overtly racist theories or remarks is often cited as evidence that racism is no longer the issue it once was.

Although the primary focus of this anthology is race and not racism, the two are not always easy to separate. Indeed, the current debate on the legitimacy of the concept has come to focus on the use of the term "race" as a resource to combat racism. Race can be employed as an oppressive device, but once it has been embedded into the institutional structures of society, the concept of race is often needed to combat those structures. This recalls a more general truth: discussions of race tend to be highly contextualized. What is liberatory at one time and place can be oppressive at another. However much care one takes, this remains a highly charged, unstable, discourse. As a result, discussions of race threaten always to create further misunderstandings. The optimism that assumes that dialogue is automatically a way forward is nowhere so likely to be misplaced. And yet, if attention is given to the history of race theory, which is what at least half of the present anthology offers, there is at least the hope of dispelling some of the ignorance that still surrounds the notion of race.

Robert Bernasconi
The University of Memphis

Notes

1 The debate was initiated by Anthony Appiah's "The Uncompleted Argument: Du Bois and the Illusion of Race," *Critical Inquiry*, Autumn 1985, 12(1), p. 35.

2 Appiah called this "thing" like "race", which he was forced to posit, a "racial identity." Its most important feature for him was that talk of racial identities did not entail a belief in racial essences, even though it made reference to a history of racial essences. This is not the place to debate Appiah's conception, but it is hard not to come to the conclusion that he thereby conceded under another name most of what had made his initial view distinctive. In other words, Appiah's initial approach led nowhere. It is also striking that, to develop his new

view, Appiah drew on Sartre, albeit he reads Sartre through Ian Hacking. K. Anthony Appiah, "Race, Culture, Identity: Misunderstood Connections," *Color Conscious*, (Princeton: Princeton University Press, 1996), pp. 78–82.

3 Gilles Deleuze and Félix Guattari, *Qu'est-ce que la philosophie?*, Paris, Minuit, 1991, p. 13; trans. Hugh Tomlinson and Graham Burchell, *What is Philosophy?*, New York, Columbia University Press, 1994, p. 8.

4 *Qu'est-ce que la philosophie?*, p. 13; trans. *What is Philosophy?*, p. 7.

5 I. Kant, "Von den verschiedenen Racen der Menschen," *Gesammelte Schriften*, (Berlin: Walter de Gruyter, 1902-), pp. 429–43. Kant revised and expanded the essay in 1777. An English translation by Jon Mark Mikkelsen under the title "Of the Different Human Races," can be found in *The Idea of Race*, eds. R. Bernasconi and T. Lott, (Indianapolis: Hackett, 2000), pp. 8–22.

6 I. Kant, "Über den Gebrauch teleologischer Principien in der Philosophie," *Gesammelte Schriften*, (Berlin: Walter de Gruyter, 1902-), pp. 159–84. The page numbers to this edition are contained in parentheses within the main body of Jon Mark Mikkelsen's translation in Chapter 2 (this volume).

7 See Tommy Lott, "Du Bois on the Invention of Race," *The Invention of Race*, (Oxford: Blackwell, 1999), pp. 47–66.

8 Frantz Fanon, *Peau noire, Masques blancs*, (Paris: Seuil, 1952), p. 87; trans. Charles Lam Markmann, *Black Skin, White Masks*, (New York: Grove Press, 1967), p. 80.

9 Simone de Beauvoir, *La force des choses*, (Paris: Gallimard, 1963), p. 620; trans. Richard Howard, *Hard Times. Force of Circumstances II*, (New York: Paragon, 1992), p. 314.

10 For a full list of Merleau-Ponty's teaching at that time, see Hugh Silverman, "Translator's Preface," in M. Merleau-Ponty, *Consciousness and the Acquisition of Language*, (Evanston: Northwestern University Press, 1973), pp. xxxvi–ix.

PART I

KANT AND THE INVENTION OF RACE

1

WHO INVENTED THE CONCEPT OF RACE?

Kant's Role in the Enlightenment Construction of Race

Robert Bernasconi

Who invented the scientific concept of race? This question admits of a variety of answers depending on what one takes to be decisive about the concept and on whether one believes that what defines the moment in which a technical term is introduced is the first usage of the word in the required sense or the definition that secures its status and influence. It will quickly become clear that by "the inventor of the concept of race" I mean the one who gave the concept sufficient definition for subsequent users to believe that they were addressing something whose scientific status could at least be debated. The terms and basis of the definition might continue to be scrutinized, but, so long as the term was being used only loosely, it made no sense to contest the concept. The invention of the concept of race in this sense took place some time after the introduction of the broad division of peoples on the basis of color, nationality, and other inherited characteristics that could not be overcome subsequently, as religious differences could be overcome by conversion.[1] One need only think of the purity of blood statutes of fifteenth-century Spain that were used against the *conversos*, Jews who had converted to Christianity but who were still not accepted. Then there were the debates in sixteenth-century Spain when the opponents of Bartolomé de Las Casas justified the mistreatment of Native Americans on the grounds that they were not human. One can also look at the Atlantic trade in African slaves that began in the sixteenth century and was already a large operation in the seventeenth century. It was possible for the Spanish or the English to exploit Jews, Native Americans, and Africans, as Jews, Native Americans, and Africans, without having the concept of race, let alone being able to appeal to a rigorous system of racial classification. We have no difficulty identifying these as cases of racism, but they were not sustained by a scientific concept of race. However, the introduction of that concept lent an air of apparent legitimacy to these practices. By investing the concept of race with a scientific status, members of the academy certainly have in the past contributed to making racism more respectable and have even seemed to provide a basis for it, but the academy of itself is now virtually powerless to undo those effects. However, we can at least try to throw some light on that history.

In the first section of this paper, I introduce some of the main candidates for the title of the inventor of the concept of race and give a preliminary assessment of their claims to that title. The remainder of the paper is largely concerned with providing supporting evidence for this outline. I begin that task by identifying, in the second section of my paper, the main concern that called for the specific concept of "race" that Kant introduced. I find it in the revival of the theory of polygenesis in seventeenth-century Europe as a response to the growing awareness of the diversity of peoples across the world. Even though polygenesis had relatively few proponents and tended not to be presented with scientific rigor, it represented such a clear challenge to the Biblical narrative that Kant could not ignore it. In the third section, I examine Buffon's rule for the identification of species which is at the center of much of the discussion of race in the second half of the eighteenth century, not least because it served the proponents of monogenesis. In the fourth section, I turn to the question that obsessed so many European scientists at that time, the question of why Africans are black. It is in this context that one can best approach the crucial question of the relation between race and teleology. In the fifth and final section, I show that the concept of race played a part in a decisive debate conducted in Germany during the final decades of the eighteenth century. it was during this debate that the reality of race was contested for the first time. Today, when there is once again a philosophical debate being conducted about the reality of race,[2] it is worth recalling the outlines of that first debate, not least because philosophical debates have a habit of repeating themselves.

I

It is usually agreed that the term "race" was first used in something like its contemporary meaning at the end of the seventeenth century. Europeans had long been aware of the multiplicity of different peoples and had often embellished their sense of it with tales of fabulous monsters. Since the end of the fifteenth century, Europeans had been increasingly exposed to travel reports written by missionaries, traders and explorers that detailed some of the differences between peoples, although that was rarely their main focus of attention. On some occasions "specimens" were brought back by travellers to exhibit to the curious. However, in the sixteenth and seventeenth centuries, the primary issue raised by the diversity of peoples was theological and focused on the question of baptism.[3] It was not until the end of the seventeenth century that European scholars attempted to organize the mass of information now available to them and to sort the different peoples into a few groupings. In 1684 an anonymous essay, now usually attributed to François Bernier, acknowledged four or five different types. He did not give them all names, but they correspond roughly to Europeans, Africans, Orientals and Laplanders, while allowing for the possibility of two additional types, the Native Americans and the Hottentots. Within the first group, that included Europeans, he also placed Moroccans, Egyptians, and Indians. What made Bernier's classification so important retrospectively was not the list itself, but the fact that he employed the term "race" for the purpose. Nevertheless, his title, "A new division of the earth, according to the different species or races of men who inhabit it," with its equation of race and species, also indicates that the terminology was not yet fixed or precise.[4] The absence of any distinction between race and species is reflected in Leibniz's response to Bernier.

> I remember having read somewhere, but I cannot locate the passage again, that a certain traveler had divided humans into certain tribes, races, or classes. He gave one particular race to the Lapps and Samoyedes, another to the Chinese and neighboring peoples, another to Negroes, and still another to the Caffres, or Hottentots. Further, in America, there is a marvelous difference between the Galibs, or Caribs, who are very brave and indeed spirited, and the people of Paraguay, who seem to be children or novices all their lives. That does not prevent all human beings who inhabit the earth from being of the same race, which has been altered by different climates, just as we see that beasts and plants change their nature and improve or degenerate.[5]

The distinction between race and species, that would preoccupy subsequent theorists, is here elided for lack of a clear terminology.

That Bernier was not particularly interested in proposing a rigorous system of classification is shown not only by the fact that he did not name the races, but also by the way he allotted over half of his brief essay to his observations of where he had seen beautiful women, which he acknowledged was everywhere. The fact that that the issue of sexual desire and the stereotyping of women was part of the first discourse on race should not surprise us given its subsequent history. However, Bernier also anticipated one of the most disputed terms of the scientific debate over race when, in the only theorizing on the notion of race or species that he pursued, he referred to different seeds (*semences*): beauty "arises not only from the water, the diet, the soil, and the air, but also from the seed which must be peculiar to certain races or species."[6] Bernier may not have taken the task of classifying peoples very far, but during the eighteenth century it was increasingly performed using the methods developed for the classification of plants and animals in the burgeoning discipline of natural history. Even so, the status accorded to the types into which varieties of peoples were grouped was left unclear. This was reflected in the lack of a consistent terminology for describing those types. "Race" was only one of many words used for this purpose. It was not accorded a privilege and its application in this context does not seem to have stopped it from being used more often in other ways. Some scholars have sought the origin of specifically racial antagonism in the desire of certain capitalist interests to find a basis for their exploitation of Native Americans and Africans,[7] but these interests seem to have been satisfied with broad designations loosely defined. There is clear evidence that many slave owners were attentive to the country of origin of their slaves and in some cases assisted them in their attempts to perpetuate a sense of national groupings.[8] The initial pressure leading to the development of the concept of race, insofar as it was called to make sense of diversity in the appearance and customs of different peoples, seems to have come from reconciling the information provided by the travelogues, both new and old, with the religious narrative through which Europeans understood the meaning of history. However, these forces were in play for some time before they gave rise within the academy to a determinate notion of race. The delay in producing the concept of race needs to be the focus of investigation as much as its eventual introduction does. Indeed, even one hundred years after Bernier, the term "race" was, according to one authority, still characterized "by [the] total absence of any precise meaning."[9]

The idea of a single author of the concept of race is at best only a useful fiction, but I shall argue that, if any one person should be recognized as the author of the first theory of race worthy of the name, it should be the German philosopher Immanuel Kant. There is no shortage among Kant's writings of remarks that would today unquestionably be characterized as racist. Although the most notorious comment is his remark in *Observations on the Feeling of the Beautiful and Sublime*, that the fact that someone was completely black from head to toe was clear proof that what he said was stupid,[10] it is by no means the most problematic. Because I have discussed Kant's racism elsewhere,[11] I shall concentrate here on the philosophical motivation for his definition of race as a "class distinction between animals of one and the same line of descent (*Stamm*), which is unfailingly transmitted by inheritance" (AA VIII 100).

Kant expended more energy on securing the concept of race than one would ever guess from the secondary literature about him. In 1775 Kant published the first version of "Of the Different Human Races" (AA II 429–43) as the preliminary announcement for his lectures on *Physical Geography*.[12] Kant regularly lectured on Anthropology and on Physical Geography at the University of Königsberg. Both courses included discussions of race drawn from his own independent reading of the travelogues, which were still the main source of information for the natural scientists of his day. However, they did not provide the same level of theoretical discussion to be found in "Of the Different Human Races." Kant prefaced the first publication of the essay with a statement that the essay, like the lecture course it was advertising, was more like a game than profound investigation (AA II 429), but this warning was dropped when he expanded the essay for republication in 1777.[13] The two versions of this essay were in fact Kant's only publications between the 1770 inaugural lecture and the first edition of the *Critique of Pure Reason* in 1781. However, an even better guide to Kant's preoccupation with the concept of race is that he came to its defense during the 1780s, when he was completing the critical project. Even though "Of the Different Human Races" was reprinted again in 1783,[14] Kant published "Bestimmung des Begriffs einer Menschenrasse" in November 1785. In this essay Kant largely reiterates his earlier position. It is probable that he felt obliged to do so as a result of Herder's denial of race in the second part of his *Ideen zur Philosophie der Geschichte der Menschheit*, which had appeared in August of the same year. However, in 1786, under the title "Still More About the Human Races," Georg Forster attacked Kant's position. Georg Forster, who favored empirical science, challenged Kant's distinction between natural history and natural description, a distinction Kant had employed to justify giving a role to teleological explanation in science.[15] Georg Forster was better placed than most to marshall the information about the South Pacific which reached Europe in the second half of the eighteenth century through reports of the voyages of George Anson, Samuel Wallis, Phillip Carteret, Louis Antoine de Bougainville, and James Cook.[16] Georg Forster had accompanied his father on Captain Cook's voyage and assisted his father with the task of writing a report on the voyage.[17] It was small wonder therefore that Kant, in his reply early in 1788 in "On the Use of Teleological Principles in Philosophy," retreated from some of his empirical claims and turned to a discussion of method (AA VIII 157–84).[18] This essay, which was predominantly concerned with race, was not in any sense an interruption of the writing of his major philosophical works. Indeed, it appears that it was in the course of this controversy that Kant recognized that he needed to expand his Critique of Taste into what we now know as the *Critique of Judgment* by adding the second part on the Critique of Teleological Judgement.[19] A number of the most important questions posed in the course of the Critique of Teleological Judgment can be understood as suggested by issues Kant raised in his essay on race fifteen years earlier.

My claim about Kant's place in the construction of the scientific concept of race is not new. In the 1920s Walter Scheidt maintained that although Buffon was the first anthropologist, Kant was the originator of "the first theory of race which really merits the name."[20] There is no doubt that Scheidt had arrived at this conclusion after a careful study of the history of the concept, although perhaps because he was Director of the Rassenbiologische Institut of the Hanseatic University at Hamburg, there might have been suspicion that he had been misled by a desire to find support for the concept from such an exalted source. However, Kant's role in establishing the concept of race has been widely acknowledged by historians of the concept of race.[21] It is only philosophers who have ignored it, until Emmanuel Eze restated the argument for them.[22] Even so, a great deal more work needs to be done, both to establish the context of Kant's discussion of race with reference to his sources and to clarify the various aspects of Kant's theory of race that have been treated largely in isolation from each other. Before exploring Kant's theory, I will examine other possible candidates for the dubious honor of being the inventor of the concept of race.

The Swedish researcher, Carolus Linnaeus, certainly contributed to what would subsequently become race thinking in the twelve editions of his *Systema naturae sive regna tria naturae* that were published from 1735 until his death. Linnaeus was the first to include human beings within a formal classification of animals and plants. He included under the heading *homo sapiens* four geographical varieties, corresponding not only to the four regions of the world then recognized by Europeans, but also to the medieval theory of the four humors.[23] Although a great deal is sometimes made of the fact that they were not organized hierarchically, Linnaeus's descriptions included not only physical differences but also differences in character, clearly derived in large part from stereotypes already emerging in the travel literature. So one finds in the tenth edition of 1758, after the feral or wild man, the following classes: *homo americanus*, who was allegedly obstinate, content, free, and governed by habit; *homo Europaeus*, who was allegedly gentle, very acute, inventive and governed by customs or religious observances (*ritus*); *homo Asiaticus*, who was allegedly severe, haughty, covetous, and governed by opinions; and *homo Africanus*, who was allegedly crafty, indolent, negligent and governed by caprice.[24] However, although Linnaeus took great care in making his classifications and subjected them to constant revision, he made little attempt to clarify the status of the varieties thus differentiated. There was a tension in his works between his theoretical commitment to the constancy of species and the clear evidence to the contrary that was available to him.[25] The above list was followed by a record of *homo monstrosus* after whom Linnaeus proceeded to *homo troglodytes*. Linnaeus also appears to have been willing to try to accommodate in his *Systema natura* that for which he did not have clear evidence.[26]

From the outset, Buffon presented his theory as an alternative to that of Linnaeus. He began the publication of his *Histoire naturelle générale et particulière* in 1749 with a discussion of methodology that rejected the classifications of Linnaeus as arbitrary.[27] In spite of the fact that Buffon tended to disdain questions of classification and nomenclature, it has sometimes been claimed that Buffon was the originator of the concept of race.[28] The importance of Buffon's definition of species and the means by which he secured it is undeniable. To Buffon, a species was "a constant succession of similar individuals that can reproduce together" (HN IV 384–5). The definition, presented in his essay on the ass from 1753, was widely disseminated, so that, for example, it is quoted verbatim in Diderot's *Encyclopédie*.[29] The definition was accompanied by an account of how one separates one species from another: the mark of separation lay where a pair of individuals are unable to reproduce with each other across successive generations. Often known as Buffon's rule, it seems to have been expounded by John Ray in the seventeenth century.[30] According to Buffon, species were fixed and constant, although he did concede that the general prototype that was found in the first individual and that was imprinted in all subsequent individuals left some room for variation (HN IV 215–16). This variation was represented by the various types, breeds, or races, but those terms themselves remained without clear definition.[31]

The argument that Buffon introduced a determinate concept of race is hampered by his failure not only to propose a definition of race as he did of species, but also to use the term with any consistency. The best evidence that he was working toward a precise notion of race is to be found in "On the Degeneration of Animals" where, in 1766, Buffon indicated that quasi-permanent change from an original stock could take place as a result of climate, geography and especially food. In this context Buffon came to acknowledge "constant and general characters by which one recognizes the races and even the different nations which compose the human genus" (HN XIV 316). However, this formulation is not as decisive as it might appear to be. In 1753 in his essay on "The Ass," Buffon had already applied his rule and the notion of degeneration to the variations within the human species. There he had focused on the differences between Blacks and Whites, Laplanders and Patagonians, but the addition of Giants and Dwarfs to the list, as well as mention of the enormous legs of certain people in Ceylon and the occurrence of six fingers and toes in certain families, shows that he did not consider that his framework was sufficient to establish a new category (HN IV 387–9). Indeed, he explicitly warned against doing so. Having identified the difference between two species on the basis that they cannot give rise to a succession of individuals that can mix, he added:

> This is the most fixed point that we have in Natural History; all other resemblances and differences that we can grasp in the comparison of beings, are neither so constant, real, nor certain. These intervals are also the sole lines of separation that one will find in our work. We shall not divide beings otherwise than they are in fact. Each species, each succession of individuals which reproduce and cannot mix will be considered apart and treated separately, and we shall not use *families*, kinds, orders and classes which are set by Nature. (HN IV 385–6).

Even after 1766 Buffon demonstrated no clear commitment to the terminology of race, still less an interest in clarifying its theoretical status.

A word should also be said about Blumenbach's claim to being the originator of the anthropological concept of race.[32] Although his name is often mentioned in this regard, Kant's credentials over against Blumenbach are easily secured. Kant's first essay on race, "Of the Different Human Races," was published in 1775, some months before Johann Friedrich Blumenbach submitted *De generis humani varietate nativa* as his dissertation for the doctorate in medicine to the University of Göttingen at the age of twenty-three.[33] Furthermore, one needs to attend to the history of the publication of Blumenbach's treatise. It was twice republished, in 1781 and 1795, but the revisions between the first and second editions were extensive and those between the second and third were such that the latter is better thought of as a new book, albeit published under the same title. All three editions were written in Latin, and it was not until the third edition, which was the first to be translated into German, that the terms *gens* and *gentilitius* began to predominate in a way that suggests that Blumenbach had begun to develop a concept of race. In the first edition he had relied almost exclusively on the same general term that had been used by Linnaeus: *varietas*.[34] Furthermore, while it is true that Blumenbach's system of classification was more complex than Kant's, which was based almost solely on color, in the first edition Blumenbach did not include any theoretical reflection on the status of these varieties, other than to say that the different human varieties run into each other so that no definite limits can be drawn between them (GHV1 40–1; NVM 98–9), a position he repeated in the third edition (GHV3 285 and 322; NV 203–4 and 224; NVM 264 and 275). Indeed in his *Handbuch der Naturgeschichte* Blumenbach explicitly acknowledges that Kant was the first to distinguish precisely races and varieties.[35] By setting out clearly the distinction between race and variety, where races are marked by hereditary characteristics that are unavoidable in the offspring, whereas the distinguishing marks of varieties are not always transmitted, Kant introduced a language for articulating permanent differentiations within the notion of species (AA VIII 180n). Buffon had not argued for a clear distinction along these lines because he was not concerned with organizing in a systematic way the raw data provided by travellers.

Another indication of Blumenbach's relation to Kant can be found in the former's defense of color as a way of differentiating the races. From the outset Kant relied almost exclusively on color for his classification of the races, even though this led to severe difficulties. Already in 1775, the year of Kant's first essay on race, it was becoming clear that the appeal to color as a criterion could not be sustained without anomalies. For example, in that year, John Hunter of Edinburgh included under the label "light brown," Southern Europeans, Sicilians, Abyssinians, the Spanish, Turks, and Laplanders, and under the label "brown," Tartars, Persians, Africans on the Mediterranean, and the Chinese.[36] In 1786 Forster directly challenged Kant's appeal to color by presenting him with the case of two people of two different races having a child that was the same color as both the parents.[37] Color was simply not a viable indicator. It is ironic that at the very time that Kant was giving the concept of race intellectual coherence, his criterion for distinguishing the different races was collapsing. And yet it is some measure of the growing proximity of Kant and Blumenbach that, although in 1775 Blumenbach had dismissed color as an indicator of human varieties, on the grounds that so many additional factors contribute to the differences (GHV1 50–7; NVM 107–13), some twenty years later, with specific references to Kant's 1785 and 1788 essays on race, he granted that color is the most constant character of the human varieties (GHV3 114–15; NV 91; NVM 207).

Some commentators have made much of Kant's own acknowledgment of his debt to Blumenbach, but the balance of the debt goes in the other direction, as I shall show later. It is not usually noticed that in his essay on teleology, which is one of the places where Kant praised Blumenbach's notion of a formative drive or *Bildungstrieb* (AA VIII 180n), Kant also argued for a distinction between "race" and "variety" (AA VIII 163–5). Kant again acknowledged the importance of the notion of *Bildungstrieb* in the *Critique of Judgment* but in the context of showing Blumenbach's conformity with Kant's long-standing attempt to unite the teleological and mechanical frameworks (AA V 424).[38] The growing proximity of Kant and Blumenbach is confirmed by Christoph Girtanner's *Über das Kantische Prinzip für die Naturgeschichte* of 1796.[39] Girtanner dedicated his book on race to Blumenbach, with whom he had studied from 1780 to 1782, and in his *Anthropology* Kant endorsed Girtanner's book as "in keeping with my principles" (AA VII 320). Not only is Kant's chronological primacy secured, but so is the importance of his theoretical contribution, even if it was Blumenbach and the Göttingen school who, by undertaking empirical research, such as the measurement of skulls, set the tone for nineteenth-century research in Germany not just for the science of race but the biological sciences generally. Unlike Kant, Blumenbach did not base his account on Buffon's rule of fertile progeny, which he recognized as an entirely impractical criterion for scientists to have to utilize, condemning them to endless attempts to persuade different types from different parts of the world to copulate (GHV3 67–9; NV 59–60; NVM 188–9). Blumenbach relied on morphological considerations and the application of a revised version of Buffon's notion of degeneration. However, it was through Blumenbach that Kant's concept of race came to have an impact on the larger scientific community. Kant's writings on race seem to have disappeared from view until the advent of Darwinism reopened some of the theoretical issues, and interest in them was revived.[40]

II

Although skin color and hair texture offered a way of organizing the growing mass of data on the ever increasing number of peoples known to European scientists, there were other more pressing issues that went to the very heart of Europe's conceptual framework at that time. The general problem was that of how to account for the variety and dispersion of such apparently different peoples from a single pair within a timeframe of only a few thousand years as a literal reading of the Bible demanded.[41] One solution that was offered from time to time was that some of these peoples were simply not human. This had, for example, been the focus of the debate in sixteenth-century Spain about Native Americans. Another possibility was to question the Biblical chronology. Isaac La Peyrère, whose *Praeadamitae* was first published in 1655, introduced a further possibility by becoming the first European in modern times to articulate in any detail a theory of polygenesis.

Ironically, one of La Peyrère's main motives for proposing polygenesis was to combat anti-Semitic activity, although his underlying hope appears to have been that once Christians behaved responsibly toward Jews, then the Jews would convert to Christianity, thereby introducing the Messianic Age.[42] However, there were also other considerations that led him to pre-Adamism, including the problem of accounting for the multiplicity of different peoples, news of whom had been brought back to Europe by the explorers.[43] The initial version of La Peyrère's manuscript, *Praeadamitae*, was never published and so is now known only on the basis of criticisms made of it, especially that by Grotius in 1643. Grotius argued that the inhabitants of North and South America were descendants of Viking explorers, so that appeal to polygenesis was unnecessary in that case.[44] In *Praeadamitae* La Peyrère responded that when the Vikings arrived in Greenland they already found the Eskimos and that Grotius had provided no answer as to where they came from.[45] However, the published version of *Praeadamitae* is largely dominated by the problem of writing a coherent narrative that reconciled the Biblical story of the creation of Adam with the more extended chronologies proposed by the Chaldaeans, Egyptians, Greeks and Chinese. La Peyrère resolved the problem by declaring the legitimacy of all the accounts. The Adamite account was true only of the Jews, even if its significance extended beyond the Jews. Rejecting the Church Fathers who had insisted on reading the Biblical account as applying to all humanity, La Peyrère wrote:

> Truly they would pity themselves, if they should hear or see those things which are discovered in the East and West Indies in this clear-sighted age, as also a great many other countries full of men, to which it is certain none of Adam's posterity ever arrived.[46]

Although the question of the extent of La Peyrère's influence is still a matter of speculation, and even though it did not resolve the question of whether Native Americans, Africans, and Europeans in spite of their different origins were each of them human, there is some evidence that the theory of polygenesis did find support among some slaveholders before the end of the seventeenth century.[47] In 1774 Edward Long in his influential *History of Jamaica* gave a new lease of life to polygenesis by appealing to it in support of slavery.[48] However, he did not need a concept of race to proclaim his particular brand of racism. As we shall see, the concept of race was introduced to buttress the case against polygenesis.

Buffon was a particularly important figure in the debate against polygenesis, not only because he was an unambiguous supporter of the claim that there was only one human species (HN III 529–30), but especially because his "rule" appeared to provide scientific support for this claim. Buffon had argued that any two animals that can procreate together are of the same species, if their issue can also procreate. Following this rule it was clear that all dogs were of the same species, but that a horse and an ass were not because their issue, a mule, cannot procreate. The fact that all human beings, however different they are, are able to procreate and have fertile offspring, led Buffon to the conclusion that they all belong to the same species. It is a testimony to Buffon's importance that Henry Home, Lord Kames, defended polygenesis largely by attacking Buffon.

Kames introduced his *Sketches of the History of Man* by asking "whether all men be of one lineage, descended from a single pair, or whether there be different races originally distinct."[49] It quickly became clear that Kames favored the second alternative. Kames even had some fun at Buffon's expense with the latter's notion of degeneration. According to Kames, people degenerate in a climate to which they are not suited by nature, except around Charleston where Europeans die so fast from the heat that they do not have time to degenerate (SHM I 11). However, Kames's serious point was that people do not adapt to a new climate, but that different races are fitted by nature for different climates (SHM I 10). Hence Kames posed the following question to Buffon:

> But is he seriously of opinion, that any operation of climate, or of other accidental cause, can account for the copper colour and smooth chin universal among the Americans, the prominence of the *pudenda* universal among Hottentot women, or the black nipple no less universal among female Samoides? (SHM I 12)

Although Kames seems to have had little doubt as to the conclusion that should be drawn from the evidence, he was reluctant to express it directly, placing it in quotation marks so as to avoid having to take full responsibility for it:

> "That God created many pairs of the human race, differing from each other both externally and internally; that he fitted these pairs for different climates, and placed each pair in its proper climate; that the peculiarities of the original pairs were preserved entire in their descendants; . . . " (SHM I 38–9)

That the Biblical account of the creation of a single pair is "not a little puzzling" was as much as he was willing to say outright at the outset. Later in the book he returned to the topic that had occupied La Peyrère and argued for the separate origin of the American Nations (SHM II 70–2). However, even here, in an effort to assuage believers in the Biblical account, he proposed a way of reconciling his account with theirs:

> . . . supposing the human race to have been planted in America by the hand of God later than the days of Moses, Adam and Eve might have been the first parents of mankind, i.e. of all who at that time existed, without being the first parents of the Americans. (SHM II 75)

Voltaire, by contrast, not only contested the Biblical account openly. His opposition to the Bible seems to have been one of his main reasons for adopting polygenesis.

In his adherence to polygenesis, Voltaire was more concerned with polemic than with argument. In his *Essai sur les moeurs et de l'esprit des nations* he was satisfied with the claim that "only the blind could doubt that the Whites, the Blacks, the Albinos, the Hottentots, the Laplanders, the Chinese, the Americans, are entirely different races."[50] This was not meant as an exhaustive list. Voltaire was also open to the possibility of further types that had disappeared. Elsewhere, albeit in a text that was first published posthumously in 1784, Voltaire was even more direct in declaring that "bearded Whites, wooly haired Blacks, yellow-skinned peoples with their long manes, and beardless men do not come from the same man."[51] However, Voltaire, who had been a leading advocate of the importance of Indian and especially Chinese civilization, was critical of Africa. He offered a hierarchical model in which Blacks were not only not at the highest level, but adding insult to injury, placed explicitly above "apes and oysters."[52]

Kant's 1775 essay on race included an attack on the theory of "local creations" in the context of which Voltaire was mentioned explicitly (AA II 440; IR 19).[53] Kant's interest in defending monogenesis emerged in other writings also. In January 1786, Kant published "Speculative Beginning of Human History" in which he argued that the speculation of philosophy about the first beginnings coincided with the account to be found in Genesis, including the fact of a single original pair (AA VIII 110).[54] Two years later, Kant returned to the issue when Georg Forster revived the theory of "local creations."[55] Fully aware that polygenesis was deprived of the rhetoric of human brotherhood as a tool to combat racism, Forster simply responded: "Let me ask whether the thought that Blacks are our brothers has ever anywhere even once abated the raised whip of the slave driver was put away."[56] Although polygenesis lent itself to those who wanted to defend the enslavement of Africans, one cannot establish a correlation between these two positions.[57] Although it is significant that the concept of race was given precision in an effort to combat polygenesis, that does not constitute an ethical defence of the concept, any more than La Peyrère's good intentions in introducing Preadamism are relevant to assessing its merits. However, it does alert us to the complexity of the issues being discussed.

The fact that the scientific concept of race was developed initially in Germany rather than in Britain or America suggests that it was not specifically the interests of the slaveowners that led to its introduction, but rather, as Kant's essays themselves confirm, an interest in classification and above all the attempt to provide a theoretical defense of monogenesis.[58] The appeal of monogenesis in large measure lay in its conformity to the Biblical account, but it also lent itself to discussions of "human fraternity," so that within the context of the late eighteenth century the idea of race was a resource for those who opposed slavery, just as polygenesis lent itself to the upholders of slavery, without there being any necessary connection between one's position on the monogenesis-polygenesis dispute and one's position on slavery. Nevertheless, none of this means that there was not a strong connection between the concept of race and racism. What the natural historians and philosophers in Europe knew about the different human varieties or races came from travel reports that were increasingly being written with an eye to the debate over slavery.

III

Kant's originality in this context arises from the fact that, having adopted Buffon's rule so as to defend monogenesis, he articulated a theory of race that is not to be found in Buffon. Before examining Kant's appeal to Buffon's rule it is worth recalling some of the objections raised against it by Lord Kames. It was perhaps inevitable that in a book like Buffon's *Histoire naturelle* that took forty years to publish and which contained some thirty-six volumes, there would be some inconsistency, especially as Buffon was constantly receiving new information and even conducting his own experiments to satisfy his curiosity on matters of contention. Kames did not seem to notice that Buffon still entertained the longstanding stories about the fertile coupling of Orangutans and African women, which would undermine the use of Buffon's rule to defend monogenesis,[59] but he found a number of inconsistencies that were damaging to Buffon's rule for differentiating species. Indeed, Kames found that in a recent volume of the *Natural History* Buffon had apparently deprived himself of the privileged example that he had used for promoting the rule when he conceded that the offspring of a horse and an ass was not barren (HN XII, 223). Kames also focused on the artificiality of Buffon's rule. Kames conceded that Providence had usually been careful to remove the possibility of mixed breeds, except where, as in the case of dogs, it was harmless (SHM I 5). The complaint against Buffon was that the rule had not been established without a single exception and so was a clear example of a *petitio principii* (SHM I 6). Kames argued that if Buffon was able to tell, for example, that animals in America were of a different species from those in Europe on the basis of their dissimilarities without having to wait to see if they could procreate, then the differences between certain tribes of men should be equally obvious and independent of any procreation criterion (SHM I 8). However, what is particularly significant for my purposes is the way Kames conducted the debate, when he found Buffon providing clear examples in his *Natural History* of exceptions to his own rule, such as the mixture of a he-goat and a ewe or of a camel and a dromedary. Kames quoted Buffon as saying of the camel and the dromedary that "they are one species; but their races are different, and have been so past all memory."[60] Kames countered by asking why Buffon did not simply say that they were two species of the same genus, as he had no evidence that they derived from the same source: "If our author will permit me to carry back to the creation the camel and the dromedary as two distinct races, I desire no other conclusions" (SHM I 7). Even though Kames had found a passage in which Buffon had distinguished races from species, he was under no pressure to debate the concept of race with Buffon because Buffon used the term inconsistently and without definition.

In spite of the difficulties noticed by Lord Kames or the doubts that Buffon himself expressed in relation to the interbreeding criterion in 1766 in his section on the "Degeneration of the Animals," Kant took Buffon's rule that animals that generate fertile young belong to the same physical genus as his starting-point. Races are deviations within this genus which maintain themselves over protracted generations, even when displaced geographically, and which produce hybrids or mulattoes, that exhibit the characteristics of both races when they interbreed with other deviations or races. With this definition Kant secured the unity of humanity as a natural genus. However, there were other advantages to be gained by the introduction of the language of "race." First, Kant explained that by presenting the large number of apparently different types as "races" of the same genus he was providing a "physical system for the understanding" (AA II 434n; DHR 13n). Kant believed that it was necessary for the understanding to reduce the great number of different kinds (*Arten*) to races of the same genus so that it was not overwhelmed by the data. Second, the account of races was charged with the task of showing the reason for the diversity of human deviations. Kant called the science dedicated to this task natural history (*Naturgeschichte*), as opposed to natural description (*Naturbeschreibung*) (AA II 443; DHR 22). However, it should not be confused with the distinction between Buffonian natural taxonomy organized according to kinship and the artificial divisions of

Linnaeus, which was a form of labeling. Kant introduced the distinction between natural and artificial divisions at the beginning of the essay (AA II 429; DHR 8), but although he adopted Buffon's title "natural history" to describe the activity he was proposing, he meant by it something very different from what Buffon had proposed. Indeed, when still defending the distinction between natural history and natural description in "On the Use of Teleological Principles in Philosophy," he pointed to the work of Linnaeus and not that of Buffon as an example of natural history, albeit he did not have in mind Linnaeus's system of classifications (AA VIII 161–2). That was why Kant eventually in the *Critique of Judgment* had to renounce Buffon's phrase "natural history" and propose instead the phrase "archaeology of nature" to describe the work he proposed of speculating on how the various families of creatures arrived at their current state on the basis of the assumption that nature is organized purposively (AA V 419 and 428n; CJ 304–5 and 315n). Because Kant clearly locates his concept of race within natural history, it has a radically different theoretical status from that it would have if Kant had located it within natural description instead. Although Kant seems to have given a different weight to this distinction at the end of the 1780s than he did in 1777, this change in no small measure reflects the theoretical work that had to be done to sustain the concept of race.

Already in "Of the Different Human Races," Kant was concerned with the kind of causality that produced the races. Kant proposed a review of the entire human genus over the whole earth with a view to finding either the natural or the purposive causes of the various deviations, depending simply on whichever kind of cause was most readily discernible (AA II 435; DHR 14). More specifically, Kant attempted to explain differences in skin color, as this was the basis on which he distinguished the four fundamental races: Whites, Blacks, Hindustanic, and Kalmuck. Kant's explanation of the production of these differences was in terms of the effects of air and sun, but he argued that these developments must have been preformed and could not be understood as simply a product either of chance or the application of mechanical laws alone. Kant argued that by the solicitude of nature, human beings were equipped with seeds (*Keime*) and natural predispositions (*Anlagen*) that were developed or held back depending on climate (AA II 434–5; DHR 13–14). That is to say, the seeds of all the races were latent from the start in everyone, and the appropriate seed was actualized to serve a purpose that arose from the circumstances. The thrust of Kant's account, therefore, was to support the use of teleology within biology as opposed to providing merely mechanical explanations, as had become the tendency. Mechanical explanations would allow for the effects of climate to produce further changes in species or parts of the species. This was a possibility Kant rejected, just as he rejected all evolutionary theories. Such changes that had occurred were all preformed. They were also irreversible.

Although Kant had already indicated in 1775 that race is an ex-speciation which cannot return to the original stem, it was only in 1777 that he made absolutely clear that the races, once formed resist further remodeling (AA II 442; DHR 21). This was crucial. He emphasized the same point in the 1785 essay (AA VIII 105) and again in 1788 (AA VIII 166). Race cannot be undone by further differences in climate. It is permanent. Whichever germ was actualized by the conditions, the other germs would retire into inactivity.[61] It was also in 1777 that Kant first identified the stem genus as

White (AA II 441; DHR 20). Buffon had already argued in 1749 that "White appears to be the primitive color of Nature" (HN III 502).[62] However, Kant was not rehearsing Buffon's argument which relied on the claim that Blacks can have White children but that the reverse cannot happen. Kant did not concede until 1785 that, because it is now impossible to reproduce the original stock, we will never be able to tell for sure what it was like (AA VIII 82). See also (AA V 420; CJ 306).

In appealing to the idea of "pre-existing seeds" Kant was adopting a view that had arisen in the seventeenth century under the influence of Malebranche and that came to be associated with certain works of Charles Bonnet in the early 1760s.[63] Buffon had explicitly rejected the language of germs when he dismissed attempts to refer generation back to God, on the grounds that they placed it beyond the reach of human investigation (HN II 32–3). However, it can be argued that both Bonnet and Buffon were trying to solve the same problem that faced all mechanical theories of generation of how a complex order could be created from an originally chaotic arrangement of particles. Indeed, Buffon's appeal, in his essay on the horse, to the idea of a general prototype of every species that is found in the first of its kind, which in turn acts as an external model and internal mold of all the individuals of the species (HN IV 215–16), was not so distant from Bonnet.[64] Kant's introduction of Bonnet's vocabulary in an essay whose main framework was formed by Buffon was not therefore as extraordinary as it might otherwise appear. Nevertheless, no reader of Kant could underestimate the significance of the fact that he replaced Buffon's simply mechanical explanation of the diversity of human types with an account that appealed to teleological causes.[65]

IV

Early discussions of the various human types were by no means always focused on Africans. A great deal of attention and animosity was reserved for Lapps and often Native Americans were placed below all the other types. However, insofar as color was regarded as the most striking characteristic differentiating the various types and insofar as Whites considered themselves clearly superior to everyone else, then one obvious way of organizing these types hierarchically that occurred to Europeans was from white to black.[66] Even before the last quarter of the eighteenth century, which was when the proslavery faction became directly involved in providing descriptions of Africa that served their cause, European travellers to Africa were only too happy to support this growing prejudice against Africans by exaggerating what they observed in an effort to gain the public's attention.[67] The blackness of Africans was not only a subject of theoretical speculation, it became the characteristic around which all the prejudices against Africans were gathered. Already in 1728 Ephraim Chambers wrote: "The origin of *Negroe's* [sic], and the cause of that remarkable difference in complexion from the rest of mankind, has much perplexed the naturalists; nor has any thing satisfactory been yet offered in that head."[68] That it had been possible at one time to pose the question without any hint of the prejudice with which it subsequently became infused can be illustrated by turning to Sir Thomas Browne. When he explored the question "Of the Blackness of Negroes," it was a strictly theoretical inquiry, and even if he did not go so far as to ask why Whites were white, in the course of dismissing the account of the "curse of Ham," he did not neglect to ask why observers would consider it a curse to be that color.[69] For Browne it was quite clear that beauty could not "reasonably" be associated with one color over another, as beauty is determined by what custom leads one to regard as natural: "And by this consideration of Beauty, the Moors also are not excluded, but hold a common share with all mankind."[70] The praise that is sometimes lavished on Kant for having come to a similar insight is for that reason not fully deserved (AA V 234; CJ 82).[71] He was repeating a standard observation of the time, but it is noteworthy that the emphasis is no longer, as in Bernier, that there are beautiful women everywhere, but that each culture has its own idea of what constituted human beauty.

The problem, of why Blacks were black, obsessed scientists throughout the eighteenth century. Some anatomists sought and sometimes claimed to find a physiological explanation, such as black bile.[72] Although most natural scientists were inclined to include some environmental explanation in terms of air, food, or climate, not least because it could easily be reconciled with a belief in Adam as the source of all mankind,[73] on its own this ran counter to the evidence that skin color was transmitted largely unchanged across generations. Buffon favored the environmental explanation of color but he was unusual in being prepared to draw the consequences. He insisted in 1749 that if Africans were brought North their skin color would lighten, albeit slowly and that possibly they would end up as white as northerners (HN III 523–4). In his essay "On the Degeneration of Animals" Buffon even described a possible experiment to establish this. He proposed transporting some Blacks from Senegal to Denmark, the country of white skin, blonde hair and blue eyes. If the Blacks were enclosed "with their women" and all possibility of crossbreeding excluded, he suggested that we would learn how long it would take to "reintegrate (*réintégrer*) in this respect the nature of man" (HN XIV 314). The term "reintegrate," of course, had its source in Buffon's belief that white was the original color. A similar question arose in the course of Kant's debate with Forster. Kant held that one showed one's "true" color only in a mild climate: "one can more correctly judge in France the color of a Negro, who has lived there a long time, or better still was born there, insofar as that determines his or her class distinction from other men, than one can judge it in the fatherland of the Blacks" (AA VIII 92). Indeed, Kant claimed that the true color of the South Sea Islanders was not yet known for certain and would not be until one of them was born in Europe (AA VIII 92), a proposition to which Georg Forster, who had taken the trouble to travel to the South Pacific, objected strongly.[74] However, one important characteristic of Kant's theory is that he excluded the possibility of any such reintegration as described by Buffon. This was a decisive difference because it established the distinction between, on the one hand, race as a permanent characteristic that is unfailingly inherited and, on the other hand, characteristics, such as hair color, sickness or deformity, for which there was only a tendency to hereditary transmission (AA VIII 93–4). It was this distinction that in "On the Use of Teleological Principles in Philosophy" was redrawn as a distinction between race and variety, thereby challenging Blumenbach to introduce a similar distinction, as noted earlier (AA VIII 180n).

Kant speculated about the physical basis for blackness, appealing to iron particles in 1777 (AA II 440) and to phlogiston in 1785 (AA VIII 103). But the most important consequence of Kant's interest in the question of the color of Africans was that it seems to have kept him focused on the question of the adequacy of mechanistic explanations offered in isolation from teleology. In Kant's first essay on race the purposive nature of racial (which meant for him color) differences was assumed but not argued on the basis that because neither chance nor mechanical laws could have brought about the developments that enabled organic bodies to adapt to the climates into which they first moved, those developments must be construed as preformed (AA II 435; DHR 14). He was more direct in the 1785 essay when he wrote that the purposive nature of color was visible in the Negro race (AA VIII 103).[75] However, for the other races, Kant was obliged simply to assume that color was purposive. And yet it was from the presence of purposiveness that Kant inferred the existence of seeds (AA VIII 102). The blackness of Blacks provided Kant with one of his most powerful illustrations of purposiveness within the biological sphere. But perhaps it worked as a powerful example among his White audience because it addressed their fascination with the fact of Blackness.

However, the issue in "On the Use of Teleological Principles in Philosophy," as in the second part of the *Critique of Judgment*, is a much larger one and it arises in relation to a new point of contact between Kant and Blumenbach. What brought Kant and Blumenbach together was Kant's recognition that in his notion of *Bildungstrieb* or formative drive, Blumenbach had gone beyond natural description and an account of mechanical forces to posit a teleology in nature. Like his book on human varieties, Blumenbach's essay on the *Bildungstrieb* appeared in three very different versions. The first, published in 1780, was barely twenty pages.[76] The following year it was expanded into a treatise of some 87 pages.[77] In 1789, Blumenbach published a text of 116 pages on the *Bildungstrieb* that was reprinted two years later.[78] Blumenbach had discovered the *Bildungstrieb* while conducting some experiments on polyps while on holiday. He found that if their arms or tentacles were cut off, they would grow again within a few days, albeit they would be smaller (B3 28–9). On this basis he came to posit in the unformed generative matter of organized bodies a lifelong drive that initially takes on a determinate form, maintains it lifelong, and reproduces itself where possible, if it is in any way mutilated (B3 31).

Because Blumenbach's essay was an attack on Haller's conception of preformed seeds, it appears to be in stark contrast with Kant's theory of race, which also appeals to seeds. However, the appearance is somewhat deceptive.[79] Blumenbach's argument against preformed seeds was based on the existence of hybrids. Indeed, in the 1781 edition, Blumenbach even appealed to the fact that the mixing of pure varieties, such as Blacks and Whites, produces mulattoes and blendings (B2 60), an example which lay at the heart of Kant's reflections on race. The theory of seeds that Blumenbach is attacking is the same as that found in the theory of evolution that Kant rejects in section 81 of the Third Critique. Indeed, if Kant ends that section by applauding Blumenbach's account of the *Bildungstrieb*, he has done much more than take over this notion from Blumenbach (AAV 424; CJ 311). The whole way Kant frames the issue as a question of the advantages of the theory of epigenesis over that of evolution was taken from Blumenbach (B3 13–14).[80] I judge Kant to have been quite genuine in his praise for Blumenbach when in 1790 he wrote to thank Blumenbach for sending him *Über den Bildungstrieb* (B3) in which Blumenbach's combination of the physico-mechanical principle of explicating organic nature was in line with his own recent work (AA XI 185).[81] It is worth noting that although Blumenbach had only recently arrived at the theory of epigenesis, Kant had long maintained it, as is reflected in the *Critique of Pure Reason*.[82] The transformation of Blumenbach's philosophy of science in the ten years after 1788 was largely toward a form of Kantianism.[83] However, Kant preferred to emphasize the conformity of his views with those of Blumenbach, because Blumenbach brought to Kant a scientific legitimacy that Kant was unable to provide on his own account. The advantage to Kant is nowhere clearer than in Blumenbach's adoption of the Kantian language of race. Even though it is far from clear that Blumenbach fully recognized the status Kant gave to the concept of race, which is one of the subjects of the next section, he came to frame his discussion of human varieties, like Kant, in terms of the conjunction of the physico-mechanical and teleological principles (GHV3 82–3; NV 69; NVM 194).

V

That Kant's three essays on race are important sources for understanding the genesis of the *Critique of Judgment* has been recognized by a number of Kant scholars.[84] Indeed, Girtanner, Kant's contemporary, already saw the relevance of the *Critique of Judgment* for Kant's discussions of race.[85] Kant seems to have decided to address the vexed problem of the grouping of species by taking the model he had developed in his investigation of race and extending it to cover broader groupings of species.[86] In drawing on this model Kant not only described how creatures of a less purposive form gave birth to others "better adapted to their place of origin" (AA V 419; CJ 305), thereby recalling the way climate served to develop the races, he also returned to the language of "predisposition": "nothing is to be taken up into the generative force that does not already belong to one of the being's undeveloped original predispositions" (AA5 420; CJ 306). For Kant, when certain individuals undergo accidental change leading to the altered character being taken up into the generative force (*Erzeugungskraft*) and thereby becoming hereditary, this has to be judged as the development of a purposive predisposition already in the species for the sake of its preservation:

> If we find that the altered character of these individuals becomes hereditary and is taken up into their generative force, then the only proper way to judge it is as the development, on [a given] occasion, of a purposive predisposition that was originally present in the species and that serves the preservation of the kind (*Art*). (AA V 420; CJ 305–6)[87]

This sentence so clearly evokes what Kant had said about racial differences that it is no surprise to find one English translator introducing "race" as a translation of *Art* in the last sentence.[88] If Kant did not mention "race" explicitly in the second half of the *Critique of Judgment*, it is perhaps because he knew from his debate with Herder how controversial it still was and that it might interfere with the general acceptance of his theory.

Herder's polemic against Kant in his *Ideas on the Philosophy of the History of Humankind* and Kant's response in his reviews of the first two parts of Herder's book came to a head around the notion of race. Although an opponent of polygenesis,[89] Herder, who had attended Kant's lectures on *Physical Geography* in which the concept of race had been championed, explicitly denied the reality of race: "there are neither four nor five races, nor are there exclusive varieties on earth."[90] Herder's questioning of race did not stop him, for example, from citing Camper's studies on the angle of the head which places the head of Africans and Kalmucks closer to apes than Europeans, and which allegedly was Nature's means of discriminating the varieties of creation as they approximate to the most perfect form of beauty in human beings (IGM 134–35). But Herder believed that the language of race was divisive. He opened his criticism of the concept of race in these terms:

> Nature has provided for each kind and given each one its own inheritance. She has distributed the apes in as many species and varieties and spread them out as far as she could spread them; you human, however, should honour yourself. Neither the pongo nor the gibbon is your brother, whereas the American and the Negro certainly are. You should not oppress him, nor murder him, nor steal from him; for he is a human being just as you are; you may not enter into fraternity with the apes. (IGM 255; PH 25–6)

Herder understood peoples as the fundamental units of history and, although he primarily conceived of them in cultural terms, their biological basis was retained in his works, as when he wrote of "the original root-character of a nation" (*die ursprungliche Stammgebilde der Nation*) (IGM 255–6; PH 26). Whereas Kant was among those who advocated a division into only four or five kinds, Herder advocated recognition of the diversity of human peoples; whereas Kant focused on color divisions, Herder saw continuity: "the colors run into one another" (IGM 256; PH 26). Like Blumenbach, Herder believed that if we only knew more about the different peoples, we could perhaps complete the shadings of the portraits of these peoples without finding a single break (IGM 231).[91] Whereas Kant regarded the division of races as permanent, according to Herder, "the characters of peoples are gradually extinguished in the general run of things" (IGM 685).

Herder disagreed with Kant on the role the latter gave to seeds. Herder in the first part of the *Ideas* complained: "No eye has ever seen these preformed seeds, lying ready ever since the creation; what we observe from the first moment of a creature's genesis are effective *organic powers*." (IGM 171) In his anonymous review of the first part of Herder's *Ideas* Kant merely noted this difference and attacked Herder as the one who was explaining the obscure by the more obscure (AA VIII 48 and 53–4; OH 31 and 37). In his review of the second part of the *Ideas*, in which Herder had denied race explicitly, Kant took up the argument more directly. Herder had acknowledged that the inner vital principle modifies itself according to variations in external conditions, most notably climate. Kant proposed that if these adaptations were limited to a certain number of variations and were such that, once established, they could no longer revert to the original form or change into another type, then it would be legitimate to reintroduce the contested language of seeds and original dispositions (AA VIII 62; OH 48). In this way Kant attempted to persuade Herder that his objections to the notion of seeds applied to an account of seeds that was not Kant's own and that Herder could readily accommodate Kant's conception, properly understood. However, it might seem Kant did not have a good response for Herder's accusation that the seeds were somewhat mysterious. Kant described them as limitations that cannot be rendered comprehensible (AA VIII 62–3; OH 68).

That is why, when Kant referred Herder's hostility to classification based on hereditary colorization to Herder's not yet having "clearly determined the concept of a race" (AA VIII 62; OH 47), something more was at stake than the conception of seeds. At issue was the conception of scientific investigation that afforded them a status. In the *Critique of Pure Reason* Kant distinguished those people who assume that there are certain hereditary characteristics in each nation and race and those who insist that in all such cases nature made the same provision for all and that such differences that one does find are due to external and accidental conditions (KrV A667, B695). Kant negotiated the two positions by granting that we cannot speak from insight into the nature of the objects concerned. He made clear, however, that looking for order in nature, such as Leibniz and Bonnet did in proposing what came to be known as the chain of being, is a legitimate and excellent regulative principle of reason (KrV A668; B696). This same insight governed all Kant's writings on race and is most clearly expressed in his observation that the word *variety*, but not the word *race*, belongs to the description of nature and that nevertheless an observer of nature finds the word *race* necessary from the viewpoint of natural history (AAVIII 163). This is what underlies Kant's crucial explanation of the status of the concept of race, whereby it corresponds to nothing in the world, but nevertheless is "necessary from the viewpoint of natural history":

> What is a *race*? The word certainly does not belong in a systematic description of nature, so presumably the thing itself is nowhere to be found in nature. However, the *concept* which this expression designates is nevertheless well established in the reason of every observer of nature who supposes a conjunction of causes placed originally in the line of descent of the genus itself in order to account for a self-transmitted peculiarity that appears in different interbreeding animals but which does not lie in the concept of their genus. (AA VIII 163)[92]

A similar insight at a more general level can be found in the *Critique of Judgment*. If one applies what Kant says about regulative concepts in the *Critique of Judgment* to his discussions of race, then Kant is saying that in the present state of our knowledge the idea of race imposes itself. It is also what underlies his observations in notes written when preparing his response to Forster, which read: "to accept that any part of a creature which adheres constantly to the species is without purpose is just like accepting that an event in the world has arisen without a cause" (AA XXIII 75). As Kant understood it, racial differences called for a purposive account.[93] To this extent, Kant was right to say that Herder had not yet clearly understood what he meant by the concept of race. Nevertheless, Herder's debate with Kant about race for all of its misunderstandings was a philosophical debate that shows that the concept had finally reached sufficient precision in Kant to allow one to say he brought it to fruition.

The scientific concept of race underwent many changes after Kant introduced it. At times the reality of race was not in question. Race was a given. However, now that the reality of race is being questioned by Appiah on the grounds that it is no longer in conformity with our best scientific knowledge, one must still ask whether we can do without it. In response to Appiah, Lucius Outlaw has argued, "As we struggle to realize social justice with harmony in America, given this nation's history of race relations, we are unable to do away with the notion of 'race.'"[94] When he writes that we cannot do away with the notion of race, Outlaw seems to be proposing an argument about strategy within a particular context, rather than a Kantian style argument about whether or not race still imposes itself on us according to some regulative principle of reason. But if we acknowledge, as Appiah does, that our current ways of talking about race are the residue of earlier views, then it is prudent to develop a deeper understanding of the history of race thinking as well as of racial practices.[95]

Notes

1 See Richard Popkin, "The Philosophical Bases for Modern Racism," *The High Road to Pyrrhonism*, San Diego, Austin Hill Press, 1980, pp. 79–102.

2 The debate was initiated by Anthony Appiah, "The Uncompleted Argument," *Critical Inquiry*, 1985, 12, p. 35: "The truth is that there are no races: there is nothing in the world that can do all we ask 'race' to do for us."

3 For example, Lewis Hanke, *Aristotle and the American Indians*, Bloomington, Indiana University Press, 1959, esp. pp. 44–73. John Locke, *An Essay concerning Human Understanding*, Oxford, Oxford University Press, 1975, pp. 454–5. See Robert Bernasconi, "Locke's Almost Random Talk of Man: The Double Use of Words in the Natural Law Justification of Slavery," *Perspektiven der Philosophie*, 18, 1992, pp. 293–318.

4 Anon. "Nouvelle division de la Terre, par les differentes Especes ou Races d'hommes qui l'habitent, envoyée par un fameux Voyageur à Monsieur *****[sic] à peu prés en ces termes," *Journal des scavans*, Monday 24 April, 1684, pp. 148–55; trans. "A new division of the earth, according to the different species or races of men who inhabit it, sent by a famous traveller to Mons. , [sic] nearly in these terms," in T. Bendyshe, "The History of Anthropology," Appendix 1, in *Memoirs Read before the Anthropological Society of London*, vol. 1, 1863–64, pp. 360–4. Bendyshe's translation has now been reprinted in *The Idea of Race*, eds. Robert Bernasconi and Tommy Lott, Indianapolis, Hackett, 2000, pp. 1–4.

5 G. W. Leibniz, *Otium Hanoverium sive Miscellanea*, 2nd ed., Leipzig, Christian Martin, 1737, pp. 37–8. That the essay attributed to Bernier is meant is confirmed at *Miscellanea*, pp. 158–9.

6 Anon., "Nouvelle division de la Terre," p. 153; trans. "A new division of the earth," p. 364.

7 For example, Oliver C. Cox, *Caste, Class and Race*, New York, Doubleday, 1948, pp. 330–6.

8 Nicholas Hudson, "From 'Nation' to 'Race': The Origin of Racial Classification in Eighteenth-Century Thought," *Eighteenth-Century Studies*, 29 (3) Spring 1996, pp. 250–2. For evidence of the perpetuation of national distinctions among slaves, Hudson cites James Walvin, *Black Ivory. A History of British Slaves*, Washington, D.C., Howard University Press, 1992, p. 173. For a more detailed assessment of the evidence as it relates especially to the early period, see John Thornton, *Africa and Africans in the Making of the Atlantic World, 1400–1680*, Cambridge, Cambridge University Press, 1992, pp. 183–205.

9 Winthrop D. Jordan, *White over Black. American Attitudes Toward the Negro, 1550–1812*, New York, W. W. Norton, 1977, p. 489. Jordan, whose comment was made in the context of a discussion of Jefferson's *Notes on Virginia* from 1787, was almost certainly discussing only English language usage and perhaps only its usage in the USA. Nevertheless, the comment is still telling.

10 I. Kant, *Beobachtungen über das Gefühl des Schönen und Erhabenen, Gesammelte Schriften*, Berlin, de Gruyter, 1902, vol. II, p. 255; trans. John T. Goldthwait, *Observations on the Feeling of the Beautiful and Sublime*, Berkeley, University of California Press, 1973, p. 113. Whenever possible German reference will be to the Akademie Ausgabe, abbreviated as AA followed by the volume number. On Kant's "witticism" see Ronald A. T. Judy, *(Dis)forming the American Canon*, Minneapolis, University of Minnesota Press, 1993, esp. pp. 108–17.

11 Robert Bernasconi, "Kant as an Unfamiliar Source of Racism," in *Philosophers on Race*, eds. T. Lott and J. Ward, Oxford, Blackwell, forthcoming.

12 Two very different editions of the *Physische Geographie* were published in Kant's lifetime: the authorized version in two volumes edited by Friedrich Theodor Rink and published by Gobbels and Unzer in Königsberg in 1802 has formed the basis of all subsequent editions, but the unauthorized edition in four volumes published by Gottfried Bollmer of Mainz and Hamburg between 1801 and 1805 remains a largely neglected source of information about Kant's extensive knowledge of the travel literature of his day.

13 This version can now be found in a new translation by Jon Mark Mikkelsen in *The Idea of Race*, pp. 8–22. Henceforth DHR.

14 I. Kant, "Von der verschiedenen Racen der Menschen," *Der Philosoph für die Welt*, ed. J. J. Engel, Reuttlingen, Joh. Georg Fleischhauer, 1783, Part 2, pp. 100–31. The Akadamie Ausgabe does not list this edition, which my cursory examination suggests is an unchanged version of the 1777 text.

15 Georg Forster, "Noch etwas über die Menschenrassen," *Werke* 8, ed. Siegfried Scheibe, Berlin, Akademie Verlag, 1991, pp. 142–3.

16 See P. J. Marshall and G. Williams, *The Great Map of Mankind*, Cambridge, Harvard University Press, 1982, pp. 258–98.

17 Johann Reinhold Forster, *Observations made during a Voyage round the World*, eds. Nicholas Thomas et al., Honolulu, University of Hawaii Press, 1996. On Georg Forster's role in the book, see Thomas P. Saine, *Georg Forster*, New York, Twayne Publishers, 1972, p. 24.

18 An English translation by Jon Mark Mikkelsen is given in chapter 2. Because references to the Academy edition are given in parentheses within the main body of the translation, I have not included references to the translation in this paper.

19 See F. C. Beiser, *The Fate of Reason. German Philosophy from Kant to Fichte*, Cambridge, Harvard University Press, 1987, p. 155.

20 Walter Scheidt, "Beiträge zur Geschichte der Anthropologie. Der Begriff der Rasse in der Anthropologie und die Einteilung der Menschenrassen von Linné bis Deniker," *Archiv für Rassen- und Gesellschaftsbiologie* 15, 1924, p. 383; trans. "The Concept of Race in Anthropology and the Divisions into Human Races from Linneus to Deniker," *This is Race*, ed. Earl W. Count, New York, Henry Schuman, 1950, p. 372. It is worth noting that Count also provides an English translation of "Von der verschiedenen Racen der Menschen," but it is incomplete and follows more closely the 1777 edition than the 1775 edition in spite of giving the earlier date. "On the Distinctiveness of the Races in General," *This is Race*, pp. 16–24.

21 For example, Wilhelm A. Mühlmann, *Geschichte der Anthropologie*, Bonn, Universitäts-Verlag, 1948, p. 60 and Earl W. Count, *This is Race*, p. 704.

22 Emmanuel Eze, "The Color of Reason: The Idea of 'Race' in Kant's Anthropology," *Anthropology and the German Enlightenment: Perspectives on Humanity*, ed. Katherine M. Faull, Lewisburg, Bucknell University Press, 1995, pp. 219–20.

23 Carolus Linnaeus, *Systema naturae*, Facsimile of the First Edition, eds. M. S. J. Engel-Ledeboer and H. Engel, Nieuwkoop, B. de Graaf, 1964. See Gunnar Broberg, "Homo Sapiens. Linnaeus's Classification of Man," *Linnaeus. The Man and His Work*, ed. Tore Frängsmyr, Canton, Science History Publications 1994, pp. 156–94.

24 The Latin text of the 1758 edition is quoted by T. Bendyshe, "The History of Anthropology," *Memoirs Read before the Anthropological Society of London*, vol. 1, 1863–64, pp. 424–6. A partial English translation can be found in Winthrop D. Jordan, *White over Black*, Baltimore, Penguin, 1969, pp. 220–1. However, I have modified Jordan's translation to reflect the ambiguity of *ritus*.

25 James L. Larson, *Reason and Experience. The Representation of Natural Order in the Work of Carl von Linné*, Berkeley, University of California Press, 1971, pp. 98–9.

26 Londa Schiebinger, *Nature's Body. Gender in the Making of Modern Science*, Boston, Beacon Press, 1993, pp. 80–1.

27 George Louis le Clerc, Comte de Buffon, "Premier Discours. De la manière d'étudier et de traiter l'Histoire Naturelle," *Histoire Naturelle, Générale et Particulière, avec la description du cabinet du Roi*, Paris, De l'imprimerie royale, 1749, vol. 1, pp. 1–62, esp. 37–40. All further references to this edition are designated HN followed by the volume number.

28 See, for example, Michèle Duchet, *Anthropologie et Histoire au siècle des lumières*, Paris, François Maspero, 1971, pp. 270–3 and Phillip Sloan, "The Gaze of Natural History," *Inventing Human Science*, eds. Christopher Fox, Roy Porter and Robert Wokler, Berkeley, University of California Press, 1995, p. 135.

29 Eds. D. Diderot and d'Alembert, *Encyclopédie ou Dictionnaire Raisonné des Sciences, des Arts et des Métiers*, Elmsford, NY, Pergamon Press Reprint of 1777 edition, vol. 5, p. 957.

30 Frank W. P. Dougherty, "Buffons Bedeutung für die Entwicklung des anthropologischen Denkens im Deutschland der zweiten Hälfte des 18. Jahrhunderts," *Die Natur des Menschen*, eds. Gunter Mann and Franz Dumont, Soemmerning Forschungen VI, Stuttgart, Gustav Fischer, 1990, p. 255.

31 Paul L. Farber, "Buffon and the Concept of Species," *Journal of the History of Biology*, 5 (2), 1972, p. 278.

32 For example, M. F. Ashley Montagu, *Man's Most Dangerous Myth: The Fallacy of Race*, New York, Columbia University Press, 1945, p. 28.

33 Ivan Hannaford presents Kant's "On the Different Races of Man" as an answer to Blumenbach, but he focuses on the *Anthropology* and seems largely unconcerned with Kant's essays on race. See *Race. The History of an Idea in the West*, Baltimore, Johns Hopkins University Press, 1996, pp. 218–19. It is not clear to me why the chronology is so often ignored so as to make Kant's essay a response to Blumenbach. More than one commentator, while stating correctly that Blumenbach was born in 1752, even moved the date of the first edition of *De generis humani varietate nativa* forward from 1775 to 1770. Kenneth A. R. Kennedy, "Race and Culture," *Main Currents in Cultural Anthropology*, eds. Raoul and Frada Naroll, Englewood Cliffs, Prentice Hall, 1973, pp. 142 and 151. See also Michael Banton, "The Classification of Races in Europe and North America: 1700–1850," *International Social Science Journal*, 39 (1), 1987, p. 47.

34 Io. Frid. Blumenbach, *De generis humani varietate nativa*, Göttingen, Vandenhoeck, 1776. Henceforth GHV1. See also the second edition: Io. Frid. Blumenbach, *De generis humani varietate nativa*, Göttingen, Vandenhoek, 1781. Henceforth GHV2. The third edition was the only one translated into German. *De generis humani varietate nativa*, Göttingen, Vandenhoeck et Ruprecht, 1795; trans. Johann Gottfried Gruber, *Über die naturlichen Verschiedenheiten im Menschengeschlechte*, Leipzig, Breitkopf und Hartel, 1798. Henceforth GHV3 and NV respectively. The first and the third edition are translated by Thomas Blendyshe in Johann Friedrich Blumenbach, *On the Natural Varieties of Mankind*, London: Longman,

Green, Longman, Roberts, & Green, 1865. Henceforth NVM. Blumenbach's linguistic usage is discussed by Eric Voeglin, "The Growth of the Race Idea," *Review of Politics*, 2, 1940, p. 297.

35 J. F. Blumenbach, *Handbuch der Naturgeschichte*, fifth ed. Göttingen, Heinrich Dieterich, 1797, p. 23n. Blumenbach also praised the precision of the distinctions by which Kant authorized the concept of race and other related terms in his conversations with Gruber. See NV 259–61.

36 John Hunter, "An Inaugural Disputation of the Varieties of Man," appended to Blumenbach, *On the Natural Varieties of Mankind*, p. 367.

37 Forster, "Noch etwas über die Menschenrassen," p. 148.

38 See the translation by Werner S. Pluhar, *Critique of Judgment*, Indianapolis, Hackett, 1987, p. 311. Henceforth CJ.

39 Christoph Girtanner, *Über das Kantische Prinzip für die Naturgeschichte*, Göttingen, Vanderoek und Ruprecht, 1796. On Girtanner, see Phillip R. Sloan, "Buffon, German Biology and the Historical Interpretation of Biological Species," *British Journal for the History of Science*, vol. 12, no. 41, 1979, pp. 137–141.

40 Kant's essays on race were reprinted with other related works and some commentary by Fritz Schultze in *Kant und Darwin*, Jena, Hermann Dufft, 1875.

41 For example, see Matthew Hale, *The Primitive Origination of Mankind, Considered and Examined According to the Light of Nature*, London, William Godbid, 1677. For Hale's discussion of La Peyrère, see sect. 2, ch. 7, pp. 174–203.

42 Richard H. Popkin, *Isaac La Peyrère*, Leiden, E. J. Brill, 1987, pp. 7–8.

43 La Peyrère, *Apologie de la Peyrère*, Paris, 1663, pp. 19–20 and *Lettre de la Peyrère à Philotine*, Paris, 1658, pp. 111–13, both cited by R. H. Popkin, *Isaac La Peyrère*, Leiden, E. J. Brill, 1987, p. 15.

44 R. H. Popkin, *Isaac La Peyrère*, pp. 6 and 80.

45 [Isaac la Peyrère,] *Systema Theologicum ex Praeadamitarum Hypothesi*, 1655, Book IV, ch. 14, pp. 251–5; trans. *Man before Adam*, Book IV, ch. 14. See also R. H. Popkin, *Isaac La Peyrère*, pp. 11 and 47.

46 Isaac la Peyrère, *Systema Theologicum*, p. 252; trans. *Man before Adam*, p. 276. Punctuation modified.

47 Morgan Godwyn, *The Negro's and Indians Advocate*, London, 1680, pp. 15–18.

48 Edward Long, *The History of Jamaica*, photomechanical reproduction of the 1774 edition, London, Frank Cass, 1970, vol. 2, p. 356.

49 This formulation of the question is found first in the second edition. Henry Home, Lord Kames, *Sketches of the History of Man*, Edinburgh, William Creech, 1778, vol. 1, p. 2. All subsequent references will be to the first edition: *Sketches of the History of Man*, Edinburgh, W. Creech, 1774. Henceforth SHM (followed by the volume number).

50 Voltaire, *Essai sur les moeurs et l'esprit des nations*, Oeuvres complètes, vol. 11, ed. Louis Moland, Paris, Garnier Frères, 1878, p. 12.

51 Voltaire, *Traité de métaphysique*, ed. W. H. Barber, *The Complete Works of Voltaire*, vol. 14, Oxford, The Voltaire Foundation, 1989, p. 423.

52 Ibid., p. 452. Voltaire also advocated the idea of a hierarchy of "degrees descending from man to the animal" when he placed albinos beneath Blacks (*nègres*) and Hottentots but above apes. *Essai sur les moeurs*, vol. 2, Oeuvres complètes, vol. 12, pp. 367–8.

53 Blumenbach also specified his opposition to polygenesis. GHV1 40–1; NVM 98. GHV3 65–6; NV 58; NVM 188.

54 I. Kant, "Conjectural Beginning of Human History," *On History*, ed. Lewis White Beck, Indianapolis, Bobbs-Merrill, 1963, p. 54. Henceforth OH.

55 Ludwig Uhlig, *Georg Forster*, Tübingen, Max Niemeyer, 1965, pp. 57–62.

56 Georg Forster, "Noch etwas über die Menschenrassen," p. 154.

57 Hans-Konrad Schmutz, "Friedrich Tiedemann (1781–1861) und Johann Friedrich Blumenbach (1752–1840) – Anthropologie und Sklavenfrage," *Die Natur des Menschen*, eds. G. Mann and F. Dumont, pp. 353–63, esp. 354.

58 Nevertheless the advocates of slavery came to see that the science of racial differences could be used to support their case. This is never more clear than in the transmission of the European science of race to the USA. See, for example, the presentation of Julien Joseph Virey's *Histoire naturelle du genre humain* in J. H. Guenebault, *Natural History of the Negro Race*, Charleston, D. J. Dowling, 1837.

59 Phillip R. Sloan, "The Idea of Racial Degeneracy in Buffon's *Histoire Naturelle*," *Racism in the Eighteenth Century*, ed. Harold E. Pagliano, Cleveland, Case Western Reserve University, 1973, pp. 309–10.

60 The source of the quotation is HN XI 211.

61 See Arthur O. Lovejoy, "Kant and Evolution," *Forerunners of Darwin: 1745–1859*, eds. Bentley Glass, Owsei Temkin, and William L. Straus, Baltimore: Johns Hopkins Press, 1959, p. 188.

62 Later, in 1775, in the second volume of the *Suppléments* Buffon explored the possibility that the Black race might be older than the White race. This led him to speculate in 1778 that Whites were an improved race, the first truly civilized culture, and indeed the only variety of mankind worthy of being called people. See also J. H. Eddy, "Buffon, Organic Alterations, and Man," *Studies in History of Biology*, vol. 7, eds. William Coleman and Camille Limoges, Baltimore, Johns Hopkins University Press, 1984, p. 35.

63 See Peter J. Bowler, "Preformation and Pre-existence in the Seventeenth Century," *Journal of the History of Biology*, 4 (2) 1971, pp. 221–44; and Elizabeth B. Gasking, *Investigations into Generation*, London, Hutchinson, 1967.

64 This is the argument of Peter J. Bowler, "Bonnet and Buffon: Theories of Generation and the Problem of Species," *Journal of the History of Biology*, 6 (2), 1973, pp. 259–81.

65 Jean Ferrari, "Kant, lecteur de Buffon," *Buffon 88*, ed. Jean Gayon, Paris, Vrin, 1992, p. 159.

66 Philip D. Curtin, *The Image of Africa. British Ideas and Action, 1780–1850*, Madison, University of Wisconsin Press, 1964, p. 39.

67 "Travellers have exaggerated the mental varieties far beyond the truth, who have denied good qualities to the inhabitants of other countries, because their mode of life, manners and customs have been excessively different from their own." John Hunter, "An Inaugural Disputation on the Varieties of Man," p. 352.

68 *Cyclopaedia: Or an Universal Dictionary of Arts and Sciences* (1728), s. v. "Negro's [sic]." Cited by J. H. Eddy, "Buffon, Organic Alterations and Man," *Studies in the History of Biology*, eds. William Coleman and Camille Limoges, vol. 7, 1984, p. 25.

69 Sir Thomas Browne, *Pseudoxia*, Works, vol. 2, ed. Charles Sayle, Edinburgh, John Grant, 1927, pp. 383–4.

70 Ibid., p. 385.

71 Sandor Gilman gives Kant too much credit for what appears to be a common trope. See *On Blackness without Blacks*, Boston, G. K. Hall, 1982, pp. 33–4. Compare also Adam Smith, *The Theory of Moral Sentiments*, eds. D. D. Raphael and A. L. Macfie, Oxford, Oxford University Press, 1976, p. 199.

72 J. H. Eddy, "Buffon Organic Alterations and Man," pp. 25–7.

73 A. Owen Aldridge, "Feijoo and the Problem of Ethiopian Color," *Racism in the Eighteenth Century*, ed. Harold A. Pagliaro, Cleveland, The Press of Case Western University, 1973, pp. 265 and 275.

74 Georg Forster, "Noch etwas über die Menschenrassen," pp. 134–7.

75 It seems to me that it is to this passage that Kant must be referring when he wrote in 1788 that in a short essay on human races he had tried to show the necessity of resorting to teleological principles where theory proves inadequate (AA VIII 159). For an alternative, see J. D. McFarland, *Kant's Concept of Teleology*, Edinburgh University Press, 1970, p. 61n.

76 J. Blumenbach, "Über den Bildungstrieb und seinen Einfluss auf die Generation und Reproduktion," *Göttingsches Magazin der Wissenschaft und Literatur* 1, no. 5, 1790, pp. 247–66.

77 Johann Friedrich Blumenbach, *Über den Bildungstrieb und das Zeugungsgechäfte*, Göttingen, Johann Christian Dieterich, 1781. Henceforth B2.

78 Johann Friedrich Blumenbach, *Über den Bildungstrieb*, Göttingen, Johann Christian Dieterich, 1791. Henceforth B3.

79 Kant went out of his way to show that the language of preformation could still be used to describe the theory of epigenesis Blumenbach embraced (AAV 423; CJ 311). Furthermore, Girtanner persisted with the language of seeds. *Über das Kantische Prinzip*, p. 11.

80 It is worth noting that section 80 of the *Critique of Judgment* with its praise of comparative anatomy, especially bone structure, was already clearly about Blumenbach.

81 I thus disagree with James Larson's understanding of the letter in "Vital Forces: Regulative Principles or Constitutive Agents," *Isis* 70, 1979, p. 237.

82 See J. Wubnig, "The Epigenesis of Pure Reason," *Kant Studien* 60, 1968–69, pp. 147–57.

83 See Timothy Lenoir, "Kant, Blumenbach, and Vital Materialism in German Biology," *Isis*, 71, 1980, p. 77. Unfortunately, in this essay Lenoir ignores Kant's 1775 essay, so that Kant's originality is not fully appreciated.

84 In addition to the works by Lovejoy, Beiser, Lenoir, McFarland, and Zammito listed elsewhere in these notes, see Paul Bommersheim, "Der Begriff der organischen Selbstreguitation in Kants *Kritik der Urteilskraft*," *Kant Studien* 23, 1919, pp. 209–20; Manfred Riedel, "Historizismus und Kritizismus. Kants Streit mit G. Forster und J. G. Herder," *Kant Studien*, 72, 1981, pp. 41–57; and John H. Zammito, *The Genesis of Kant's Critique of Judgment*, Chicago, University of Chicago Press, 1992, pp. 213–18.

85 Christoph Girtanner, *Über das Kantische Prinzip für die Naturgeschichte*, pp. 17–30. See also Theodor Elsenhans, *Kants Rassentheorie und ihre bleibende Bedeutung*, Leipzig, Wilhelm Engelman, 1904, pp. 40–52.

86 Timothy Lenoir, "Teleology Without Regrets. The Transformation of Physiology in Germany: 1790–1847," *Studies in the History of Philosophy and Science*, 12, 1981, pp. 307–8.

87 This passage was important to Girtanner. He quoted it at *Über das Kantische Prinzip für die Naturgeschichte*, p. 20.

88 J. H. Bernard in *Critique of Judgment*, New York, Hafner, 1951 at p. 269.

89 J. G. Herder, *Auch eine Philosophie der Geschichte zur Bildung der Menschheit*, eds. J. Brummack and M. Bollacher, Frankfurt, Deutscher Klassiker, 1994, p. 11.

90 J. G. Herder, *Ideen zur Philosophie der Geschichte der Menschheit*, ed. M. Bollacher, Frankfurt, Deutscher Klassiker, 1989, p. 256. Henceforth IGM. A translation by Tom Nenon of the crucial chapter can be found in *The Idea of Race*, pp. 23–6. Henceforth PH.

91 Blumenbach insisted on the same point particularly in the first two editions of his treatise. GHV1 40–1 and 50; NV 98–9 and 107. See also GHV2 48–9 and 64.

92 Few commentators have recognized the importance of these sentences. Exceptions include Phillip R. Sloan, "Buffon, German Biology and the Historical Interpretation of Biological Species," pp. 133–4 and Andrea Figl, "Immanuel Kant und die wissenschaftliche Werke des Rassismus," *Zeitschrift für Afrika Studien* 13/14, 1992, pp. 10–11. Unfortunately, this second essay came to my notice too late to take full advantage of it.

93 Herder and Kant shared the idea that the history of mankind should be written with reference to a conception of nature according to which nothing arises aimlessly. However,

they approached the task very differently. For example, Herder had a greater respect for the distinctness of different peoples than Kant and believed that every people contributed to the idea of humanity by virtue of the realization of their own dispositions. See R. Bernasconi, "'Ich mag in keinen Himmel wo Weisse sind'," *Acta Institutionis Philosophiae et Aestheticae* (Tokyo), vol. 13, pp. 69–81. I intend to explore elsewhere the question of Kant's difficulties rewriting his cosmopolitanism with his view of races. Some indication of the problems can be found in Mark Larrimore, "Sublime Waste: Kant on the Destiny of the 'Races'," in *Civilization and Oppression*, ed. Catherine Wilson, *Canadian Journal of Philosophy*, Supplementary volume 25, pp. 99–125.

94 Lucius Outlaw, *On Race and Philosophy*, New York, Routledge, 1996, p. 157.

95 K. Anthony Appiah, "Race, Culture, Identity," in *Color Conscious*, New Jersey, Princeton University Press, 1996, p. 38.

2

ON THE USE OF TELEOLOGICAL PRINCIPLES IN PHILOSOPHY (1788)

Immanuel Kant*

[159] If we understand by *nature* the sum-total of everything that exists determinately according to laws and by world (as nature properly so-called) these things together with their supreme cause, we can attempt to investigate nature following two different methods. The first of these methods is called *physics*, the second *metaphysics*. The method of physics is *theoretical* and employs only such purposes as can be known to us through experience. By contrast, the method of metaphysics is *teleological* and can employ only a purpose established by pure reason for its end. I have demonstrated elsewhere that, in metaphysics, reason cannot secure the *complete* end it desires (with regard to knowledge of God) following the theoretical method of natural investigation. Consequently, the teleological method is the only one that remains for metaphysics. The deficiencies of inadequate theory will, therefore, have to be supplemented not by natural purposes that rest only upon the evidence of experience, but instead by a purpose determinately given *a priori* by pure practical reason (in the Idea of the highest good). In a little essay on the human races, I have tried to demonstrate a similar warrant, indeed a need, to proceed from a teleological principle where theory forsakes us. However, both of these cases include a demand to which understanding submits only reluctantly, and one which can give rise to misunderstanding.

In every investigation of nature, reason properly appeals first to theory and only later to a determination in terms of purposes. No appeal to teleology or practical purposiveness can make up for the deficiencies of theory. We always remain ignorant about efficient causes even when we are able to make plausible the appropriateness of our assumption by appealing to final causes, be they from nature or our will. This complaint seems to be most justified when (as in that metaphysical case) even practical laws must take precedence in order to specify, first of all, the purpose for the sake of which I intend to determine the concept of a cause. This concept, however, is one which has nothing to do with the nature of the object [160] but seems instead to be only a preoccupation with our own ends and needs.

* Translated by Jon Mark Mikkelsen

It is always difficult to agree on principles in those cases where reason has a double, reciprocally limiting interest. What is more, it is difficult just to understand principles of this kind because they concern the method of thinking prior to determining the object and the conflicting claims of reason render the perspective from which one has to consider the object ambiguous. Two essays of mine concerning two very different subjects of varying importance have been subjected to keen examination in the present publication. In one of these I was simply *not understood*, which I had expected, but in the other I was *well understood* beyond all expectation. Both articles were written by gentlemen of superior talent, youthful vigor, and blossoming reputation. In one of these I came under suspicion of wanting to answer a question concerning the *physical* investigation of nature by means of religious documents; in the other I was freed from suspicion of wanting to do damage to religion by means of a proof of the deficiency of a *metaphysical* investigation of nature. In both cases the difficulties are to be understood as resting upon a warrant not yet sufficiently brought to light that would allow the teleological principle to be used where theoretical sources of knowledge do not suffice. The use of this warrant must nevertheless be so limited that the right of *precedence* be secured for theoretical-speculative investigation in order, first of all, to test its full capacity for such inquiry. (Pure reason rightly demands, in the course of this test, that it justify – particularly in the case of metaphysical investigations – this capacity in advance and, in general, its presumption to rule on anything at all. However, this process might also fully reveal the *condition of the cognitive capacities*, thereby permitting us to count on the trust that we place in them.) This freedom shall always remain open to theoretical-speculative investigation. Much of the disagreement in these matters rests upon concern over this possible damage to religion. Such concern threatens the free use of reason. However, if this concern were to be lifted, I believe that the obstacles to agreement could easily be cleared away.

In the *Teutschen Merkur* of October/November 1786, Councilor Georg Forster presented objections against an explanation published in the *Berliner Monatschrift* for November 1785 concerning my previously expressed opinion about the concept and origin of the *human races*. [161] These objections, it seems to me, arose simply from a misunderstanding of the principle from which I began. Indeed, this famous man found it difficult from the very beginning to establish in advance a *principle* on the basis of which the natural scientist might even be led *in the investigation* and observation of nature. In particular, he found it difficult to find a principle on the basis of which we might differentiate the mere *description of nature* from the kind of observation that furthers the study of *natural history*, thereby rendering this distinction illicit. But this unpleasant disagreement can also be easily cleared up.

As for the first dubious claim, it surely cannot be doubted that nothing purposive would ever be found in nature by means of simple empirical groping about without a guiding principle that might direct one's search: for *to observe* means nothing less than to organize experience *methodically*. I am ever thankful for the purely empirically minded traveler and the story he tells, especially when he provides us with coherent knowledge of things that reason can make use of for the purpose of theory. But if someone were to ask him about something that he hadn't considered observing, he would typically answer: "I certainly could have taken note of that had I known that someone would ask me about it." Indeed, Forster himself follows the lead of the

Linnaean principle of the perseverance of the character of the pollinating parts in plants without which the systematic *natural description* of the plant kingdom would not be so gloriously ordered and widely extended as it is. But, unfortunately, it is quite true that many individuals are so careless as to carry their ideas into their own observations (even the great naturalist himself probably took the similarity of characters, due to certain examples, as an indication of the similarity of the powers of plants). Thus, the lesson for *those who reason too quickly* (which presumably does not pertain to either of us) is well established; but this misuse of the rule certainly cannot nullify its validity.

Let us return, however, to the subject of the contested, indeed entirely rejected distinction between the description of nature and natural history. If by the latter one wanted to understand a *narrative account* of natural events to which human reason cannot extend, e.g., the first appearance of plants and animals, then to be sure, as Forster says, this would be a science for gods, who were present at the time of creation or who were themselves the creators, and not one for human beings. A science of *natural history* would, by contrast, concern itself with investigating the connection between certain present properties of the things of nature and their causes in an earlier time in accordance with causal laws that we do not invent but rather derive from [162] the forces of nature as they present themselves to us, pursued back, however, only so far as permitted by analogy. Indeed, this would be of a kind of natural history that is not only possible, but one which is attempted frequently enough, as, for example, in the theories of the earth formulated by careful natural scientists (among which the theories of the famous *Linnaeus* also find their place). These individuals may have accomplished much or little through their research. Likewise, Forster's conjecture concerning the origin of the *Negro* certainly does not belong to the description of nature, but instead only to natural history. This distinction lies in the nature of things; and in making this distinction I am demanding nothing new but instead only the careful separation of one activity from the other, because they are totally *heterogeneous*. Further, if the description of nature makes its appearance as science in all the full splendor of a great system, natural history can only offer us fragments or shaky hypotheses. But even if natural history can, at the present time (and perhaps for ever), only be presented more in outline than in a work of practicable science (i.e., an activity in which one might find a blank space already marked out for the answers to most questions), such efforts are not, I hope, without value. For the result of separating and presenting natural history as a special science distinguishable from the description of nature is that one might not do something with supposed insight for one of these two kinds of investigation which properly belongs to the other. I also hope that we might become more definitely acquainted with the sphere of real knowledge in natural history (for we already possess some knowledge of natural history) along with knowledge of the boundaries and principles of such knowledge lying in reason itself, according to which this knowledge might be extended in the best possible manner. One must make allowances to me for the awkwardness of my exposition in these matters, since I have come to know so much harm in other cases caused by the carelessness of allowing the borders of the sciences to run into one another (as I have pointed out, not exactly to everyone's liking). I am now nevertheless thoroughly convinced that an entirely new light often dawns for the sciences through the mere analysis of heterogeneous things that had previously been supposed to be indistinguishably mixed together. Through such analysis many inadequacies which could previously be hidden behind exotic claims of knowledge are no doubt uncovered, but many previously proscribed, genuine sources of knowledge are also opened up where one would not even have supposed them to exist. The greatest difficulty in this supposed innovation has its source merely in the name. The word *history*, when used to express the same meaning as the Greek historia (tale, description), has already been too much and too long in use for us easily to ascribe it [163] another meaning that can uniquely designate the natural science of origins. The problem is indeed even greater in this case, since one cannot, without difficulty, find another, appropriate term for this science.[1] But resolving the linguistic difficulty in differentiating these two sciences can certainly not remove the difference in the things. Presumably, the cause of this difference of opinion concerning the things themselves has also been the cause of exactly the same unpleasantness which we find in discussions of the concept of a *race*, namely, an unavoidable departure from *classical* expressions. We encounter here what *Sterne* said on the occasion of a dispute about physiogonomy after his whimsical ideas had put all the faculty of the University of Strasburg in an uproar: the logicians might have settled the matter *had they not been pushed to a definition*. What is a *race*? The word certainly does not belong in a systematic description of nature, so presumably the thing itself is nowhere to be found in nature. However, the *concept* which this expression designates is nevertheless well established in the reason of every observer of nature who supposes a conjunction of causes placed originally in the line of descent of the genus itself in order to account for a self-transmitted peculiarity that appears in different interbreeding animals but which does not lie in the concept of their genus. The fact that the word race does not occur in the description of nature (but instead, in its place, the word *variety*) cannot keep an observer of nature from finding it necessary from the viewpoint of natural history. This observer must nevertheless clearly specify how this word is being used, as we wish to attempt in this essay.

The designation *race* to indicate a *radical* peculiarity that announces a common descent – along with several such persistently transmitted characters not admissible only to the same genus of animal but instead to the same line of descent – is not improperly conceived. I would render it through *deviate form* (progenies *classifica*) in order to distinguish a race from a *degeneration* (degeneratio s. progenies *specifica*),[2] [164] something which one cannot allow because it runs counter to the laws of nature (in the preservation of its species in unchangeable form). The word progenies indicates that the species were not originally divided up as species of the same genus through so many different *lines of descent*, but instead that these species first appeared in the developing characters of successive generations. Hence, they are not really species of different *kinds*, but *deviate forms*, even though they are still so distinct and persistent that they are justifiably distinguishable as classes.

According to these preliminary concepts, the *human genus* (following the general characteristics of this term as it is used in the description of nature) could, in a system of nature, be divided into a *line* (or lines) *of descent*, races, or deviate forms (progenies classificae), and different *human stocks* (varietates nativae). The last of these does not, however, contain invariable characteristics passed on according to a given law. Consequently, it does not contain the characteristics needed for a division into classes. But all of this remains a mere idea of the kind showing how reason might unite the greatest diversity in generation with the greatest unity of descent. Observations which make the unity of descent discernible must determine if there really is such a kinship in the human genus. And now we see clearly that we must be led by a determinate principle in order merely to be able *to observe*, that is, in order to give due attention to those things that are an indication of descent and not merely character similarities. This is because we are concerned in these investigations with a task of natural history and not a description of nature and simple methodological classification. When someone takes up the investigation of nature without using such a principle, he will have to search again; for that which he needs, in order to decide whether there might exist a real or merely nominal kinship among created things, will not present itself to him on its own.

There can be no more certain indication of the diversity of the original line of descent than the impossibility of producing fertile offspring through the interbreeding of two human groups of different heredity. [165] However, such interbreeding is successful and not impossible. Thus, the great variety of form is no obstacle to at least possibly finding a common descent for these two groups, since, notwithstanding this difference, they could *unify* themselves through procreation in a product which contains both characters. In this way, they have been able, beginning from one line of descent which originally concealed in itself the predispositions for the development of both characters, to *divide* themselves into so many races through procreation. Reason will not, without need, proceed from two principles if it can make do with one. However, the more certain indication of hereditary peculiarities as the distinctive mark of just so many races has already been introduced. There is nevertheless still something to be noted about hereditary *varieties* that provides a reason for naming one or the other human stocks (family- and folk-stocks).

A variety is a hereditary peculiarity which does not lend itself to classification because it does not inevitably reproduce itself; for this sort of persistence of hereditary character is already required just to legitimate the division into classes needed for the description of nature. A form which reproduces the character of the nearest parents in propagation *only occasionally* – and often only from one side (from the father or mother) – is no distinctive mark from which we can know the lineage from both parents, e.g., the difference between blondes and brunettes. Just so, race or deviate form is an *inevitable* hereditary peculiarity which certainly justifies division into classes, but not into specific classes, because the inevitable half-breed resemblance (that is, the *fusing together* of the characters of their difference) at least makes it not impossible to regard their inheritable, given difference – which can be seen in their original line of descent – as *unified* in simple predispositions and as gradually developed and *separated* only through natural reproduction. For one cannot make a kind of animal into a particular species if it belongs with another in one and the same system of reproduction. Genus and species would, consequently, in natural history, signify one and the same thing, namely, the hereditary peculiarities which cannot be unified in one common descent. But that hereditary, peculiarity which can exist together with another peculiarity is either necessarily hereditary, or it isn't. In the first case, it determines the character of a *race*; in the other case, it determines the character of a *variety*.

Concerning that which in the human genus can be called a *variety*, I here now remark that, with respect to varieties, we may also not regard nature [166] as formed in full freedom, but instead, in the same way as with racial-characters, as only developing, and to be viewed as if they were predetermined in this way through original predispositions. This is so because we also find an appropriate regularity in *this* and the same sorts of cases of purposiveness that cannot be the work of chance. Every portrait painter, who thinks about his art, can similarly confirm what Lord *Shaftesbury* has already noted, namely, that a certain originality – or, as it were, a real uniqueness – will be found in the face of every human being. This originality determinately marks the individual as to particular purposes which they do not have in common with any other individual even if it is clearly beyond our ability to decipher these marks. We ascribe truth to a picture correctly depicting life that is also well-executed, that is, to a picture that is not simply taken from the imagination. But in what does this truth lie? Without doubt, it lies in a definite proportion of one of the many parts of the face to all the others, which, by means of this proportion, expresses an individual character that embodies a dimly represented purpose. No part of the face, even if it appears to us to be out of proportion, can, therefore, be altered in the painting – while leaving the remainder unchanged – without it being immediately noticeable to the expert eye. Thus, whether or not the expert has seen the original, he can tell which of the two contains genuine nature and which fiction when it is compared with that portrait copied from nature. The variety among human beings even from the same race was in all probability inscribed just so purposively in the original line of descent in order to establish – and, in successive generations, to develop – the greatest diversity for the sake of infinitely diverse purposes, just as the difference among races establishes fewer but more essential purposes. The difference, however, prevails, so that the final predispositions – after they have once developed (which must have occurred already in the most ancient times) – does not allow any new forms of this kind to emerge, nor the old forms to be extinguished. On the other hand, the first – at least according to our knowledge – predisposition seems to announce a nature inexhaustible in new characters (outer as well as inner).

With respect to varieties, nature seems to prevent the *fusing together* of characters because this is contrary to her purposes, namely, to preserve a diversity of characters. On the other hand, nature at least permits, even if she does not encourage, the fusing together of characters with respect to racial differences, because through this the progeny will be suited for several [167] climates, although none of those produced by such fusing are suited for several climates to the degree as was the first variant form. For, as far as common opinion is concerned, children (from our class of whites) should inherit from the parents on one side the distinguishing marks which belong to the variety (such as stature, facial form, skin color, and even many infirmities, inner as well as outer). (As people say: the child has this from the father, it has that from its mother.) I cannot, however, after giving closer attention to the notion of a family line, agree to this common view. The children take after, if not equally the mother or father, still either the family of the one or the other unmixed. And if the aversion to the interbreeding of close relatives no doubt surely has for the most part moral grounds, since the sterility of the offspring might not prove sufficient to prevent such interbreeding, its wide range – extending even to barbarian tribes – gives occasion to suppose that the reason for this might, in some distant way, lie in nature itself. For nature does not want the old forms to be reproduced constantly, but rather that all the diversity that she had placed in the original seeds of the human line of descent should be displayed. Likewise, a certain degree of uniformity, such as that which is found in a family line or even in a folk-stock, cannot ascribe its character to the half-breed variant form (which in my opinion does not occur with respect to varieties). For the preponderance of reproductive power in one or the other partners of venerated couples can – through effect and counter-effect from the original, great differentiation of characters (by which the resemblances to the one side becomes less frequent) – diminish the diversity and bring about a certain uniformity (which is visible only to unfamiliar eyes), such that nearly all children sometimes resemble either the paternal or maternal stock. This, however, is only a preliminary opinion of mine which I leave to the reader to judge as he pleases. More importantly, nearly everything that one might, in other animals, call a variety (such as size, qualities of the skin, etc.) looks half-breedish. For this conclusion – if one, as is reasonable, considers humans (with respect to their reproduction) according to an analogy with animals – seems to comprise an objection to my distinction of races from varieties. To decide whether or not this is so, one must take a higher standpoint in order to account for this natural arrangement of things. Specifically, one must assume that reasonless animals, [168] whose existence can have value merely as a means, must have been outfitted for different uses already in their original predispositions (as are the different breeds of dogs, which, according to *Buffon*, are all derived from a common line of descent of sheep dog). By contrast, the greater uniformity of purpose in the human genus does not require such a large difference of natural forms that take after one another. The natural forms necessarily taking after one another might, therefore, have been allowed to be established only for the preservation of the species in a few superior climates differing only slightly from one another. However, it is not really necessary for me to say anything to give credence to my account of the reason why there are varieties, since I only wanted to defend the concept of *race*.

After the resolution of this verbal disagreement, which is frequently more responsible for bickering than any disagreement over principles, I hope now to meet a lesser obstacle to the statement of my kind of explanation. Forster agrees with me in that he at least finds an inheritable peculiarity among different human forms, namely, between the *Negro* and other humans, that is great enough to prevent us from viewing it as a simple play of nature and the result of merely accidential imprints. This inheritable peculiarity requires instead predispositions incorporated originally in the line of descent and a specific natural arrangement. This point of agreement in our theories is no doubt important and also makes possible reconciliation in consideration of the mutual principles of explanation. Instead of the common, superficial way of presenting these matters which takes all differences in our species to be of the same kind, namely, to be merely accidental and as ever appearing and disappearing as ordained by external circumstances, we can declare all investigation of this kind to be superfluous, and, in saying this, the belief in the persistence of species in the same purposive form to be empty. There remain only two differences in our theories, which, however, are not so far apart from one another to constitute a dispute that cannot possibly be resolved. The *first* difference is that Forster believes that only certain supposed heritable characters, namely those which distinguish the *Negro* from all other men, are the only ones which deserve to be viewed as originally implanted, while I, by contrast, would judge several others (those of the *Asian-Indians* and the *Americans*, in addition to those of *whites*) to be equally well justified for the complete classificatory division. The *second* difference, which is not so much concerned with observation (the description of nature) as with supposed theory (natural history), is that Forster [169] finds two original lines of descent necessary for the sake of explaining these characters, while, in my opinion it is possible – and more appropriate for an explanation of a philosophical type – to look on these characters (which I, along with Forster, believe to be original characters) as a further development of purposive primary predispositions implanted in the line of descent. But this is also not so great a disagreement that reason should not be able to offer a hand in resolving it, if one remembers that the physical, first source of organic being and human reason in general remains just as unfathomable for both of us as do the half-breed resemblances in the reproduction of the same species. Since it does not secure the slightest bit more for rational comprehensibility to assume, as Forster does, that the system of seeds was separated from the very beginning and isolated into two lines of descent, but that they were later, in the mixing of the previously separated seeds, again harmoniously melted together, than to assume, as I do, that the evolving seeds were distinct but originally implanted in one and the same line of descent *purposively suited for the first general populating of the earth* through their offspring, Forster should not be reluctant to concede to his two stocks an equal claim to special, original, implanted seeds. Further, my hypothesis carries with it the advantage of not requiring different local creations, since it is not at all possible to suppose an economy of *teleological* explanations in the case of organized beings in order to supplant them with physical explanations with regard to the preservation of their kind; but the latter kind of explanation – that is, the kind of explanation befitting natural science – imposes thereby no new burden beyond that which it can never be rid of anyway, namely, that of following *the principle of purposes*. Besides, it was only through the discoveries of his friend, *Sömmering*, the famous philosophical anatomist, that Forster finds the difference between the Negro and other men more important than they would have liked. For they would gladly have viewed all heritable characters as having vanished into one another and as merely accidental shadings. But this splendid man even affirms the perfect purposefulness of the development of the Negro with reference to his motherland,[3] although a comprehensible fitness to his climate is not so equally to be perceived in the bony structure of the head [170] as is to be found in the organization of the skin; for the skin is the great instrument for discharging everything that should be eliminated from the blood. Hence, Sömmering seems to understand *this* from all of the remaining elements of the exceptional natural arrangement pertaining to the development of the Negro (of which the quality of the skin is an important part), since this, for the anatomist, presents the clearest mark of truth. These, therefore, are the reasons why Forster should not be reluctant to concede to his two stocks an equal claim to special, original, implanted seeds suitable for the entire stock. To come to this conclusion, however, it must also be proven that there are other, equally persistent transmittable characteristics in fewer number, according to the gradation of climate, which do not blend into one another but which are instead rather sharply divided, whether or not these characteristics conform to those already accepted by the art of anatomy. Whether it is necessary to assume several, or only one, common line of descent is, however, something about which we can, hopefully, eventually still reach agreement.

To concur with my view would, therefore, be only to raise the difficulties which Forster backs off from, not so much in consideration of the principle itself, but rather in considering the difficulty of adapting it to all of the cases to which it applies. In the first section of his article of October 1786, p. 70, Forster introduces a guide to the skin color of the peoples who live in the regions of northern Europe extending through Spain, Egypt, Arabia, and Abyssinia to the equator, but which, beginning from the equator, is extended even further, in reversed gradations corresponding to the climatic shift in the temperate southern zone, to include the peoples of the lands inhabited (in his view) by the Kassernians and Hottentots. This guide presents Forster's view that the skin color of all these peoples – from southern Europe to the tip of Africa – can be proportionately calibrated to the climate of the land, changing from brown to black and back again to brown (whereby he supposes, although without proof, that the Kasserians and Hottentots are descended from colonies in central Africa that migrated to the tip of Africa, and that these migrating peoples were, merely through the effect of climate, gradually transformed into Kassernians and Hottentots). All of this so surprised Forster that he wondered how anyone could still overlook it. We must, however, even more justifiably wonder how anyone could have overlooked the distinctive characteristics of the inevitable half-breed offspring, which is sufficiently determinate and provides the only basis for making decisions about everything at issue in these matters. [171] For neither the interbreeding of northern Europeans with those of Spanish blood, nor the interbreeding of the Mauritanians or Arabs (and presumably also their near relatives, the Habessinians) with Circassian women, supports at all the rule presumably derivable from Forster's color guide. We also have no reason to judge their color – which is firmly established by one side or the other of the family line – according to that which the sun of their land imprints upon each individual in the last example as something different than what one judges olive-skinned individuals to be among whites. Concerning, however, the ways in which the Kassernians and, to a lesser degree, the Hottentots, are similar to the Negroes in that same part of the world, cases which would presumably pass the test of half-breed offspring: it is in the highest degree probable that they might be nothing other than the bastard offspring of a Negroid people who interbred with the offspring of Arabs who have frequented this coastal area ever since the earliest times. For how else could it be that one does not find the same supposed gradations of skin color among the peoples living on the west coast of Africa, where nature instead makes a sudden jump from the olive-skinned Arabs or Mauritanians to the blackest Negroes in Senegal without going first through the intermediate rung represented by the Kassernians? This case also invalidates the experimental test suggested by Forster (p. 74). This test is decisive throughout Forster's article and it should have proven the unacceptability of my principle. Specifically, the test should show that the dark brown Habessinian interbred with a female Kassernian would not produce an intermediary stock according to color, because both colors are the same, namely, brownish black. For Forster assumes that the depth of the brown color of the Habessinian, like that of the Kassernians, might be inherent, and indeed such that an intermediary color must necessarily be given in the offspring produced by interbreeding with a white. Were this so, the test would certainly turn out as Forster wants. However, he would also prove nothing against me, because the differences of the races is not to be judged according to that which is the same in them, but rather according to that which is different. One would only be able to say that there might also be deep brown races which distinguish themselves from Negroes or their descendants according to *other distinguishing characteristics* (for example, bone structure); for only with respect to these characteristics would the offspring produce a hybrid and my catalogue of colors would only be increased by one. If, on the other hand, the deep color which the Habessinian – who grew up in his own land – bears is not passed on, but is instead, like that of a Spaniard who might have been raised from childhood in the same land, then without doubt his natural color would yield an intermediary type of offspring with that of the Kassernians, but one which, because of the additional, coincidental coloration caused by the [172] sun, would remain hidden and seem to be of the same human type (when judged according to color). Therefore, this projected test proves nothing against the usefulness of necessarily heritable skin color for distinguishing different races, but rather only the difficulty of correctly determining skin color, in so far as it is hereditary, according to place when the sun covers it over with accidental coloration. However, this projected test does confirm the legitimacy of my demand to give preference to *offspring* from parents of the same race living *in foreign lands* for the purpose of distinguishing different races.

Of the latter, we now have a deciding example in the Asian–Indian skin color of a small band of people who have been reproducing in our northern lands for several centuries, namely, the *gypsies*. That they are an *Asian–Indian* people is proven by their speech independently of their skin color. But nature remains so persistent in preserving their skin color that, if indeed one can follow their presence in Europe back twelve generations, they still turn up so perfect that, had they grown up in India, no difference would, in all probability, be found between them and those who were born in India. To say now that one would have to wait still twelve times twelve generations until the northern air had fully bleached out the inherited color would mean to put off the natural scientist with dilatory answers and to look for excuses. To pass off their color as a mere variety – somewhat like the skin color of the olive-skinned Spaniard compared to that of the Danes – means to doubt the imprint of nature. For when they interbreed with our old native born they inevitably produce half-breed children who are not subject to the same laws to which the race of whites is subject with respect to any one of its characteristic varieties.

However, the most important counter-argument to Forster's views appears on pages 155–6. In the event that this counter-argument were established, it might be proven – were one also to concede to me my notion of *original predispositions* – that the fitness of human beings to their mother lands could not co-exist *with their dispersion* over the face of the earth. Forster, on the other hand, still thinks it entirely defensible to say that *precisely those* human beings *whose predisposition* makes them suited *for this* or that *climate* would be born here or there through a wise act of Providence. But, he continues, how then has this same Providence become so short-sighted not to think of a *second transplanting*, when that seed, were it fitted only for one climate, would become totally without purpose? [173]

As for the first point, one might remember that I did not assume that these primary predispositions were *divided among different* kinds of human beings but instead that they were *united* in the first human couple. For if this were not the case there might have been several different *lines of descent*. Thus the descendants of this first human couple, for whom the *complete* original predisposition is still undivided for all future deviate forms, were (potentially) fitted for all climates. Their seed could, in other words, have developed in such a way that would make them fitted for that one region of the earth into which they or their early offspring might have wandered. A special, wise act of Providence is not, therefore, required to bring them to such places to which their predispositions are fitted. Rather, the seed making them fitted for such a climate through the way in which they are organized for a specific region of the earth developed there, where they, who accidentally came into a certain region, stayed for generations. The development of these predispositions conforms, in short, according to my view, to the places. Forster, however, mistakenly thinks that the places must somehow have been sought out that conform to the already developed predispositions. All this is understood, however, to have happened only in the earliest times and to have lasted long enough (for a gradual populating of the earth) in order, first and foremost, to provide a people having a permanent place to live the requisite influence of climate and land needed for the development of those predispositions fitted to this place. This, then, is the point in his account where he asks: but how, then, did this same intelligence – which had previously calculated so correctly which lands and which seeds should come into conjunction with one another – all at once become so short-sighted that it did not foresee the need for *a second transplanting*? (For lands and seeds *must*, according to the foregoing account, *always* come together if one also wants to claim that it wasn't an intelligence that might just so carefully have equipped them for this task, but instead only the same nature which had – so thoroughly, purposefully, and inwardly – first outfitted the organization of animals for their preservation as well.) For through this process, the inborn peculiarities that are useful for only one climate will thereby become entirely without purpose, etc.

As for the second point of this objection, I concede that this intelligence – or, if one prefers, this purposive nature working in conformity with seeds that had, through transplantation, already developed further – did not actually give much consideration to the fact that it might be accused of being unwise and short-sighted, even if it had not done all this. To the contrary, nature has prevented human beings from mistakenly exchanging one climate for another – especially the warm for the cold – through their established fitness to a specific climate. For nature, working on her own, checks this calamitous adaptation to a new region [174] by those inhabitants of an old region whose natural dispositions have already become adapted to the old region. Where, for example, have Asian–Indians or Negroes ever attempted to spread out into northern lands? The descendants of those exiled in northern lands (like the Creole *Negroes* or *Asian–Indians* known as gypsies) have never wanted to become a stock useful to settled farmers or craftsmen.[4] [175]

However, even those cases that Forster believes to pose an insurmountable difficulty for my principle are cast in the most advantageous light. For these cases, when viewed in a certain way, can solve problems that no other theory has any power to resolve. I assume that there have been as many generations from the time of the beginning of the human genus through the gradual development of the variant form, whose present predispositions are fully adapted to a climate, as is required to account for the development of these predispositions. I also assume that the distribution of these variant forms, caused for the most part by powerful natural revolutions, could have occurred over a considerable part of the earth with only insignificant increases in the kinds of variant forms. If through these causes a small band of people of the old world is driven from southern regions to northern ones, then the development of this variant form must gradually come to a standstill. To be consistent with what was previously stated, however, this development is perhaps not yet complete, but a place has also been made for a complimentary development of predispositions (namely, the predispositions needed for a northern climate). Assume, then, that this human stock were to migrate even further northwards toward America – a view which, admittedly, has the highest possibility. Before this band of people could move again from this part of the world to the south, its natural predispositions would already be as developed as much as possible. This development, were it then complete, would have made all further variant formation for a new climate impossible. Consequently, a race would then be established which, in the event that it moved south again, is forever one and the same for all climates. But, in actuality, this race would belong suitably to no climate, because the change in the southern variant form was interrupted in the middle of its development, before its departure, by the northerly climate. So, the persistent condition of these human bands had already been established. Indeed, *Don Ulloa* (an especially important witness who knew native American inhabitants from both hemispheres) affirms that the characteristic appearance of the natives of this continent has been found to be thoroughly similar. (Their color, for example, has been described by a recent seafarer, whose name I cannot presently give with certainty, as *iron rust* mixed with *oil*.) But the fact that their natural disposition has not yet reached a *complete* fitness for any one climate provides a test that can hardly offer another explanation [176] why this race, too weak for hard labor, too indifferent for diligence, and unfit for any culture, still stands – despite the proximity of example and ample encouragement – far below the Negro himself, who undoubtedly holds the lowest of all remaining levels by which we designate the different races.

Now consider all other possible hypotheses to account for this phenomenon! If one does not wish to add to the special creation of the Negro, already proposed by Forster, a second special creation, namely, that of the American Indian, there remains no other answer than that America is either too *cold* or too *new* ever to produce a deviate form such as the Negro or the yellow Indian, or to have already produced them in the short time since America has been populated. The first claim, concerning the warm climate of the continent, has now been sufficiently refuted. As for the *second* claim, namely, that, if one only had sufficient patience to wait a few thousand years, the Negro would someday (at least as far as heritable skin color goes) also appear here through the gradual influence of the sun, one would first have to be certain, before supporting this view, that sun and air can bring about such an engrafting simply in order to defend oneself against the *objections* that this purely assumed consequence, so loosely stated and shifted around at pleasure, could indeed have come about in the way it is said to have. But since this view is itself still very much subject to doubt, can any one imagine presenting a lesser, merely arbitrary assumption, contrary to the *facts?*

There is an important validation of the derivation of invariable hereditary differences through early, purposeful development in a human line of descent for the preservation of the kind of predispositions that can be found together. This validation can be found in the fact that the races that actually developed are not dispersed through this process *sporadically* (in all parts of the world, in one and the same climate, of the same type), but are instead dispersed *cycladicly* in small, unified bands of people. These bands may even have been formed from smaller groups that were divided within the boundaries of a region which happened to meet up with one another. Thus, the *pure* descent of the *yellow-skinned* peoples are confined within the borders of *Hindustan*, while *Arabia*, which is not far away and which occupies for the most part the same latitude, holds no yellow-skinned peoples. However, neither of these regions holds any *Negroes*, who are to be found only in *Africa* between *Senegal* and *Cape Negro* (and more widely in the interior of this continent). In fact, neither yellow-skinned peoples nor Negroes are to be found in all of America. Indeed, no racial character whatsoever of the old world can be found among the peoples of the Americas (excepting the *Eskimo*, [177] who, according to various features taken from their appearance, as well as by their abilities, appear to be later arrivals from one of the old continents). Each of these races is virtually isolated. They also share the same climate, yet are still distinguished from one another through an inseparable, appended feature that is surely transmitted through their ability to reproduce. Consequently, they make the opinion that the origin of the second of these two races as a result of climate unlikely. They corroborate instead the presumption of a universal kinship among offspring through unity of descent. But we can at the same time determine the *cause* of the classical distinction among these different races. This cause does not lie in the climate, but comes from within these peoples themselves. The distinction must also have required a long time to make its effect fitted to the place of propagation. Then, after all this had finally taken place, new deviate forms were no longer possible because there was no further displacement of these peoples. The distinction can be viewed then as arising from nothing other than a gradually, purposefully developing *original predisposition* laying in the line of descent and limited to a certain number of features according to the chief differences resulting from atmospheric influences. The scattered races of the *Papuans*, which belong to the south Asian islands that extend eastward to the Pacific Ocean, seem to seriously weaken this argument. I, along with Captain *Forrester*, have called these people Kaffirs (because he has found reasons not to classify them with the Negro, presumably partly because of their skin color, and partly because of their head and beard hair, which, contrary to the characteristic features of the Negro, can be combed out to a presentable length). But the wondrous dispersion of still other races, namely, the Haragorans, and, more certainly, peoples similar to the pure Asian–Indian line of descent, rehabilitate the argument, because the fact of such dispersion also weakens the case for the effect of climate on their inherited traits inasmuch as these traits, so dissimilar, do not all come out at the same latitude. Hence, there are, in all probability, good reasons not to view these peoples as aborigines, but rather as foreigners who were – for who knows what reasons – driven from the regions where they had previously lived. (These Papuans were probably from Madagascar and were perhaps driven into this new region because of a powerful upheaval of the earth, which moved from west to east.) As for the inhabitants of *Frewill Island*, I can only state from memory (perhaps incorrectly) the report of *Carterets*. But if memory serves me well, one will look for evidence of the development of racial differences in the presumed place of residence of their line of descent on the *continent* and not on the islands [178], which, to all appearances, were first populated through an operation of nature completed long ago.

So much then for the defense of my theory of the derivation of the inheritable variety of organic creatures from one and the same *natural genus* (species naturalis, in so far as these creatures are united through their ability to reproduce and could have originated from one common line of descent).[5] This notion of a *natural genus* is, however, to be distinguished from an *artificial genus* (species artificialis, in so far as these creatures merely share a common, purely comparative, characteristic). The first of these notions belongs to a natural history. The second belongs to a description of nature. I want then next to say something more about the origin of Forster's peculiar system. We both agree that in a system of natural science everything must be explained *naturally*, or else nothing would belong to this science. I have followed this maxim so carefully that a perspicacious gentleman (O. C. R. *Büsching*, in a review of a previously noted work of mine) makes me into *a naturalist*, if only, as he adds, one *of a certain type*, because of my use of expressions referring to the intention, wisdom, care, etc., of nature. For I do not find it advisable to use theological language in discussions that concern the mere knowledge of nature and how far it extends (although it is totally proper to express oneself teleologically in these cases). I follow this maxim in order to point out quite carefully the boundaries of every type of knowledge.

But this same maxim, that everything in natural science must be explained naturally, points, at the same time, to the limits of natural science. [179] For one has reached the boundary of natural science when one uses the last of all explanatory reasons that can still be time-tested by *experience*. When experience ends and one begins to explain natural phenomena by appealing to material forces that one has personally invented and which only operate according to unheard of laws, incapable of proof, one has already gone beyond natural science. It hardly matters in these cases whether we still call natural things causes, since one is, at the same time, ascribing powers to them, the existence of which cannot by any means be proven, and whose very possibility can, only with difficulty, be reconciled with reason. The concept of an organized being presupposes that this thing should be a matter in which everything stands in the reciprocal relationship of ends and means to one another. Such a being can be conceived only as a *system of final causes*. Consequently, only teleological types of explanation are left to account for the possibility of such a being, at least for *human* reason, but a physico-mechanical type explanation can never be used in such cases. Thus, physics cannot ask where all organization itself originally came from. The answer to this question, if it is available to us at all, would obviously lie *outside* natural science, in *metaphysics*. I, for my part, derive all organization from *organic beings* (through reproduction) and account for later forms (of this sort of natural thing) through laws of gradual development from *original predispositions* (of the kind that one frequently finds in the transplantation of plants). I assume that these predispositions were to be found in the organization of the line of descent. To explain, however, how the line of descent itself might have *come into existence* is a task that lies completely beyond the boundaries of any physics possible for human beings. I certainly believed, therefore, that I had to hold myself within these boundaries.

For these reasons, I fear nothing that might arise from a Court of Inquisition against Forster's system (for that would be to presume a jurisdiction outside its proper domain); and even if I were to submit crucial cases to a philosophical *jury* (p. 166) of pure naturalists I can hardly believe that their verdict would come out favourable for him. Consider, for example, the following passages from Forster's work:

> This earth in labor (p. 80) gives birth from her womb – impregnated by the slime of the sea – to animals and plants without procreation from beings like them; the regional production of organic genera thereby established gives rise in *Africa* to its particular kind of human being (the Negro) and in *Asia* to its own (all the others) (p. 158); the kinship of everything – from humans to whales and even further in a natural chain[6] of organic being (extending, presumably, to mosses and lichens) [180] – that derives from this productive process (p. 77) exists not merely in a comparative system of likenesses but is instead part of a system of reproduction descended from a common line of descent.

The natural scientist would not recoil from these passages as he might from some monster (p. 75) (for this is a game with which many a person has certainly amused themselves, but then given up because nothing is to be gained by it). He would, however, shrink away from it were he to consider that he had strayed from the fertile grounds of natural science into the desert of metaphysics. I know, in addition to this, yet another *unmanly* fear, namely, to shrink back from everything that reason releases from her first principles. For this makes it possible for reason to wander about in unbounded imagination. Perhaps Forster has done a favor to some *hyper-metaphysician* and wanted to provide material for his own fantasy that he might himself be amused by later (for there are also those people who are not even acquainted with the elementary concepts of sound natural science and who behave as if to scorn them and go heroically in quest of conquests).

True metaphysics knows the limits of human reason. Among other limits, true metaphysics recognizes reason's hereditary defect, which she can never disavow, namely, that true metaphysics can or may devise *a priori* absolutely no *fundamental powers* (because she would thereby be concocting nothing but empty concepts). True metaphysics can instead, learning from experience, do nothing more than reduce its concepts of those fundamental powers to the smallest number possible (in so far as these powers only appear to be different, but are fundamentally identical). When these powers are to be of value for physics they are to be sought in the *world*; but when they are of concern to metaphysics (that is to say, when they are of concern to that which is not dependent on anything else) they must always be sought *outside the world*. We can, however, have no other concept of a fundamental power (since we know it only through the relation of cause upon an effect) and can find no other name for it than that which is taken from the effect and which expresses precisely this relation.[7] [181] Now the concept of an organized being is the concept of a material being possible only through the relation of all that which is contained in it existing reciprocally as ends and means (as, in fact, every anatomist, as physiologist, also presumes when considering such beings). A fundamental power through which organization might be produced must, therefore, be thought of as a purposive, efficient cause. Indeed, it must be thought of as the sort of cause that could not possibly have the effect that it does, were it not for these purposes. We recognize this power *according to its determining grounds*, however, through experience solely within ourselves, namely, through experience of our understanding and will as a cause of the possibility of certain products set up entirely according to purposes, that is, through our experience of *works of art*. Understanding and will are, for us, fundamental powers, of which the latter, in so far as it is determined by the former, is a capacity to produce something in accordance with an *Idea*, which is called a purpose. We should not, however, independent from all experience, devise any new fundamental powers that might purposefully have an effect upon a thing which did not have its determining ground in an Idea. Therefore, the concept of a being that has the capacity to act *purposefully* of itself, but *without purpose* or intention lying in itself or its cause – as a special fundamental power, for which there is no example in experience – is entirely fanciful and empty. There is, in other words, not the slightest assurance that this concept [182] could ever correspond to any object whatsoever. The cause of organized beings might, therefore, be found *in* the world or *outside* of the world. Consequently, we must either abandon all efforts to determine their cause or conceive of an *intelligent being* in addition to ourselves. The point of all this is not that we had realized (as the late Mendelssohn and others believed) that such an effect would be *impossible* were there no other cause, but rather that we would need to *invent* a fundamental power in order to explain another cause, with the exclusion of a final cause. But reason has no authority to go so far as that, because it would then have no difficulty in explaining *whatever* it wished to explain *however* it wished.

⋆ ⋆ ⋆

And now to draw the result from all this! *Purposes* have a direct connection to *reason*, be they unknown or our own. However, in order to place purposes in an unknown reason we must first lay down the foundations of our own reason, if only analogically to an unknown reason, because purposes simply cannot be represented at all without doing this. Purposes are either purposes of *nature* or of *freedom*. No human being appreciates *a priori* that there must be purposes in nature, but we can very well appreciate *a priori* that there must be a connection between causes and effects. Consequently, the use of the teleological principle is, in the consideration of nature, always empirically conditioned. The same might be said with regard to purposes of freedom if such purposes must be specified prior to the objects of volition through the agency of nature (in needs and inclinations) as the determining grounds of action, since we make these things into purposes simply in order to decide what we can do through a rational comparison of these needs and inclinations with one another and with their sum total. The critique of practical reason shows nevertheless that there are pure practical principles through which reason is determined *a priori*. These pure practical principles also specify *a priori*, therefore, the purpose for which reason exists. Thus, if the use of teleological principles is to be of any value for explaining nature, the ultimate basis of the purposive connection can never be fully specified or sufficiently determined for all purposes, since such use is always limited by empirical conditions. One must instead expect this purposive connection to come from a *pure theory of purpose*. (This theory can be of no other kind than that which is concerned with purposes of *freedom*.) The principle *a priori* of this theory embodies the relationship of reason in general to the totality of all purposes and can only be practical. However, since a pure practical [183] teleology, i.e., a moral teleology, is intended to realize its purposes in the world, it cannot be allowed to pass over the *possibility* that these purposes can be realized in the world. A pure practical teleology cannot, in other words, be allowed to ignore transcendental philosophy in considering the *final causes* that might thereby be given as well as the fitness of the *supreme world cause* to be the efficient cause of a totality of purposes. Hence, it also cannot ignore considering the possibility of a natural *teleology* or the possibility of nature in general, since these are also issues addressed by transcendental philosophy. For were it to ignore these issues, it would also pass over an opportunity to secure the objective reality for the practical pure theory of purpose with respect to the possibility of such objects in our daily practice, that is, objects of purposes which it prescribes as having an effect in the world.

In both respects, *the author of the letter concerning the critical philosophy* has demonstrated, in exemplary fashion, his talent, insight, and praiseworthy way of thinking applying each of these usefully to universal necessary purposes. And if it indeed be an imposition on the superb editor of the present publication, which seems to tread too close to modesty, I could not fail to beg of him to permit me to insert in his journal my recognition of the service of the unnamed author of this letter, who was, until recently, also unknown to me, in order to make a contribution to the joint concerns of speculative as well as practical reason, pursued according to fixed principles, as I have attempted to do. The talent for giving an illuminating and even charming presentation of a dry, distilled theory without damage to its thoroughness is so rare (if only allowing for the age of the author) and, all the same, so useful. I do not want to say this merely as a recommendation, but instead to extend publicly my thanks for the clarity of insight, the understanding, and the persuasiveness that is bound up with these qualities. I feel myself bound, in fact, to extend such thanks to that individual who has supplemented my work in ways so as to facilitate understanding that I could never have supplied.

I also want to take this opportunity to touch briefly on the charge that an alleged contradiction has been discovered in a work of considerable scope, before one has fully comprehended it. These contradictions disappear altogether on their own, however, when one examines them in connection with everything else. In the *Leipziger Zeitung* (1787, No. 94) a passage from the Introduction of the *Critique of Pure Reason*, p. 3, 1. 7 (1787 edition), is given together with another, from shortly thereafter, p. 5, 11. 1–2. These passages seem to stand in direct contradiction. For in the first passage I said that knowledge *a priori* is called pure when it is [184] not *mixed* with anything empirical. As an example of the opposite of this, this sentence followed: everything *changeable* has a cause. On the other hand, I offer on page 5 this same sentence as an example of pure knowledge *a priori*, that is, as a kind of knowledge that is not dependent upon anything empirical. I have, therefore, admittedly appealed to two different meanings of the word *pure*, although in the work as a whole I am concerned only with the second of these meanings. To be sure, I could have averted misunderstanding by using a different sentence as an example of the first meaning of *pure*, such as: everything accidental has a cause. For here there is absolutely nothing empirical *mixed* in. But who considers all occasions for misunderstanding?

Exactly the same sort of thing has befallen me with a note to the Preface of the *Metaphysical Foundations of Natural Science*, pp. xvi–xvii, where I represent the Deduction of the categories as important, but not as *ultimately necessary*, while I studiously asserted the latter view in the *Critique*. But one easily sees that the categories are viewed in the *Metaphysical Foundations* only from a *negative* point of view, namely, only in order to demonstrate that it would not be possible by means of the categories *alone* (without sensible intuition) to come to any knowledge of a thing, since this is already clear if one also only refers to the *Exposition* of the categories (as pure logical functions applied to objects in general). However, because we make use of these categories and because through this use they really belong to the *knowledge* of objects (of experience), the possibility of the *a priori* objective validity of such concepts in relation to the empirical must be expressly demonstrated. For if we do not do this, the categories would be judged to be entirely without meaning or not really to have *originated* empirically. This, however, was the *positive* point of view with respect to which the *Deduction* is, to be sure, indispensably necessary.

I just now learned that the author of the above-mentioned letter is Councilor *Reinhold*, recently appointed professor of philosophy in Jena, an addition to the faculty which cannot be other than very advantageous to this renowned university.

Notes

1 I would suggest the word *physiography* for the description of nature and *physiogony* for natural history.

2 The nomenclature of classes and orders expresses completely and without any ambiguity a *logical* distinction that *reason* makes among its concepts for the purpose of simple *comparison*; but *genera* and *species* can also signify the *physical* distinction that *nature* herself makes among her creatures with respect to their *procreation*. The character of a race can, therefore, suffice thereafter in order to classify creatures, but not to construct a distinct *species*, since this could also signify à distinct descent that we do not wish to understand by use of the term race. It is obvious that we do not use the word class in the extended meaning that it has in the *Linnaean* system; but we also use it for grouping things together for a completely different purpose.

3 Concerning the physical differences between the Negro and the Europeans, *Sömmering* writes, p. 79: "One finds characteristics in the build of the Negro which make him most perfect for his climate, perhaps as perfect as the Europeans." This splendid man also doubts (in the same publication, p. 44) *D. Schott's* view that the more skillfully organized skin of the Negro improves the release of harmful matter. However, when one combines this with *Lind's* reports (on the diseases of the Europeans, etc.) about the harmfulness of the air phylogistized by swampy wooded areas around the Gambia river, which was, so swiftly, so deadly to English sailors, that view gains much probability, since Negroes live all the same in this region as in their element.

4 The last remark is not introduced in this context as conclusive, but it is nevertheless not insignificant. In *Sprengel's* Contributions, Fifth Part, pp. 287–92, a knowledgeable man states, in opposition to Ramsay's desire to make use of all Negro slaves as *free* workers, that, among the many thousand freed Negroes that one meets in America and England, he is acquainted with no instance in which any one of them has ever pursued an occupation that one can really call *work*. To the contrary, he says that when such slaves get their freedom they immediately give up the easy work they had previously been forced to do as slaves in order to become hawkers, *miserable* innkeepers, livery stable workers, always going fishing or hunting, or, in one word, petty hustlers. One also finds exactly the same pattern of behavior in the gypsies among us. The same author notes that it is not in some way or other the northern climate that might possibly make them disinclined to work; for when they must

wait behind the wagons of their masters or, on the worst winter nights, in the cold entrances to the theatre (in England), they hold up much better than they do when threshing, ditch digging, or carrying cargo, etc. Should one not conclude from this that there still exists, apart from the *ability* to work, an immediate drive for activity independent of all enticement to work (presumably the drive for persevering, which we call industry), that is specifically interwoven with certain natural predispositions, and that Indians as well as Negroes bring with them and pass on to their offspring no more of this impulse when living in other climates than what they had needed and received from nature for their preservation in their old motherland, and that this inner predisposition might be extinguished just so little as the outwardly perceivable? However, the much smaller needs in those lands and the little trouble required to satisfy only them requires no great predisposition for keeping oneself busy.

I want here to quote something else from *Marsden's* thorough description of Sumatra (see Sprengel's Contributions, Sixth Part, pp. 198–99):

"The color of their (the *Rejangs*) skin is usually *yellow* without the admixture of red, which the copper color brings out. They are almost universally somewhat lighter in complexion than the Mestizo in other regions of India. The white color of the inhabitants of Sumatra, *in comparison with other people of exactly the same climate*, is to my mind a stronger proof that the color of the skin depends in no way directly upon the climate. (He says precisely the same thing about the children of Europeans and Negroes born there in the second generation and supposes that the darker color of the Europeans, who have stayed here a long time, might be a consequence of the many diseases of the gall bladder to which everyone there is exposed.) I must also mention here that the hands of the natives and Mestizo are unusually cold, not considering the hot climate" (an important detail which indicates that the characteristic properties of the skin do not necessarily arise from superficial external causes).

5 To belong to one and the same line of descent does not directly signify generation from a single original *pair*; it only says that the diversity that we find in a certain animal genus may not – simply on the basis of that diversity – be regarded as arising from so many original differences. If the first human line of descent was comprised then of just so many individuals (of both sexes), which were nonetheless of the same kind, I can derive existing human beings equally well from one single pair as from many pairs. Forster suspects me of wanting to claim on the strength of expert authority the latter possibility as a fact. But it is just an idea that follows quite naturally from the theory. As for the difficulty that human kind would have been poorly secured from flesh-eating animals had it begun from a single pair, this cannot pose a serious difficulty for the sort of account he offers, since his all-begetting earth would only allow that these animals had been produced later than human beings.

6 Concerning this idea, which has become very popular primarily through *Bonnet*, the memoir of Professor *Blumenbach* (Handbook of Natural History, 1779, Lecture No. 7) deserves to be read. This observant, reasonable man ascribes the *formative impulse*, by means of which he has cleared up so many issues in the theory of reproduction, not to inorganic matter, but instead only to the rank of organized beings.

7 For example, *imagination* in human beings is an effect which we do not recognize as the same as other effects of the mind. Hence, the power to which it corresponds can only be called the power of imagination (as a fundamental power). In the same way, the powers of repulsion and attraction are, among those things that fall under the heading of moving powers, *fundamental powers*. Many different researchers have believed that it was necessary to assume a single fundamental power to account for the unity of substance. Many of them have even believed that they had identified it in so far as they merely gave a *common name* to different fundamental powers, e.g., the sole fundamental power of the soul might be called

the world's power of representation. This would be no different than if I were to say that the only fundamental power of matter is the moving power because repulsion and attraction both fall under the common concept of motion. We need to know, however, if repulsion and attraction can be *derived* from this common concept, which is not possible. For *lower-order* concepts can never be derived from the *higher-order* ones according to what is different in them. As for the unity of substance, it seems that the concept of the unity of fundamental powers is contained in the very concept of such a unity. But this delusion rests upon an improper definition of *power*. For this power is not that *which* contains the ground of the actuality of the accidents (that is the substance); it is instead merely the *relation* of the substance to the accidents *in so far as* it contains the ground of their actuality. However, different relations can certainly be attributed to the substance (without doing harm to its unity).

PART II

DU BOIS AND THE CONSERVATION OF RACES

3

DU BOIS'S ANTHROPOLOGICAL NOTION OF RACE

Tommy Lott

Despite the fact that Du Bois is widely known for his sociological and historical research on African-Americans, not much attention has been given to his anthropological writings, or the anthropological notion of race underlying his lifelong commitment to the study of black people.[1] Views presented on all sides of the current debate regarding his definition of race in "The Conservation of Races" have been woefully negligent in this regard.[2] His commitment to the biological categories of race in "The Conservation of Races" has been a source of criticism, but his account of these categories has gone largely unremarked. One consequence of this neglect is that his insistence on sociohistorical criteria to define race has generated confusion. He is understood by some commentators to have rejected the biological view of race, while others have taken him to task for inconsistently relying on a biological view that he ought to have rejected given his argument against it.[3] Although I believe this line of criticism is not completely without merit, I will show that it fails to appreciate the status Du Bios accorded science, especially anthropology, in his account of race.

In *Dusk of Dawn*[4] Du Bois indicates his awareness of the "contradiction" in his earlier account in "The Conservation of Races" by means of a facetious characterization of his earlier commitment to the biological view. He refers (p. 100) to that earlier commitment as something that went unquestioned in the nineteenth century. But that essay is so remarkable because of the revisionist concept of race Du Bois proposed as an alternative in that context.[5] His assessment of a "contradiction" in his earlier view refers not only to the inconsistent criteria used to classify races, but also to a shift in his later view. This shift, however, seems to point more to a change in the prevailing view, for there is no difference in the concept of race he employed in "The Conservation of Races" and in *Dusk of Dawn*.

As a practicing scientist conducting field research at the turn of the century Du Bois faced a strategic problem of how to confront and dismantle the concept of race that had been constructed by racist scientists. In his anthropological writings his primary aim was to vindicate black people and their cultural heritage. This propagandistic aspect of his scientific work has led some commentators to overlook, or diminish, its value as a contribution to science.[6] Du Bois, however, couched his proposal for a long-range empirical study of black people in terms of its far-reaching implications for science.[7]

The scientific basis for the widely held belief that black people are inferior had been articulated in terms of biology, specifically the theory of evolution applied to the development of racial groups. Du Bois was well aware of the prevalence of this view. In *Dusk of Dawn* he tells us that, as a student at Harvard,

> I began to face scientific race dogma: first of all, evolution and the "Survival of the Fittest." It was continually stressed in the community and in classes that there was a vast difference in the development of the whites and the "lower" races; that this could be seen in the physical development of the Negro. I remember once in a museum, coming face to face with a demonstration: a series of skeletons arranged from a little monkey to a tall well-developed white man, with a Negro barely outranking a chimpanzee. Eventually in my classes stress was quietly transferred to brain weight and brain capacity, and at last to the "cephalic index."[8]

It is important to note here that what immediately follows this passage is Du Bois's frequently cited memoir of Heinrich von Treitschke's classroom remarks regarding the inferiority of mulattoes. I want to highlight a seldom noticed connection between Du Bois's citing of his museum experience and his citing of von Treitschke's classroom remarks. His publication, in 1906, of "The Health and Physique of the Negro-American" for the eleventh Atlanta University conference, documents the extent to which these experiences may have motivated his anthropological research. In that particular study, more than any other, his attempt to rectify a false anthropological view of black people displayed a particular concern with the collection of empirical data on so-called "mulattoes." More importantly, the anthropological account of race he presented in the 1906 Atlanta University study – which included charts and comparative data on brains, as well as an endorsement of Ripley's use of hair and Sergi's use of the "cephalic index" as biological racial markers – is consistent with the view presented in his later anthropological writings.[9] And, as I will argue, in many respects this view undergirds his argument regarding racial identity and group progress in "The Conservation of Races."

It may be unwise to invest too heavily in the veracity of Du Bois's comment in *Dusk of Dawn* regarding the change his concept of race underwent since "The Conservation of Races." He cites the first article of his proposed racial creed in that pamphlet, which proclaimed "Negro people as a race have a contribution to make to civilization," to draw in question the biological view of race it presupposed.

> [A]s I face Africa I ask myself what is it between us that constitutes a tie which I can feel better than I can explain?... On this vast continent were born and lived a large portion of my direct ancestors going back a thousand years or more. The mark of their heritage is upon me in color and hair. These are obvious things, but of little meaning in themselves; only important as they stand for real and more subtle differences from other men. Whether they do or not, I do not know nor does science know today.[10]

After minimizing the importance of "the physical bond" he cites the "social heritage of slavery" and "the discrimination and insult" as "the real essence of this kinship."[11]

These remarks can lead unwary readers to assume that the change of view to which he refers aimed to resolve a "contradiction" in his earlier thinking about race. Since, in his later reflections, he identified the historical experience of oppression as the real essence of the bond between Africans and African–Americans, and dismissed the physical bond as unimportant, he clearly gave up his earlier commitment to a biological view of race. The tension between the biological and sociohistorical criteria of race is resolved in favor of the latter.[12]

Whether Du Bois can resolve this tension in his view of race by opting for wholly sociohistorical criteria remains an open question.[13] I want to draw attention to some of his remarks in the *Dusk of Dawn* passage just quoted that seem to indicate that the tension remained as a source of a similar inconsistency. His talk of a "social heritage" of oppression that binds together "not simply the children of Africa, but extends through yellow Asia and into the South Seas" suggests that other nonwhites share a common history of oppression with black people. To make this point about cross-racial oppression, however, he invoked a biological racial distinction between "the children of African" and "yellow Asians." The tension between biological and sociohistorical criteria remained in his later view because his anthropological view of black people was a crucial component of his scientific account of their sociohistorical development.

Notice that in *Dusk of Dawn* he does not deny a role for physical differences, insisting that they are "only important as they stand for real and more subtle differences." By "real and more subtle differences," of course, he meant *cultural* differences. He misleadingly suggests that he gave up his earlier commitment to a biological view of race when, in fact, he only gave up the argument he presented in "The Conservation of Races" that black people, as a racial group, have a unique cultural contribution to make to civilization. In *Dusk of Dawn* he treats his earlier claim regarding the potential development of black people as simply something about which there is no scientific knowledge. While he seems to have believed that scientific knowledge of race is not possible, the anthropological study he published in 1906 was motivated by his belief that the matter of race simply had not been properly investigated.

The Anthropological View in "The Conservation of Races"

The question Du Bois raised in "The Conservation of Races" of whether African–Americans have a special duty to retain their racial identity and not to seek absorption into the white mainstream was ambiguous as between biology and culture. Elsewhere I have interpreted the imperative for group loyalty he sought to establish as a call for *cultural* preservation.[14] Here I will emphasize those remarks which suggest a biological reading of this question. In *Dusk of Dawn* he ridiculed his earlier assumption that group development, which is primarily a cultural process, may be biologically determined. The argument in "The Conservation of Races," however, is dominated by his notion of "intermingling," which is primarily a biological process. I want to consider what Du Bois meant by "intermingling" to indicate how his anthropological notion of race fits into the theory of development he employed in "The Conservation of Races."

Surprisingly, Du Bois's statement against absorption can be read as a *condemnation* of intermingling, a stance that seems to go against the grain of his sociohistorical definition of race. Consider, for instance, his assertion regarding his African heritage. "My mother's folk were closer and yet their direct connection, in culture and race, became tenuous." In this statement he refers not only to a loss of African culture.[15] Indeed, the tenuousness of the biological racial connection between his mother's relatives and their African ancestors was due to the former's having intermingled with Europeans and other mixed-bloods.

His stance against intermingling is difficult to understand when we consider his appeal to the history of racial intermingling to discredit the racial categories of science. He admitted that when the "contradictory criteria" of race are sorted out the "final word" of science is that "we have at least two, perhaps three, great families of human beings – the whites and Negroes, possibly the yellow race. That other races have arisen from the intermingling of the blood of these two."[16] The fact that he does not state his monogenetic theory of human origin in "The Conservation of Races" may have some bearing on why certain details of his account changed so dramatically in his later anthropological writings. His belief that all humans originate from a single race was consistently maintained elsewhere.[17] But his acknowledgment of the yellow race as one of the main racial groups is tentative in the passage just quoted from "The Conservation of Races." This contrasts sharply with his much more categorical statement in a later book, *The World and Africa.* There he identified three main "subtypes," including Mongoloids, that were defined in terms of physical differences that developed from a long history of inbreeding.[18] In *Dusk of Dawn* he tells us that changes in his anthropological view were due partly to his having to keep up with new anthropological findings.[19]

The most significant change in his anthropological view was his shift from the view in "The Conservation of Races" that white and Negro are the two primary races to the view, in *The World and Africa*, that Negroids and Mongoloids are primary, with Caucasoids listed last as "a type between these, possibly formed by their union, with bleached skins and intermediate hair."[20] This shift occurred as early as his groundbreaking anthropological study of African–American physical types in 1906.[21] He presented empirical data to show, not only that the prevailing scientific view of mulattoes as physically and mentally degenerate was mistaken, but also that the intermingling of African–Americans with other races has yielded physical evidence to support Giuseppi Sergi's Mediterranean theory of the origin of the white race.[22]

The idea of racial intermingling thoroughly informs Du Bois's anthropological view with respect to biology and culture. As early as "The Conservation of Races" he maintained that the historical development of various groups of people has been along "physical race lines," but adds "the great characteristic of this growth has been the differentiation of spiritual and mental differences between great races of mankind and the integration of physical differences." Racial intermingling has been an important biological ingredient in the "whole process which has brought about these race differentiations." With respect to the growth and development of the Teuton nations Du Bois points to their common history and culture as more important than "their race identity and common blood."[23] He seems to ignore important differences between Teuton nation-states and diaspora black people. For example, common history and culture accounts for the *cleavage* among the different Teuton nations, all of whom represent white people. When he refers to the "larger races" as "far from homogeneous" he illustrates this by focusing on the intraethnic interminglings of cultural groups within each of the main biological groups. What stands out are his remarks that Negroes, including mulattoes, are "the most indefinite" and that "Hindoos" include "traces of widely different nations." This is as close as he gets in this passage to acknowledging *biological* intermingling, although in his statement regarding the origin of humans he suggested, in passing, that the white and black races have intermingled to produce the yellow race. Not yet having arrived at his view of whites as originating from the intermingling of Mongoloid and Negroid blood, in "The Conservation of Races" he only hinted at his belief that, due to a long history of intermingling, there is very little biological difference between the races.[24]

How then are we to understand Du Bois's stance against racial intermingling given the fundamental role it plays in his anthropolgical theory? He seems to grant priority to sociohistorical criteria of race, not so much because he wanted to deny a role for the physical, but because he believed the prevailing scientific account of the physical aspects of black and white people had been misguided by racism.

> There is, of course, nothing more fascinating than the question of the various types of mankind and their intermixture. The whole question of heredity and human gift depends upon such knowledge; but ever since the African slave trade and before the rise of modern biology and sociology, we have been afraid in America that scientific study in this direction might lead to conclusions with which we were loath to agree; and this fear was in reality because the economic foundation of the modern world was based on the recognition and preservation of so-called racial distinctions.[25]

By relying on racial classifications he employed an empirical method to challenge the scientific basis for racial classifications. He culled from the work of other anthropologists evidence to show that the claim of "pure" or "unmixed" blood is groundless.[26] In his study of African-American physical types he wanted to demonstrate on scientific grounds that, due to the historical intermingling of races, apparent physical differences between racial groups are deceptive as regards common blood.

Du Bois was particularly concerned with showing that there is no scientific basis for the widely held view that black people are inferior subhumans incapable of developing a civilization. In all of his anthropological writings he stressed that the cultural development of a group has little to do with physical characteristics. He points out that history provides many cases in which physical differences have simply been ignored in the social formation of nations. Indeed, the multiracial history of Egypt and Ethiopia are discussed at length to establish that they included black blood.[27] In keeping with his theory of development, he stated in "The Conservation of Races" that when "vast families" came together to form cities "purity of blood was replaced by the requirement of domicile."[28] Although he had modern Europe in mind, his point was that history has demonstrated that it is possible for group identity to transcend physical differences. This multiracial view of group identity, however, seems inconsistent with his stance against racial intermingling.

Biological Determinism, Free Will, and Group Progress

As a call for group loyalty, Du Bois's claim regarding the transcendence of physical differences was focused on African–Americans. He tailored the idea of group identity based largely on sociohistorical criteria to fit the social situation faced by African–Americans as a group composed of mulattoes and mixed-bloods.[29] From personal experience he knew that "all members of the Negro race were not black and that the pictures of my race which were current were not authentic nor fair portraits" and realized that the racial identity of African–Americans could not be rendered strictly in terms of biological criteria.[30] Yet he did not embrace the idea of a broader multiracial national identity that would include white Americans – an idea that would have been more in keeping with his model of ancient Egypt. In the context of a racially segregated American society he instead argued for a more specific group identity closer to his model of the modern Teuton nations described in "The Conservation of Races." Just as various Europeans groups had bonded on the basis of "first, their race identity and common blood; secondly, and more important, a common history, common laws and religion, similar habits of thought and a conscious striving together for certain ideals of life" to progress as nations, African–Americans ought to retain their race identity and common blood to progress as a group.[31]

The influence of Herbert Spencer's social Darwinism is reflected in Du Bois's proposal for group development, yet in many respects that proposal also constituted a critique of biological determinism.[32] Within Spencer's evolutionist conceptual frame Du Bois's sociological research emphasized environmental factors to challenge, with empirical data, the current scientific status of black people as inferior to all other races.[33] In *Dusk of Dawn* he tells us,

> Herbert Spencer finished his ten volumes of *Synthetic Philosophy* in 1896. The biological analogy, the vast generalizations, were striking, but actual scientific accomplishment lagged. For me an opportunity seemed to present itself. I could not lull my mind to hypnosis by regarding a phrase like "consciousness of kind" as a scientific law. But turning my gaze from fruitless word-twisting and facing the facts of my own social situation and racial world, I determined to put science into sociology through a study of the condition and problems of my own group.[34]

He was especially concerned with the negative implications of Spencer's biological determinism for policy directed toward the uplift of African–Americans. He maintained that "[W]e are subject to the same natural laws as other races." But within the constraints imposed by "the constitution of the world" he emphasized the operation of free will in human affairs.[35] Defining sociology as "the science of free will" he spoke of it as "the Science that seeks [to measure] the limits of Chance in human conduct."[36]

With his long-range study of African–Americans in mind, Du Bois argued that the task of sociology was to investigate the operations of free will and natural law in human affairs. His definition of race in "The Conservation of Races" contains a reference to the "voluntary and involuntary striving together" that brings in the matter of collective action.[37] His use of the term "striving" with regard to the shared cooperative activities of different racial groups reflects a Darwinian dimension of his theory of development. He presented a picture of various groups of people in different parts of the world engaged in various collective actions to achieve certain goals. By striving to realize its particular ideal for the advancement of civilization each racial group is pursuing the ultimate goal of cultural pluralism which will guide the world "nearer and nearer that perfection of human life."[38] While the English, German and Romance nations have already developed their particular messages, the Slavs have just begun and the complete message of the whole race of black people has not yet been given. The development of "Negro genius" can be achieved by "only Negroes bound and welded together... inspired by one vast ideal."[39] The aim of the long-range study he proposed was to demonstrate, by historical investigation, sociological interpretation, and statistical and anthropological measurement, that black people are "capable to a degree of improvement and culture."[40]

Although Du Bois's interest in the scientific study of black people was motivated by a desire for social change, he understood his proposed project to be on the cutting edge of science. He wanted to put science into sociology by subjecting to empirical test the grand theories of social scientists. In his proposal for a long-range study he argued that the study of African–Americans would advance the cause of science in general and that "No such opportunity to watch and measure the history and development of a great race of men ever presented itself to the scholars of a modern nation."[41] He believed social scientists had gone astray by "still thinking in terms of theory and vast and eternal laws" rather than in terms of "local studies."[42] With the idea of testing these theories and laws in mind, he maintained that because African–Americans were a "concrete group of living beings artificially set off by themselves," they provided a "laboratory experiment" for "noting influences of climate and physical environment, and particularly of studying the effect of amalgamating two of the most diverse races in the world."[43] The proposed long range study of African–Americans had a twofold thrust: to advance sociology as a science as well as to provide scientific knowledge of black people.

Du Bois's stance against intermingling had a direct connection with his interest in the scientific study of black people.[44] In "The Conservation of Races" he claimed,

> [I]f in America it is to be proven for the first time in the modern world that not only are Negroes capable of evolving individual men like Toussaint the Saviour, but are a nation stored with wonderful possibilities of culture then their destiny is not a servile imitation of Anglo-Saxon culture, but a stalwart originality which shall unswervingly follow Negro ideals.[45]

His memorable formulation of the concept of double consciousness in this essay rests on the idea that, in the American context of legally imposed racial segregation, "commingled blood" can foster a dilemma of whether to strive to be an American, or a Negro. Opting for sociohistorical criteria of African–American racial identity was a means of addressing the "incessant self-questioning and the hesitation that arises from it" that stifles "combined race action."[46] With regard to identity, his proposed definition of race emphasized sociohistorical criteria to avoid the dilemmas that arise from the fact that the biological racial types offered by science are based on physical criteria that, due to the history of racial intermingling, are contradictory. As some commentators have noted, he did not propose that sociohistorical criteria replace the biological criteria.[47] He spoke of race in this sociohistorical sense as an "invention" that various European nations had used to realize their group ideals. An important lesson to be drawn from history, according to Du Bois, is that racial identity has played an important role in guiding the collective actions that led to the modernization of European nations. A similar invention by African–Americans would allow widely different physical types within the race to embrace their African–American identity. Overcoming the self-questioning and hesitation caused by double consciousness will then enable the entire spectrum of African–Americans to engage in collective actions that will contribute to the progress of the group.[48]

Du Bois's Pragmatic Essentialism

It is not difficult to notice the extent to which Du Bois's scientific orientation to the study of black people was influenced by his philosophical background.[49] In "The Conservation of Races," his concern with the natural laws governing race development, stated rather inspiringly in his talk of the voluntary and involuntary strivings of a developing race, evolved by 1904 into a question of "how much of natural law there is in human conduct."[50] He maintained that this was the question sociology must address in order to become a true science and set out in the Atlanta University studies "to make in truth the science of human action a true and systematic statement of the verifiable facts as ascertained by observation and measurement."[51] By posing the issue of natural law and human action in terms amenable to empirical investigation, he gave a pragmatic turn to a seemingly philosophical question. He rejected Herbert Spencer's attempt to account for human action "in eternity" as too all encompassing. He proposed instead to address this question by studying "limited fields of human action." The scientific gain would be "at last careful, cautious generalization and formulation" and "a real knowledge of natural law as locally manifest."[52]

Du Bois's scientific orientation to these philosophical issues was matched by his scepticism toward science. In *Black Folk Then and Now* he claimed, "In fact it is generally recognized that no scientific definition of race is possible." He pointed out that because physical differences fade into each other "so insensible . . . we can only indicate the main division of men in broad outlines."[53] He then dismissed the question of how many races as unscientific and a matter of philosophical speculation. How do we reconcile his posing the question of race development in terms of an empirical study of free will and collective action, with his frequently expressed scepticism regarding the possibility of acquiring scientific knowledge of race?

The scepticism expressed by Du Bois is consistent with his pragmatism regarding the use of scientific methods to acquire knowledge. Consider, for instance, his criticism of Frederick Hoffman's use of statistical data to show that the death-rate of African–Americans was due to the influence of certain race traits. Du Bois pointed out that statistics is "after all nothing but the application of logic to counting, and no amount of counting will justify a departure from the severe rules of correct reasoning."[54] He referred to Hoffman's "absurd conclusion" that black people are "shown to be on a downward grade" and offered an alternative interpretation of Hoffman's data. Although most of his criticisms focused on Hoffman's "unscientific use of the statistical method" his chief objection had more to do with Hoffman's bias. But rather than charge Hoffman with the promotion of antiblack racism, Du Bois instead cordially offered him a way out. "[M]ost persons . . . would feel surer of the author's fairness and judgment if he more candidly admitted the contingent character of his broader conclusions."[55] These remarks suggest a more general scepticism regarding the use of "anthropometrical inquiry" to reach such broad conclusions. Nevertheless, this scepticism did not inhibit Du Bois from welcoming further scientific interest. He availed himself of the opportunity to recommend that what was needed in research on black people was the kind of project he undertakes in *The Philadephia Negro*, a study of black people "in limited localities."[56]

The racial bias of scientists writing about black people was a reason Du Bois often gave to distrust a lot of what passed as scientific literature, but his critique of their scientific practice did not amount simply to a charge of racism. He was even more critical of Joseph Tillinghast's book, *The Negro in Africa and America*, because it represented another attempt to establish that "the Negro is slowly but surely tending to revert toward savagery or extinction."[57] Although he criticized Tillinghast's conclusions as contrary to "the best available evidence," he thought the author's greatest shortcoming was his "coming to universal conclusions on so narrow a basis of induction."[58] Tillinghast's conservative political perspective clearly influenced his analysis, and Du Bois does not fail to mention this, yet the criticism of Tillinghast's fallacious reasoning is strictly a point about his scientific method.

Realizing that no truly scientific study of black people had ever been conducted Du Bois became set on correcting the prevailing scientific view with empirical evidence. A major shortcoming of social science research on black people was the inability of biased scientists to deal with "contradictory social facts" that require "systematic interpretation."[59] Hoffman's data, for example, excluded two-thirds of the black population, sometimes excluded women, and ignored comparative data, while Tillinghast's account simply lacked any empirical ground, compounded by a gross ignorance of comparative anthropology. In these reviews Du Bois revealed his general scepticism toward any scientific study of black people that was not empirically well-grounded, while championing the need for more scientific research on black people.

The purpose of the long-range study he proposed for the Atlanta University conferences was to correct the prevailing scientific view by providing ongoing research that was systematic and empirical. In "The Development of a People" he addressed the question of policy in the face of contradictory social facts. He cited the issue of illiteracy among African–Americans to illustrate how confusion regarding social policy occurs when policy is based on a nonsystematic use of empirical data. His comparative view of development, stated more philosophically in "The Conservation of Races," is now presented as a theory that would provide the guiding principles for scientific investigation. This theory permits the question of what counts as satisfactory advance in education, for instance, to be formulated from a comparative standpoint. To determine whether black people have progressed, the steps they have taken must be considered in relation to the steps other groups have taken in similar circumstances.[60]

Du Bois included anthropological measurement, along with statistical data, under the rubric "empirical method." In addition to local studies he wanted to study the "physical appearance and pecularities" of African–Americans.[61] Commentators sometimes interpret his opposition to the racism in scientific practice to mean he was opposed to *all* biological views of race.[62] Although he criticized scientists who only pretended to engage in empirical study, he often cited others to support his view. His selective use of anthropological research was guided by a special interest in presenting an alternative to Spencer's biological determinism. He conceived the anthropological study in "The Health and Physique of the Negro-American" in terms of a "laboratory experiment" in which grand theories, such as Spencer's, could be tested. In the absence of reliable empirical data on black people he borrowed as much as was available from current anthropological research to support his view of race. He also constructed an ingenious study of African–Americans, as a group of "living beings," to provide empirical proof of Sergi's theory.

I have cautioned against fully accepting Du Bois's suggestion in *Dusk of Dawn* that his view of race shifted away from the biological notion, especially if this is taken to imply that by sociohistorical groups "transcending" physical differences he meant to reject biological racial classification altogether.[63] Notwithstanding his conviction that racial classifications are not well established by science he was not entirely opposed to their use. He rejected the notion of pure unmixed races yet, in his Atlanta University study of the health and physique of African–Americans, he not only distinguished mixed and unmixed, but within the mixed group he distinguished between mulatto, quadroon and, especially important for his theory of racial origin, "white types with Negro blood."[64] His sceptical attitude towards scientific definitions of race did not preclude his use of the language of racial types. But how could he declare, on the one hand, that there are no unmixed races and, on the other, employ a category referring to "unmixed Negroes"?

The 1906 Atlanta University study included data that dealt with the question of whether there is a correlation between moral character and the "mixed" or "unmixed" racial composition of African–Americans. Du Bois needed biological categories to carry out this research. But having discovered Sergi's Mediterranean theory, he well understood that these categories misrepresent themselves. It was strictly on pragmatic grounds that he justified employing racial categories, which he based on measurable physical differences established with visual evidence. The series of photographs he published in "The Health and Physique of the Negro-American" was meant to parallel the Greek and Roman statuary Sergi used to establish his biological classification of ancient Afro-Mediterranean types.[65]

Even with visual evidence at hand there remain grounds for scepticism regarding the empirical study of the physical characteristics of people. In several places Du Bois acknowledged problems with his use of racial classifications based on physical characteristics. To set up his study of the "physical peculiarities" and "interesting physiognomies" of African–Americans he had to forego relying on data from the census for 1850 and 1890, which inaccurately reported the mulatto population at 11.2% and 15% respectively. He pointed out that both figures were understatements and because local studies were too restricted in area, they provided too narrow basis of induction.[66] In the absence of accurate data he reports his own personal classification of 40,000 African–Americans in the Black Belt rural districts, but mostly in Atlanta and Savannah.[67] He distinguished between black people who were "to all appearances of unmixed Negro blood," those who "had without doubt more white than Negro blood," those classified as "brown," but who in most cases had some white blood, and those whom he was "not sure whether their color was due to white blood or to the fact that they were descendants from brown Africans."[68] The inherent fallability of making these distinctions is revealed in his general estimate that one-third of the African–American population have recognizable traces of white blood and the other two thirds may have white blood, but with "few traces of it." Although he claims that this conclusion is based on "available data and the results of fairly wide observation," he admits that "This, of course, is partial guess work."[69] By this he meant first that observation cannot reveal whether an African–American has white blood. Even more significant for the nature and purpose of this particular study was his acknowledgment that visual perception is an inadequate means of identifying mulattoes who have the physical characteristics of a white person.

The sceptical attitude Du Bois built into the framework of his study served to bolster his pitch for a more careful study of African–American physical types. He stated that in the present study he wanted only "to indicate in a general way the interesting matter which is open for observation."[70] But the subjective factors involved in observation could not have been more problematic than in the case of a group of people with "such infinite variation in the proportion of Negro and white blood."[71] He selected photographs of fifty-six young black men and women whom he had known personally over a ten-year period. On the basis of observable physical characteristics such as skin color, hair, and facial features he distinguished four sets of African–American physical types: Negro, Mulatto, Quadroon, and White with Negro Blood. "The main types for separate study would be the full blooded Negroes and those with a quarter, half and three-quarters of white blood."[72] He stated that the focus of this study will be the latter group and recommended the former for future study. But if we consider his focus on mulattoes in this study in the light of the problem of "contradictory criteria" he mentioned earlier in "The Conservation of Races," he seems to have meant to undermine the whole business of constructing racial categories.

Du Bois confronted head on the question of how the investigator is to ascertain the proper category for each individual by pointing out the complication of "the intermarriage of persons of mixed blood."[73] Knowledge of the family background of the individuals in a study of this sort is necessary because physical characteristics do not always correlate with ancestry, hence, it cannot be assumed that a mulatto has one white parent or grandparent. He included a diagram of the family tree of a person who would be considered mulatto based on physical appearance and pointed out that "no full blood white appeared among his ancestors for four or five generations and yet he himself may be half or three-fourths white."[74] Some of his remarks question the use of visual perception to ostensively define African–Americans. "The types are only provisionally indicated as the lines are by no means clear in my own mind." He seems to have only a tentative commitment to the biological racial categories he employed. They were considered merely "a workable division . . . so far as that is possible without exact scientific measurements." He qualifies his categorization of people as Quadroon Types (with more than one-half and less than seven-eights) with the remark "so far as I can ascertain."[75] And, in the case of people with less than one-eighth Negro blood (Octoroons and White types) he states that there are no "real numbers" because in an unknown number of cases they are indistinguishable from whites.

Needless to say, Du Bois's sceptical view of racial categories did not deter him from employing biological racial classifications with a vengeance. In the next section I will discuss the place of his study of African–American physical types in his vindication project. Here I want to highlight an important relation between his scepticism and his pragmatic justification of the use of biological categories. In section one of his study he extensively quotes Ripley on the Aryan myth and Sergi on the Mediterranean race to show that European races are intermingled with African blood. He turns in section two to a similar consideration of racial diversity in Africa, again utilizing extensive quotations from the publications of Ratzel, Denniker and Boas that were published after "The Conservation of Races." His discussion of African–Americans in section four is prefaced with the claim regarding intermingling he had sought to establish in section one regarding Europeans and in section two regarding Africans. He pointed out that the assumption that there is a pure Negro type is an error because African–Americans are racially blended with a wide cross section of the African population and "to a larger extent than many realize" with European and African blood.[76]

He seems to have believed that racial intermingling in Europe and Africa, established on the basis of the current findings of anthropological research, remained speculative from the standpoint of concrete evidence. Responding to James Bryce's recommendation that the subject of "intermingling of blood" be given more scientific attention, he conceived his study of African–American physical types as the first such investigation. His focus on mulattoes can be understood in strictly scientific terms – they were the right specimens for scientific study in "one of the most interesting anthropological laboratories conceivable."[77] He wanted to demonstrate Sergi's theory regarding past racial intermingling, namely, that "white and black blood can make as good an Egyptian type today as five thousand years ago."[78] Under the category of White types with Negro Blood he included subcategories based on the European physical types the individual most resembled "either accidentally or because of real blood relationship."[79] In addition to Sergi's Latin type, he referred to various photographs to indicate Celtic, English or Anglo-American, and Germanic types that sometimes descended from two black parents. With regard to this special category his more pervasive scepticism emerges in his remark that, "In none of these ten cases would the casual observer notice the Negro blood."[80] In his endeavor to prove that the biological concept of race is misguided because all races are intermingled he needed biological racial categories to present evidence to undermine the scientific mythology that served as a justification of those very categories.

He maintained that there is no scientific knowledge of race because there has been no empirical study of racial intermingling. For this reason he had a particular interest in studying the mulatto.[81] His study of the mulatto in "The Health and Physique of the Negro-American" was meant to be his version of a "queer *reductio ad absurdum*" regarding racial distinctions based on physical characteristics.[82]

> The human species so shade and mingle with each other that not only indeed is it impossible to draw a color line between black and other races, but in all physical characteristics the Negro race cannot be set off by itself as absolutely different.[83]

There is no way to overcome scepticism regarding the use of racial categories in the case of racial intermingling in which "Negro blood" is indiscernible. Du Bois wanted to demonstrate that a scientific definition of race is not possible by showing that even the most experienced observer has reason to be sceptical given that racial classifications require ostensive definitions based on visual perception, which, in this case, is unreliable.

To the Eye of the Historian and Sociologist

The biological categories of race Du Bois defined in terms of physical characteristics were an essential feature of his project to correct the systematic erasure of black people from history. In *Black Folk Then and Now* he indicated the importance of anthropology in this regard.

> The racial identity of the Ethiopians has often been disputed. There is no question but that they were dark brown or black people. If, however, scientists go beyond that and, like Reisner, apparently confine the designation "Negro" to black people with close-curled hair, flat noses, thick lips and prognathism, many of the Ethiopians were not Negroes; although there is distinct evidence of the wide prevalence of precisely this type of Negro among the blacks of Ethiopia; but according to such definition, most black people of Africa and the world are not Negroes and never were, leaving the number of "pure" Negroes too small to form a race.[84]

This, of course, was also an implication of the "queer" *reductio* he had employed earlier in his Atlanta University study. But not the only one.[85] From the broader perspective of his vindication project he aimed to do more than simply undermine the prevailing view of white people as a pure race. In the case of historical research, the lack of scientific knowledge of black people was compounded by "a certain irritating silence" that implied "the Negro has no history."[86] He employed the insight of his *reductio* argument to represent both sides of the "contradictory criteria" of race. Rather than allow the erasure of black people from history on racially biased, but nonetheless technical scientific grounds, he employed scientifically defined racial categories to establish their presence.[87]

With regard to the racial identity of ancient Egyptians his agnostic statement in "The Conservation of Races" is replaced in *Black Folk Then and Now* with a much more definite claim regarding Negro blood. Of special interest is his statement that "They seem to have stood in relationship nearest the Negro race in earliest times, and then gradually through the infiltration of Mediterranean and Semitic elements became what would be described in America as a light mulatto stock of octoroons or quadroons."[88] Here he seems to be tacitly relying on the racial categories he ostensibly defined using photographic evidence in his Atlanta University study to argue that if a stock of mulattoes in America count as members of the Negro race then so do the Egyptians who have the same physical characteristics.[89]

Herskovits thought Du Bois may have gone too far in seeking to vindicate black people. Among a list of criticisms he sent Du Bois regarding the manuscript for *Black Folk Then and Now* was his objection to assigning racial categories to prehistoric people. Herskovits probably had in mind Du Bois's statement that "It may well be that Africa rather than Asia was the birthplace of the human family and ancient Negro blood the basis of the blood of all men."[90] Rather than follow Horskovits's suggestion and change his view, instead Du Bois asserted a somewhat different version of it in a later work. "It seems reasonable to suppose that Negroids originating in Africa or Asia appeared first as Negrillos."[91] Du Bois's refusal to capitulate to pressure from Herskovits to give up using racial classifications in this questionable case seems to have been influenced by his very strong commitment to the use of science to vindicate the past achievements of black people.

In two of his later writings on anthropology Du Bois refers to the Negroids of Grimaldi, a prehistoric group anthropologists regarded as the earliest "representatives of *homo sapiens*" yet found in Europe.[92] He wanted to establish that black people had introduced an advanced form of sculpture into early European civilization. To ignore Herskovit's objection may very well have been a mistake, but what is important to note here is that Du Bois's decision to remain committed to this view was deliberate.[93] For largely pragmatic reasons he employed the racial categories of science to establish a black presence in history with full awareness of his own scepticism toward scientific definitions of race.

Du Bois's stance against intermingling was partly due to his understanding of the nature of race and cultural contacts throughout history. He often compared the situation of various groups of black people in the West Indies and South America with the situation of black people in the United States. Unlike the South America case, in which "whites will absorb the Negro," or the West Indian case in which the whites will be absorbed into a "mulatto race," in the United States "The real bar to race amalgamation at present . . . is the spreading and strengthening determination of the rising educated classes of blacks to accept no amalgamation except through open legal marriage."[94] While this assertion certainly reflected his personal attitude toward interracial marriage it seems that he also had historical reasons to support his view of racial amalgamation in the United States. In a summary of the topics discussed at the First Universal Races Congress, held in London in 1911 he included the following statement regarding racial intermingling on a list of the major findings:

> The most fruitful cause of race crossing is ill-will – as illustrated by war, conquest, slavery, exploitation and persecution – for where there exists mutual respect the differences in differing traditions, etc., make it almost an invariable rule that intermarriage is avoided – as shown by any two nations friendly to each other . . . that the rate of crossing decreases with the increase of interracial and international amity.[95]

Given the role of slavery, with its "system of concubinage," in the history of racial intermingling in America Du Bois had a historical basis for attributing his moral opposition to intermingling to African–Americans as a group.[96]

In his unpublished essay on "Miscegenation" (1935) he presents a more complex, somewhat ambivalent, vision of the future of racial intermingling in the United States.

> Nor is there any doubt but that continued residence of white and black people together in this country over a sufficiently long term of years will inevitably result in complete absorption, unless strong reasons against it, in place of mere prejudice, are adduced... [E]ither amalgamation will take place gradually and quietly by mutual consent, or by equally peaceful methods the groups will seek separate careers or even separate dwelling places, either in the same or different lands.[97]

These remarks reflect an important shift in the moral and political implications of Du Bois's call for the scientific study of race. His earlier concern in "The Conservation of Races" with the question of group development and race uplift is displaced here by a different concern with the question of "how fast and under what conditions this amalgamation ought to take place?" In what appears to be an update of the pitch he made in 1897 he again recommended that to address this issue, "the nation needs the guidance of careful and unbiased scientific inquiry."[98]

There is perhaps strong enough reason to suspect that he gave up the idea of a unique cultural message that black people would contribute to civilization because he discovered, after Boas's commencement address at Atlanta University in 1906, that black people had already made great cultural contributions to the growth and development of civilization.[99] I want to emphasize another line of thought in his writings. In "The Future of Africa in America" (1942), he seems to have pronounced the question of development a dead issue.

> The contrast between the white and dark populations of America can no longer for a moment be considered a contrast between cultivated and the uncultivated... [A]t the head of both these groups you will find a small but undeniable proportion of Negroes and Indians side by side with the larger proportion of whites and with no essential differences in ability and creativeness... There is no scientist of repute today who for a moment would declare that biological differences between white folk and black consign an individual of either race inevitably to a lower status.[100]

His view of development no longer entailed the idea of a unique cultural message, because he began to shift toward a view of black people and black culture as providing an alternative path to modernization.[101] He protests in *Dusk of Dawn* the fact that civilization in the twentieth century has turned into a "vast Frankenstein monster" and a "White Imperial Industry!"[102] More important than this metaphorical reference to global capitalism was the belief he expressed that the accomplishments of white people might have been achieved by black, brown, and yellow people with different results.[103] As his view of civilization shifted so did his view of the scientific study of race. In *Dusk of Dawn* he asserted, "Certainly modern civilization is too new and has steered too crooked a course and been too much a matter of chance and fate to make any final judgment as to the abilities of mankind." In his later writings Du Bois seems to have arrived at a view of the value of Western civilization quite different from the one he had presented at the turn of the century. He no longer believed that the vindication of black people required a scientific study of their development from "primitive" to "civilized."[104]

Notes

1 This is the case in otherwise quite valuable research devoted specifically to his view of science and race. See Faye V. Harrison and Donald Nonini, eds., Special Issue: W. E. B. Du Bois and Anthropology, *Critique of Anthropology* 22.3 (1992), Lee D. Baker, *From Savage to Negro: Anthropology and the Construction of Race*, 1896–1954 (University of California Press, 1998), Shamoon Zamir, *Dark Voices: W. E. B. Du Bois and American Thought*, 1888–1903 (Chicago: University of Chicago Press, 1995), Rutledge M. Dennis, ed., W. E. B. Du Bois: The Scholar as Activist, *Research in Race and Ethnic Relations*, vol. 9 (1996), Michael B. Katz and Thomas J. Sugrue, eds., *W. E. B. Du Bois, Race, and the City: The Philadelphia Negro and Its Legacy* (Philadelphia: University of Pennsylvania Press, 1998), Bernard W. Bell, Emily R. Grosholz and James B. Stewart, eds., *W. E. B. Du Bois On Race and Culture* (New York: Routledge, 1996), William, Toll, *The Resurgence of Race: Black Social Theory from Reconstruction to the Pan-African Conferences* (Philadelphia: Temple University Press, 1979).

2 Bernard R. Boxill, "Du Bois on Cultural Pluralism" in Bernard W. Bell, et al., eds., *Du Bois on Race and Culture*, 57–85; Lucius Outlaw, " 'Conserve' Races? In Defense of W. E. B. Du Bois" in Bernard W. Bell, et al., eds., *W. E. B. Du Bois on Race and Culture*, 15–37. Anthony K. Appiah, "The Uncompleted Argument: Du Bois and the Illusion of Race," in Henry Louis Gates, Jr. ed. *"Race," Writing, and Difference*, (Chicago: University of Chicago Press, 1986), 21–37, Robert Gooding-Williams, "Outlaw, Appiah, and Du Bois's 'The Conservation of Races' " in Bernard W. Bell, et al., eds., *W. E. B. Du Bois on Race and Culture*, 39–56, Kenneth Mostern, "Three Theories of the Race of W. E. B. Du Bois" *Cultural Critique* 34 (1996): 27–63 and Thomas C. Holt, "W. E. B. Du Bois's Archaeology of Race: Re-Reading 'The Conservation of Races' " in Michael Be. Katz and Thomas J. Sugrue, eds. *W. E. B. Du Bois, Race, and the City*, 61–76.

3 See Baker, *From Savage to Negro*, 112 and Appiah, "The Illusion of Race," 27–9.

4 W. E. B. Du Bois, *Dusk of Dawn: An Essay Toward an Autobiography of a Race Concept* (New York: Schocken Books, 1971).

5 For a discussion of the "Linnaean web" of scientific opinion regarding race that was prevalent at the turn of the century, see Thomas F. Gossett, *Race: The History of an Idea in America* (Dallas: Southern Methodist University Press, 1963), 82–3, cited in Arnold Rampersad, *The Art and Imagination of W. E. B. Du Bois* (New York: Schocken Books, 1976), 60.

6 According to Kenneth Manning, for instance,

> His was a lone (or lonely) voice crying in the wilderness. Yet even he did not challenge, in a consistent or forthright way, the scientific arguments for black inferiority. His commentary through *The Crisis* broaches a range of disciplines speaking to the condition of blacks, but he and other black intellectuals said surprisingly little about science.

Kenneth R. Manning, "Race, Science, and Identity" in Gerald Early, ed., *Lure and Loathing* (New York: Penguin Books, 1994), 324. Arnold Rampersad expressed the following view regarding the Atlanta University studies.

> Certain volumes, such as *The Health and Physique of the Negro American* (1906), with its photographs of black American facial types and cephalic and skeletal measurements, *and*

Morals and Manners among Negro Americans (1914), now seem mementos of largely discredited intellectual approaches.

Arnold Rampersad, *The Art and Imagination of W. E. B. Du Bois*, 55. With regard to M. J. Herskovits's *Anthropometry of the American Negro* (New York: Columbia University Press, 1930), Du Bois would later claim, "No other careful studies of mulatto physique have been made, although Atlanta University (Publications No. 11) brought together much interesting data." "Miscegenation" (1935) in *Against Racism: Unpublished Essays, Papers, Addresses, 1887–1961* ed. Herbert Aptheker, (Amherst: University of Massachusetts Press, 1985), 98. For a more favorable assessment of the Atlanta university studies see Elliott Rudwick, "W. E. B. Du Bois as Sociologist" in James E. Blackwell and Morris Janowitz, eds. *Black Sociologists: Historical and Contemporary Perspectives* (Chicago: University of Chicago Press), 46–7.

7 See W. E. B. Du Bois, "The Study of the Negro Problems," section 5, *Annals of the American Academy* (January 1898): 15–21 and "The Atlanta Conferences" *Our Monthly Review*, 1.3 (March 1904): 85–90. See also *Dusk of Dawn*, 64–5: *The Autobiography of W. E. B. Du Bois: A Soliloquy on Viewing My Life from the Last Decade of Its First Century* (New York: International Publishers, 1968), 198–204; letter to John W. Davis 23 August 1948 in Herbert Aptheker ed. *The Correspondence of W. E. B. Du Bois Volume III Selections, 1944–1963*, (Amherst: University of Massachusetts Press, 1978), 208–10. For a discussion by Du Bois of the question of propaganda see W. E. B. Du Bois, "Phylon: Science or Propaganda" *Phylon* 5.1 (1944): 5–9.

8 *Dusk of Dawn*, 98.

9 W. E. B. Du Bois, "The Health and Physique of the Negro-American," *Atlanta University Studies*, no. 11 (Atlanta, Georgia 1906): 13–39. I cite the following editions of Du Bois's anthropological writings: *The Negro* (Millwood, N.Y.: Kraus-Thomson, 1975/1915 rpt.); *Africa, Its Geography, People and Products* (Millwood, N.Y.: Kraus-Thomson 1977/1930 rpt.); "Miscegenation" (1935) in Herbert Aptheker ed. *Against Racism: Unpublished Essays, Papers, Addresses, 1887–1961*, 90–102; *Black Folk Then and Now: An Essay in the History and Sociology of the Negro Race* (New York: Henry Holt, 1939); "The Future of Africa in America" (1942) in Herbert Aptheker ed. *W. E. B. Du Bois Unpublished Essays 1937–1944*, (Amherst: University of Massachusetts Press, 1985), 173–84; *The World and Africa: An Inquiry into the Part which Africa has Played in World History* (New York: International Publishers, 1946).

10 *Dusk of Dawn*, 116–17.

11 *Dusk of Dawn*, 117.

12 Robert Gooding-Williams cites this passage as an indication of Du Bois's shift from the biological concept to a sociohistorical concept. See note 17 of his Introduction to W. E. B. Du Bois, *The Souls of Black Folk* (Boston: Bedford, 1997), 26. In a similar vein Bernard Bell cites Du Bois's address to the Grand Boule to mark this shift. He quotes the following remarks, "This group . . . was not simply a physical entity, a black people, or people descended from black folk. It was, what all races really are, a cultural group." W. E. B. Du Bois, "The Talented Tenth Memorial Address" in Henry Louis Gates, Jr. and Cornel West, *The Future of the Race* (New York: Alfred A. Knopf, 1996), 159–77, cited in Bell, "Genealogical Shifts in Du Bois's Discourse on Double Consciousness as the Sign of African American Difference" in Bell, et al., eds., *W. E. B. Du Bois on Race and Culture*, 92. Thomas Holt cites a similar passage from *Darkwater* to indicate this shift. Du Bois asserted,

There are no races, in the sense of great, separate, pure breeds of men, differing in attainment, development, and capacity. There are great groups, – now with common history, now with common interests, now with common ancestry; more and more common experience and present interest drive back the common blood and the world today consists, not of races, but of the imperial commercial groups of master capitalists, international and predominantly white; the national middle classes of the several nations, white, yellow, and brown, with strong blood bonds, common languages, and common history; the international laboring class of all colors; the backward, oppressed groups of nature-folk, predominantly yellow, brown, and black.

W. E. B. Du Bois, *Darkwater: Voices from Within the Veil* ed. by Herbert Aptheker (Millwood, N.Y.: Kraus-Thomson, 1975; 1920rpt.), 98. Bell does not seem to notice Du Bois's remark in the Grand Boule address that African-Americans were "not simply a physical entity." Holt ignores Du Bois's abundant use of biological racial categories in the quote from *Darkwater.* See also James B. Stewart, "In Search of a Theory of Human History," in Bell, et al., *W. E. B. Du Bois on Race and Culture*, 274.

13 Various interpretations of Du Bois's appeal to sociohistorical criteria to define race are offered by Anthony K. Appiah, "The Uncompleted Argument: Du Bois and the Illusion of Race," in Henry Louis Gates, Jr., ed. *"Race," Writing, and Difference*, 21–37; Lucius Outlaw, "'Conserve' Races? In Defense of W. E. B. Du Bois," 15–37, Robert Gooding-Williams, "Outlaw, Appiah, and Du Bois's 'The Conservation of Races'," 39–56, Kenneth Mostern, "Three Theories of the Race of W. E. B. Du Bois" *Cultural Critique* 34 (1996): 27–63; Thomas C. Holt, "W. E. B. Du Bois's Archaeology of Race: Re-Reading 'The Conservation of Races'" in Michael B. Katz and Thomas J. Sugrue, eds. *W. E. B. Du Bois, Race, and the City*, 61–76; Bernard R. Boxill, "Du Bois on Cultural Pluralism," 57–85; Baker, *From Savage to Negro*, 112–13.

14 Tommy L. Lott, "Du Bois on the Invention of Race" *Philosophical Forum* 19.1–3 (Fall–Spring 1992–93): 166–87.

15 *Dusk of Dawn*, 116.

16 "The Conservation of Races", 6. Du Bois cited Friedrich Ratzel and Thomas Huxley as his authorities. In the bibliography of "The Health and Physique of the Negro-American" there is no citation for Huxley, but he lists Ratzel's *The History of Mankind*, translated by A. J. Butler (New York: Macmillan, 1904), 2 vols. In the bibliography for "Miscegenation" (1935) he lists only Butler's 1896 translation of volume one (p. 101).

17 See "Health and Physique," 14–15; *The Negro*, 21; *Africa, Its Geography, People and Products*, 9; *Black Folk Then and Now*, 1939, 4; *The World and Africa*, 1946, 85.

18 *The World and Africa*, 85–6.

19 *Dusk of Dawn*, 103.

20 *The World and Africa*, 85–6.

21 In "The Health and Physique of the Negro-American," Du Bois's employed a list of Ripley's and Sergi's main findings regarding hair texture, color and cranial features. With regard to his monogenetic theory of racial origin he quoted Ripley's view. "The European races, as a whole, show signs of a secondary or derived origin; certain characteristics, especially the texture of the hair, lead us to class them as intermediate between the extreme primary types of the Asiatic and the Negro races respectively." This is followed by another quote from Sergi to support Du Bois's claim that this primitive group was a "colored" race: "If, therefore, as all consistent students of natural history hold today, the human races have evolved in the past from some common root type, this predominant dark color must be

regarded as the more primitive." Sergi's theory was the basis for Du Bois's statement regarding the order and priority of origin: "[T]he so-called Negro races... separated from the primitive human stock some ages after the yellow race and before the Mediterranean race." "Health and Physique," 15, 18. In the bibliography for the Atlanta University study Du Bois listed G. Sergi, *The Mediterranean Race: A Study of the Origin of European Peoples* (London: Walter Scott, Charles Scribner's Sons, 1901). In the bibliography for *The Negro* he listed volume forty of The Contemporary Science Series, ed. by H. Ellis (London: Scott Publishing Co., Ltd., 1901). In the bibliography for "Miscegenation" (1935) a 1967 reprint by Humanities Press is listed. It is worth noting that there is no reference to Sergi's book in either the footnotes or the bibliographies of *Black Folk Then and Now* and *The World and Africa*.

22 G. Sergi, *The Mediterranean Race*, 233–65.

23 "The Conservation of Races," 8.

24 See "The Conservation of Races," 8–9. But compare this with his full statement in "The Health and Physique of the Negro-American." (See note 21) "We have, then, in the so-called Negro races to do with a great variety of human types and mixtures of blood representing at bottom a human variation which separated from the primitive human stock some ages after the yellow race and before the Mediterranean race, and which has since intermingled with these races in all degrees of admixture so that today no absolute separating line can be drawn." (p. 18) Cf. *Black Folk Then and Now*, 1.

25 *Dusk of Dawn*, 103. In *The World and Africa* Du Bois points out with regard to the three main biological types: "less than two-thirds of the living peoples of today can be decisively allotted to one or the other of the definite subspecies" (p. 85).

26 "Health and Physique," 13–18.

27 Du Bois cites Arnold Toynbee's *Study of History* (London: Oxford University Press, 1934) as an example. See *The World and Africa*, 99. In his introduction to Du Bois's *The Negro*, Herbert Aptheker reports that a passage comparing "Prehistoric and early dynastic Egyptians" with "a light mulatto stock of quadroons or octoroons." was excised from chapter three by the editor. See *The Negro*, 9. A different version of the excised statement appears in *Black Folk Then and Now* (p. 22). In a chapter on Egypt in *The World and Africa* Du Bois makes the same point, and adds an important sceptical remark regarding the use of scientific racial categories. "Many of the yellow peoples from the East filtered in and gradually there evolved a type which we know and would call a mulatto type, although that word brings the notion of a mixture of primary races" (p. 105).

28 "Conservation of Races," 9.

29 Du Bois cites his own family background to illustrate this point. See *Dusk of Dawn*, 103–16. He complained that "Most American students have the curious habit of studying Negroes in America indiscriminately without reference to their blood mixture and calling the result a study of the Negro race." "Miscegenation," 98.

30 *Dusk of Dawn*, 100.

31 "The Conservation of Races," 8.

32 With apparent ignorance of Du Bois's 1897 pamphlet bearing a similar title, an essay critical of Spencer's views appeared in a leading sociology journal in 1900. The criticism carries two very interesting implications for interpreting Du Bois's early view of development. Spencer's detractor was concerned with how the term "race preservation" was being used

> without pausing to reflect why one group of individuals should be called the race rather than another, or why the preservation of one group should be more 'justifiable' than the preservation of another group.... To this must be added that the introduction of the

terminology of traditional ethics into the province of natural science is both illogical and dangerous.

Antonio Llano, "The Race-Preservation Dogma" *American Journal of Sociology* 5.4 (January 1900): 488–9. If we bear in mind Du Bois's early view of the talented tenth and his talk of a "duty" to conserve the race we can see the extent to which he negotiated these criticisms in his adaptation of Spencer's philosophical view to fashion an empirically grounded theory of group development for African–Americans. See Herbert Spencer, *Principles of Sociology* (New York: Appleton, 1898) vol. 1, sections 275 and 277. Du Bois seems to be ridiculing Spencer when he claims in *Dusk of Dawn* that, "I could accept evolution and the survival of the fittest, provided the interval between advanced and backward races was not made too impossible." (p. 99) This earlier acceptance is captured in his statement in 1898 that "We have here going on before our eyes the evolution of a vast group of men from simpler primitive conditions to higher more complex civilization." See Du Bois, "The Atlanta Conferences," 85.

33 For a critical discussion of Du Bois's "environmental perspective" in *The Philadelphia Negro* (Philadelphia: University, Ginn & Co, 1899) see Kevin Gaines, *Uplifting the Race: Black Leadership, Politics, and Culture in the Twentieth Century* (Chapel Hill: University of North Carolina Press, 1996), 161 ff. and Michael Katz and Thomas Sugrue, eds., *W. E. B. Du Bois, Race, and the City*, Introduction, 24–5.
34 *Dusk of Dawn*, 51. See also Du Bois, *Autobiography*, 205–6.
35 "Conservation of Races," 5.
36 See "The Atlanta Conferences," 85 and W. E. B. Du Bois, "Sociology Hesitant," 6–8 unpublished essay, Du Bois Collection, University of Massachusetts, Amherst, quoted in Dan S. Green and Edwin D. Driver, "W. E. B. Du Bois: A Case Study in the Sociology of Sociological Negation" *Phylon* 37.4 (1976): 313. I thank Ronald Judy for providing me a copy of Du Bois's essay soon to be published in *Boundary 2*.
37 "Conservation of Races," 7.
38 "Conservation of Races," 9. For a discussion of Du Bois's account of cultural pluralism see Boxill, "Du Bois on Cultural Pluralism."
39 "Conservation of Races", 10.
40 Du Bois, *Autobiography*, 201. The proposal is presented in W. E. B. Du Bois, "The Study of the Negro Problems" *The Annals of the American Academy of Political and Social Science*, 11 (January 1898) 1–23, abridged rpt. in Dan S. Green and Edwin D. Driver, eds. *W. E. B. Du Bois on Sociology and the Black Community* (Chicago: University of Chicago Press, 1978), 81–3. See also James B. Stewart, "W. E. B. Du Bois's Theory of Social and Cultural Dynamics" in Bell et al., eds. *W. E. B. Du Bois on Race and Culture*, 261–88.
41 *Autobiography*, 201. In *Dusk of Dawn* he stated, "[I]f I could have carried it out as completely as I conceived it, the American Negro would have contributed to the development of social science in this country an unforgettable body of work" (p. 63).
42 *Dusk of Dawn* 60–61. Cf. Du Bois, *Autobiography*, 200.
43 *Dusk of Dawn*, 61.
44 According to Du Bois, "The careful exhaustive study of the isolated group is the ideal of the sociologist of the twentieth century." "The Atlanta Conferences," 85. He believed this isolation would not end soon. He stated in "The Health and Physique of the Negro-American" that "At present those who dislike amalgamation can best prevent it by helping to raise the Negro to such a plane of intelligence and economic independence that he will

never stoop to mingle his bood with those who despise him." (p. 39) In *Dusk of Dawn* he stated,

> Nor again was there any idea of racial amalgamation. I resented the assumption that we desired it. I frankly refused the possibility while in Germany and even in America gave up courtship with one "colored" girl because she looked quite white, and I should resent the inference on the street that I had married outside my race (p. 101).

In "Miscegenation" (1935) he stated,

> Indeed, the question of the extent to which whites and blacks in the United States have mingled their blood, and the results of this intermingling, past, present and future, is, in many respects, the crux of the so-called Negro problem in the United States.... They are glad that slavery has disappeared; but their hesitation now is to how far complete social freedom and full economic opportunity for Negroes is going to result in such racial amalgamation as to make America octoroon in blood. It is the real fear of this result and inherited resentment at its very possibility that keeps the race problem in America so terribly alive (p. 96).

45 "Conservation of Races," 10.
46 "Conservation of Races," 11.
47 Outlaw, "'Conserve' Races? In Defense of W. E. B. Du Bois," 27–8.
48 Du Bois's remark in "The Conservation of Races" that "the best blood... cannot be marshalled to do the bidding of the race," as well as his use of "absorption," "commingled blood" and "self-obliteration" seem to have a particular application to mulattoes. In "The Health and Physique of the Negro-American" he pointed out that "Comparisons will inevitably arise between the blacks and mixed bloods. In regard to the latter much friction and prejudice must be cleared away." (p. 36) See also his discussion of mulattoes and group loyalty in *Dusk of Dawn*, 101.
49 Although Du Bois cited Josiah Royce, George Herbert Palmer, and George Santayana, and William James as his philosophy teachers at Harvard, I have in mind primarily James. See *Dusk of Dawn*, 38–9 and *Autobiography*, 143, 148. He claimed: "I became a devoted follower of James at the time he was developing his pragmatic philosophy.... William James guided me out of the sterilities of scholastic philosophy to realist pragmatism." *Autobiography*, 133, 148. For a discussion of William James's influence on Du Bois see Nancy Ladd Muller, "Du Boisian Pragmatism and 'The Problem of the Twentieth Century'" in *Critique of Anthropology* 22.3 (1992): 319–37; Cornel West, "W. E. B. Du Bois: The Jamesian Organic Intellectual" in *The American Evasion of Philosophy* (Madison: University of Wisconsin Press, 1989); Zamir, *Dark Voices*, 79–80; Cynthia D. Schrager, "Both Sides of the Veil: Race, Science, and Mysticism in W. E. B. Du Bois" *American Quarterly* 48.4 (December 1996): 551–86; Adolph Reed, Jr., *W. E. B. Du Bois and American Political Thought: Fabianism and The Color Line* (New York: Oxford University Press, 1997), 99–105; James Campbell, "Du Bois and James" *Transactions of the Charles Pierce Society* 15.3 (Summer 1992): 569–81; Henry Louis Gates, Jr., "Introduction" in W. E. B. Du Bois, *The Souls of Black Folk* (New York: Bantam, 1989), vii–xxiv.
50 "The Atlanta Conferences," 85.
51 He speaks of "groping after a science – after reliable methods of observation and measurement." "The Atlanta Conferences," 85–6.
52 "The Atlanta Conferences," 85.

53 *Black Folk Then and Now*, 13–14. For a similar claim see *The Negro*, 15; *Africa, Its Geography, People and Products*, 9; *The World and Africa*, 116.

54 W. E. B. Du Bois, Review of Frederick L. Hoffman, Race Traits and Tendencies of the American Negro (New York: Macmillan, 1896) in *Annals of the American Academy of Political and Social Science* (1897): 129.

55 Du Bois, Review of Hoffman, 128.

56 Du Bois, Review of Hoffman, 133. In *Dusk of Dawn* Du Bois stated "I lived to see every assumption of Hoffman's "Race Traits and Tendencies" contradicted" (p. 99).

57 W. E. B. Du Bois, Review of Joseph Alexander Tillinghast, *The Negro in Africa and America* (American Economic Association, 1902) in *Political Science Quarterly* 18.4 (December, 1902): 695–7.

58 Du Bois, Review of Tillinghast, 697.

59 Du Bois presented the following examples: "we find among American Negroes today, at the very same time, increasing intelligence and increasing crime, increasing wealth and disproportionate poverty, increasing religious and moral activity and high rate of illegitimacy in births. . . ." Review of Hoffman, 132.

60 W. E. B. Du Bois, "The Development of a People" *International Journal of Ethics* 14 (1904): 295.

61 Du Bois, "Health and Physique," 29.

62 On Du Bois's criticisms of racist scientists see, for example, his denunciation of Woods Hutchinson's columns on black people as scientifically uninformed and racist. "Scientists" *The Crisis* 13 (November 1916): 11, rpt. in Herbert Aptheker, ed. *Selections from* The Crisis, *1911–1925*, 128. Similarly, he criticized Walter Wilcox for his preface to Joseph Tillinghast's *The Negro in Africa and America.* On Du Bois and the biological view of race see Baker, *From Savage to Negro*, 113; Boxill, "Du Bois on Cultural Pluralism," 65; Mostern, "Three Theories of the Race of W. E. B. Du Bois"; David W. Blight and Robert Gooding-Williams, Introduction to *The Souls of Black Folk* (Boston: Bedford Books, 1997), 8–9.

63 In "The Conservation of Races" Du Bois remarked "they [races] perhaps transcend scientific definition" (p. 7) and "spiritual, psychical, differences – undoubtedly based on the physical, but infinitely transcending them" (p. 8).

64 "Health and Physique," 35–6.

65 "Health and Physique," 15. See note 82 below for Du Bois's remarks that suggest this justification.

66 "Health and Physique," 29.

67 His population included 10,000 rural residents in the Black Belt and the rest from the two cities near the Black Belt. "Health and Physique," 29.

68 "Health and Physique," 30.

69 "Health and Physique," 30.

70 "Health and Physique," 30.

71 "Health and Physique," 30.

72 "Health and Physique," 30.

73 "Health and Physique," 30.

74 "Health and Physique," 30. Dubois seems to be responding to a criticism of the method of "classification by observation" raised by Monroe Work in a memorandum on the brain and racial difference Du Bois included in section three (pp. 25–6).

75 "Health and Physique," 35. By "exact scientific measurement" Du Bois had in mind the measurement of the cranio-facial skeletal characteristics. He quoted and later paraphrased Sergi's claim that these physical characteristics are "the guiding thread in anthropological research." (pp. 16, 18) With regard to the common assumption that the Negro race is

easiest to distinguish because of its "pronounced physical characteristics," Du Bois claimed that "Exacter studies and measurements prove this untrue." (p. 16) Following Sergi, he meant that the physical development of the skin and intermediate "soft" parts vary, while the cranio-facial skeletal characteristics remain uniform.

76 "Health and Physique," 28.

77 "Health and Physique," 29. For a similar use of the laboratory metaphor with regard to the anthropological study of black people see Melville J. Herskovits, *The New World Negro: Selected Papers in AfroAmerican Studies* (Indiana University Press/Minerva, 1969), 1–41.

78 "Health and Physique," 36.

79 "Health and Physique," 36.

80 "Health and Physique," 36.

81 In "The Atlanta Conferences" Du Bois stated, "We do not even know the number of mixed bloods, the extent of the mixture, the characteristics, stature, or ability of the mixed; and yet there is scarcely a man or woman who would not be able or willing at a moment's notice to express a full and definite opinion concerning American Mulattoes, both here and everywhere, in time and eternity" (p. 86).

82 "Health and Physique," 16. In *The World and Africa* Du Bois may have been reflecting on his earlier use of racial classifications in "The Health and Physique of the Negro-American" when he stated, "It would therefore be helpful to science if the broad hypothetical division of men into three or five great groups in accord with physique and culture were provisionally maintained to facilitate, but certainly not to obstruct, further study. This was the scientific status of the race theory early in the twentieth century, and in accord with this we spoke of three "races" – Caucasoid, Negroid, and Mongoloid – as comprising mankind, knowing well that no scientifically accurate definition of these races could be made which would not leave most of mankind outside the limits" (p. 116).

83 "Health and Physique," 16.

84 *Black Folk Then and Now*, 17. In *Africa, Its Geography, People and Products* he insisted that there are no "pure" cultures. "Culture arises from the contact and mixture of groups of men" (p. 10).

85 Aptheker reports that a reviewer for *The Negro* had proposed a change of title from The Negro Race because this is "perhaps a misnomer, since Dr. Du Bois makes it clear that there is, strictly, no such thing." *The Negro* (New York: Holt, 1915/rpt. 1975 Kraus Thomas), 6.

86 *Black Folk Then and Now*, vii.

87 Du Bois quoted a scientific definition of race in terms of the "morphological and metrical features . . . derived from their common descent" given by Earnest Hooton, *Up from the Ape* (New York: Macmillan, 1931), 397. His paraphrase of Hooton is preceded by the remark that "we mean by Race today, not a clearly defined and scientifically measured group."

88 *Black Folk Then and Now*, 22.

89 Du Bois pointed out in *The Negro* that, "The mulatto is as typically African as the black man and cannot logically be included in the 'white' race, especially when American usage includes the mulatto in the Negro race" (p. 14).

90 *Black Folk Then and Now*, 14.

91 *The World and Africa*; 88.

92 *Black Folk Then and Now*, 3; *The World and Africa*, 87. See also Frances Hoggan, "Prehistoric Negroids and Their Contribution to Civilization" *Crisis* (1911): 171–2.

93 See Herbert Aptheker, Introduction, *Black Folk Then and Now*, (Millwood, N. Y.: Kraus-Thomson, 1975), 9.

94 "Health and Physique," 38. In "Miscegenation" (1935) he pointed out that

> The bitterest protest and deepest resentment in the matter of inter-breeding has arisen from the fact that the same white race which today resents race mixture in theory has been chiefly responsible for the systematic misuse and degradation of darker women the world over, and has literally fathered millions of half-castes in Asia, Africa and America (p. 95).

See also "The Future of Africa in America" (1942).

95 "Races," *Crisis 2* (August 1911): 177–8, in Herbert Aptheker, ed. *Writings in Periodicals Edited by W. E. B. Du Bois Selections from* The Crisis, *Volume 1 1911–1925*, (Millwood, N.Y.: Kraus-Thomson 1983), 13–15.

96 *The Negro*, 185. Much later in "India's Relation to Negroes and the Color Problem" (1965) he reasserts his stance against racial intermingling in the United States.

> American Negroes have long considered that their destiny lay with the American people; that their object was to become full American citizens and eventually lose themselves in the nation by continued intermingling of blood. But there are many things that have happened and are happening in the modern world to show that both these lines of thought are erroneous.

Andrew Paschal, ed. *W. E. B. Du Bois: A Reader* (New York: Macmillan, 1971), 282.

97 "Miscegenation," 100.

98 "Miscegenation," 100. Du Bois made the pitch for funding of his "laboratory experiment" as late as 1948. See Du Bois to John W. Davis, New York City, 23 August 1948, in Herbert Aptheker, *The Correspondence of W. E. B. Du Bois: Volume III Selections, 1944–63* (Amherst: University of Massachusetts Press, 1978), 208–9.

99 A large portion of this address is reproduced in "The Health and Physique of the Negro-American," (pp. 18–21). See also W. E. B. Du Bois, "What is Civilization? Africa's Answer," *Forum* (February, 1925), rpt. in Weinberg, ed., *W. E. B. Du Bois: A Reader*, 376–81.

100 "The Future of Africa in America", 178.

101 Wilson Moses refers to Du Bois's favourable view of the West African village and his unfavorable view of the modern city to indicate that Du Bois meant to call in question ideas of modernity and progress. Wilson J. Moses, "Culture, Civilization, and the Decline of the West," in Bell, et al., *W. E. B. Du Bois on Race and Culture*, 247. Remnants of Du Bois's claim in "The Conservation of Races" regarding "Negro genius" can be found in some of his later remarks regarding racial absorption.

> This problem of the African in America cannot be avoided. . . . His sudden physical absorption without planned social effort would result in a distinct lowering of the level of culture over wide areas. His slow absorption if accompanied by curbing and extinction of his genius is but worship of white domination.

"The Future of Africa in America", 183.

102 *Dusk of Dawn*, 149.

103 *Dusk of Dawn*, 174.

104 Du Bois discussed the decline of European civilization in the opening chapter of *The World and Africa*. In a letter to Du Bois requesting his support for the *American Committee for Anti-Nazi Literature* Boas included the statement. "For us who hold precious the

progress of civilization, this reversion of mankind to the jungle-pit appears as an incalculable calamity." Franz Boas to Du Bois, New York, N.Y., 22 April 1936, in *Correspondence*, vol. 2, 135. In a chapter from *Dusk of Dawn* titled, "The White World" Du Bois has his black interlocutor pose the following question:

> Admitting that the problem of native human endowment is obscure, there is no corresponding obscurity in spiritual values. Goodness and unselfishness; simplicity and honor; tolerance, susceptibility to beauty in form, color, and music . . . In all these mighty things, the greatest things in the world, where do black folk and white folk stand? (p. 147).

4

THE CONSERVATION OF RACES

W. E. Burghardt Du Bois

The American Negro has always felt an intense personal interest in discussions as to the origins and destinies of races: primarily because back of most discussions of race with which he is familiar, have lurked certain assumptions as to his natural abilities, as to his political, intellectual and moral status, which he felt were wrong. He has, consequently, been led to deprecate and minimize race distinctions, to believe intensely that out of one blood God created all nations, and to speak of human brotherhood as though it were the possibility of an already dawning to-morrow.

Nevertheless, in our calmer moments we must acknowledge that human beings are divided into races; that in this country the two most extreme types of the world's races have met, and the resulting problem as to the future relations of these types is not only of intense and living interest to us, but forms an epoch in the history of mankind.

It is necessary, therefore, in planning our movements, in guiding our future development, that at times we rise above the pressing, but smaller questions of separate schools and cars, wage discrimination and lynch law, to survey the whole question of race in human philosophy and to lay, on a basis of broad knowledge and careful insight, those large lines of policy and higher ideals which may form our guiding lines and boundaries in the practical difficulties of every day. For it is certain that all human striving must recognize the hard limits of natural law, and that any striving, no matter how intense and earnest, which is against the constitution of the world, is vain. The question, then, which we must seriously consider is this: What is the real meaning of Race; what has, in the past, been the law of race development, and what lessons has the past history of race development to teach the rising Negro people?

When we thus come to inquire into the essential difference of races we find it hard to come at once to any definite conclusion. Many criteria of race differences have in the past been proposed, as color, hair, cranial measurements and language. And manifestly, in each of these respects, human beings differ widely. They vary in color, for instance, from the marble-like pallor of the Scandinavian to the rich, dark brown of the Zulu, passing by the creamy Slav, the yellow Chinese, the light brown Sicilian and the brown Egyptian. Men vary, too, in the texture of hair from the obstinately straight hair of the Chinese to the obstinately tufted and frizzled hair of the Bushman. In measurement of heads, again, men vary; from the broad-headed Tartar to the medium-headed European and the narrow-headed Hottentot; or, again in language, from the highly-inflected Roman tongue to the monosyllabic Chinese. All these physical characteristics are patent enough, and if they agreed with each other it would be very easy to classify mankind. Unfortunately for scientists, however, these criteria of race are most exasperatingly intermingled. Color does not agree with texture of hair, for many of the dark races have straight hair; nor does color agree with the breadth of the head, for the yellow Tartar has a broader head than the German; nor, again, has the science of language as yet succeeded in clearing up the relative authority of these various and contradictory criteria. The final word of science, so far, is that we have at least two, perhaps three, great families of human beings – the whites and Negroes, possibly the yellow race. That other races have arisen from the intermingling of the blood of these two. This broad division of the world's races which men like Huxley and Raetzel [sic] have introduced as more nearly true than the old five-race scheme of Blumenbach, is nothing more than an acknowledgment that, so far as purely physical characteristics are concerned, the differences between men do not explain all the differences of their history. It declares, as Darwin himself said, that great as is the physical unlikeness of the various races of men their likenesses are greater, and upon this rests the whole scientific doctrine of Human Brotherhood.

Although the wonderful developments of human history teach that the grosser physical differences of color, hair and bone go but a short way toward explaining the different roles which groups of men have played in Human Progress, yet there are differences – subtle, delicate and elusive, though they may be – which have silently but definitely separated men into groups. While these subtle forces have generally followed the natural cleavage of common blood, descent and physical peculiarities, they have at other times swept across and ignored these. At all times, however, they have divided human beings into races, which, while they perhaps transcend scientific definition, nevertheless, are clearly defined to the eye of the Historian and Sociologist.

If this be true, then the history of the world is the history, not of individuals, but of groups, not of nations, but of races, and he who ignores or seeks to override the race idea in human history ignores and overrides the central thought of all history. What, then, is a race? It is a vast family of human beings, generally of common blood and language, always of common history, traditions and impulses, who are both voluntarily and involuntarily striving together for the accomplishment of certain more or less vividly conceived ideals of life.

Turning to real history, there can be no doubt, first, as to the widespread, nay, universal, prevalence of the race idea, the race spirit, the race ideal, and as to its efficiency as the vastest and most ingenious invention for human progress. We, who have been reared and trained under the individualistic philosophy of the Declaration of Independence and the *laisser-faire* philosophy of Adam Smith, are loath to see and loath to acknowledge this patent fact of human history. We see the Pharaohs, Caesars, Toussaints and Napoleons of history and forget the vast races of which they were but epitomized expressions. We are apt to think in our American impatience, that while it may have been true in the past that closed race groups made history, that here in conglomerate America *nous avons changer tout cela* – we have changed all that, and have no need of this ancient instrument of progress. This assumption of which the

Negro people are especially fond, can not be established by a careful consideration of history.

We find upon the world's stage today eight distinctly differentiated races, in the sense in which History tells us the word must be used. They are, the Slavs of eastern Europe, the Teutons of middle Europe, the English of Great Britain and America, the Romance nations of Southern and Western Europe, the Negroes of Africa and America, the Semitic people of Western Asia and Northern Africa, the Hindoos of Central Asia and the Mongolians of Eastern Asia. There are, of course, other minor race groups, as the American Indians, the Esquimaux and the South Sea Islanders; these larger races, too, are far from homogeneous; the Slav includes the Czech, the Magyar, the Pole and the Russian; the Teuton includes the German, the Scandinavian and the Dutch; the English include the Scotch, the Irish and the conglomerate American. Under Romance nations the widely-differing Frenchman, Italian, Sicilian and Spaniard are comprehended. The term Negro is, perhaps, the most indefinite of all, combining the Mulattoes and Zamboes of America and the Egyptians, Bantus and Bushmen of Africa. Among the Hindoos are traces of widely differing nations, while the great Chinese, Tartar, Corean and Japanese families fall under the one designation – Mongolian.

The question now is: What is the real distinction between these nations? Is it the physical differences of blood, color and cranial measurements? Certainly we must all acknowledge that physical differences play a great part, and that, with wide exceptions and qualifications, these eight great races of to-day follow the cleavage of physical race distinctions; the English and Teuton represent the white variety of mankind; the Mongolian, the yellow; the Negroes, the black. Between these are many crosses and mixtures, where Mongolian and Teuton have blended into the Slav, and other mixtures have produced the Romance nations and the Semites. But while race differences have followed mainly physical race lines, yet no mere physical distinctions would really define or explain the deeper differences – the cohesiveness and continuity of these groups. The deeper differences are spiritual, psychical, differences – undoubtedly based on the physical, but infinitely transcending them. The forces that bind together the Teuton nations are, then, first, their race identity and common blood; secondly, and more important, a common history, common laws and religion, similar habits of thought and a conscious striving together for certain ideals of life. The whole process which has brought about these race differentiations has been a growth, and the great characteristic of this growth has been the differentiation of spiritual and mental differences between great races of mankind and the integration of physical differences.

The age of nomadic tribes of closely related individuals represents the maximum of physical differences. They were practically vast families, and there were as many groups as families. As the families came together to form cities the physical differences lessened, purity of blood was replaced by the requirement of domicile, and all who lived within the city bounds became gradually to be regarded as members of the group; i.e., there was a slight and slow breaking down of physical barriers. This, however, was accompanied by an increase of the spiritual and social differences between cities. This city became husbandmen, this, merchants, another warriors, and so on. The *ideals of life* for which the different cities struggled were different. When at last cities began to coalesce into nations there was another breaking down of barriers which separated groups of men. The larger and broader differences of color, hair and physical proportions were not by any means ignored, but myriads of minor differences disappeared, and the sociological and historical races of men began to approximate the present division of races as indicated by physical researches. At the same time the spiritual and physical differences of race groups which constituted the nations became deep and decisive. The English nation stood for constitutional liberty and commercial freedom; the German nation for science and philosophy; the Romance nations stood for literature and art, and the other race groups are striving, each in its own way, to develope for civilization its particular message, its particular ideal, which shall help to guide the world nearer and nearer that perfection of human life for which we all long, that "one far off Divine event."

This has been the function of race differences up to the present time. What shall be its function in the future? Manifestly some of the great races of today – particularly the Negro race – have not as yet given to civilization the full spiritual message which they are capable of giving. I will not say that the Negro race has as yet given no message to the world, for it is still a mooted question among scientists as to just how far Egyptian civilization was Negro in its origin; if it was not wholly Negro, it was certainly very closely allied. Be that as it may, however the fact still remains that the full, complete Negro message of the whole Negro race has not as yet been given to the world: that the messages and ideal of the yellow race have not been completed, and that the striving of the mighty Slavs has but begun. The question is, then: How shall this message be delivered; how shall these various ideals be realized? The answer is plain: By the development of these race groups, not as individuals, but as races. For the development of Japanese genius, Japanese literature and art, Japanese spirit, only Japanese, bound and welded together, Japanese inspired by one vast ideal, can work out in its fullness the wonderful message which Japan has for the nations of the earth. For the development of Negro genius, of Negro literature and art, of Negro spirit, only Negroes bound and welded together, Negroes inspired by one vast ideal, can work out in its fullness the great message we have for humanity. We cannot reverse history; we are subject to the same natural laws as other races, and if the Negro is ever to be a factor in the world's history – if among the gaily-colored banners that deck the broad ramparts of civilization is to hang one uncompromising black, then it must be placed there by black hands, fashioned by black heads and hallowed by the travail of 200,000,000 black hearts beating in one glad song of jubilee.

For this reason, the advance guard of the Negro people – the 8,000,000 people of Negro blood in the United States of America – must soon come to realize that if they are to take their just place in the van of Pan-Negroism, then their destiny is *not* absorption by the white Americans. That if in America it is to be proven for the first time in the modern world that not only Negroes are capable of evolving individual men like Toussaint, the Saviour, but are a nation stored with wonderful possibilities of culture, then their destiny is not a servile imitation of Anglo-Saxon culture, but a stalwart originality which shall unswervingly follow Negro ideals.

It may, however, be objected here that the situation of our race in America renders this attitude impossible; that our sole hope of salvation lies in our being able to lose our race identity in the commingled blood of the nation; and that any other course would merely increase the friction of races which we call race prejudice, and against which we have so long and so earnestly fought.

Here, then, is the dilemma, and it is a puzzling one, I admit. No Negro who has given earnest thought to the situation of his people in America has failed, at some time in life, to find himself at these cross-roads; has failed to ask himself at some time: What, after all, am I? Am I an American or am I a Negro? Can I be both? Or is it my duty to cease to be a Negro as soon as possible and be an American? If I strive as a Negro, am I not perpetuating the very cleft that threatens and separates Black and White America? Is not my only possible practical aim the subduction of all that is Negro in me to the American? Does my black blood place upon me any more obligation to assert my nationality than German, or Irish or Italian blood would?

It is such incessant self-questioning and the hesitation that arises from it, that is making the present period a time of vacillation and contradiction for the American Negro; combined race action is stifled, race responsibility is shirked, race enterprises languish, and the best blood, the best talent, the best energy of the Negro people cannot be marshalled to do the bidding of the race. They stand back to make room for every rascal and demagogue who chooses to cloak his selfish deviltry under the veil of race pride.

Is this right? Is it rational? Is it good policy? Have we in America a distinct mission as a race – a distinct sphere of action and an opportunity for race development, or is self-obliteration the highest end to which Negro blood dare aspire?

If we carefully consider what race prejudice really is, we find it, historically, to be nothing but the friction between different groups of people; it is the difference in aim, in feeling, in ideals of two different races; if, now, this difference exists touching territory, laws, language, or even religion, it is manifest that these people cannot live in the same territory without fatal collision; but if, on the other hand, there is substantial agreement in laws, language and religion; if there is a satisfactory adjustment of economic life, then there is no reason why, in the same country and on the same street, two or three great national ideals might not thrive and develop, that men of different races might not strive together for their race ideals as well, perhaps even better, than in isolation. Here, it seems to me, is the reading of the riddle that puzzles so many of us. We are Americans, not only by birth and by citizenship, but by our political ideals, our language, our religion. Farther than that, our Americanism does not go. At that point, we are Negroes, members of a vast historic race that from the very dawn of creation has slept, but half awakening in the dark forests of its African fatherland. We are the first fruits of this new nation, the harbinger of that black tomorrow which is yet destined to soften the whiteness of the Teutonic to-day. We are that people whose subtle sense of song has given America its only American music, its only American fairy tales, its only touch of pathos and humor amid its mad money-getting plutocracy. As such, it is our duty to conserve our physical powers, our intellectual endowments, our spiritual ideals; as a race we must strive by race organization, by race solidarity, by race unity to the realization of that broader humanity which freely recognizes differences in men, but sternly deprecates inequality in their opportunities of development.

For the accomplishment of these ends we need race organizations: Negro colleges, Negro newspapers, Negro business organizations, a Negro school of literature and art, and an intellectual clearing house, for all these products of the Negro mind, which we may call a Negro Academy. Not only is all this necessary for positive advance, it is absolutely imperative for negative defense. Let us not deceive ourselves at our situation in this country. Weighted with a heritage of moral iniquity from our past history, hard pressed in the economic world by foreign immigrants and native prejudice, hated here, despised there and pitied everywhere; our one haven of refuge is ourselves, and but one means of advance, our own belief in our great destiny, our own implicit trust in our ability and worth. There is no power under God's high heaven that can stop the advance of eight thousand thousand honest, earnest, inspired and united people. But – and here is the rub – they *must* be honest, fearlessly criticising their own faults, zealously correcting them; they must be *earnest.* No people that laughs at itself, and ridicules itself, and wishes to God it was anything but itself ever wrote its name in history; it *must* be inspired with the Divine faith of our black mothers, that out of the blood and dust of battle will march a victorious host, a mighty nation, a peculiar people, to speak to the nations of earth a Divine truth that shall make them free. And such a people must be united; not merely united for the organized theft of political spoils, not united to disgrace religion with whoremongers and ward-heelers; not united merely to protest and pass resolutions, but united to stop the ravages of consumption among the Negro people, united to keep black boys from loafing, gambling and crime; united to guard the purity of black women and to reduce that vast army of black prostitutes that is today marching to hell; and united in serious organizations, to determine by careful conference and thoughtful interchange of opinion the broad lines of policy and action for the American Negro.

This, is the reason for being which the American Negro Academy has. It aims at once to be the epitome and expression of the intellect of the black-blooded people of America, the exponent of the race ideals of one of the world's great races. As such, the Academy must, if successful, be

(a) representative in character
(b) impartial in conduct
(c) firm in leadership.

It must be representative in character; not in that it represents all interests or all factions, but in that it seeks to comprise something of the *best* thought, the most unselfish striving and the highest ideals. There are scattered in forgotten nooks and corners throughout the land, Negroes of some considerable training, of high minds, and high motives, who are unknown to their fellows, who exert far too little influence. These the Negro Academy should strive to bring into touch with each other and to give them a common mouthpiece.

The Academy should be impartial in conduct; while it aims to exalt the people it should aim to do so by truth – not by lies, by honesty – not by flattery. It should continually impress the fact upon the Negro people that they must not expect to have things done for them – THEY MUST DO FOR THEMSELVES; that they have on their hands a vast work of self-reformation to do, and that a little less complaint and whining, and a little more dogged work and manly striving would do us more credit and benefit than a thousand Force or Civil Rights bills.

Finally, the American Negro Academy must point out a practical path of advance to the Negro people; there lie before every Negro today hundreds of questions of policy and right which must be settled and which each one settles now, not in accordance with any rule, but by impulse or individual preference; for instance: What should be the attitude of Negroes toward the educational qualification for voters? What should be our attitude toward separate schools? How should we meet discriminations on railways and in hotels? Such questions need not so much specific answers for each part as a general expression of policy, and nobody should be better fitted to announce such a policy than a representative honest Negro Academy.

All this, however, must come in time after careful organization and long conference. The immediate work before us should be practical and have direct bearing upon the situation of the Negro. The historical work of collecting the laws of the United States and of the various States of the Union with regard to the Negro is a work of such magnitude and importance that no body but one like this could think of undertaking it. If we could accomplish that one task we would justify our existence.

In the field of Sociology an appalling work lies before us. First, we must unflinchingly and bravely face the truth, not with apologies, but with solemn earnestness. The Negro Academy ought to sound a note of warning that would echo in every black cabin in the land: *Unless we conquer our present vices they will conquer us;* we are diseased, we are developing criminal tendencies, and an alarmingly large percentage of our men and women are sexually impure. The Negro Academy should stand and proclaim this over the housetops, crying with Garrison: *I will not equivocate, I will not retreat a single inch, and I will be heard.* The Academy should seek to gather about it the talented, unselfish men, the pure and noble-minded women, to fight an army of devils that disgraces our manhood and our womanhood. There does not stand today upon God's earth a race more capable in muscle, in intellect, in morals, than the American Negro, if he will bend his energies in the right direction; if he will

> Burst his birth's invidious bar
> And grasp the skirts of happy chance,
> And breast the blows of circumstance,
> And grapple with his evil star.

In science and morals, I have indicated two fields of work for the Academy. Finally, in practical policy, I wish to suggest the following *Academy Creed:*

1 We believe that the Negro people, as a race, have a contribution to make to civilization and humanity, which no other race can make.
2 We believe it the duty of the Americans of Negro descent, as a body, to maintain their race identity until this mission of the Negro people is accomplished, and the ideal of human brotherhood has become a practical possibility.
3 We believe that, unless modern civilization is a failure, it is entirely feasible and practicable for two races in such essential political, economic and religious harmony as the white and colored people of America, to develop side by side in peace and mutual happiness, the peculiar contribution which each has to make to the culture of their common country.

4 As a means to this end we advocate, not such social equality between these races as would disregard human likes and dislikes, but such a social equilibrium as would, throughout all the complicated relations of life, give due and just consideration to culture, ability, and moral worth, whether they be found under white or black skins.

5 We believe that the first and greatest step toward the settlement of the present friction between the races – commonly called the Negro Problem – lies in the correction of the immorality, crime and laziness among the Negroes themselves, which still remains as a heritage from slavery. We believe that only earnest and long continued efforts on our own part can cure these social ills.

6 We believe that the second great step toward a better adjustment of the relations between the races, should be a more impartial selection of ability in the economic and intellectual world, and a greater respect for personal liberty and worth, regardless of race. We believe that only earnest efforts on the part of the white people of this country will bring much needed reform in these matters.

7 On the basis of the foregoing declaration, and firmly believing in our high destiny, we, as American Negroes, are resolved to strive in every honorable way for the realization of the best and highest aims, for the development of strong manhood and pure womanhood, and for the rearing of a race ideal in America and Africa, to the glory of God and the uplifting of the Negro people.

PART III

NARDAL AND RACE CONSCIOUSNESS

5

PAULETTE NARDAL, RACE CONSCIOUSNESS AND ANTILLEAN LETTERS[1]

T. Denean Sharpley-Whiting

Should one see in the tendencies here expressed a sort of implicit declaration of war upon Western culture and the white world in general? We want to eliminate such ambiguity so as to leave no doubt . . . . Without it we would have never become conscious of who we really are.

Paulette Nardal

Coined between 1936–1937 by Martiniquan poet Aimé Césaire during the writing of his now celebrated *Cahier d'un retour au pays natal*, Negritude, as a poetics, a philosophy of existence, a literary, cultural, and intellectual movement, signified the birth of a new literature among black Francophone writers, a "New Negro" from the Francophone world, a metaphorically rich pan-Africanism in French. While the neologism is readily traceable to Césaire, the mapping of the concept of Negritude as the inauguration of a black humanism, as a "theory of black cultural importance and autonomy"[2] was the stuff of a panoply of critical works.

Before the 1935 publication of *L'Etudiant noir*, a one-issue journal sponsored by the Association des Etudiants martiniquais en France that featured, according to Georges Ngal, "les deux textes fondateurs du mouvement de la Négritude," ("The two founding texts of the Negritude movement")[3] Aimé Césaire and the Senegalese poet Léopold Sédar Senghor, there were a number of Francophonic novelistic and journalistic precursors that equally treated the themes of assimilation, colonialism, identity, and black consciousness. These were most notably, René Maran's 1921 Prix Goncourt-winning *Batouala: véritable roman nègre* with its incendiary anti-colonialist preface, Suzanne Lacascade's 1924 *Claire-Solange, âme africaine*, and the journals, *La Race* Nègre (1927–1986), *Le Cri des Nègres* (1931–1935), *La Revue du monde noir* (1931–1932), and the June 1932 publication of the Marxist-Surrealist pamphlet *Légitime Défense* However, it was not until September 1931 that Senghor made the acquaintance of Césaire and the Guyanese Léon-Gontron Damas, the third voice of this poetic trilogy, thus setting the stage for their collective exploration of their conflicting identities, the "tormenting question" in the words of Senghor, of "who am I?," their experiences of being black, African and African-diasporic, and French.[4] For Césaire and Damas, "in meeting Senghor, [they] met Africa."[5] Through Damas and Césaire, Senghor's horizon was opened to the dynamism of the literary and cultural worlds of West Indians and African Americans living in Paris in the 1930s.

For their part, Césaire, Senghor, and Damas, the designated founders of this poetics in the French-speaking world, provide a conspicuously masculine genealogy of their critical consciousness, tracing "the awakening of their race consciousness" to the writers of the Harlem Renaissance, specifically Claude McKay, Langston Hughes, James Weldon Johnson, and Sterling Brown, Dubois's journalistic organ for the National Advancement of Colored People (NAACP), *The Crisis*, Carter G. Woodson's *Opportunity*, medium for the National Urban League, and Alain Locke's 1925 anthology *The New Negro: An Interpretation*. As Senghor revealed, "[T]he general meaning of the word [Negritude] – the discovery of black values and recognition for the Negro of his situation – was born in the United States of America."[6]

But if African–American writers of the 1920s radicalized the consciousness of these young and aspiring Francophone black writers, if the race-conscious New Negro of the United States planted the seeds of negritude in their collective imagination, then the three future negritude poets also received inspiration from Cuban writer Nicolas Guillén, Haitian writers Jacques Roumain and Jean Price-Mars, and deployed as tools of critical engagement Frobenius and Delafosse's ethnology and Breton's surrealism.[7]

While a general consensus among the founding poets around Negritude's literary historiography and philosophical commitment to affirming blacks' "being-in-the-world" exists, Césaire, Damas, and Senghor experienced and expressed their negritudes differently. In a series of interviews with sociologist Lilyan Kesteloot at the 1959 Black Writers and Artists Conference in Rome sponsored by *Présence Africaine*, Césaire responded that he experienced his Negritude as the acknowledgement of "a fact, a revolt, and the acceptance of responsibility for the destiny of [my] race." For Senghor, Negritude represented "black cultural patrimony, that is to say, the spirit of its civilization," while Damas regarded it as the explicit "rejection of an assimilation that negated his spontaneity and as a defense for his condition as Negro and Guyanese."[8] The tones and styles of Damas's 1937 *Pigments* and Césaire's oft-analyzed *Cahier* (1939) are periodically anguish-ridden, volatile, critiquing slavery, the colonial system, the utter fallaciousness of the French program of assimilation, suffering from feelings of exile, evoking biting sarcasm, and searching for an identity and culture rooted in Africa, blackness, and the West Indies.

In "Trève," Damas writes:

> Enough letting-go-of
> licking-up-to
> taking-the-leavings
> and
> of an attitude
> of super-assimilation.[9]

Tired of the mimetic existence lived by the colonized, knowing full well, in the prophetic words of Frantz Fanon, that "wherever he goes, the Negro remains a

Negro,"[10] that assimilation requires a "negation of spontaneity," Damas revolts against the inauthenticity of this existence in "Solde":

> I feel ridiculous
> In their shoes
> in their dinner jackets . . .
> I feel ridiculous
> among them an accomplice . . .
> hands hideously red
> from the blood of their
> ci-vi-li-za-tion.[11]

Damas realizes that the *devenir français* process necessitates loss, repression, rejection, negation. With their bloodied hands, the colonized will have murdered themselves in trying to assimilate into a culture, a "*ci-vi-li-za-tion*," that denegates indigenous cultures and peoples as it claims to civilize. The poet laments this loss in "Limbé," the creole word for "Blues" or "Spleen":

> Give me my black dolls
> so that I may play with them
> the naïve games of my instincts
> I become myself once more
> myself anew
> of that which yesterday I was
> Yesterday
>   Without complexity
>   Yesterday
> when the hour of uprooting came . . .[12]

The poet wants to return to the pre-colonial black world, an era of innocent games, where naiveté and spontaneity supposedly reigned before the physical uprooting of black bodies for production, before European cultural and racial domination.

Damas's slow-burning ire reaches a boil in Césaire's *Cahier*:

> Because we hate you you and
> your reason, we identify with the
> precocious dementia of the burning madness
> of tenacious cannibalism.[13]

Reason, Absolute Truth, Logic – the ideals of the European Enlightenment – are renounced by Césaire in favor of the madness, the illogical, the uncivilized, indeed cannibalistic tendencies, ascribed to blacks by Europeans. Césaire recognizes the Manichean nature of the colonial world. If the Negro is but a "jungle savage,"[14] "a corrosive element, the depository of maleficent powers,"[15] then Césaire, as he writes in the *Cahier*, "accepts, accepts, accepts . . . entirely without reserve" the lot of his race[16]. His revolt against Europe and alienated Antilleans consists partly of this acceptance.

Unlike Damas's and Césaire's wounds associated with exilic existence, that is, the state of "inhabit[ing] one place," as Michael Seidel notes in *Exile and the Narrative Imagination*, "and remember[ing] or project[ing] the reality of another,"[17] in this case, sub-Saharan Africa and the Antilles, Senghor's ancestral ties to Africa were solidly traceable and his cultural memory of Africa remained clearly, if not romantically, intact. Growing up in the rural villages of Djilor and Joal in Senegal, Senghor's two collections of poetry, *Chants d'ombre* (1945) and *Hosties noires* (1948) represent rather mythical "pilgrimages to the ancestral fountains," of his "childhood universe" interjected with anti-colonialist tropes:

> At the foot of my Africa, crucified these four hundred years yet still breathing...
> Lord forgive those who made guerrillas of Askias who turned my princes into sergeants.
> Made houseboys of my servants, and laborers of my country folk, who turned my people into proletariat
> For you must forgive those who hunted my children like wild elephants...
> You must forgive those who stole ten million of my sons in their leprous ships...
> Yes, Lord, forgive France, which hates all occupations and imposes hers so heavily on me
> That have made my Mesopotamia, the Congo, a vast cemetery beneath the white sun.[18]

Senghor recounts France's crimes against Africa, while simultaneously imploring the Lord for forgiveness for France. Written after World War II, Senghor makes mention of the rather touchy subject of the German Occupation in this "Peace Prayer," a subject France is still grappling with today. Occupied, oppressed, humiliated by the Occupation, France hypocritically continued to shine its "white sun" over parts of the *dark continent*, gradually turning the idyllic Africa of Senghor's boyhood into a wasteland, a vast cemetery, as it emptied out the continent's natural resources, including black boys and men to fight for its freedom. Senghor knew first hand the impact of France's liberation wars on Africa: he was drafted into the French army in World War II and detained in a prison camp until the end of the war; his elder brother was gassed while serving France in World War I.

Despite negritude's cultural currency in the 1930s and 1940s, it has not been without its critics regarding its self-reflexive exoticism and its socio-political efficacy. Early on in "Orphée Noir" ("Black Orpheus"), his 1948 preface to Senghor's *Anthologie de la nouvelle poésie nègre et malgache de langue française*, Jean-Paul Sartre described Negritude, much to the chagrin of Senghor and *Présence Africaine* editor Alioune Diop, as an "anti-racist racism," as a negative stage in the dialectics of history invented to be destroyed in a move towards synthesis, a universal humanism.[19] Negritude was thus not for Sartre the answer to "the black problem" in France and the Francophone world, but a necessary step toward resolution. Writer and literary critic Wole Soyinka insists that Negritude was reactionary, advocating a return to the past and feeding into a notion of a black Essence. In his essays "De la négritude" and "De l'Exotisme," René Ménil, onetime Negritude proponent, Marxist, philosopher, and co-founder with Aimé Césaire of the Martiniquan literary magazine *Tropiques*, equally critiqued Negritude as a form of black exoticism, as an 'appetitive self-consciousness,' unable to free itself from its ideological straitjacket, its becoming other, hence contributing to continuing European imperialism in the Martiniquan context.[20] And, Marcien Towa, in

Poésie de la négritude: approche structuraliste (1983), writes that Césaire's Negritude was "ouvertement politique" ("openly political"), an "authentic revolutionary Negritude" as opposed to Senghor's "bon nègre" ("good Negro") Negritude.[21]

It is perhaps undeniable that in their zeal, their anti-assimilationist stances, and their resistance to colonialism's cultural fleecing of the black world, Negritude writers lapsed into a reductive essentialism, an evocation of a specifically "black sensibility," "black spirit," "black soul." Yet every movement, concept, and poetics has its place and time in history. To Charles de Gaulle's declaration that "between America and Europe, there is only the ocean and some dust",[22] to questions regarding the existence of culture in the Antilles and civilization in Africa, for the 1930s and 1940s, Negritude, with its affirmation of blackness, vindication of Africa, promotion of a culturally engaged literature in the face of French assimilationist propaganda, *les missions civilisatrices* in Africa, and nauseating French paternalism, represented a radically progressive and self-actualizing alternative.

Negritude flew in the face of Cardinal Verdier's 1939 Introduction to the anthology *L'homme de couleur* in which French colonial policy is praised as benevolent and humanitarian, indeed, humanizing:

> Nothing is more moving than this gesture of the Frenchman, taking his black brother by the hand and helping him to rise. This hierarchic but nonetheless real collaboration, this fraternal love stooping towards the blacks to measure their possibilities of thinking and feeling; this gradual initiation to all the arts of sciences; . . . helping them progress toward an improved physical, social and moral well-being . . . This is . . . France's colonizing mission . . . .[23]

Negritude would throw down an important gauntlet to French colonialism, exposing it as a "murderous humanitarianism"[24] in the words of the Paris Surrealist Group, as wholly self-serving in its "hierarchic collaboration," self-affirming in its "fraternal love." While Damas denounced French assimilationist policy in his 1938 ethnography *Retour de Guyane* as "the cunning instrument of domination,"[25] Léopold Senghor, also included in Cardinal Verdier's volume, methodically presented "that which the black man brings" to his world, to his culture, to humanity in his essay of the same title "Ce que l'homme noir apporte."

Hence, it was not until the 1950s that René Ménil took negritude to task in "De la négritude."[26] And while Frantz Fanon recognized that the "black soul was but a white artifact" in the 1952 publication of *Peau noire, masques blancs*, within this same text writings by negritude poets were scattered throughout.[27] Whatever its conceptual and practical shortcomings, in its engagement with issues of race, identity, color, assimilation, alienation, and exile, Negritude, as a race-conscious movement, raised questions that have continuing relevance in contemporary black Francophone African and Caribbean letters and philosophical thought.

At this juncture I would like to shift the terrain of this essay. While Senghor et al. recite a curiously masculinist, albeit pan-Africanist, literary historiography of Negritude, one Francophone woman intellectual in particular, however, played a pivotal role in shaping the philosophical commitments, indeed, the evolution of this literary movement in the 1930s. Paulette Nardal, as editor of *La Revue du monde noir* and hostess of weekly Sunday salons at her residence outside of Paris, was the veritable conduit through which the negritude poets passed. The Martiniquan Nardal literally provided a cultured place (her apartment) and literary space (*La Revue du monde noir*) for male intellectual coming-of-age, as it was within the pages of the review and Nardal's apartment that Damas, Césaire, and Senghor read and mingled with Harlem Renaissance writers. Yet, Paulette Nardal's landmark essay "Eveil de la conscience de race chez les étudiants noirs" "Awakening of race consciousness among Black students," published in the sixth and final issue of *La Revue du monde noir* in April 1932, marked the inauguration of three major and lasting components of negritude thought, that is, pan-Africanism, the affirmation of peoples of the African diaspora and their cultural productions, and the validation of African civilizations.

Born in 1896 to a rather affluent black family in François, Martinique, Paulette Nardal was the eldest of the four *soeurs* Nardal. Educated at the Colonial College for Girls in Martinique, she perfected her English in the British West Indies. She would later attend the Sorbonne, specializing in French and English literature and language. She taught English for a year in Martinique until she returned to Paris where she became a journalist. Nardal wrote articles for one of the long-standing black newspapers, *La Dépeche africaine*, among others in Paris.[28]

In 1931, Paris became a safe haven of sorts for the African–American community fleeing racial oppression in America. Josephine Baker was performing at the Casino de Paris and the Folies Bergères, and Langston Hughes, Claude McKay, Countee Cullen, Jean Toomer, Alain Locke, and Nella Larsen could be seen in cafes and at the various salons in the 1930s. 1931 was also the year of the Exposition Coloniale at the Bois de Vincennes where blackness was showcased, celebrated, and simultaneously exoticized. On the eve of all this cultural activity in Paris, the Sunday salons at 7 rue Hébert in Clamart, a suburb of Paris, began. Its hosts were Andrée, Jane, and Paulette Nardal. Drinking *thé à l'anglaise* and speaking in French and English, the hosts and their guests danced, discussed interracial and colonial problems, racist injustices, current events, examined the precarious position of men and women of color in France, and reflected on the attention to things black generated by the Exposition Coloniale.[29] It was under these circumstances, these lively intellectual and diasporic exchanges, that the idea for a monthly, bilingual, multiracial collaborative review was born under the directorship of the Haitian Dr. Léo Sajous, a specialist on Liberian issues, and Paulette Nardal. While Nardal helped to edit, translate, and arrange the journal, her title – General Secretary – reflected a typically supportive feminine role. She maintained that Dr. Sajous was Director of the monthly. The offices for *The Review of the Black World* were located at 45 Rue Jacob in the student-filled Left Bank. According to Nardal, "This review, this movement, it was something that had to happen. It happened like that, like a sudden dawning. At this time, people were ready to read such a review."[30]

The first issue of the journal appeared in November 1931. Its pan-Africanist and race-conscious raising objectives were boldly declared in "Ce que nous voulons faire":

> To give to the intelligentsia of the blak [sic] race and their partisans an official organ in which to publish their artistic, literary and scientific works.
>
> To study and to popularize by means of the press, books, lectures, courses, all which concerns NEGRO CIVILIZATION and the natural riches of Africa, thrice sacred to the black race.

> The triple aim which *La Revue du Monde Noir* will pursue will be: to create among Negroes of the entire world regardless of nationality, an intellectual, and moral tie, which will permit them to better know each other, to love one another, to defend more effectively their collective interests and to glorify their race.
>
> By this means, the Negro race will contribute, along with thinking minds of other races and with all those who have received the light of truth, beauty and goodness to the material, the moral and the intellectual improvement of humanity.
>
> The motto is and will continue to be:
> For PEACE, WORK and JUSTICE.
> By LIBERTY, EQUALITY and FRATERNITY.
>
> Thus, the two hundred million individuals which constitue [sic] the Negro race, even though scattered among the various nations, will form over and above the latter a great Brotherhood, the forerunner of universal Democracy.[31]

With its grandiose mission, the managing editors sought out and published articles, reviews, poetry, short stories, editorials, and letters to the editor in a section called the "Negroes' Letterbox" on a variety of topics related to Africa and the African diaspora in Cuba, the United States, Liberia, Ethiopia, and the Francophone Antilles. Articles such as "The Problems of Work in Haiti," "The Negroes and Art," "Reflections on Islam," "The Negro in Cuba," reprints of ethnologist Frobenius's "Spiritism in Central Africa," and novelistic extracts by Walter White and poetry by Claude McKay and Langston Hughes appeared within its pages.

As the review received part of its funding from the Ministry of the Colonies, subjects of an overtly political nature were to be expressly avoided. Its cultural emphasis has, thus, led critics, among them Etienne Léro, who was initially inspired by the journal, to characterize *La Revue du monde noir* as "rosewater," as apolitical, bourgeois, and assimilationist.[32] Clearly, as the journal's aim states, the review targeted a particular class of blacks and their "partisans:" the educated of the races. The articles found within the review's six issues, specifically those written by Antilleans on the Antillean situation *vis-à-vis* French culture, do indeed advocate a democratic collaboration between "white, Western culture"[33] and the black world. The notion of a total abandonment of white, Western culture for all things African represents, for Nardal, a return to "obscurantism," to the unknown. Moreover, she is not interested in "declar[ing] a war on upon Western culture and the white world in general" (p. 31). And yet, the review's very presence on the cultural scene as an instrument through which to "glorify their race" and "defend their collective interests," undermined white cultural hegemony and signified a political and culturally politicizing intent. While the journal, communitarian in its approach and aspirations, naively assumed that all black peoples, or at least those members of the black intelligentsia to which it was directed, had common interests, its goals, rather novel ones for the era, were to globalize Negro consciousness. It never challenged the social constructivity of racial categories, rather it proudly donned the mantle of Negroness and endeavored to affirm the Negro's being in the world through cultural, artistic, and scientific works. Using the rhetoric of *Les Droits de l'homme*, of liberty, equality, and fraternity and the principles of the Enlightenment – "light of truth, beauty, goodness" – to foreground their pan-Africanism, the editors of *The Review of the Black World* further endeavored to bring about a new humanism made up of enlightened minds of all races that displaced the normative model of democracy that was explicitly white. It is then no small wonder that the French police and colonial administrators, believing the contributors had ties to Communists and American Garveyites, kept abreast of the activities of the journal's contributors,[34] that the review, plagued by funding issues after colonial administrators withheld further monetary support, ceased publication after a mere six issues, and that in its sixth and final issue Paulette Nardal would write a politically charged philosophical and historical essay that would not only broach the subject of colonialism and its effects on the evolution of the modern Antillean writer, but implore students and aspiring writers to engage with the "riches that the past of the black race and the African continent offers them." In effect, Nardal called dangerously for the awakening of race conscious in the psyche of cultural workers and intellectuals, a displacement of Frenchness as the embodiment of culture; she explicitly linked race and the experiences of racialized subjects to cultural productivity, a linking that would definitively formalize the course and commitments of Negritude in the latter part of the 1930s and 1940s.

In the opening sentence of the six-page article, Paulette Nardal asserts that she is concerned with this awakening among Antilleans in particular. Witnessing a modification in attitudes towards race and racial problems among the younger and older generations of Antilleans in 1930s Paris, Nardal writes: "A few years ago, we might even say a few months, certain subjects were simply taboo in Martinique.... One could not speak of slavery nor proclaim pride in being of African descent without being considered a fanatic or at the very least eccentric" (p. 25). Just what brought on this marked transformation in the Antillean Negro's consciousness? Through a literary historiography, Nardal proceeds systematically to outline this evolution. Race consciousness among a number of Antilleans was stirred in the late nineteenth century. This racial stirring was initially brought on when the native left the colony for the metropolis. Exile and feelings of non-belonging, or as Nardal writes, "uprooting and ensuing estrangement," created a sensation of difference, oftentimes a *malaise*. The writer for the first time was forced to live his/her blackness, experience their difference. However, the Antillean writer never explicitly articulated this conflict. Rather the writer seemed bent on immersing him/herself more deeply in the culture of the metropolis in order to avoid confronting this consciousness; the writer was content to imitate rather than create for fear of giving life to this difference through their art. Creativity would force the writer to confront his/her situation.

Nardal then compares and contrasts the development of race conscious literature among African–Americans to that of Antilleans. In effect, because of the persistence and virulence of American racism, the African–American writer has been consistently confronted with the "race problem," thus, their identity as black. The African–American like the Antillean passed importantly through the imitative phase because of their initial uprooting and forced immersion into a foreign and hostile environment; their creative expressions were necessarily imitative. The African–American writer then passes through Nardal's next phase: "literature of controversy and moral protest" amidst antislavery agitation (p. 26). Various fictional memoirs such as Harriet Wilson's *Our Nig, or Sketches from the Life of a Free Black* (1859), slave narratives such as Harriet

Jacob's powerful *Incidents in the Life of a Slave Girl* (1861) and Frederick Douglass's classic *Narrative* (1845), which, for Nardal, attempt to appeal to a sense of morality, pity, and moral indignation, would necessarily characterize this stage of African–American letters. From 1880 onwards, the African–American writer enters into a period where s/he ascends to, in Nardal's words, "veritable culture" (p. 27). Through W. E. B. Du Bois's social protest literature, Paul Lawrence Dunbar's "school of racial realism," and the poetry of Claude McKay and Langston Hughes, reprinted in the pages of the *Review*, Nardal insists that one can "observe that the Americans, having thrown off all inferiority complexes, tranquilly express their individual dark-skinned selves without fear or shame" (p. 27).[35]

The Antillean writers' broaching of racial themes in literary productions developed less rapidly. Nardal attributes this slower awakening to the cultural and historical differences between French and US race policies. The ideals of the French Republic, its perceived racial liberalism, and assimilation policy effectively obfuscated the very real issues of domination and its attendant results in the area of cultural production: alienation. The Antillean writer up until 1914 was consistently and consciously imitative, lapsing into the standard forms of exoticism practiced by European writers, as they wrote "lovingly of their native islands" (p. 28). For Nardal, no race pride can be found in this literature; strangers celebrated the islands with more appreciation and real attachment than the indigenous poets and writers who continued to model "their artistic productions after those of the metropolis" (p. 28). Ever diplomatic and measured, Nardal levels a veiled critique at the West Indian literary bourgeoisie. In effect, their literary productions have been hitherto mediocre, unimaginative, "no way inferior to those of the French writers," but certainly not distinguishable (p. 28). Taking his cue from Nardal, poet Etienne Léro, and a frequent contributor to *The Review of the Black World*, would acerbically write, just two months after Nardal's journal ceased publication in April 1932, "Misère d'une poésie" in the June 1932 Marxist-surrealist manifesto *Légitime Défense:*

> The West Indian writer, stuffed to bursting with white morality, white culture, white education, white prejudice, fills his little books with a swollen image of himself. Merely to be a good imitation of the white man fulfills both his social and his poetic requirements.... he does not want to "make like a nigger" in his poems. It is a point of honor with him that a white person could read his entire book without ever guessing the author's pigmentation.... He will stifle his originality in order to be considered "civilized." Because of this borrowed personality, his poetry is hardly better than pastiche... Some indigestible mix of French *esprit* and classical humanities has produced these babblers and the soothing syrup of their poetry.[36]

Nardal writes that between the period of conscious imitation of the literature of the metropolis by West Indian writers and the present, there was another stage in which theories by Marcus Garvey, the organization of the first Pan-African Congress incited commentary. Negro journals and studies on the history of Guadeloupe emerged and within René Maran's preface to *Batouala* "a generous indignation stir[ed]" (p. 28). However, Nardal finds these Literary efforts perplexing on the question of race: "These works remain still," she writes, "the tributaries of white Western culture. In none of them is expressed faith in the future of the race and the necessity to create a feeling of solidarity between the different groups of Blacks disseminated throughout the globe" (p. 29). Antillean writers still avoided racial subjects. Objective observation, rather than reflective subjectifying narratives dominated these writerly endeavors. Race was still a thorny issue for the writer who was still more interested in expressing their Frenchness, in *becoming French*. The idea that there was a future in blackness, a "future of the race" and that there was a particular lived experience of blackness that could somehow create feelings of transracial solidarity was beyond the comprehension of the Antillean writer. Race may exist; blackness may exist, but it was not accorded a crucial role in the formation of an Antillean identity, hence a grand place in the scheme of Antillean letters.

Paulette Nardal then moves on to a discussion of the veritable awakening of race consciousness among Antilleans. Parallel to the aforementioned string of developments and commentaries, indicative of some stirring of race consciousness within the Antillean, was the veritable awakening of race consciousness, the desire to secure the future of the race in the annals of cultural history and the need for race solidarity among a group of Antillean women students:

> The women of color living alone in the metropolis, who until the Colonial Exhibition, were certainly less favored than their male compatriots who have enjoyed easy successes, have long before the latter, felt the need of a racial solidarity that would not be merely material. They were thus aroused to race consciousness. (p. 29)

In this passage, Nardal asserts clearly that Antillean women were at the vanguard of the cultural revolution that would later be called Negritude and identified as male. It was the women who recognized a need for racial solidarity, who had first experienced a veritable race consciousness; it was the women who "passed, just as their Black American counterparts, through a period of revolt" (p. 29). In providing a literary historiography of race consciousness among Antilleans, Nardal's essay also reveals itself as an official record of black women's collective cultural praxes in a Francophone Antillean context. She would again elaborate upon the black feminine dimensions of this newly found and celebrated race consciousness among French-speaking black intellectuals in the 1930s four years later in a June 1936 interview-essay, "Black Paris", with Eslanda Goode Robeson, Paul Robeson's wife. Nardal's text, in effect, demands that literary critics, historians and philosophers reconsider black Francophone women's contributions to Negritude's intellectual history.

In her chronicling of the evolution of race consciousness among the women, Nardal describes the curious situation of black male privilege and black female circumscription in matters of race, sex, and class. Unlike their black and mulatto male counterparts in France, who threw themselves successfully, according to Nardal one might add, into the pursuit of French women, the educated women of color were isolated, ignored by fellow Antilleans and unable to be fully accepted into French culture other than on certain defined interracial terms.[37] The desire for a community in Paris, their "uprooting," she continues, "had been the starting point of their evolution." While the celebrated literary men of the era sidestepped their responsibilities to become engaged writers, and a number of Antillean male students partook of the fruit of French (sexual) liberalism in full swing, these young race women threw themselves into the study of subjects on the black race and on their respective countries (p. 30). What began as a descriptive essay, tracing the evolution of racial themes in the writings of the African diaspora, winds down with earnest prodding on the continued need for academic, literary, scientific, and artistic engagements with questions of race. Nardal suggests optimistically that some Antillean writers are on the brink of entering into "the last phase" of the evolution noted in African–American letters and that *The Review of the Black World* fully intends to publish these writers. However, the journal never fulfilled its promise. The funding by the Ministry of the Colonies had been withdrawn.

Yet, Paulette Nardal's prophetic last essay ushered in a stream of writing by Antillean and African students. Confronted with French metropolitan racism, a "Negro" identity had been foisted upon Antilleans and Africans. This imposition was doubly shocking for the Antillean who, according to Fanon in *Black Skin, White Masks*, thought that Negroes were Senegalese. Nardal's reaction was to encourage Antilleans to accept their being in the world as blacks, as Negroes, extol, research, and write about blackness, the race. Appearing to have heeded her call, three students whose names would be forever associated with Negritude explored other areas during their courses of study: the nineteen-year old Aimé Césaire began to examine the theme of the South in African–American literature; Damas traced African survivals in the West Indies; and Senghor, who was writing on Baudelaire, began to study African ethnography and languages.[38] Among the women she undoubtedly influenced was Martiniquan student Suzanne Roussy. In 1937, Roussy would return to Martinique as Suzanne Roussy-Césaire. Troubled by what she perceived as a cultural void and the continuing imitative nature of Martiniquan writing, she, along with her husband Aimé Césaire and René Ménil, co-founded *Tropiques* in 1941.

Notes

1 From the forthcoming *Gendering Negritude: Race Women, Race Consciousness, Race Letters, 1924–1945.*

2 Janet Vaillant, *Black, French and African: A Life of Léopold Sédar Senghor* (Cambridge, MA and London: Harvard University Press, 1990), p. 1.

3 Georges Ngal, "*Lire . . .*" *Le Discours sur le colonialisme* (Paris and Dakar: Présence Africaine, 1994), p. 13.

4 Vaillant, *Black, French, African*, p. 90.

5 Vaillant, *Black, French, African*, p. 91.

6 Léopold S. Senghor, "Problematique de la négritude," *Présence Africaine* 78 (1971): 12–14.

7 André Gide's *Voyage au Congo* was a French precursor to black Francophone literary anticolonial resistance.

8 Lilyan Kesteloot, *Black Writers in French: A Literary History of Negritude*, translated by Ellen Conroy Kennedy (Washington, DC: Howard University Press, 1991), pp. 119–20.

9 Léon G. Damas, "Trève" in *Pigments* (Paris: Présence Africaine, 1962).

10 Fanon, *Black Skin, White Masks* (New York: Grove, 1967), p. 173.

11 Damas, "Solde" in *Pigments.*

12 Damas, "Limbé" in *Pigments.*

13 Aimé Césaire, *Cahier d'un retour au pays natal* (Paris: Présence Africaine, 1956), pp. 47–8.

14 Frantz Fanon, *Black Skin, White Masks*, p. 12.

15 Frantz Fanon, *The Wretched of the Earth* (New York: Grove Press, 1963), p. 41.
16 Aimé Césaire, *Cahier*, pp. 76–7.
17 Cited in Marjorie Salvodon's "Contested Crossings: Identities, Gender, and Exile in *Le baobab fou*," in T. Denean Sharpley-Whiting and Renée T. White eds. *Spoils of War: Women of Color, Cultures, and Revolutions*, (Lanham, MD: Rowman & Littlefield Publishers, 1997), p. 113.
18 Léopold S. Senghor, "Prière de paix," *Hosties noires*, (Paris: Seuil, 1948), pp. 148–52.
19 See Lilyan Kesteloot's discussion in *Black Writers in French*. (See note 8.)
20 Michael Richardson, *Refusal of the Shadow: Surrealism and the Caribbean* (London: Verso, 1996), pp. 1–30.
21 See Belinda Jack's discussion in *Negritude and Literary Criticism: The History and Theory of "Negro-African" Literature in French* (Westport, CT: Greenwood Press, 1990).
22 Cited in René Ménil's *Tracées: Identité. Négritude, esthètique aux Antilles* (Paris: Èditions Robert Laffont, 1985), p. 27. The original statement by de Gaulle: "Entre Amérique et l'Europe, il n'y a que l'Océan and quelques poussières!"
23 Cardinal Verdier, "*L'homme de couleur* (Paris: Plon, 1939), p. xi.
24 The Surrealist Group in Paris, "Murderous Humanitarianism" in Nancy Cunard's *Negro: An Anthology* (New York: Ungar, 1970), pp. 352–3.
25 Damas, *Retour de Guyane* (Paris, 1938), p. 97
26 See essay in Ménil's *Tracées: Identité, négritude, esthètique aux Antilles*. (See note 22.)
27 In his essay "On National Culture" in *The Wretched of the Earth*, Fanon also challenged these "men of culture" to engage with the culture of today and leveled a subtle critique of Léopold Senghor after the 1959 Black Writers and Artist Conference in Rome in a footnote of that chapter.
28 See Eslanda Goode Robeson, "Black Paris" in *Challenge* (June 1936), pp. 9–12.
29 Louis Achilles, "Preface" to *Revue du monde noir* (Paris: Jean-Michel Place, 1992), p. xv.
30 Louis Achilles, "Preface," p. xiii. Achilles was a relative of Nardal. Her words are taken from an interview he conducted with her in Martinique.
31 The Management, "Our Aim," *Review of the Black World* (Paris: Jean-Michel Place, 1992).
32 See Jacque Louis Hymans, *Léopold Sédar Senghor: An Intellectual Biography* (Edinburgh: University Press of Edinburgh, 1971), pp. 42–3.
33 Nardal, "Awakening of Race Consciousness," *Review of the Black World* (Paris: Jean-Michel Place, 1992), p. 30. All citations are from a re-translation of this essay. From hereafter page numbers will be included in the textual analysis.
34 Janet Vaillant, *Black, French, African*, p. 95.
35 Nardal does not mention any US black women writers in this essay. However she does discuss a US black woman orator's recital in Geneva and Cambridge in the first issue of the journal.
36 Etienne Léro, "Misère d'une poésie," *Légitime Défense*, pp. 10–12.
37 See Eslanda Goode Robeson, "Black Paris," *Challenge* (June 1936): 10. Being ever the cultured woman, Nardal says "friend." But one could well imagine other less desirable terms of interaction. She further states that many of the French women pursued by men of color were from a lower socio-economic class and that on the island those liaisons would have been frowned upon. The educated Antilean woman, much more sensitive to the class issue, according to Nardal, was less willing to interact with white men not of her class. Conversely, race prevented many educated French men from interacting with serious intentions with Antillean women. Writer Mayotte Capécia, in her award-winning *Je suis martiniquaise* (Paris: Corrêa, 1948), would express this same sentiment with respect to interracial relationships with Frenchmen.
38 Vaillant, *Black, French, African*, p. 98.

6

THE AWAKENING OF RACE CONSCIOUSNESS[1]

Paulette Nardal*

I shall study this awakening more specifically among Black Antilleans. Their attitude about matters of race has certainly changed. A mere few years ago, one might even say a few months, certain subjects were taboo in Martinique. Woe to those who dared broach them! One could not speak of slavery nor proclaim pride in being of African descent without being considered a fanatic or at the very least eccentric. Such matters roused no deep chord in the young or the old.

Now this quasi-contemptuous indifference seems to have transformed itself into a startled interest among the older generation and a genuine enthusiasm among the younger.

However, race consciousness among certain Antilleans had already been awakened as a result of their leaving their small native lands. The uprooting and ensuing estrangement they felt in the metropolis, where Blacks have not always enjoyed such consideration as has been witnessed since the Colonial Exhibition, gave them, despite their white Western[2] education, a Negro[3] soul. Yet, this state of mind was never externalized.

The Antillean attitude towards their own race, so different from that of Black Americans, can easily be explained by the liberalism that characterizes French race politics *vis-à-vis* peoples of color. Sieburg's book *Is God French*? contains, among other things, a very judicious observation regarding the assimilative force of the French spirit.[4] According to the German writer, the absence of color prejudice among the French is owing to their certainty of turning the Negro, in a relatively short time, into a true Frenchman. Besides, it is natural that Antilleans, products of race-mixing, black and white, imbued with white Western culture, and ignorant of the history of the black race, should in the end turn towards the element which honors them the most.[5]

The situation among Black Americans was quite different. Though they were not of pure racial origins either, the systematic scorn displayed by white America towards them inspired them to look for some reasons, from a historical, cultural and social point of view, for pride in the past of the black race. Consequently the idea of race, because

* Annotated re-translation by T. Denean Sharpley-Whiting

of the necessity to resolve the racial problem plaguing the United States from the moment of the abolition of slavery, became the core of their concerns.

It would be interesting to explore the repercussions of this situation on African–American literature. As is the case with nearly all colonized people, three characteristic periods may be noted in the intellectual evolution of Black Americans. First, a period of indispensable acquisitions during which the Blacks imported from Africa had to learn a new language and adapt to a hostile environment. This is a period of black absorption. From a literary point of view, Blacks could only docilely imitate the works of their white models. Only certain slave narratives retain all of their original freshness and genuine emotion thanks to the use of the African–American dialect. During the anti-slavery struggle, we witness the dawning of a literature of controversy and moral protest where the oratorical genre is deftly cultivated and oftentimes with success. Increasing calls to pity characterize the poetic production then. There remain from this epoch a considerable number of documents, papers, which, from a historical point of view, are undoubtedly valuable.

From 1880 onwards, Black Americans rose to true culture. Two opposing tendencies emerged. On one side, Dunbar, poet and novelist, who used both patois and English, represented, if we may say so, the school of racial realism. On the other, Du Bois continued, as it were, the literature of social protest by advocating civil and cultural rights for Blacks equal to that of whites. But it is under the influence of Braithwaite that modern authors, starting in 1912, without abandoning Negro themes and the emotional intensity due to their ancestral sufferings, took these themes as the starting point of their inspiration and gave them universal purport. Our readers have had, through the verse of Claude McKay, an inkling of this new attitude. And more recently still, through the poems of Langston Hughes, they have been able to observe that the Americans, having thrown off all inferiority complexes, tranquilly express their "individual black-skinned selves without fear or shame."

This interesting intellectual evolution of the Black American leads us to ask ourselves: where does the Antillean, who has developed intellectually in a relatively more favorable milieu now stand in this evolution?

If racial concerns can hardly be found in the literary productions of the period following the abolition of slavery in the Antilles, it is because the "Great Elders" were busy struggling for liberty and political rights for the various categories of the black race on Antillean soil.[6] From a purely literary point of view, these elders and their successors, among whom we may cite the Martinicans Victor Duquesnay, Daniel Thaly, Salavina, the Guadelopean Oruno Lara, and many Haitian writers and poets, represent the phase of orientation towards the literature of the conquering race, which lasted until roughly 1914. But if the intellectual evolution of Black Americans has been rapid, that of the Black Antillean might be called prodigious. During the romantic period in Europe, the productions of Antillean writers are in no way inferior to those of French writers, not to mention such Antilleans of genius like the father and son Dumas and José Maria de Hérédia.

Needless to say, if we examine the works of these precursors, we find there the glorification of small, far-away homelands, the "Islands of Beauty" (exoticism is already in fashion), but nothing resembling race pride. Indeed, they speak lovingly of their native islands, but it so happened that a stranger celebrated them with still more blissfulness and (see Lafcadio Hearn, *Esquisses Martiniquaises*[7]) and showed more appreciation for and real attachment to the islands' distinct racial types. Their successors will continue to model their artistic productions after those of the metropolis.

However, between this period and the present may be classed a generation of men whose racial leanings are being channeled through literature or political and humanitarian concerns. Certain ideas are brewing. One is commenting on the theories of Marcus Garvey. The first Pan-Negro Congress is organized. Literature gives us *Batouala* by René Maran – who received the Prix Goncourt in 1920 – a "novel of objective observation," as the author himself writes in his preface, where, nonetheless, a generous indignation stirs. Later there was the publication of the first Black journal in Paris, *Les Continents*, which disappeared within a few months. We must also cite an essay "Heimatlos" written by a young man from Guyana who, during his time, had a certain success, but has since died. The first Black journal of longstanding in Paris was *La Dépêche Africaine*, whose director, Maurice Satineau, wrote a much appreciated history of Guadeloupe under the ancien régime. In this journal, the movement that was to culminate in *The Review of the Black World* emerged. In the Antilles, it is important to note the remarkable works of Jules Monnerot – *Contributions to the History of Martinique* – and more recently, *Les Galeries Martiniquaises*, a valuable document that the author, Césaire Philémon, dedicated to his small homeland, and in which matters of race are treated with more frankness than usual.

In none of these works is the black question studied in itself, as we can plainly attest. These works remain still the tributaries of white, Western culture. In none of them is expressed faith in the future of the race, and the necessity to create a feeling of solidarity between the different groups of Blacks disseminated throughout the globe.

However, parallel to the aforementioned isolated efforts, the aspirations that were to crystallize around *The Review of the Black World* asserted themselves among a group of Antillean women students in Paris. The women of color living alone in the metropolis, who until the Colonial Exhibition were less favored than their male compatriots who have enjoyed easy successes, have felt long before the latter the need for a racial solidarity that would not be merely material. They were thus aroused to race consciousness. The feeling of uprooting, felicitously expressed in Robert Horth's "A Thing of No Importance," published in the second issue of *The Review of the Black World*, had been the starting point of their evolution.

After having been trained obediently in the school of thought of their white models, they have perhaps passed, like their Black American brothers, through a period of revolt. But, with maturity, they became less severe, less intransigent, since they have understood that everything is relative. Their present position is the middle ground.

In the course of their evolution, their intellectual curiosity has turned toward the history of their race and their respective countries. They were thus led to deplore the absence of such interesting material in the educational programs implemented in the Antilles. Instead of despising their backward compatriots or losing faith in the possibility of the black race ever equaling the Aryan race, they began to study. And as a matter of course, when the occasion came to select a subject for a paper or thesis, their preference turned to that which had become the object of their concerns: the black race. For the first time, one of the female students took "The Work of Mrs. Beecher-Stowe (*Uncle Tom's Cabin* – Puritanism in New England") as a subject for the Diplôme d'Etudes supérieures d'anglais.[8] Later on, another male student of English studied Lafcadio Hearn's works on the Antilles. Still another female student of French endeavored to analyze the works of Jean Antoine Nau and the memoirs of Father Labat. We must say that at that time, Afro-American writers were completely unknown in France. But the interest of Antillean students in their own race had begun to be awakened. We have been informed that many students of English are preparing papers on Afro-American writers hitherto neglected, in spite of their evident value, in the surveys of American literature compiled by French academics professors.

Let us hope that the students who are preparing for degrees in History and Geography will take advantage of the riches that the past of the black race and the African continent offers them. Let us also hope that they will soon give us the occasion to analyze within the pages of this Review some masterful doctoral theses. In this realm, they have had two distinguished precursors. Félix Eboué, Administrator-in-chief of the Colonies, has for many years studied the ethnology of certain African peoples. And there is also Grégoire Micheli, member of the International Institute of Anthropology, who has contributed remarkable articles to this Review, and has devoted all his efforts to the study of the ancient religions of South America. On the other hand, we know that René Maran's new novel *Le Livre de Brousse*, whose translation is to appear in America, and will be in all likelihood his masterpiece, constitutes a real and splendid rehabilitation of African civilization. It is worth nothing that a certain number of our young friends seem to have spontaneously arrived at the last phase that we have observed in the intellectual evolution of Black Americans. If they [Antilleans] do continue to treat purely Occidental subjects, it is today in an extremely modern form and they attempt simultaneously to highlight characteristic racial themes as our readers will be able to verify in a series of interesting poems that we are soon going to publish.

Should one see in the tendencies here expressed an implicit declaration of war upon Western culture and the white world in general? We want to eliminate such ambiguity so as to leave no doubt. We are fully conscious of our debts to white, Western culture and we have no intention of discarding it in order to promote a return to I know not what obscurantism. Without Western culture, we would have never become conscious of who we really are. But we want to go beyond this culture in order to give to our brethren, with the help of white scientists and all the friends of Blacks, the pride of belonging to a race whose civilization is perhaps the oldest in the world. Once informed of that civilization, they will no longer despair of the future of their race, of which a portion seems presently lethargic. They will tender to their backward brothers a helping hand and endeavor to understand and love them better...

Notes

1 The essay was originally announced under the French title *L'Eveil de la conscience de race chez les étudiants noirs*. Nardal's English translation was: "Awakening of the Race Consciousness among Negro Students." When it was published, it appeared as "Eveil de la, Conscience de Race." Nardal generally translates "Noir" as "Negro" (for instance, Antillean Negroes from Noirs Antillais). In reference to black or African–Americans, Nardal uses interchangeably Afro-Americans, Negro Americans. We will often translate "Noir" as "Black" unless

"Negro" is more appropriate and use "Black Americans," "African–Americans," and Afro-Americans." This re-translation will attempt to stay as close to Nardal's translation of her essay as possible so as not to lose the style and voice of the author. Modifications however are necessary in places to clarify the meaning, bearing in mind that Nardal was more at home in French than English. It must be noted that Nardal uses the masculinist language that seemed to dominate writing of this era. Where possible, I opt for gender-neutral phrases. This is not always possible however. Hence, the proceeding is, in effect, a "modified translation" of the 1932 English translation. All endnotes have been added.

2 Here we have chosen to replace "education Latine" with "white Western education" instead of Latin. For today Latin does not have the same exclusionary geographic or cultural connotations as in Nardal's time, e.g. Latin America and Latin Americans. The addition of "white" is meant to draw attention to the fact that the Western world is not and has never been a wholly white one. Whites make up only a part of the Western world and its culture.

3 The original was "âme nègre"

4 Friedrich Sieburg, *Dieu est-il Français?*, traduit d l'allemand (Paris: Bernard Grasset, 1930), pp. 76–82.

5 Here Nardal translates "finissent par se tourner vers l'élément qui leur faisait le plus honneur" as "should in end return to the element that honored them most." Her translation does not clearly express the original French. In effect, since Antilleans are ignorant of black history, they would hold in esteem the element with which they were most familiar and that provided a sense of honor: the white element.

6 Unlike the United States, which maintained a one-drop rule with regards to the racial category black and the denial of political and social rights, under French governance, mulattoes, quadroons, octoroons shared certain privileges and rights denied their darker Antillean brethren. Hence, the struggle for equality was as much an internal political and social struggle as it was against French colonial policy.

7 Lafcadio Hearn, *Two Years in the French West Indies* (New York: Harper, 1890).

8 According to Michel Fabre, it was Paulette Nardal herself who wrote on Harriet Beecher Stowe. See *From Harlem to Paris: Black American Writers in France 1860–1980* (Urbana: University of Illinois Press, 1991), p. 152.

PART IV

THE NEGRITUDE MOVEMENT

7

BLACK ORPHEUS[1]

Jean-Paul Sartre

When you removed the gag that was keeping these black mouths shut, what were you hoping for? That they would sing your praises? Did you think that when they raised themselves up again, you would read adoration in the eyes of these heads that our fathers had forced to bend down to the very ground? Here are black men standing, looking at us, and I hope that you – like me – will feel the shock of being seen. For three thousand years, the white man has enjoyed the privilege of seeing without being seen; he was only a look – the light from his eyes drew each thing out of the shadow of its birth; the whiteness of his skin was another look, condensed light. The white man – white because he was man, white like daylight, white like truth, white like virtue – lighted up the creation like a torch and unveiled the secret white essence of beings. Today, these black men are looking at us, and our gaze comes back to our own eyes; in their turn, black torches light up the world and our white heads are no more than chinese lanterns swinging in the wind. A black poet – unconcerned with us – whispers to the woman he loves:

> Naked woman, black woman
> Dressed in your color which is life . . .
>
> Naked woman, dark woman,
> Firm fleshed ripe fruit, somber ecstasies of black wine, . . .[2]

and our whiteness seems to us to be a strange livid varnish that keeps our skin from breathing – white tights, worn out at the elbows and knees, under which we would find real human flesh the color of black wine if we could remove them. We think we are essential to the world – suns of its harvests, moons of its tides; we are no more than its fauna, beasts. Not even beasts:

> These gentlemen from the city
> These proper gentlemen
> Who no longer know how to dance in the evening by moonlight
> Who no longer know how to walk on the flesh of their feet
> Who no longer know how to tell tales by the fireside . . .[3]

Formerly Europeans with divine right, we were already feeling our dignity beginning to crumble under American or Soviet looks; Europe was already no more than a geographical accident, the peninsula that Asia shoves into the Atlantic. We were hoping at least to find a bit of our greatness reflected in the domesticated eyes of the Africans. But there are no more domesticated eyes: there are wild and free looks that judge our world.

Here is a black man wandering:

to the end of
the eternity of their boulevards
with cops . . .[4]

Here is another one shouting to his brothers:

Alas! Alas! Spidery Europe is moving its
fingers and its phalanxes of ships . . .[5]

Here is:

the cunning silence of Europe's night . . .[6]

in which

. . . there is nothing that time does not dishonor.[7]

A negro writes:

At times, we will haunt Montparnasse and Paris,
Europe and its endless torments, like memories
or like malaises . . .[8]

and suddenly France seems exotic in our own eyes. She is no more than a memory, a malaise, a white mist at the bottom of sunlit souls, a back-country unfit to live in; she has drifted towards the North, she is anchored near Kamchatka: the essential thing is the sun, the sun of the tropics and the sea "lousy with islands" and the roses of Imangue and the lilies of Iarive and the volcanos of Martinique. Being [*L'Être*] is black, Being is made of fire, we are accidental and far away, we have to justify our mores, our technics, our undercooked paleness and our verdigris vegetation. We are eaten away to the bones by these quiet and corrosive looks:

Listen to the white world
horribly weary of its immense effort
its rebel articulations crackling under hard stars,
its steel-blue stiffnesses piercing mystical flesh
listen to its exhibitionist victories trumpeting its defeats
listen to its wretched staggering with grandiose alibis
Have pity on our naïve omniscient conquerors.[9]

There we are, *finished*; our victories – their bellies sticking up in the air – show their guts, our secret defeat. If we want to crack open this finitude which imprisons us, we can no longer rely on the privileges of our race, of our color, of our technics: we will not be able to become a part of the totality from which those black eyes exile us, unless we tear off our white tights in order to try simply to be men.

If these poems shame us however, they were not intended to: they were not written for us; and they will not shame any colonists or their accomplices who open this book, for these latter will think they are reading letters over someone's shoulder, letters not meant for them. These blacks are addressing themselves to blacks about blacks; their poetry is neither satiric nor imprecatory: it is a *becoming conscious*. "So," you will say, "in what way does it interest us, if it is only a document? We cannot enter into it." I should like to show in what way we can gain access to this jet-black world; I should like to show that this poetry – which seems racial at first – is actually a hymn by everyone for everyone. In a word, I am talking now to whites, and I should like to explain to them what blacks already know: why it is necessarily through a poetic experience that the black, in his present condition, must first become conscious of himself; and, inversely, why black poetry in the French language is, in our time, the only great revolutionary poetry.

⋆ ⋆ ⋆

It is not just by accident that the white proletariat rarely uses poetic language to speak about its suffering, its anger or its pride in itself; neither do I think that workers are less gifted than our bourgeois sons: "talent" – that efficacious grace – loses all meaning when one claims that it is more widespread in one *class* than in another. Nor is it hard work that takes away their capacity for song: slaves used to drudge even harder and yet we know of slave hymns. It must therefore be recognized that it is the present circumstances of the class struggle that keep the worker from expressing himself poetically. Oppressed by technics, he wants to be a technician because he knows that technics will be the instrument of his liberation; he knows that it is only by gaining professional, economic and scientific know-how that he will be able someday to control business management. He now has a profound practical knowledge of what poets have called Nature, but it is a knowledge he has gained more through his hands than through his eyes: Nature is Matter for him – that crafty, inert adversity that he works on with his tools; Matter has no song. At the same time, the present phase of his struggle requires of him continual, positive action: political calculation, precise forecasting, discipline, organization of the masses; to dream, at this point, would be to betray. Rationalism, materialism, positivism – the great themes of his daily battle – are least propitious for the spontaneous creation of poetic myths. The last of these myths – the famous "Upheaval" – has withdrawn under the circumstances of the struggle: one must take up the matter that is most urgent, gain this and that position, raise this salary, decide on that sympathy strike or on some protest against the war in Indo-China: efficiency alone matters. And, without a doubt, the oppressed class must first find itself. This self-discovery, however, is the exact opposite of a subjective examination of oneself: rather, it is a question of recognizing – in and by action – the objective situation of the proletariat, which can be determined by the circumstances of production or of redistribution of property. Unified by an oppression which is exerted on each and every one, and reduced to a common struggle, workers are hardly acquainted with the inner contradictions that fecundate the work of art and that are harmful to the *praxis*. As far as they are concerned, to know themselves is to situate themselves within the context of the great forces that surround them; it requires them to determine both their exact position in their class and their function in the Party. The very language they use is free from the slight loosening of the screws, the constant frivolous impropriety, the game of transmissions which create the poetic Word. In their business, they use well-defined technical terms; and as for the language of revolutionary parties, Parain has shown that it is *pragmatic*: it is used to transmit orders, watch-words, information; if it loses its exactness, the Party falls apart. All of this tends more and more rigorously to eliminate the subject; poetry, however, must in some way remain subjective. The proletariat has not found a poetry that is sociological and yet finds its source in subjectivity, that is just as subjective as it is sociological, that is based on ambiguous or uncertain language and that is nevertheless as exalting and as generally understood as the most precise watch-words or as the phrase "Workers of all countries, unite" that one reads on doors in Soviet Russia. Lacking this, the poetry of the future revolution has remained in the hands of well-intentioned young bourgeois who found their inspiration in their personal psychological contradictions, in the dichotomy between their ideal and their class, in the uncertainty of the old bourgeois language.

Like the white worker, the negro is a victim of the capitalist structure of our society. This situation reveals to him his close ties – beyond the nuances of skin color – with certain classes of Europeans who, like him, are oppressed; it incites him to imagine a privilege – less society in which skin pigmentation will be considered a mere fluke. But even though oppression itself may be a mere fluke, the circumstances under which it exists vary according to history and geographic conditions: the black is a victim of it *insofar as he is black* and by virtue of being a colonized native or a deported African. And since he is oppressed within the confines of his race and because of it, he must first of all become conscious of his race. He must compel those who throughout the centuries have vainly tried, because he was a negro, to reduce him to the status of a beast, to recognize that he is a man. On this point, there is no means of evasion, or of trickery, no "passing" that he can consider: a Jew – a white man among white men – can deny that he is a Jew, can declare himself a man among men. The negro cannot deny that he is negro, nor can he claim that he is part of some abstract colorless humanity: he is black. Thus he has his back up against the wall of authenticity: having been insulted and formerly enslaved, he picks up the worked "nigger" which was thrown at him like a stone, he draws himself erect and proudly proclaims himself as black, in the face of the white man. The unity which will come eventually, bringing all oppressed peoples together in the same struggle, must be preceded in the colonies by what I shall call the moment of separation or negativity: this anti-racist racism is the only road that will lead to the abolition of racial differences. How could it be otherwise? Can blacks count on a distant white proletariat – involved in its own struggles – before they are united and organized on their own soil? And furthermore, isn't there some need for a thorough work of analysis in order to realize the identity of the interests that underlie the obvious difference of conditions? The white worker benefits somewhat from colonization, in spite of himself: low as his standard of living may be, it would be even lower if there were no colonization. In any case, he is less cynically exploited than the day laborer in Dakar or St. Louis. The technical equipment and industrialization of the European countries make it possible for measures of socialization to be immediately applicable there; but as seen from Senegal or the Congo, socialism seems more than anything else like a beautiful dream: before black peasants can discover that socialism is the necessary answer to their immediate local claims, they must learn to formulate these claims jointly; therefore, they must think of themselves as blacks.

But this becoming conscious is different from that which Marxism tries to awaken in the white worker. In the European worker, class consciousness is based on the nature of profit and unearned increment, on the present conditions of the ownership of the instruments for work; in brief, it is based on the objective characteristics of the *situation* of the proletariat. But since the selfish scorn that whites display for blacks – and that has no equivalent in the attitude of the bourgeois towards the working class – is aimed at the deepest recesses of the heart, negroes must oppose it with a more exact view of black *subjectivity*; consequently race consciousness is based first of all on the black soul, or, rather, – since the term is often used in this anthology – on a certain quality common to the thoughts and conduct of negroes which is called *negritude*. There are only two ways to go about forming racial concepts: either one causes certain subjective characteristics to become objective, or else one tries to interiorize objectively revealed manners of conduct; thus the black who asserts his negritude by means of a revolutionary movement immediately places himself on the terrain of Reflection, either because he wishes to recognize in himself certain objectively established traits of the African civilizations, or because he hopes to discover the Essence of blackness in the well of his heart. Thus subjectivity reappears: the relation of the self with the self; the source of all poetry, the very poetry from which the worker had to disengage himself. The black who asks his colored brothers to become conscious of themselves is going to try to present to them an exemplary image of their negritude and will look into his own soul to grasp it. He wants to be both a beacon and a mirror; the first revolutionary will be the harbinger of the black soul, the herald – half prophet and half partisan – who will tear negritude out of himself in order to offer it to the world; in brief, he will be a poet in the literal sense of the word "vates." Furthermore, black poetry has nothing in common with heartfelt effusions: it is functional, it answers a need which is defined in precise terms. Leaf through an anthology of contemporary white poetry: you will find a hundred different subjects, depending upon the mood and interests of the poet, depending upon his condition and his country. In the anthology which I am introducing to you here, there is only one subject that all the poets attempt to treat, more or less successfully. From Haiti to Cayenne, there is a single idea: *reveal* the black soul. Negro poetry is evangelic, it announces the good news: negritude has been rediscovered.

However, this negritude, which they wish to fish for in their abyssal depths, does not fall under the soul's gaze all by itself: in the soul, nothing is given. The herald of the black soul has gone through white schools, in accordance with a brazen law which forbids the oppressed man to possess any arms except those he himself has stolen from the oppressor; it is through the shock of white culture that his negritude has passed from the immediacy of existence to the reflective state. But at the same time, he has more or less ceased to live his negritude. In choosing to see what he is, he has become split, he no longer coincides with himself. And on the other hand, it is because he was already exiled from himself that he discovered this need to reveal himself. He therefore begins by exile. It is a double exile: the exile of his body offers a magnificent image of the exile of his heart; he is in Europe most of the time, in the cold, in the middle of grey crowds; he dreams of Port-au-Prince, of Haiti. But this is not enough: in Port-au-Prince, he was already in exile; the slavers had torn his fathers out of Africa and dispersed them. And *all* of the poems in this book – except those which were written in Africa – show us the same mystical geography. A hemisphere: in the foreground – forming the first of three concentric circles – extends the land of exile, colorless Europe; then comes the dazzling circle of the Islands and of childhood, which dance the round dance around Africa; the last circle is Africa, the world's navel, pole of all black poetry – dazzling Africa, burnt, oily like a snake's skin, Africa of fire and rain, torrid and thickly wooded; Africa – phantom flickering like a flame, between being and nothingness, more *real* than the "eternal boulevards with cops"[10] but absent, disintegrating Europe with its black but invisible rays, Africa, out of reach, an *imaginary* continent. The extraordinary good luck of black poetry lies in the fact that the anxieties of the colonized native have their own grandiose and obvious symbols which need only to be gone into deeply and to be meditated upon: exile, slavery, the Africa-Europe couple and the great Manichean division of the world into black and white. This ancestral bodily exile represents the other exile: the black soul is an Africa from which the negro, in the midst of the cold buildings of white culture and technics, is exiled. An ever-present but concealed negritude haunts him, rubs against him; he himself rubs up against its silky wing; it palpitates and is spread throughout him like his searching memory and his loftiest demands, like his shrouded, betrayed childhood, and like the childhood of his race and the call of the earth, like the swarming of insects and the indivisible simplicity of Nature, like the pure legacy of his ancestors, and like the Ethics that ought to unify his truncated life. But if he turns around to look his negritude in the face, it vanishes in smoke; the walls of white culture – *its* science, *its* words, *its* mores – rise up between it and him:

> Give me back my black dolls, so that I may play with them
> my instinct's simple games
> that I may remain in the shadow of its laws
> recover my courage
> my audacity
> feel me as me
> me renewed through what I was yesterday
>   yesterday
>   without complexity
>   yesterday
> when the uprooting hour came . . .
> they have ransacked the space that was mine[11]

However, the walls of this culture prison must be broken down; it will be necessary to return to Africa some day: thus the themes of return to the native country and of re-descent into the glaring hell of the black soul are indissolubly mixed up in the *vates* of negritude. A quest is involved here, a systematic stripping and an *askesis* accompanied by a continual effort of investigation. And I shall call this poetry "Orphic" because the negro's tireless descent into himself makes me think of Orpheus going to claim Eurydice from Pluto. Thus, through an exceptional stroke of poetic good luck, it is by letting himself fall into trances, by rolling on the ground like a possessed man tormented by himself, by singing of his angers, his regrets or his hates, by exhibiting his wounds, his life torn between "civilization" and his old black substratum; in short, it is by becoming most lyrical, that the black poet is most certain of creating a great collective poetry: by speaking only of himself, he speaks for all negroes; it is when he seems smothered by the serpents of our culture that he is the most revolutionary, for he then undertakes to ruin systematically the European knowledge he has acquired, and this spiritual demolition symbolizes the great future taking-up of arms by which blacks will destroy their chains. A single example will suffice to clarify this last remark.

In the twentieth century, most ethnic minorities have passionately endeavored to resuscitate their national languages while struggling for their independence. To be able to *say* that one is Irish or Hungarian, one must belong to a collectivity which has the benefit of a broad economic and political autonomy; but to *be* Irish, one must also *think Irish*, which means above all: think *in* Irish. The specific traits of a Society correspond exactly to the untranslatable locutions of its language. The fact that the prophets of negritude are forced to write their gospel *in French* means that there is a certain risk of dangerously slowing down the efforts of blacks to reject our tutelage. Having been dispersed to the four corners of the earth by the slave trade, blacks have no common language; in order to incite the oppressed to unite, they must necessarily rely on the words of the oppressor's language. And French is the language that will furnish the black poet with the largest audience, at least within the limits of French colonization. It is in this goose-pimply language – pale and cold like our skies, and which Mallarmé said was "the neutral language *par excellence* since our spirit demands an attenuation of variegation and of all excessively brilliant color" – in this language which is half dead for them, that Damas, Diop, Laleau, Rabéarivelo are going to pour the fire of their skies and of their hearts: it is through this language alone that they can communicate; like the sixteenth-century scholars who understood each other only in Latin, blacks can meet only on that trap-covered ground that the white has prepared for them: the colonist has arranged to be the eternal mediator between the colonized; he is there – always there – even when he is absent, even in the most secret meetings. And since words are ideas, when the negro declares in French that he rejects with the other; he sets up the enemy's thinking-apparatus in himself, like a crusher. This would not matter: except that this syntax and vocabulary – forged thousands of miles away in another epoch to answer other needs and to designate other objects – are unsuitable to furnish him with the means of speaking about himself, his own concerns, his own hopes. The French language and French thought are analytical. What would happen if the black genius were above all synthetical? The rather ugly term "negritude" is one of the few black contributions to our dictionary. But after all, if this "negritude" is a definable or at least a describable concept, it must subsume other more elementary concepts which correspond to the immediate fundamental ideas directly involved with negro consciousness: but where are the words to describe them? How well one understands the Haitian poet's complaint:

This obsessing heart which does not correspond
To my language, nor to my customs,
And on which encroach, like a clinging-root,
Borrowed feelings and the customs
Of Europe, feel this suffering
And this despair – equal to no other –
Of ever taming with words from France
This heart which came to me from Senegal.[12]

It is not true, however, that the black expresses himself in a "foreign" language, since he is taught French from childhood and since he is perfectly at ease when he thinks in the terms of a technician, of a scholar or of a politician. Rather, one must speak about the slight but constant difference that separates what he says from what he would like to say, whenever he speaks about himself. It seems to him that a Northern Spirit steals his ideas from him, bends them slightly to mean more or less what he wanted; that white words drink his thoughts like sand drinks blood. If he suddenly gorges himself, if he pulls himself together and takes a step backward, there are the sounds lying prostrate *in front of him* – strange: half signs and half things. He will not speak his negritude with precise, efficacious words which hit the target every time. He will not speak his negritude *in prose*. As everyone knows, every poetic experience has its origin in this feeling of frustration that one has when confronted with a language that is supposed to be a means of direct communication.

The reaction of the *speaker* frustrated by prose is in effect what Bataille calls the holocaust of words. As long as we can believe that a pre-established harmony governs the relationship between a word and Being, we use words without seeing them, with blind trust; they are sensory organs, mouths, hands, windows open on the world. As soon as we experience a first frustration, this chattering falls beyond us; we see the whole system, it is no more than an upset, out-of-order mechanism whose arms are still flailing to *indicate* in emptiness; in one fell swoop we pass judgment on the foolish business of naming things; we understand that language is in essence prose, and that prose is in essence failure; Being stands erect in front of us like a tower of silence, and if we still want to catch it, we can do so only through silence: "to evoke, in an intentional shadow, the object '*tu*' by allusive words, never direct, reducing themselves to the same silence."[13] No one has better stated that poetry is an incantatory attempt to suggest Being in and by the vibratory disappearance of the word: by insisting on his verbal impotence, by making words mad, the poet makes us suspect that beyond this chaos which cancels itself out, there are silent densities; since we cannot keep quiet, we must *make silence with language*. From Mallarmé to the Surrealists, the final goal of French poetry seems to me to have been this auto-destruction of language. A poem is a dark room where words are knocking themselves about, quite mad. Collisions in the air: they ignite each other with their fire and fall down in flames.

It is in this perspective that we must situate the efforts of the "black evangelists." They answer the colonist's ruse with a similar but inverse ruse: since the oppressor is present in the very language that they speak, they will speak this language in order to destroy it. The contemporary European poet tries to dehumanize words in order to give them back to nature; the black herald is going to *de-Frenchifize* them; he will crush them, break their usual associations, he will violently couple them

with little steps of caterpillar rain
with little steps like mouthfuls of milk
with little steps like ball-bearings
with little steps like seismic shocks
yams in the soil stride like gaps of stars[14]

Only when they have regurgitated their whiteness does he adopt them, making of this ruined language a solemn, sacred superlanguage, Poetry. Only through Poetry can the blacks of Tananarive and of Cayenne, the blacks of Port-au-Prince and of Saint-Louis, communicate with each other without witnesses. And since French lacks terms and concepts to define negritude, since negritude is silence, these poets will use "allusive words, never direct, reducing themselves to the same silence" in order to evoke it. Short-circuits of language: behind the flaming fall of words, we glimpse a great black mute idol. It is not only the black man's self-portrayal that seems poetic to me; it is also his personal way of utilizing the means of expression at his disposal. His position incites him to do it: even before he thinks of writing poetry, in him, the light of white words is refracted, polarized and altered. This is nowhere more manifest than in his use of two connected terms – "black-white" – that cover both the great cosmic division – "day and night" – and the human conflict between the native and the colonist. But it is a connection based on a hierarchical system: by giving the negro this term, the teacher also gives him a hundred language habits which consecrate the priority of white over black. The negro will learn to say "white like snow" to indicate innocence, to speak of the blackness of a look, of a soul, of a crime. As soon as he opens his mouth, he accuses himself, unless he persists in reversing the hierarchy. And if he reverses it *in French*, he is already poetizing: can you imagine the strange savor that an expression like "the blackness of innocence" or "the darkness of virtue" would have for us? That is the savor which we taste on every page of this book, when, for example, we read:

Your round, shining, black satin breasts...
this white smile
of eyes
in the face's shadow
awaken in me this evening
deaf rhythms...
which intoxicate, there in Guinea
our sisters
black and naked
and inspire in me
this evening
black twilights heavy with sensual anxiety
for
the soul of the black country where the ancients
are sleeping

lives and speaks
this evening
in uneasy strength, along the small of your back...[15]

Throughout this poem, black is color; better still, light; its soft diffuse radiance dissolves our habits; the *black* country where the ancients are sleeping is not a dark hell: it is a land of sun and fire. Then again, in another connection, the superiority of white over black does not express only the superiority that the colonist claims to have over the native: more profoundly, it expresses a universal adoration of *day* as well as our night terrors, which also are universal. In this sense, these black men are re-establishing the hierarchy they have just upset. They don't want to be poets *of nights*, poets of vain revolt and despair: they give the promise of dawn; they greet

the transparent dawn of a new day.[16]

At last, the black man discovers, through the pen, his baleful sense of foreboding:

Negro black like misery[17]

one of them, and then another, cries out:

Deliver me from my blood's night[18]

Thus the word *black* is found to contain *all Evil* and *all Good*, it covers up an almost unbearable tension between two contradictory classifications: solar hierarchy and racial hierarchy. It gains thereby an extraordinary poetry, like self-destructive objects from the hands of Duchamp and the Surrealists; there is a secret blackness in white, a secret whiteness in black, a fixed flickering of Being and Non-being which is perhaps nowhere expressed as well as in this poem by Césaire:

My tall wounded statue, a stone in its forehead; my great inattentive day
flesh with pitiless spots, my great night flesh with day spots.[19]

The poet will go even further; he writes:

Our beautiful faces like the true operative power
of negation.[20]

Behind this abstract eloquence evoking Lautréamont is seen an extremely bold and subtle attempt to give some sense to black skin and to realize the poetic synthesis of the two faces of night. When David Diop says that the negro is "black like misery," he makes black represent deprivation of light. But Césaire develops and goes into this image more deeply: night is no longer absence, it is refusal. Black is not color, it is the destruction of this borrowed clarity which falls from the white sun. The revolutionary negro is negation because he wishes to be complete nudity: in order to build his Truth, he must first destroy the Truth of others. Black faces – these night memories which haunt our days – embody the dark work of Negativity which patiently gnaws at concepts. Thus, by a reversal which curiously recalls that of the humiliated negro – insulted and called "dirty negro"[21] when he asserts his rights – it is the privative aspect of darkness that establishes its value. Liberty is the color of night.

Destructions, *autodafés* of language, magic symbolism, ambivalence of concepts: all the negative aspects of modern poetry are here. But it is not a matter of some gratuitous game. The situation of the black, his original "laceration," the *alienation* that a foreign way of thinking imposes on him in the name of assimilation, all oblige him to reconquer his existential unity as a negro, – or, if you prefer, the original purity of his plan – through a gradual *askesis*, beyond the language stage. Negritude – like liberty – is a point of departure and an ultimate goal: it is a matter of making negritude pass from the immediate to the mediate, a matter of *thematizing* it. The black must therefore die to white culture in order to be reborn with a black soul, like the Platonic philosopher whose body embraces death in order to be reborn in truth. This dialectical and mystical return to origins necessarily implies a method. But this method is not presented as a set of rules to be used in directing the spirit. Rather, it becomes one with whoever applies it; it is the dialectical law of successive transformations which lead the negro to coincidence with himself in negritude. It is not a matter of his *knowing*, nor of his ecstatically tearing himself away from himself, but rather of both discovering and becoming what he is.

There are two convergent means of arriving at this original simplicity of existence: one is objective, the other subjective. The poets in our anthology sometimes use one, sometimes the other, and sometimes both of them together. In effect, there exists an objective negritude that is expressed by the customs, arts, songs and dances of the African populations. As a *spiritual exercise*, the poet will prescribe allowing himself to be fascinated by primitive rhythms, letting his thoughts run in traditional forms of black poetry. Many of the poems included here are called tams-tams, because they borrow from the nocturnal tambourine players, a percussive rhythm which is sometimes sharp and regular, sometimes torrential and bounding. The poetic act, then, is a dance of the soul; the poet turns round and round like a dervish until he faints; he has established his ancestors' time in himself, he feels it flowing with its peculiar violent pulls; he hopes to find himself in his rhythmic pulsation; I shall say that he tries to make himself possessed by his people's negritude; he hopes that the echoes of his tam-tam will come to awaken timeless instincts sleeping within him. Upon leafing through this collection, one will get the impression that the tam-tam tends to become a genre of black poetry, just as the sonnet or the ode was a genre of our poetry. Others, like Rabémananjara, will be inspired by royal proclamations, still others will draw from the popular well of the Hain-tenys. The calm center of this maelstrom of rhythms, songs, shouts, is the poetry of Birago Diop, in all its majestic simplicity: it alone is at *rest* because it comes directly from Griot narratives and oral tradition. Almost all the other attempts have something contorted, taut and desperate about them because they aim at *becoming a part* of folkloric poetry rather than emanating from it. But however far he may be from "the black country where the ancestors are sleeping,"[22] the black is closer than we to the great period when, as Mallarmé says, "the word creates Gods." It is practically impossible for our poets to resume some closeness with popular traditions: ten centuries of scholarly poetry separate them from such traditions; furthermore, folkloric inspiration is drying up: at the very best, we could only imitate its simplicity from a distance. The blacks of Africa, on the contrary, are still in the great period of mythical fecundity and French-language black poets are not just using their myths as a form of diversion as we use our epic poems: they allow themselves to be spellbound by them so that at the end of the incantation, negritude – magnificently evoked – may surge forth. This is why I call this method of "objective poetry" *magic*, or charm.

Césaire, on the contrary, chose to backtrack into himself. Since this Eurydice will disappear in smoke if Black Orpheus turns around to look back on her, he will descend the royal road of his soul with his back turned on the bottom of the grotto; he will descend below words and meanings, – "in order to think of you, I have placed all words on the mountain-of-pity" – below daily activities and the plan of "repetition," even below the first barrier of reefs of revolt, with his back turned and his eyes closed, in order finally to touch with his feet the black water of dreams and desire and to let himself drown in it.[23] Desire and dream will rise up snarling like a tidal wave; they will make words dance like flotsam and throw them pell-mell, shattered, on the shore.

> Words go beyond themselves; and just as the old geography is done for, the high and the low (words) do not allow diversion either towards heaven or towards earth. . . . On the contrary, they operate on a strangely flexible range at one level: on the gaseous Level of an organism both solid and liquid, black and white day and night.[24]

One recognizes the old surrealistic *method* (automatic writing, like mysticism, is a method: it presupposes an apprenticeship, exercises, a start along the way). One must dive under the superficial crust of reality, of common sense, of reasoning reason, in order to touch the very bottom of the soul and awaken the timeless forces of desire: desire which makes of man a refusal of everything and a love of everything; desire, the radical negation of natural laws and of the possible, a call to miracles; desire which, by its mad cosmic energy, plunges man back into the seething beast of Nature and, at the same time, lifts him above Nature through the affirmation of his Right to be unsatisfied. Furthermore, Césaire is not the first negro to take this road. Before him, Etienne Léro had founded *Légitime Défense*. "*Légitime Défense*," says Senghor, "was more a cultural movement than a review. Starting from the Marxist analysis of the society of the 'Islands,' it discovered, in the Antilles, descendants of African negro slaves, who had been kept in the dulling condition of the proletarian for three centuries. It affirmed that only surrealism could deliver him from his taboos and express him in his entireness."

However, if one compares Léro with Césaire, one cannot help but be struck by their dissimilarities, and this comparison may allow us to measure the abyss that prevents a black revolutionary from utilizing white surrealism. Léro was the precursor; he invented the exploitation of surrealism as a "miraculous weapon" and an instrument for reconnaissance, a sort of radar with which one probes the depths of the abyss. But his poems are student exercises, they are mere imitations: they do not go beyond themselves; rather, they close in on each other:

> The ancient heads of hair
> Glue to the branches floors of empty seas

Where your body is only a memory
Where Spring trims its nails
Helix of your smile thrown far away
On the houses we will have nothing to do with.[25]

"The helix of your smile," "the spring which trims its nails": we recognize in these the preciousness and gratuitousness of surrealistic imagery, the eternal process that consists of throwing a bridge between two extremely unrelated or separated terms and hoping – without really believing – that this "throw of the dice"[26] will uncover some hidden aspect of Being. It does not seem to me that, either in this poem or in the others. Léro demands the liberation of the black: at the very most he lays claim to a categorical liberation of the imagination; in this completely abstract game, no combination of words evokes Africa even remotely. If these poems were taken out of the anthology and the name of their author hidden, I would defy anyone at all, white or black, not to attribute them to a European contributor to *La Révolution Surréaliste* or *Le Minotaure*. The purpose of surrealism is to rediscover – beyond race and condition, beyond class, behind the fire of language – dazzling silent darknesses which are no longer opposed to anything, not even to day, because day and night and all opposites are blended in them and suppressed; consequently, one might speak of the impassiveness and the impersonality of the surrealist poem, just as there is a Parnassian impassiveness and impersonality.

A poem by Césaire, on the contrary, bursts and wheels around like a rocket; suns turning and exploding into new suns come out of it; it is a perpetual surpassing. It is not a question of the poem becoming part of the calm unity of opposites; but rather of making *one* of the opposites in the "black–white" couple expand like a phallus in its opposition to the other. The density of these words thrown into the air like stones from a volcano, is found in negritude, which is defined as being *against* Europe and colonization. What Césaire destroys is not *all* culture but rather white culture; what he brings to light is not desire for *everything* but rather the revolutionary aspirations of the oppressed negro; what he touches in his very depths is not the spirit but a certain specific, concrete form of humanity. With this in mind, one can speak here about *engaged* and even *directed* automatic writing, not because there is any meditative intervention but because the words and images perpetually translate the same torrid obsession. The white surrealist finds within himself the trigger; Césaire finds within himself the fixed inflexibility of demands and feeling. Léro's words are feebly organized around vague general themes through expansion and a relaxing of logical ties; Césaire's words are pressed against each other and cemented by his furious passion. Between the most daring comparisons and between the most widely separated terms, runs a secret thread of hate and hope. For example, compare "the helix of your smile thrown far away" – which is the product of a free play of the imagination as well as an invitation to revery – with

and the radium mines buried in the abyss of my innocence
will jump by grains
into the feeding-trough of birds
and the stars' stere

will be the common name of fire-wood
gathered from the alluvium of the singing veins of night[27]

in which the "disjecta membra" of the vocabulary are so organized as to allow the supposition that there is a black "*Art Poétique.*"

Or read:

Our beautiful faces like the true operative power of negation[28]

Also read:

Seas lousy with islands cracking in the roses' fingers
flame-thrower and my lightning-struck body intact.[29]

Here we find the apotheosis of the fleas of black misery jumping in the water's hair, islands in a stream of light, cracking under the fingers of the celestial delouser: dawn with rose-colored fingers, the dawn of Greek and Mediterranean culture – snatched from the sacrosanct Homeric poems by a black thief – whose enslaved princess's fingernails are suddenly controlled by a Toussaint Louverture in order to crack the triumphant parasites of the negro sea; the dawn, which suddenly rebels and is metamorphosed, which opens fire like that savage weapon of whites, the flame-thrower, the weapon of scientists, the weapon of executioners, strikes the tall black Titan with its white fire, and he arises intact and eternal in order to begin the assault on Europe and heaven. In Césaire, the great surrealist tradition is realized, it takes on its definitive meaning and is destroyed: surrealism – that European poetic movement – is taken from the Europeans by a Black man who turns it against them and gives it a rigorously defined function. I have pointed out elsewhere how the whole of the proletariat completely shut itself off from the destructive poetry of Reason: in Europe, surrealism languishes and pales, rejected by those who could have given it a transfusion of their own blood. But at the very moment when it is losing contact with the Revolution, it is, in the Antilles, grafted onto another branch of the universal Revolution; it develops into an enormous somber flower. Césaire's originality lies in his having directed his powerful, concentrated anxiety as a negro, as one oppressed, as a militant individual, into this world of the most destructive, free and metaphysical poetry at the moment when Eluard and Aragon were failing to give political content to their verse. And finally, *negritude-object* is snatched from Césaire like a cry of pain, of love and of hate. Here again he follows the surrealist tradition of *objective* poetry. Césaire's words do not describe negritude, they do not designate it, they do not copy it from the outside like a painter with a model: they *create* it; they compose it under our very eyes: henceforth it is a thing which can be observed and learned; the subjective method which he has chosen joins the objective method we spoke about earlier: he ejects the black soul from himself at the very moment when others are trying to interiorize it; the final result is the same in both cases. Negritude is the far-away tam-tam in the streets of Dakar at night; voodoo shouts from some Haitian cellar window, sliding along level with the roadway; the Congolese mask; but it is also this poem by Césaire, this slobbery, bloody poem full of phlegm, twisting in the dust like a cut-up worm. This double spasm of absorption and excretion beats out the rhythm of the black heart on every page of this collection.

What then, at present, is this negritude, sole anxiety of these poets, sole subject of this book? It must first be stated that a white man could hardly speak about it suitably, since he had no inner experience of it and since European languages lack words to describe it. I ought then to let the reader encounter it in the pages of this collection and draw his own conclusions about it. But this introduction would be incomplete if, after having indicated that the quest for the Black Grail represented – both in its original intention and in its methods – the most authentic synthesis of revolutionary aspirations and poetic anxiety, I did not show that this complex notion is essentially pure Poetry. I shall therefore limit myself to examining these poems objectively as a cluster of testimonies and to pointing out some of their principal themes. Senghor says: "What makes the *negritude* of a poem is less its theme than its style, the emotional warmth which gives life to words, which transmutes language into speech." It could not be more explicitly stated that negritude is neither a state nor a definite ensemble of vices and virtues or of intellectual and moral qualities, but rather a certain affective attitude towards the world. Since the beginning of this century, psychology has renounced its great scholastic distinctions. We no longer believe that the "acts" of the soul are divided into volitions or actions, cognitions or perceptions, sentiments or blind passiveness. We know that a feeling is a definite way of establishing our relation with the world around us, that it involves a certain comprehension of this universe. It is a tension of the soul, a choice of oneself and of another, a way of going beyond the raw facts of experience; in short, a *project* quite like the voluntary act. To use Heidegger's language, Negritude is the Negro's being-in-the-world.

Furthermore, here is what Césaire tells us about it:

> My negritude is not a stone with its deafness flung out against the clamor of the day
> My negritude is not a dead speck of water on the dead eye of the earth
> my negritude is neither a tower nor a cathedral
> it plunges into the red flesh of the ground
> it plunges into the ardent flesh of the sky
> it perforates the opaque pressure of its righteous patience.[30]

Negritude is portrayed in these beautiful lines of verse more as an act than as a disposition. But this act is an *inner* determination: it is not a question of *taking* the goods of this world in one's hands and transforming them; it is a question of *existing* in the milieu of the world. The relation with the universe remains an *appropriation*. But this appropriation is not technical. For the white, to possess is to transform. Certainly, the white worker uses instruments which he does not possess. But at least his techniques are his own: if it is true that the personnel responsible for the major inventions of European industry comes mainly from the middle classes, at least the trades of carpenter, cabinet-maker, potter, seem to the white workers to be a true heritage, despite the fact that the orientation of great capitalist production tends to remove their "joy in work" from them. But it is not enough to say that the black worker uses instruments which are lent to him; techniques are also lent him.

Césaire refers to his black brothers as:

Those who have invented neither gunpowder nor compass
those who have never tamed either steam or electricity
those who have explored neither the seas nor the sky...[31]

But this haughty claim of non-technicalness reverses the situation: what could pass as a deficiency becomes a positive source of wealth. A technical relation with Nature reveals Nature as simple quantity, inertia, exteriority: nature dies. By his haughty refusal to be *homo faber*, the negro gives it life again. As if the passiveness of one of the members of the "man–nature" couple necessarily produced the other's activity. Actually, negritude is not passiveness, since it "perforates the flesh of the sky and of the earth": it is "patience," and patience appears like an active imitation of passivity. The negro's act is first of all an act on oneself. The black stands erect and immobilizes himself like a bird-charmer, and things come to perch on the branches of this fake tree. A magic inveigling of the world – through silence and rest – is involved here: the white, by acting first of all on Nature, loses himself when he loses Nature; the negro, by acting first of all on himself, claims to win Nature while winning himself.

Seized, they abandon themselves to the essence of every thing
ignorant of the surfaces but seized by the movement of every thing
heedless of counting, but playing the world's game
truly the elder sons of the world
porous to all the breaths of the world...
flesh of the world's flesh palpitating from the very movement of the world.[32]

Upon reading this, one can hardly help thinking of the famous distinction between intelligence and intuition established by Bergson. Césaire rightly calls us

Omniscient and naïve conquerors...[33]

Because of his tools, the white knows all. But he only scratches the surface of things; he is unaware of duration, unaware of life. Negritude, on the contrary, is comprehension through sympathy. The black's secret is that the sources of *his existence* and the roots of Being are identical.

If one wanted to give a sociological interpretation of this metaphysics, one would say that a poetry of agriculturists is here opposed to a prose of engineers. Actually, it is not true that the black has no techniques: the relation between any human group and the exterior world is always technical in one way or another. And inversely, I shall say that Césaire is imprecise: Saint-Exupéry's airplane folding the earth below like a carpet is a means of disclosure. However, the black is first of all a peasant; agricultural technique is "righteous patience;" it trusts in life; it waits. To plant is to impregnate the earth; after that, you must remain motionless and watch: "each atom of silence is a chance for ripe fruit," each instant brings forth a hundred times more than man gave, whereas the worker finds in the manufactured product only as much as he put into it;[34] man grows along with his wheat: from minute to minute he goes beyond himself and becomes more golden; he intervenes in this watchful wait before the fragile swelling belly, only to protect. Ripe wheat is a microcosm because the cooperation of sun, wind and rains was needed for it to grow; a blade of wheat is both the most natural thing and the most improbable chance. Techniques have contaminated the white peasant, but the black peasant remains the great male of the earth, the world's sperm. His existence is great vegetal patience; his work is the yearly repetition of holy coitus. Creating and nourished because he creates. To till, to plant, to eat, is to make love with nature. The sexual pantheism of these poets is undoubtedly what will impress us first of all: it is in this that they join the dances and the phallic rites of Negro-Africans.

> Oho! Congo lying in your bed of forests, queen of tamed Africa
> May the phalli of the mountains carry your banner high
> For, through my head, through my tongue, through my belly, you are a woman,[35]

writes Senghor. And:

> and so I shall mount again the soft belly of the dunes
> and the gleaming thighs of the day...[36]

and Rabéarivelo:

> the earth's blood, the stone's sweat and the sperm of
> the world[37]

and Laleau:

> The conical drum laments under the sky
> And it is the very soul of the black man
> Sultry spasms of men in rut, lover's sticky sobs
> Outraging the calm of the evening.[38]

Here, we are far from Bergson's chaste asexual intuition. It is no longer a matter of being in sympathy with life, but rather of being in love with all its forms. For the white technician, God is first of all an engineer. Jupiter orders chaos and prescribes its laws; the Christian God conceives the world through his understanding and brings it into being through his will: the relation between the created and the creator is never carnal, except for a few mystics whom the Church looks upon with a great deal of suspicion. Even so, erotic mysticism has nothing in common with fecundity: it is the completely passive wait for a sterile penetration. We are *molded* from mud: statuettes come from the *hands* of the divine sculptor. If the manufactured objects surrounding us could worship their ancestors, they would undoubtedly adore us as we adore the All-powerful. For our black poets, on the contrary, Being comes out of Nothingness like a penis becoming erect; Creation is an enormous perpetual delivery; the world is flesh and the son of flesh; on the sea and in the sky, on the dunes, on the rocks, in the wind, the Negro finds the softness of human skin; he rubs himself against the sand's belly, against the sky's loins: he is "flesh of the flesh of this world;" he is "porous to all its breaths," to all its pollens; he is both Nature's female and its male; and when he makes love with a woman of his race, the sexual act seems to him to be the celebration of the Mystery of Being. This spermatic religion is like the tension of a soul balancing between two complementary tendencies: the dynamic feeling of being an erect phallus, and that more deaf, more patient, more feminine one of being a growing plant. Thus negritude is in its deepest origin a sort of androgyny.

> There you are
> Upright and naked
> alluvium you are and remember yourself as having been
> but in reality you are the child of this parturient shadow
> feeding on lunar lactogen[39]
> then you slowly take the form of a bole
> on this low wall jumped over by the dreams of flowers
> and the perfume of summer at rest.
> To feel, to believe that roots are pushing your feet
> and running and twisting like thirsty serpents
> toward some subterranean spring...
>
> (Rabéarivelo)[40]

And Césaire:

> Wornout mother, leafless mother, you are a flamboyant[41]
> and now wear only husks. You are a calabash tree
> and you are only a stand of *couis*....[42]

This profound unity of vegetal and sexual symbols is certainly the greatest originality of black poetry, especially in a period when, as Michel Carrouges has shown, most of the images used by white poets tend to mineralize the human being. Césaire, on the contrary, "vegetalizes," "animalizes" sea, sky and stones. More precisely, his poetry is a perpetual coupling of men and women who have been metamorphosed into animals, vegetables, stones, with stones, plants and beasts metamorphosed into men. Thus the Black man attests to a natural Eros; he reveals and incarnates it; to find a point of comparison in European poetry, one must go back to Lucretius, the peasant poet who celebrated Venus, the mother goddess, when Rome was not yet much more than a large agricultural market. In our time, only Lawrence seems to me to have had a cosmic feeling for sexuality. Even so, this feeling remains very literary in his works.

However, although negritude seems basically to be this immobile springing-forth, a unity of phallic erection and plant growth, one could scarcely exhaust it with this single poetic theme. There is another motif running through this collection, like a large artery:

> Those who have invented neither powder nor compass...
> They know the most remote corners of the country of suffering....[43]

To the absurd utilitarian agitation of the white, the black opposes the authenticity gained from his suffering; the black race is a chosen race because it has had the horrible privilege of touching the depths of unhappiness. And even though these poems are anti-Christian from beginning to end, one might call negritude a kind of Passion: the black who is conscious of himself sees himself as the man who has taken the whole of human suffering upon himself and suffers for all, even for the white.

> On the judgment day, Armstrong's trumpet will be the
> interpreter of man's sufferings.
>
> (Paul Niger)[44]

Let us note immediately that this in no way implies a resigned suffering. A while ago I was speaking about Bergson and Lucretius; I would be tempted now to quote that great adversary of Christianity: Nietzsche and his "Dionysianism." Like the Dionysian poet, the Negro attempts to penetrate the brilliant phantasm of the day, and encounters, a thousand feet under the Apollonian surface, the inexpiable suffering which is the universal essence of man. If one wished to systematize, one would say that the Black blends with the whole of Nature in as much as he represents sexual congeniality with Life and in as much as he claims he is Man in his Passion of rebellious suffering. One will feel the fundamental unity of this double movement if one considers the constantly tighter relationship which psychiatrists establish between anguish and sexual desire. There is only one proud upheaval which can be equally well described as a desire plunging its roots into suffering or as suffering fixed like a sword across a vast cosmic desire. This "righteous patience" that Césaire evokes is both vegetal growth and patience against suffering; it resides in the very muscles of the negro; it sustains the black porter going a thousand miles up the Niger under a blinding sun with a fifty-pound load balanced on his head. But if in a certain sense, one can compare the fecundity of Nature to a proliferation of suffering, in another sense – and this one is also Dionysian – this fecundity, by its exuberance, goes beyond suffering, drowns it in its creative abundance which is poetry, love and dance. Perhaps, in order to understand this indissoluble unity of suffering, eros and joy, one must have seen the Blacks of Harlem dance frenetically to the rhythm of the "blues," which are the saddest sounds in the world. In effect, rhythm cements the multiple aspects of the black soul, communicates its Nietzschian lightness with heavy dionysian intuitions; rhythm – tam-tam, jazz, the reverberation of these poems – represents the temporality of negro *existence*. And when a black poet prophesies to his brothers a better future, he portrays their deliverance to them in the form of rhythm:

> What?
> Rhythm
> sound wave in the night across the forests, nothing – or a new soul
> timbre
> intonation
> vigor
> dilation
> vibration which flows out by degrees into the marrow
> revulses[45] in its progression an old sleeping body, takes
> it by the waist
> and spins it
> and turns
> and once more vibrates in its hands, in its loins, its
> sexual member, its thighs, its vagina . . .[46]

But one must go still further: this basic experience of suffering is ambiguous; through it, black consciousness is going to become historic. In effect, whatever may be the intolerable iniquity of his present condition, it is not to that condition that the black man first refers when he proclaims that he has touched the heart of human suffering. He has the horrible benefit of having known bondage. For these poets, most of whom were born between 1900 and 1918, slavery – abolished half a century earlier – lingers on as a very real memory:

Each of my todays looks on my yesterday
with large eyes rolling with rancor with
shame
Still real is my stunned condition of the past
of
blows from knotted cords of bodies calcinated
from toe to calcinated back
of dead flesh of red iron firebrands of arms
broken under the whip which is breaking loose . . .[47]

writes Damas, a poet from Guiana. And the Haitian, Brière:

. . . Often like me you feel stiffnesses
Awaken after murderous centuries
And old wounds bleed in your flesh . . .[48]

During the centuries of slavery, the black drank the cup of bitterness to the last drop; and slavery is a past fact which neither our authors nor their fathers have actually experienced. But it is also a hideous nightmare from which even the youngest of them are not yet sure of having awakened.[49] From one end of the earth to the other, blacks – separated by languages, politics and the history of their colonizers – have a *collective memory* in common. This will not be surprising if one only recalls the French peasants who, in 1789, were still aware of the panicky terrors that went back to the Hundred Years' War. Thus when the black goes back to his principal experience, it is suddenly revealed to him in two dimensions: it is both the intuitive seizure of the human condition and the still-fresh memory of a historic past. Here, I am thinking of Pascal who relentlessly repeated that man was an irrational composite of metaphysics and history, his greatness unexplainable if he comes from the mud, his misery unexplainable if he is still as God made him; that in order to understand man, one had to go back to the *irreducible fact* of the fall.[50] It is in this sense that Césaire calls his race "the fallen race."[51] And in a certain sense I can see the *rapprochement* that can be made between black consciousness and Christian consciousness: the brazen law of slavery evokes that law of the Old Testament, which states the consequences of *Original Sin*. The abolition of slavery recalls this *other historic fact*: Redemption. The white man's insipid paternalism after 1848 resembles that of the white God after the Passion. The difference being, however, that the expiable fault that the black discovers in the back of his memory is not his own, it is that of the white; the first fact of negro history is certainly a kind of original sin: but the black is the innocent victim of it. This is why his concept of suffering is radically opposed to white dolorism. If these poems are for the most part so violently anti-Christian, it is because the religion of the whites is more clearly a mystification in the eyes of the negro than in the eyes of the European proletariat: this religion wants to make him share the responsibility for a crime of which he is the victim; it wants to persuade him to see the kidnappings, the massacres, the rapes and the tortures which have covered Africa with blood, as a legitimate punishment, deserved tests. Will you say that it also proclaims equality for all men before God? *Before God*, yes. Only yesterday I was reading in *Esprit* these lines from a correspondent in Madagascar:

> I am as certain as you that the soul of a Malagasy is worth the soul of a white. . . . Just as, before God, the soul of a child is worth the soul of his father. However, if you have an automobile, you don't let your children drive it.

One can hardly reconcile Christianity and colonialism more elegantly. In opposition to these sophisms, the black – by a simple investigation of his memory as a former slave – affirms that suffering is man's lot and that it is no less deserved for all that. He rejects with horror Christian apathy, morose sensual pleasure, masochistic humility and all the tendentious inducements to his submission; he lives the absurdity of suffering in its pure form, in its injustice and in its gratuitousness; and he discovers thereby this truth which is misunderstood or masked by Christianity: suffering carries within itself its own refusal; it is by nature *a refusal to suffer*, it is the dark side of negativity, it opens on revolt and liberty. The black promptly *historicizes himself* in as much as the intuition of suffering confers on him a collective past and assigns to him a goal in the future. Only a short while ago, he was a sheer *present* surging of timeless instincts, a simple manifestation of universal and eternal fecundity. Now he calls to his colored brothers in quite another language:

> Negro pedlar of revolt
> you have known the paths of the world
> ever since you were sold in Guinea . . .[52]

And:

> Five centuries have seen you with weapons
>   in your hands
> and you have taught the exploiting races
> passion for liberty.[53]

There is already a black *Epic*:[54] first the golden age of Africa, then the era of dispersion and captivity, then the awakening of consciousness, the heroic and somber times of great revolts, of Toussaint Louverture and black heroes, then the *fact* of the abolition of slavery – "unforgettable metamorphosis," says Césaire – then the struggle for definitive liberation:

> You are waiting for the next call
> the inevitable mobilization

for that war which is yours has known only truces
for there is no land where your blood has not flowed
no language in which your color has not been insulted
You smile, Black Boy,
you sing
you dance
you cradle generations
which go out at all hours to the
fronts of work and pain
which tomorrow will assault bastilles
onward toward the bastions of the future
in order to write in all languages
on the clear pages of all skies
the declaration of your rights unrecognized
for more than five centuries . . .[55]

Strange and decisive turn: race is transmuted into *historicity*, the black Present explodes and is temporalized, Negritude – with its Past and its Future – is inserted into Universal History, it is no longer a *state*, nor even an existential attitude, it is a Becoming; the black contribution to the evolution of Humanity is no longer savour, taste, rhythm, authenticity, a bouquet of primitive instincts: it is a dated enterprise, a patient construction and also a future. Previously, the Black claimed his place in the sun in the name of *ethnic* qualities; now, he establishes his right to life on his mission; and this mission, like the proletariat's, comes to him from his historic situation: because he has suffered from capitalistic exploitation more than all the others, he has acquired a sense of revolt and a love of liberty more than all the others. And because he is *the most oppressed*, he necessarily pursues the liberation of all, when he works for his own deliverance:

Black messenger of hope
you know all the hymns of the world
even those of the timeless building-works of the Nile.[56]

But, after that, can we still believe in the interior homogeneousness of Negritude? And how can one say that it *exists*? Sometimes it is lost innocence which had its existence in some faraway past, and sometimes hope which can be realized only within the heart of the future City. Sometimes it contracts with Nature in a moment of pantheistic fusion and sometimes it spreads itself out to coincide with the whole history of Humanity; sometimes it is an existential attitude and sometimes the objective ensemble of negro-African traditions. Is it being discovered? Is it being created? After all, there are blacks who "collaborate;" after all, in the prefaces he writes for the works of each poet, Senghor seems to distinguish between degrees of negritude. Does the poet who would be the precursor for his colored brothers invite them to *become* more negro, or does he disclose to them what they *are*, by a sort of poetic psychoanalysis? Is negritude necessity or liberty? For the authentic negro, is it a matter of conduct deriving from essences, as consequences derive from a principle, or is one a negro in the way that the religious faithful are believers, that is to say in fear and trembling, in anguish, in perpetual remorse for never being enough what one would like to be? Is it a given fact or a value? The object of empiric intuition or of a moral concept? Is it a conquest of reflection? Or does reflection poison it? Is it never authentic except when unreflected and in the immediate? Is it a systematic *explanation* of the black soul, or a Platonic Archetype which one can approach indefinitely without ever attaining it? Is it, for blacks, like our engineer's common sense, the most widely shared thing in the world? Or do some have it, like grace; and if so, does it have its chosen ones? One will undoubtedly answer this question by saying that it is all of these at once, and still other things. And I agree: like all anthropological notions, Negritude is a shimmer of Being and of an ought-to-be; it makes you and you make it: both oath and passion. But there is something more serious: the negro, we have said, creates for himself an anti-racist racism. He wishes in no way to dominate the world: he desires the abolition of ethnic privileges, wherever they come from; he asserts his solidarity with the oppressed of every color. After that, the subjective, existential, ethnic notion of *negritude* "passes," as Hegel says, into the objective, positive and precise, notion of the *proletariat*. Senghor says: "For Césaire, the 'White' symbolizes capital, just as the Negro symbolizes work. . . . Over and beyond the black-skinned men of his race, he sings about the worldwide proletarian struggle."[57] It is easy to say, not so easy to think. And it is certainly not just by accident that the most ardent cantors of Negritude are also militant Marxists. Nevertheless, the notion of race does not mix with the notion of class: the former is concrete and particular; the latter, universal and abstract; one belongs to what Jaspers calls comprehension, and the other to intellection; the first is the product of a psychobiological syncretism, and the other is a methodic construction starting with experience. In fact, Negritude appears as the minor moment of a dialectical progression: the theoretical and practical affirmation of white supremacy is the thesis; the position of Negritude as an antithetical value is the moment of negativity. But this negative moment is not sufficient in itself, and these blacks who use it know this perfectly well; they know that it aims at preparing the synthesis or realization of the human in a raceless society. Thus Negritude is for destroying itself, it is a passage and not an outcome, a means and not an ultimate end. At the moment that every black Orpheus most tightly embrace this Eurydice, they feel her vanish from between their arms. A poem by Jacques Roumain, a black communist, furnishes the most moving evidence of this new ambiguity:

Africa I have held on to your memory Africa
you are in me
Like a thorn in a wound
like a guardian mascot in the center of the village
make of me the stone of your sling
of my youth the lips of your wound
of my knees the broken columns of your humbling
however
I want to be only of your race
peasant workers of all countries.[58]

With what sadness he still retains for a moment what he has decided to abandon! With what pride as a *man* he will strip his pride as a negro for other men! He who says both that Africa is in him like "a thorn in a wound" and that he *wants* to be only of the universal race of the oppressed, has not left the empire of unhappy consciousness. One more step and Negritude will disappear completely: the negro himself makes of what was the mysterious bubbling of black blood, a geographical accident, the inconsistent product of universal determinism:

> Is it all that climate extended space
> which creates clan tribe nation
> skin race gods
> our inexorable dissimilarity?[59]

But the poet does not completely have the courage to accept the responsibility for this *rationalization* of the racial concept; one sees that he limits himself to questioning; a bitter regret is visible beneath his will to unite. Strange road: humiliated and offended, blacks search deep within themselves to find their most secret pride; and when they have found it at last, it challenges its own right to exist: through supreme generosity they abandon it, just as Philoctetes abandoned his bow and arrows at Neoptolemus. Thus the rebel Césaire finds the secret of his revolts in the bottom of his heart: he is of a royal race:

> it is true that there is in you something which has
> never been able to yield, an anger, a desire, a sadness,
> an impatience, in short a scorn, a violence . . . and now
> your veins carry gold, not mud; pride, not servitude.
> King you have been King in the past.[60]

But he immediately thrusts aside this temptation:

> My law that I cover up with a chain unbroken
> as far as the confluence of fire which violates me
> which purifies me and burns me with my prism of amalgamated
> gold. . . . I shall perish. But naked. Whole.[61]

It is perhaps this ultimate nudity of man that has snatched from him the white rags that were concealing his black armor, and that now destroys and rejects that very armor; it is perhaps this colorless nudity that best symbolizes Negritude: for Negritude is not a state, it is a simple surpassing of itself, it is love. It is when Negritude renounces itself that it finds itself; it is when it accepts losing that it has won: the colored man – and he alone – can be asked to renounce the pride of his color. He is the one who is walking on this ridge between past particularism – which he has just climbed – and future universalism, which will be the twilight of his negritude; he is the one who looks to the end of particularism in order to find the dawn of the universal. Undoubtedly, the white worker also becomes conscious of his class in order to deny it, since he wants the advent of a classless society: but once again, the definition of class is objective; it sums up only the conditions of the white worker's alienation; whereas it is in the bottom of his heart that the negro finds race, and he must tear out his heart. Thus Negritude is dialectical; it is not only not above all the blossoming of atavistic instincts; it represents the surpassing of a situation defined by free consciousnesses.

Negritude is a sad myth full of hope, born of Evil and pregnant from future Good, living like a woman who is born to die and who feels her own death even in the richest moments of her life; it is an unstable rest, an explosive fixity, a pride which renounces itself, an absolute that knows it is transitory: for whereas it is the announcer of its birth and of its death agony, it also remains the existential attitude chosen by free men and lived *absolutely*, to the fullest. Because it is tension between a nostalgic Past into which the black can no longer enter completely and a future in which it will be replaced by new values, Negritude adorns itself with a tragic beauty that finds expression only in poetry. Because it is the living and dialectical unity of so many opposites, because it is a Complex unamenable to analysis, Negritude is only the multiple unity of a hymn that can reveal both it and the flashing beauty of the Poem which Breton calls "*explosante-fixe*." Because any attempt to conceptualize its various aspects would necessarily end up showing its relativity – even though it is lived in the absolute through royal consciences – and because the poem is an absolute, it is poetry alone that will allow the unconditional aspect of this attitude to be fixed. Because it is subjectivity written in the objective, Negritude must take form in a poem, that is to say in a subjectivity-object; because it is an Archetype and a Value, it will find its most transparent symbol in aesthetic values; because it is a call and a gift; it will make itself heard and offer itself only by means of a work of art which is both a call to the spectator's liberty and absolute generosity. Negritude is the content of the poem, it is the poem like a thing of the world, mysterious and open, obscure and suggestive; it is the poet himself. One must go still further; triumph of Narcissism and Narcissus' suicide, tension of the soul beyond culture, beyond words and beyond all psychic facts, luminous night of unknowing, deliberate choice of the *impossible* and of what Bataille calls "torture" [*supplice*], intuitive acceptance of the world and refusal of the world in the name of "the law of the heart," double contradictory postulation, demanding retraction, expansion of generosity – Negritude is, in essence, Poetry. For once at least, the most authentic revolutionary plan and the most pure poetry come from the same source.

And if the sacrifice is achieved one day, what will happen then? What will happen if, casting off his negritude for the sake of the Revolution, the black no longer wishes to consider himself only a part of the proletariat? What will happen if he then allows himself to be defined only by his objective condition? If, in order to struggle against white capitalism, he undertakes to assimilate white technics? Will the source of Poetry run dry? Or in spite of everything, will the great black river color the sea into which it flows? That does not matter: each era has its poetry; in each era, circumstances of history elect a nation, a race, a class to take up the torch, by creating situations that can be expressed or that can go beyond themselves only through Poetry; sometimes the poetic *élan* coincides with the revolutionary *élan* and sometimes they diverge. Let us greet today the historic chance that will permit blacks to

> shout out the great negro cry so hard that the
> world's foundations will be shaken.[62]

Notes

1 "Orphée noir" was originally published as the preface to Léopold Sédar Senghor's anthology of "negritude poetry," *Anthologie de la nouvelle poésie nègre et malgache de langue française* (Paris: Presses Universitaires de France, 1948), pp. ix–xliv. A somewhat shortened version also appeared in October of the same year in *Les Temps modernes*, vol. 37, pp. 577–606, and some extracts also appeared in 1949 in *Présence Africaine*. vol. 6, pp. 9–14. It was reprinted the following year with the addition of two endnotes and some minor changes, mainly typographical, in *Situations, III* (Paris: Gallimard, 1949), pp. 229–86. The translation printed here is a revised version of John MacCombie's translation of the *Anthologie* version "Black Orpheus" from *The Massachusetts Review*, Autumn/Winter, 1964–65, pp. 13–52. I am grateful to *The Massachusetts Review* for permission to reprint and revise the translation. A few minor errors have been corrected and the source of all the quotations has been identified where possible. Other changes have mainly been made with the aim of making the translation more suitable for a philosophical audience. After some hesitation it was decided to maintain the use of the word "negro" to translate *nègre*. Similarly, I have retained Sartre's sexist language. However, John MacCombie's translation had the effect of exaggerating Sartre's use of this language, so the translation has been revised to more closely reflect the original. The use of italics follows the *Anthologie* version of the essay. Many of these were dropped when it was reprinted in *Situations, III*. (Ed.)

2 Léopold Senghor, "Femme noire," *Anthologie de la nouvelle poésie nègre et malgache*, p. 151. (Ed.)

3 Guy Tirolien, "Prière d'un petit enfant nègre," *Anthologie*, p. 87. (Ed.)

4 Léon-G. Damas, "Un clochard m'a demandé dix sous," *Anthologie*, p. 14. (Ed.)

5 Aimé Césaire, "Et les chiens se taisaient," *Les armes miraculeuses*, (Paris: Gallimard, 1946), p. 164. (Ed.)

6 Léopold Sédar Senghor, "A l'appel de la race de Saba," *Anthologie*, p. 152. (Ed.)

7 Cf. Jacques Rabémananjare, "Lyre à sept cordes," *Anthologie*, p. 196. (Ed.)

8 Jacques Rabémananjare, "Lyre à sept cordes," *Anthologie*, p. 201. (Ed.)

9 Aimé Césaire, "Cahier d'un retour au pays natal," *Anthologie*, p. 58. (Ed.)

10 Cf. Léon-G. Damas, *Anthologie*, p. 14. (Ed.)

11 Léon-G. Damas, "Limbe," *Anthologie*, p. 9. (Ed.)

12 Léon Laleau, "Trahison," *Anthologie*, p. 108. Sartre quotes the whole poem but omits the question mark with which it closes. (Ed.)

13 Stephan Mallarmé, "Magie," *Oeuvres complètes* (Paris: Pléiade, 1945), p. 400.

14 Aimé Césaire, "Tam-Tam II," *Les armes miraculeuses*, (Paris: Gallimard, 1946), p. 69.

15 Guy Tirolien, "L'âme du noirs pays," *Anthologie*, pp. 87–8. (Ed.)

16 Léopold Sédar Senghor, "A l'appel de la race de Saba," *Anthologie*, p. 157. (Ed.)

17 David Diop, "Souffre, pauvre Nègre," *Anthologie*, p. 176. (Ed.)

18 Léopold Sédar Senghor, "Congo," *Anthologie*, p. 169. (Ed.)

19 Aimé Césaire, "L'irrémédiable," *Les armes miraculeuses*, p. 46.

20 Aimé Césaire, "Barbare," *Anthologie*, p. 56. (Ed.)

21 David Diop, "Un Blanc m'a dit...," *Anthologie*, p. 175. (Ed.)

22 Cf. Guy Tirolien, "L'âme du noirs pays," *Anthologie*, p. 88. Sartre misquotes Tirolien who wrote *anciens*, not *ancêtres*. (Ed.)

23 Sartre seems to have confused his images here, since Orpheus was instructed not to look back while he was *ascending* from Hades, *after* he had retrieved Eurydice from Plato. (Translator's note)

24 Aimé Césaire, "L'irrémédiable," *Les armes miraculeuses*, pp. 48–9. (Ed.). The French "automatic writing" was so completely untranslatable that we have tried simply to give an English *approximation* of its sense. For those who care to consult the original French text, it runs as follows: "*Les mots se dépassent, c'est bien vers un ciel et une terre que le haut et le bas ne permettent pas de distraire, c'en est fait aussi de la vieille géographie. . . . Au contraire, un étagement curieusement respirable s'opère réel mais au niveau. Au Niveau gazeux de l'organisme solide et liquide, blanc et noir jour et nuit.*" (Translator's note)

25 Etienne Léro, "Châtaignes aux cils . . .," *Anthologie*, p. 53. (Ed.)

26 Title of a poem by Mallarmé. See *Oeuvres complètes*, pp. 453–77. (Ed.)

27 Aimé Césaire, "Avis de tirs," *Anthologie*, p. 62. (Ed.)

28 Aimé Césaire, "Barbare," *Anthologie*, p. 56. (Ed.)

29 Aimé Césaire, "Soleil serpent," *Anthologie*, p. 63. Sartre misquotes Césaire by pluralizing the first word, "sea." (Ed.)

30 Aimé Césaire, "Cahier d'un retour au pays natal," *Anthologie*, pp. 58–9. (Ed.)

31 Aimé Césaire, "Cahier d'un retour au pays natal," *Anthologie*, p. 57. (Ed.)

32 Aimé Césaire, "Cahier d'un retour au pays natal," *Anthologie*, p. 59. (Ed.)

33 Aimé Césaire, "Cahier d'un retour au pays natal," *Anthologie*, p. 57. (Ed.)

34 It is this sense that the critical (Kantian) idea expresses the point of view of the non-proletarian technician. The subject finds again in things what he has placed there. But he puts nothing there only *mentally*; it is a question of the workings of the understanding. The scientist and the engineer are Kantians. [Endnote added in *Situations, III.* –Ed.]

35 Léopold Sédar Senghor, "Congo," *Anthologie*, p. 168. (Ed.)

36 Léopold Sédar Senghor, "Chant du printemps," *Anthologie*, p. 166. (Ed.)

37 Jean-Joseph Rabéarivelo, "Cactus," *Anthologie*, p. 189. (Ed.)

38 Léon Laleau, "Sacrifice," *Anthologie*, p. 108. (Ed.)

39 "Lactogen" is a neologism in the French text as well. (Translator's note)

40 Jean-Joseph Rabéarivelo, "Traduit de la Nuit," *Anthologie*, p. 182. (Ed.)

41 *Flamboyant*: a plant found in semi-tropical countries, especially in the Antilles: a *poinciana* or *peacock flower.* (Translator's note)

42 *Couis*: apparently some kind of tree found in the Antilles. (Translator's note)

43 Aimé Césaire, "Cahier d'un retour au pays natal," *Anthologie*, p. 57. (Ed.)

44 Paul Niger, "Lune," *Anthologie*, p. 104. (Ed.)

45 *Revulses*: referring to the medical term *revulsion*: a counter-irritant. (Translator's note)

46 Paul Niger, "Je n'aime pas l'Afrique," *Anthologie*, p. 100. (Ed.)

47 Léon-G. Damas, "La complainte du nègre," *Anthologie*, pp. 10–11. (Ed.)

48 Jean-F. Brière, "Me revoici, Harlem," *Anthologie*, p. 122. (Ed.)

49 Furthermore, what is the present condition of the negro, in Cameroon, on the Ivory Coast, if not slavery, in the most rigorous sense of the term? [Endnote added in *Situations, III.* Ed.]

50 Metaphysics and history are not Pascal's terms. See *Pensées* fragment 199 (Lafuna edition) where Pascal describes human beings as composed of mind and matter. (Ed.)

51 Aimé Césaire, "Et les chiens se taisaient," *Anthologie*, p. 70. (Ed.)

52 Jacques Roumain, "Bois-d'Ébène," *Anthologie*, p. 114. (Ed.)

53 Jean-F. Brière, "Black Soul," *Anthologie*, p. 126. (Ed.)

54 Epic: the French here reads "*Geste*," as in *Chanson de Geste*; Sartre is comparing the negro Epic with the themes of Medieval French epic poetry. (Translator's note)

55 Jean-F. Brière, "Black Soul," *Anthologie*, pp. 127–8. (Ed.)

56 Jacques Roumain, "Bois-d'Ébène," *Anthologie*, p. 114. (Ed.)

57 Léopold Sédar Senghor, "Aimé Césaire," *Anthologie*, p. 55. (Ed.)

58 Jacques Roumain, "Bois-d'Ébène," *Anthologie*, p. 116. (Ed.)

59 Jacques Roumain, "Bois-d'Ébène," *Anthologie*, p. 117. (Ed.)

60 Aimé Césaire, "Et les chiens se taisaient," *Les armes miraculeuses*, p. 159. (Ed.)

61 Ibid., pp. 160–1. Sartre's quotation departs from Césaire's text in two places. *Ma loi est que je courre* (My law is what I run from) was read as *Une loi est que je courre* (There is a law that I cover up) and *Mais nu* (but naked) was read as *mais un* (but one). The errors were corrected in *Situations, III.* (Ed.)

62 Aimé Césaire, *Les armes miraculeuses*, p. 156.

8

NEGRITUDE AND MODERNITY OR NEGRITUDE AS A HUMANISM FOR THE TWENTIETH CENTURY

Léopold Senghor

Nit moo di garab u nit: It is man who is the remedy for man.
Wolof saying from Senegal

If I have chosen, today, to tell you about Negritude in its relationship with modernity, in other words, if I propose to present Negritude to you as a contemporary humanism, it is because the subject is a topical one. Many observers, even some historians and some philosophers, have pointed out that in the bosom of the world's greatest power, the United States of America, an ethnic minority – namely, the Blacks – plays a role more important than its numbers. And this in spheres as essential as art and leisure. Observers link this phenomenon to the growing influence, because of their revolt, of minorities throughout the world. They also remind us of the influence of jazz on contemporary music, as well as, prior to that, that of *Negro Art* on the Parisian school of painting, which is to say, on twentieth century art. Keeping to Euro-African relationships, some French people called us "racist" in the 1930s, when the word Negritude broke out like a nauseating bomb in Paris, right in the middle of the Latin Quarter; and today, some of Her Britannic Majesty's subjects consider *shocking*[1] the fusion in process of the Negritude movements and of the *African personality*.[2]

What is Negritude?

Getting to the matter at hand, *What is Negritude*? In a recent interview, published in the paper *Dakar-Matin*,[3] Professor Abiola Irélé, from the University of Ifé, in Nigeria, answers the question in these terms: "I am a supporter and a follower of Negritude insofar as I see, in this movement, a will to return into oneself. I even accept it as an absolutely necessary positive narcissism. I think that one should even exaggerate it, give it dimensions in proportion to the alienation. At the last Edinburgh conference,

I explained that Negritude is a philosophy that postulates a cultural action adapted to the spiritual and sociological conditions of the black man. *It is a humanism with a universal scope*". I stress the last sentence: it is the theme of this conference. If I have quoted Irélé at such length, it is because he is anglophone and because the White imperialism has attempted to use anglophone Negroes from Africa, as it does today with "marxist-leninists," to combat the Negritude movement.

But again, what is *Negritude*? If one wants to think of it seriously, one sees that the word has a double meaning: subjective and objective, particular and universal, topical and eternal – insofar as spirit is eternal. This is the first meaning of the word as defined by Irélé. In this sense Negritude is, essentially, a refusal and a commitment, it is a negation and going beyond negation through synthesis, or even better, through symbiosis.

I am referring here to my own experience, for it was in "quatrième" or "troisième" – in the third or fourth year of secondary school – that I discovered the problem and began to be militant. It was in Libermann high school, in Dakar, which was kept by the fathers of the Holy Spirit. We were, already, a handful of *protesters* who, though relatively privileged, laid claim to other privileges, including that of having white sheets. The director would dismiss us, always, to the low beds and the loincloths of our parents, denying us even the honor of having a civilization, for we were only "savages" in the etymological sense of the word, i.e., "men from the bush." I protested all the more heartily as, my father being a landowner, I had, in the countryside, lived our *Black-African civilization*, which was a certain, non-European manner, of thinking the world and of being in the world, of conceiving and of living life: a certain way of eating and working, of laughing and crying, of dancing and singing, of painting and sculpting. But also and above all, of praying. Yet the militant I was beginning to be could feel, despite everything, the weakness of this civilization, and that it was of a technical order. And I would swear to myself that I would steal from Europe the instruments of its superiority: its machines, of course, but above all the spirit of its machines, I mean its *discursive reason*.

Objectively, as a civilization, Negritude is the totality of values; not only those of the peoples of black Africa, but also of the black minorities of America, or even of Asia or the South Sea Islands. It is, as Jean-Paul Sartre puts it in "Black Orpheus,"[4] "a certain common quality to the thoughts and conduct of Negroes." *Subjectively*, Negritude is a will to take on the values of the black world, to live them oneself, after having impregnated and actualized them, but also to make them live in and through others. In this sense it is, to use Irélé's words, a "humanism with a universal scope." In order to help you have a better understanding of it, I refer you to the doctoral thesis of Erica Simon, professor at the University of Lyon but of Scandinavian origin through her mother, which is entitled *National Awakening and Popular Culture in Scandinavia*.[5] She shows how, in the nineteenth century, Scandinavian peoples, humiliated by the Great Powers as they were, searched, beyond their respective national identities, for the values of that *Spirit of the North*, which alone, could help them form, in Europe, a solid whole, cultural and political at the same time – the economic being not yet fashionable. In an article published in the *Revue de la Société des Etudes Germaniques* and entitled "The University of Grundtvig," Mrs Simon went as far as comparing the notion of Negritude to that of *Folkelighed*. I would compare it, more accurately, to that of

Northernity (Nordicité) – since one could have as well said *Negrity*, the Latin suffixes *-itudo* and *-itas* having the same abstract value.

That is to say that Negritude, as a cultural movement, is not a racism, not even an "anti-racist racism," to use Sartre's formula.[6] One knows that, under the influence of characterology, one of the inventors of which was the Franco-Senegalese philosopher Gaston Berger, ethnology has given the last blow to the idea of a unique civilization, and even more to the idea – still incarnated by the "Société européenne de Culture" – of a European civilization superior to all others. As I have been taught by Marcel Mauss and Paul Rivet, my masters at the Institute for Ethnology in Paris, each ethnic group, each people, has its own civilization, which is the succulent fruit of the geography, but also of the history and language of the race; in short, of life in society.

After having defined Negritude in this way, I would like to determine concretely its two aspects, one after the other. But in describing the second one as a living movement I will say, at the same time, to what extent it is a *humanism for the twentieth century*.

Negritude, as an objective civilization, is an idea – I mean a philosophy –, and a life, a theory and a practice, a morality and an art; but first, an *idea*. As Africanists have often noted, those that are called "primitive" do not only have a coherent philosophy, but they live off their ideas and live their ideas. I won't go that far, for only the *initiated* to the last degree, have deciphered all of the signs of the world and penetrated all of its senses. It remains that even the common Black-African – the farmer, the pastor or the fisherman – is usually eager to master, with his word, the cosmic forces, which is to say his life as a man.

Black-African philosophy, as we live it and as confirmed by Africanists themselves, is an *ontology*; a science of *being*. From one black people to another it presents many variants, even if one keeps to Africa, as I will throughout this paper; yet its significance remains the same if one knows how to interpret myths. For any science, any teaching, presents itself, in Nigritia, in the form of a myth: an analogical image. This is why I will begin, here, with the myth of creation, which is at the same time and in a significant way, the myth of the *Word*. I am borrowing it from the *Dogon* people from Mali, that Marcel Griaule[7] and his disciples have made famous.

Hence, according to the Dogon myth, it is Amma, the non-created and all-powerful God, who has created all beings and things. Previously these were, in the form of coarsely sketched ideograms, in the egg of the world, composed of double placenta. It is from this mother-egg, fertilized by the word of Amma that the first two men came out. One, having rebelled against paternal authority, introduced, besides defilement, disorder in the world, and he was changed into a fox. The other one, Nommo, put to death and then restored to life, came down from heaven to earth with an arch, which contained, besides the first eight ancestors of man, all of the animals, plants, minerals and elements inhabiting the universe.

However, all these beings were really unformed and dumb – including men, who presented themselves as dumb fish. God gives mastery of the word to Nommo, and entrusts him with teaching it. At the same time he gives techniques to unformed *existents*,[8] in the first place to men. It is thus that the learning of language coincided, not only with that of techniques, but prior to that, with the development of the human body and the perfecting if its limbs, i.e., with coming out from animality. Marx and Engels, Jaurès and Teilhard de Chardin, have said nothing else.

In the meantime, going beyond myth, we need to turn these fabulous phenomena into rational knowledge, in the sense of an explanation: coherent, but not necessarily logical. Here is the definition of philosophy. As Alfred and Maurice Croiset have written, "Greek philosophy was born on the day when a thinker attempted to give a rational and systematic explanation of the whole of things."[9]

It is precisely the case that, in many Black-African languages – as formerly in all of them, it seems –, all men, all animals, all plants, all minerals, all identifiable things, including abstract ideas, all existents are classified according to grammatical categories or "nominal classes". There are twenty-one of them in the *poular* or Peul dialect of Senegal. This classification originally corresponds, beyond phonetic, morphological and syntactical considerations, to semantic – i.e., rational – reasons. Thus relying on grammar – that is, ultimately, on language –, after Abbot Alexis Kagamé[10], Janheinz Jahn[11] discovered, in the Black-African ontology, *force* as the very essence of beings, which is expressed by the root *ntu* in Bantu. Thus, in the frame of the nominal classes, *muntu* designates "force endowed with intelligence;" *kintu* designates "the forces that act only due to the command of a Muntu;" *hantu* means "the force that localizes, in time and space, any event;" *kuntu* designates, "finally . . . "the modal force," laughter or beauty for instance, constituting "authentic forces in the eyes of the Bantu."[12] It is then the fact, precisely not of *having* the force as an attribute, but of *being* a force as substance, that makes the common quality, and, really, the identity of beings, ever since the father Placide Tempels, in translating "Bantu" thought, has established that "*being* IS *force*."[13] Every great Africanist – and the African informers and researchers in the first place – have confirmed this fundamental principle of African ontology. The latter could very well be formulated in this way: "the stuff of matter is energy."

Before going further, we need to analyze this principle, which, probably more than any other, distinguishes Black-African philosophy from classical European philosophy. Until the nineteenth century, for more than 2000 years, European thought, in neglecting the genial intuitions of a whole line of Greek philosophers, has lived more or less on Aristotle's thought, where logos, from being fluid and vibratory, has been crystallized into rigid categories, which no longer fit, no longer translate the moving, lively reality. For classical philosophy, then, beings are distinct substances, doubtless created by God, but living an independent existence: *in se* and *per se*. It is therefore a *static* ontology. For the Black-African, on the contrary and once again, being is not a substance that has force as an attribute; it is force itself that is the substance of being. *Being-force* is *energy*, that is to say a spirit, an ever moving-life, capable of growing and diminishing, of being enriched and altered. It is a *vital force*, which subtends men and animals, plants and minerals, as well as, eventually, natural phenomena: everything that is identifiable.

Therefore, rather than being side by side, separated and as if incommunicable, or at least without any action of one onto the other, each being-force, each *ntu* can influence another, due to its natural nature and its own movement; and it can do so all the more easily as the latter is *sub-ordinated*. The world of forces is, then, a system of communicating vessels: a communion of beings between themselves and within Being.

Bantu - intelligent being

For this influence is exercised, according to the system of primogeniture, starting from God – *force in itself and for itself* –, who gives force, increases it or decreases it. According to the principle of this hierarchy, there are the first human beings and the ancestors; then, among the living, the old and the young, the honest, therefore the prosperous people, as well as the others. After the human forces, there are the animal, vegetal and mineral forces, classified hierarchically according to the same rank of primogeniture, which is only the sign of pré-cellence and which translates pré-séance. This is why I said earlier: "due to its natural nature and to its own movement." For primogeniture alone is not enough. One has to add to it the actions that are good and reinforce force, and the actions that are bad, which weaken force. That is to say, this ontology primarily refers to *Man*.

We have often noted that, in the system, or rather, in the interdependent community of the universe, Man is at the same time the subject and the object of the universal movement – he is means and end, form and center. By delegation from God, the Nommo-Man teaches the Word and, thereby, completes creation, mastering the play of forces as he does, which he enriches or deprives of substance – until death. Hence the Black-African view of the universe is described in terms of *anthropocentrism* and *anthropomorphism*.

But what, exactly, is this *Man*? In every version of the Black-African philosophy, Man is presented as a complex being – the most complex after God – and as possessing several souls, which is to say several spiritual principles. Geneviève Calame-Griaule has discovered eight "souls" or *kikinu* – to which, obviously, one needs to add vital force as substance[14] –, which constitute "personality." To begin with, it is worth noting the equilibrium that the whole of these forces forms. These are divided into two groups of four, each of which contains two twins. The first group, located in the head, is made of a male principle expressing intelligence and will, and of a female principle representing intuition and emotion, to which are opposed two negative principles of an opposite meaning. The second group, located in the genitals, includes principles that are analogous, but linked to sexuality in its double aspect, physical or practical (procreation), and spiritual or sentimental (love). One already knew the importance of sexuality in Black-African civilization, yet far from being an obsession that produces imbalance, it is a whole made of elements concurring to the formation of personality. Looking at the synoptical chart of the *kikinu* provided by Geneviève Calame-Griaule, one notes that "reason and will are introduced into sexual life", while intuition and emotion, which belong with sex, are introduced into intellectual life. All the more since each human being possesses, within him or herself, the same male and female principles, with the non-exclusive predominance of the masculine or the feminine, depending on the sex. Thus Man appears to us, at the center of the Black-African *Weltanschauung*, as the equilibrium of a binary rhythm: ambivalence, or better, a *symbiosis*. This anthropocentrism, which turns into anthropomorphism, goes as far as dividing all existents, all elements of the universe, into male and female.

But how does *Man* put to work, direct and arrange the universal system of interdependent forces? Man knows cosmogony, the structures and hierarchy of the system: the – ascending or descending – series of beings and, therefore, of powers. Knowing these, Man also knows how to put them to work. But it is not useless to go back on these double-plane structures, which are more complex than they appear. There is, for human beings, a vertical plane of primogeniture, as illustrated by *age groups*, but there is also the horizontal plane of the structures, illustrated, on the one hand, by social-cultural groups or *brotherhoods*, and, on the other hand, by social-professional groups, or *corporations*. Let us not rehearse the top of the hierarchy, i.e., God; nor animals, plants and minerals; nor natural phenomena such as clouds, the wind, rain, and so on.

It is time, in connection with this horizontal or structural order, to go further into our analysis: to show more explicitly what this system of communicating vessels consists in, wherein one goes from man to rock and conversely, as if they shared in the same nature. The narratives of our evenings hum with these tales in which a woman becomes a hyena as easily as a stick turns into a warrior. "On the earth intended for men," recounts Lebeuf, following the *Fali* cosmogony from Cameroon,

> the papaye-tree rooted itself at the center and begot a first couple of human beings of opposite sex, who gave birth to two times two female twins. For their part, the Turtle and the Toad united, the former with a crocodile . . . the second with a lizard . . . and they gave birth to two couples of male twins. The latter, with the four women born of the children of the papaye-tree, constituted four couples, who are at the origin of the *Fali* people.[15]

Given that all the *ntu* can only become *beings of Being*, it follows that "engenderings" and changes, all the avatars, are merely an enrichment or an impoverishment of the same vital force: of the same *Being*. They rely on this ontological truth that every being, especially every existent, as we have seen in relation to man, is ambivalent. More precisely, it is multivalent, composed as it is of several elements, several particles of vital force – those, among others, he has received from his ancestry –, the whole of which can be submitted to variations of a moral or physical, material or spiritual origin. These variations happen in accordance with the laws of *participation*.

The word is now dropped, and beyond it, the concept that explains, after the structures, the organization and functioning of the world. The same force, then, giving life to the universe, one of its elements can, through avatar and due to the effect of certain psycho-physiological laws, pass onto another density, another form. More precisely, a certain quantity of vital force can pass from one *existent* to another one. But for this to happen, it is necessary that the two beings be united by one element at least, or any other kind of link. This link can be a *belonging* (from father to son, for example), a *correspondence* (from a color to a sound), an *analogy* (between the situations of two existents), or finally an *identity*, which facilitates everything. This is it for the nature of the link. However, the latter can unite an existent to another (for instance, a man to a tree), it can unite an element, or, more concretely, a modality to another (a sound to a color), but it can also unite a physical element to a moral modality. The list of avatars is far from being exhaustive. One could say, in a word, that the universe is a dictionary, a fabric of metaphors, a vast network – front and back – of signifiers and signifieds; yet in it the participating, or the communing correspondences, work in two directions: from sign to sign, but also of sign to sense, and conversely.

For the Black-African, even if he does not grasp all the meanings, not only every existent, but every form and every color, every sound and every smell, even every movement, until rest and silence, everything, then, is a sign, and every sign has a sense.

One could wonder why, and you will. It is, essentially, for ethnic reasons. Indeed, the ethno-characterologists have classified Black-Africans among the *Fluctuants*. Now the latter are characterized by the depth and energy of their affectivity, the rapidity and violence of their reactions. Their intelligence, which is "concreto-sensory", is more readily expressed in images rather than concepts. The richness of their inner-life, entirely turned towards the actualities of the soul, is emphasized. The *intuitive reason* of Black-Africans, their specific emotional power and imagination, used to be explained by the contrasts and violence of the African climate. *Portentosa*, or "wonder-maker", was how the Romans described Africa. But not the Greeks, for whom Africa was the continent cherished by the gods. The *Ethiopians*, which is to say Negroes, were the most ancient, the most beautiful, the most religious and the wisest of human beings, having invented religion and the law, writing and art. I refer you to the doctoral thesis that a Cameroon Jesuit, Father Engelbert Mveng, just wrote, and which is entitled *The Greek Sources of Black-African History*.[16]

Prehistory indeed confirms the opinion of the Greeks. Since the end of the Second World War, pre-historians have by their discoveries confirmed this opinion, especially de Breuil and Teilhard de Chardin's thesis, according to which it was in Africa that man emerged, for the first time, from animality.[17] For, as Teilhard explains, far from being an inhospitable land, Africa offered, on the contrary, the climate most favorable to the evolution, through sudden mutations, of the great anthropoid primates toward the *Hominoids*, then toward the Men of today. Today still, from Ethiopia to South Africa, the plateaux of Eastern Africa offer to us the grace of an earthly paradise: the pleasures of life. Among the anthropoid primates, the *Hominoids* were those who rose from this earthly paradise as standing bipeds. Thanks to the converging activity of the hand and the foot, of the hand and the brain, they would become, after several tens of millions of years, *Homines habiles*, i.e., primates that are not only omnivorous, but that are also able to build tools and use them. Able, too, doubtless, to articulate the first words of a coherent thought. That happened less than 4 million years ago, on the high plateaux of Eastern Africa.[18] "Thanks to these (hominoids) of the inferior pleistocene . . . ", writes Yves Coppens – a member of the French expedition which discovered, three years ago in the Omo valey in Ethiopia, the oldest human skeletons, dated 3,700,000 years –, "Africa presently holds, without a doubt, a lead of at least one million years, probably two, on the origin of the fabricating humanity."[19] Thus, in Africa, hominoids for 40 million years and Men for 4 million years have lived on a land where nature is generous and the climate mild. There, among the familiarity of animals and plants, of the phenomena of the earth and air, men have learned to know all existents: their shapes and movements, their activities and rests, their cries and silences, their struggles and chords. In short, among the extraordinary jumble of their links and correspondences, of their participation and union, they have learned to identify the sense that lies under the sign. These symbolic images, these *archetypal images* sleep at the back of our memories from which Negro Art makes them rise with an essential force.

Black-African Civilization

Unfortunately, I do not have time to develop these explanations about ethnic psychology, but now that they have been given, it is time to say under what circumstances and how human beings put to work, direct and coordinate the universal system of interdependent forces. We will thus be approaching the major questions constituted by *religion, morality* and *art*. But, to tell the truth, in this Black-African civilization, one of whose most characteristic traits is *unity within coherence*, art is essentially a technology, or more exactly, the whole formed by technologies in the service of ethics; the latter is, in turn, merely the practice of religion, the ontology of which, as we just explained, is dogma.

One of the great questions that human disquiet addresses *Religion* is the question of ends. In the Black-African case, why and to what does the network of vital forces tend? We will answer this question by borrowing a more modern language that takes us in the direction of "Negritude as a subject." We will answer it while underlining two traits of our ontology: the idea of fecundity and the idea of Man.

First, and once again, the idea of *Man*. It has often been said, about Black-African philosophy, that in it God was remote, indifferent, inefficient. It is not true. It would be more true to underline the role of demiurge that God ascribed to Man. It is the latter who, having received a delegation from the All-Powerful Being, completes creation. It is again Man that God has put in charge of reestablishing the order of the system when it is troubled, and of maintaining it by reinforcing it. For Creation is always to be made. Even more. God has, so to say, united all of creation, all beings in the service of the living Man as the *Existent par excellence*. Not only did animals and plants, minerals and other elements put themselves at his service, but so did the Dead, his Ancestors.

This brings us to the idea of *Fecundity*, or procreation. It is, with the idea of Force, the one that haunts, in an obsessive way, Black-African consciousness. Indeed, this has been translated in the first human works of art in the form of soapstone statuettes of fecundity, already animated by Negro rhythm. It is to this idea that creation answers. All things were therefore locked up in God's bosom, still and dumb, mere unformed sketches. If God named them with his word to give them life, it was to expand and reinforce his vital force: to make his BEING *more-being* in more and more numerous and diverse forms. In living bodies. As the Diola from Senegal say, "God holds in stock the infinity of souls to be born which, united with reincarnated souls, will come to renew indefinitely the surface of the earth."[20]

In the main function of Man, ethics mingles with mysticism, the former being merely, in fact, the latter put into practice. Since all vital forces are emanations from God and the latter's will lies in the multiplication and increase of these forces, morality will consist, for Man, in acting so as to conform to this will. This means provoking the birth of new forces and reinforcing the existing ones. And Man will act through a series of material and spiritual techniques.

In the first place, it is a question of provoking the birth of new vital forces. They will be, most of the time, only reincarnations of dead ancestors. Here we have all the ceremonies, all the rituals that surround such events and actions as marriage, birth and the giving of a name, sowing and harvesting. It is also a question of increasing the existing forces, as in professional activities: the force of the blacksmith as well as that of the weaver, and the force of the fisherman as well as that of the hunter. In addition to increasing the existing forces and creating new ones, it is also a question of restoring them when the network, the order of interdependent forces, is troubled by a mistake – intentional or not – which, like a stain, corrupts, rots the forces linked to the guilty person through the participating correspondences we analyzed earlier.

In order to play his part as a pilot, conductor, governor or, better said, as continuous creator of the world, Man uses, either simultaneously or in succession, techniques that derive at the same time from religion, craftsmanship and art. I will begin with two examples, borrowed from religion and craftsmanship: sacrifice and the forge.

In Black Africa, *sacrifice* is the essential cult act. Even in a country like Senegal, where *animists* – those who practice the traditional religion – do not represent more than 10%, sacrifice is the most common way to invoke the Deity. It is the only cult that unites all Senegalese. In Black Africa, sacrifice presents itself much more often as the gift of an object, an offering, than as the destruction of a victim. It is one of the traits of Negritude, whereby the tree gets the better of the animal. Whether it be an animal, a drink or any other kind of food, it is a matter of offering to dead ancestors earthly food that they will pass on to God. Of course, there are vital substances in the offering, such as water or blood. But the proper virtue of sacrifice is to *revitalize* these substances – in the sense of reinforcing rather than renewing. This revitalization is induced by the intention of the sacrificer, the will of the ancestors and, above all, of God; and also by the words of the sacrificer. Primordial importance of the *spoken word*. As a ringing projection of human personality, it possesses, like the human body, the "four elements" – water, air, earth, fire – to which one might add oil. Like the human being, it possesses, with the vital force, the "eight souls" I have already mentioned. To summarize, as expression of the essence of Man, containing the oil of fecundity more than any other element, the spoken word is food, but vivifying food. The spoken word is sperm.[21] In sacrifice, it is therefore the revitalized foods that the ancestors receive. This makes them relive the pleasures of life. And in return, by the grace and will of God, they increase through the sacrificer the vital forces of the people joined in prayer. In the cases of staining, or disturbance of order, there is not only revitalization, but also purification. For purification is nothing but revitalization by means of elimination of the corrupted – i.e., dead – elements.

Second example: that of the *blacksmith's* work. I refer you to the novel by Camara Laye. Son of a blacksmith, he has described for us, in his autobiographical novel entitled *The Black Child*, the work of his father on a gold jewel.[22] We will not insist on the general technique of the blacksmith, but on the particular one of the goldsmith. Now then, while he works at the jewel, the blacksmith prays – in the old sense of the term: he utters incantations. And all the while, his *griot*, his troubadour, sings his praises. And in the end, the griot starts to dance the dance of the completed jewel: of the work of art. And, in turn, the blacksmith dances "the glorious dance."

These pages by Camara Laye, which I am summarizing here, are interesting in more than one way, that show the participation, in Nigritia, of religion – which is a philosophy, craftsmanship – which is a technique, and art. Indeed, religion is at the beginning of technique, and the blacksmith received, in the past, during his apprenticeship, a religious initiation before a technical one. And the former is already present in the incantation of the blacksmith, which is a prayer to *complete* the technical work of the worker in order to give it the oil and something like the grace of beauty. For south of the Sahara, the two worlds – visible and invisible, material and spiritual, profane and religious, technical and artistic – are but the two sides of the same fabric: the same reality. When the weaver weaves, he sings. And his words are feet and hands at work, doubling the work of the shuttle and the stretcher.

I am forgetting neither the song nor the dance of the griot, which first appear to us as expressions of profane art. In Nigritia, art is never profane, never a mere distraction. The song and the dance of the griot are, on the one hand, aimed at increasing the vital force of the blacksmith – as a reward, and on the other hand, at fulfilling the beauty of the jewel by giving it ultimate grace. Yet, the blacksmith dances, in turn, to *express* his joy. For, in Nigritia, one first dances *by oneself* – if not *for oneself.* Which brings us to Negro art.

Since the beginning of the century and the stirrings of the École de Paris, since cubism and surrealism, people have talked a lot about Negro Art, both in Europe and in America. They say, sometimes, reducing it to an ethnological document, that it ignored the notion of beauty; and sometimes, confusing it with a talisman, that it was a religion or a magic. Neither of these definitions is exactly true. Negro art is all of this at the same time, and something else, and it has a deep sense of beauty. This is where I will start.

I have, among my papers, an odd text written in captivity, at the *Front-Stalag 230.* My informer, a Senegalese citizen, was describing for me ideal beauty in a young woman. That young woman is neither of an ebony color nor of a red gold color, but of a dark bronze. Her lips are finely chiseled without drooping. Her waist is thin and curved, but not excessively. *Beauty* is then, for Black-Africans, the norm, but also measure, accord: in a word, the *harmony* that unites complementary, if not contrary elements. In our *athletic* songs, the girl praises her fiancé for being "black" and "tall" – which is the norm in my ethnic group, but also for being "slender and strong." She sings:

kiin o baal, jag fo nut, jag fo ngel.

That is to say, "the black skinned man, beautiful at rest, beautiful in the arena." In fact, the ordinary word that means "beautiful" is *mos*, while *jag* means "in tune." The athlete is beautiful because he is in tune when resting at home as much as when fighting in the arena. And the beautiful poem is the one "that pleases the heart and the ear." That is to say that Negro art goes beyond the pleasure of the senses – without negating it.

Its first characteristic is to be a *total art* because it integrates all the arts while making them cooperate, as with dance and lyrical theater. Any ceremony, any public manifestation is, at the same time, an artistic activity. Still today, the complete athlete is one who knows, at the same time, how to fight and dance, sing and compose poems. The effective political meeting is one that begins and ends with singing, with dance.

The second characteristic of Negro art is to be a *technique*. Contrary to what the Europeans think, every art – dance and music, singing and poetry, sculpture and pottery, painting and weaving – is a precise technique, which comprises a theory with its own vocabulary, but also a practice aiming for efficacy. Technique then, which nevertheless plays on the twofold register of the useful and the beautiful, of the profane and the religious. The weaver's pulley is at the same time a sculpture, just like the scepter. The calabash, a household piece of equipment, is an engraving, and the loincloth, garment par excellence, is a work of tapestry. And all of these objects are magical, like the jewels, which protect more than they adorn. The work of art is a receptacle of forces that reinforce the vital force of the user and the efficacy of the instrument, itself also endowed with forces. *Negro art is a technique of essentialization toward being-more.*

I would like to illustrate these characteristics of Negro art with two examples, taken from dance and poetry.

I have always thought that *dancing* was the first art invented by Man, even before the emergence of the *Homo Sapiens*. Animals dance. It is the most spontaneous way of expressing oneself. Which is why, in Nigritia, everybody dances, and the elderly, who are the wisest, are those that dance the most. As soon as dancing is elevated into a ceremony – for the village, the brotherhood, the corporation –, it brings together all the arts, and in it every element has its own signification. Dancers wear, on their body, clothes whose shapes, textures and colors each have a sense. Their faces are hidden by masks. An orchestra, which brings together percussion instruments with melodic instruments, accompanies the dancers' steps. Not to mention the spectators who often join the dance and, most often, accompany it with their hand clapping and singing. For in Nigritia, in any ceremony, in any spectacle, one is at the same time spectator and actor.

As for dancing itself, it is a painting-sculpture in motion, thanks to the clothes, masks and paintings so displayed, but mostly thanks to the dancing steps and figures which, as expressing participating correspondences, are *rhythmic images*. I saw, several years ago in Ivory Coast, the dance of the Bull-Moon. The dancer was wearing a mask whose curves, following the law of the multivalence of the image-symbol, are at the same time moon crescent, bull's horns, horns of plenty and tubes of plenty, which is to say, expressions of *Fecundity*. And the dancer was dancing furiously, all the while expressing, in sharp movements of the feet, arms and head, the generous strength of the Bull.

I said that the crowd was singing. It was singing a poem. Let me remind you of the definition that the *Peuls* of my country give of the poem: "words pleasing to the heart and the ear." This shows that poetry is, at the same time, engraving and work of art; and also sowing – I mean efficient action – since it acts on the heart, too. For poetry is an elaborate practice of the spoken word. I won't go back over the virtues of the latter, and its fecund power. It is enough to recall that the spoken word, as fecund power, is necessary to any art; better, to any technical or professional activity. The blacksmith like the weaver, the painter like the sculptor, says, sings his work as he is working on it. Otherwise, it would not be completed because it carries vital force. We have seen this in the case of the goldsmith. But, given that the spoken word of poetry is the beautiful and good word "par excellence," we need to examine why and how beauty and goodness are mingled in it.[23] What, in Black Africa, essentially distinguishes poetry from prose, is the style or the way of saying it, but first the things said, although in Africa, one separates the content from the form even less than in Europe. For it is the form that will lead me to the substance.

I have experienced in Senegal, but also with all the Black-African ethnic groups whose poems I have read, that the poems appear, on first reading, as a tissue of comparisons and metaphors, i.e., of *catachresis*. These need to be explained because the correspondences they express, if they indeed explain essential truths, are specific to the people considered, to the village, the clan, although an experienced African – or Africanist – can easily recover, with myths, the archetypical images. Poems more than tales and stories thus say the essential: birth and death, geniuses and ancestors, work and war. They above all say it in a more concise and strong way: more dense.

Style also distinguishes poetry from prose. It is a matter of saying things – more precisely, forces and their interactions – in an unusual and strong way: in a fecund way. Hence the archaic style, which sometimes spreads to the language that often becomes obsolete. These matters of style concern vocabulary, figures of language and thought, and at last, rhythm.

Vocabulary is all the more important, in the Black-African languages, as the roots of the words are felt in their concrete value, so that words almost always carry images. I want to add that poetic vocabulary, often studded with rare words, employs a lot of proper names – of ancestors, locations, families – that are, in themselves, loaded with sense and emotions.

Yet, once again, Black-African poetry – like sculpture, painting and dance – is a string of signifying catachresis. Not only do figures of thought – comparisons, antithesis – abound, but also figures of language. Whether they be parallelisms or asymmetries, anaphoras or chiasmas, alliterations or assonances, plays on words having to do with timbre or signification, the sounds are always *pregnant* with images which tie up correspondences between things, between forces, between beings. It is an outstretched poetry, a poetry that has a direction, and in it the intention is indeed as effective as the expression. Still, the intention is more in the desire for efficacy than in the clarity of the expression. The ambivalence, the multivalence of Black Art, in which, abundant, signifying and signified terms are mingled, has often been noted. It strengthens the force, because it strengthens the mystery, of beauty.

But the latter – the expression – is effective, puts forces to work, only if the poem is itself animated by the *rhythm*: by the imperious Black rhythm, which is monotonous at first sight. In the past, every oral piece of work, including tales, was recited, declaimed in a monotonous rhythm and a very high tone. If I take the example of the athletic poems of my ethnic group, the *Serer*, those can be declaimed or sung. In both cases, the rhythm obeys strict laws, which can be expressed mathematically. There the verse is defined by a fixed number not of syllables, but of accents of intensity, as in old Germanic poetry. Poetry happens every time that an accentuated syllable intervenes at a regular interval. The gap between the number of syllables and the number of accents allows for transcending the apparent monotony in order to adapt the rhythm of the poem to that of the soul. It is this extreme freedom, above the tyranny of the basic rhythm marked by the tom-tom, which makes the originality of the Black rhythm – vibrating with syncopated and off beat notes – and that one finds again accentuated in the singing of the poem.

For the poem can obtain its full ontological efficacy only if it is sung. In most Black-African languages, there is no particular term to name the poem, which is designated by the same word as the song: *gim* in *serer* and *woi* in *wolof* from Senegal, *nii* in *dogon* from Mali. Because it is purifying and fecund, the pleasing and beneficial force of the song comes from the oil supplement it contains. This oil gives the sung word its harmony, which comes from the height of the sounds and of their melodic symbiosis. It is the reason why women's voices, and especially young women's voices, which are the highest and the most melodic, are so effective.

Thus, the poem summarizes wonderfully what I have been trying to explicate about the creative role of human beings in the world. And how would it be possible, here, not to give poetry its etymological sense of *poiesis* – of "creation?" The poem, which is to say, the rhythmical and sung word, is the perfect example of the work of art, of the act of art, which recharges the energetic batteries of the world. In a word, the poem is the fecund sperm of the world. And we will not tolerate any challenge to "Black sensuality," which exists firmly as a source of life and dream, because, precisely, there is no such thing as obsessing eroticism. Just think: there can be biological fecundity, there can be procreation, only if man, through the tenderness of his lubricated words, gently melts the heart of his wife. We have not talked enough, yet, of Black tenderness.[24]

Negritude is Attuned to the Twentieth Century

It is precisely the mission of the *New Negro*[25] to make all these values known, all the virtues of Negritude – above all, those that follow the same direction as the contemporary world and which, in symbiosis with those of other civilizations, must be used to build the Civilization of the Universal. Having started from Negritude as an object, we now turn to Negritude as a subject. The New Negro, as Jean-Paul Sartre puts it,

> wants to be both a beacon and a mirror; the first revolutionary will be the harbinger of the black soul, the herald who will tear Negritude out of himself in order to offer it to the world: half-prophet, half-partisan; in brief, he will be a poet in the literal sense of the word "vates."[26]

As I have often noted, since the *Cultural Revolution of 1889*[27], since recovery from the scientific blindness of the nineteenth century, the new discoveries of European-American culture – even in the scientific field – have been meeting, paradoxically, the intuitions and experiences, the theories and practices of Black-African civilization, while in the domain of art, there was a conscious drawing of inspiration from the values of Negritude – although not always well interpreted. These are the convergences I would like to underline first, before saying how the militants of Negritude want to draw all the consequences of these convergences of which they are conscious.

I perceived and noted these convergences, once again, at the beginning of the year, while reading the work entitled *The Gods and the Kings* – the subtitle of which is "A glance at Creative Power," by Jacques Rueff, a member of the French Academy.[28] Jacques Rueff's intention is of a philosophical order. It is to fill in the "abyss" that separates the human sciences from mathematics and the natural sciences. In short, it is – in the very spirit of philosophy, which is theory, a general view on the universe – to show that all sciences, including the natural sciences, are "social sciences." One can see how close his purpose is to Black-African philosophy, to begin with. Of course, I won't stop at this reference alone, to which I will add others, including a remarkable text by Gaetan Picon, published in 1957.[29]

As everyone knows, the first and most fundamental question that philosophy faces is an epistemological question: what is the ultimate reality, the stuff of the universe? First of all, can we grasp it and by what means? In classical philosophy, as we have already suggested, the real is an objective thing, given once and for all, situated in definite time and space, and as such, it is measurable. Of course, this "thing" can be gifted with force or spirit, but these are mere attributes, "accidents" of the substance. Naturally, "things" can be known because they can be seen, grasped and measured by the mind, by intelligence and experimentation, whereby spirit, as detached, remains at a distance. As Gaetan Picon puts it, the philosophy of discursive reason was a "visual realism." Which is why I called it *eye-reason*. According to that brilliant essayist, classical thought lasted until Hegel. I think that it lasted until the Cultural Revolution of 1889, that is to say, until Bergson, until Rimbaud's "I am Negro."[30]

Since the end of the nineteenth century, then, thanks to the new physics, to the new art, that is to say, to the new *poiesis*, to the new philosophy, we are moving away from the spirit of objectivity, i.e., *thingism* (*chosisme*). We do not think we can contemplate the thing *in se* anymore. We can only hope to grasp it alive, warm and pounding: in an *embrace*, which mingles subject and object, sensation and intelligence, experience and experimentation, passion and vision, feeling and perception.

That the *reason-embrace* holds a more and more important place in research and teaching, education and formation, is confirmed by the spread in contemporary universities, of the *human sciences* and especially, ethnology, sociology and linguistics. Even in the most abstract of sciences, namely mathematics, intuition resumes its role. And here are peoples pertaining to the *Fluctuant* ethnotype, such as the Japanese, revealing an ability to be good mathematicians. Already, at the University of Dakar, it is in medical school, as well as in mathematics, that the proportion of Black-African – or in any case, Senegalese – teachers is the strongest. I don't need to insist, for it is obvious, after everything I said in the second part of my presentation, on the fact that Black-African thought, which is "intuited, lived and based in lived-experience,"[31] easily converges with contemporary thought, which "ceases to be the thought of the world to become the actual experience of the world, the identity of the word and the real."[32]

"The identity of the word and the real," Gaetan Picon writes. I would like to stop and examine this expression in order to try to define, in relation to the Black-African idea, the role of the *Word (la parole)* in contemporary thought. For in the twentieth century, a number of philosophers, among the greatest – Kierkegaard, Heidegger and Jaspers, Sartre and Merleau-Ponty –, have considered linguistics to be one of the major instruments of philosophy, and the word to be one of its keys. It is true that linguistics had been renewed – I even want to say created – before then, by scholars, a few of which, such as Meillet and Vendryès, were my teachers at The Sorbonne; it is true that ethnologists, sociologists and writers have begun, since then, to insist on the values of signs and images, of style and communication.[33]

"Identity of the word and the real." Martin Heidegger goes even further – toward the Black-African – with his philosophy of language that leads to the following proposition: that the word is the "foundation of Being." The philosopher arrived at this point by means of a penetrating analysis of the Greek *logos*. He chose the Greeks – a people that all modern minds, from Marx to Lenin, have admired – because the Greeks are at the origin of European thought and have always managed to maintain the primordial fluidity of reason in its dual power of vision and embrace: as fecund. In order to uncover the secret, and something like the Being of the word, Heidegger started from the verb *legein* and the substantive *logos* to examine the respective yet converging evolution of their meanings and of those they had at the very origin of Greek thought in the first place: from Homer to the pre-Socratic philosophers, of which I have spoken earlier, and who wrote in verses, or at least in poetic prose. *Legein* started by meaning "to lay" or "gathered-letting-lie-before" before meaning "to present", "to ex-pose", "to say", while *logos* meant "the laying that gathers"[34] or, more explicitly, "the gathering that makes manifest", or even better, "the gathering and apprehending of the Being of the being".[35] We are not so far away from the Black-African philosophy of the word. For it too, as we saw, to speak is to gather the vital force, the Being of the being in the shape of a rough sketch, in order to lay it there by giving it a form, that is to say, existence.

Returning to Heidegger, let us note that his *logos*, like the *logos* of the Greeks, is a demiurge in its establishing and fabricating function; it is *poiesis*, which is to say production, or creation. And poetry in the modern sense of the word, too: in the sense of "saying that establishes" the holy. Like *Nommo*, the Black-African verb. This is what the German philosopher explains to us about Homer, the founder of Greek poetry, but also about Hölderlin, one of the founders of modern poetry, for whom "it is more salutary for thought to proceed through surprising things than to settle in clear things."[36]

We just saw how human beings apprehend the ultimate reality of the universe, and even how they created it. It is now a matter, for contemporary thought, of saying what this reality is or, in other words, what the stuff of the universe is. In this attempt, I will therefore refer to Jacques Rueff, who, starting from a quantic view of the universe such as that of the nuclear physicists, leads to that of sociologists and economists, of lawyers and philosophers. In his conclusion, entitled "Ultimate Confession," he summarizes his work in these terms:

I believe:

> that the individual, which is the foundation of the universe, is *wave and corpuscle, matter and spirit*;
> that it is a medium of behavior, the latter is a *spontaneous outburst* that responds to surrounding circumstances and not a passive presence, indifferent to the external world;
> that all behavior is the expression of a psychism, which is merely a manner of existing – that is to say, a way of reacting to stimuli coming from the rest of the world;

> ...
> that psychism is the internal aspect and *indeterminacy* the external aspect of one and the *same reality*, which is that of the quanta of existence, known in the living world as individuals.[37]

I have [italicized] the important words, which express contemporary ideas on the issue. I would like to show that we have already met these ideas in Black-African ontology: "the binary foundation of existence," "energy as raw material of the universe," "structure" and "interaction" as characteristics of life, "behavior"... which "always implies a certain margin of indeterminacy" and which is the manifestation of "individual psyche;" at last, "complementarity," which leads to twentieth century Humanism. These are the very same words that Jacques Rueff used as titles for the paragraphs of his book.

Even though I mentioned the *dualistic* character of the Black-African universe, I did not insist on it sufficiently. Everything is either on the right or on the left, up or down, forward or backward: more significantly, everything in Nigritia is either male or female. Beings and their modalities (forms and colors, sounds and rhythms) are grouped in twos or multiples of two. Always ruptures introduce life, such as asymmetry to break with monotonous parallelism, ternary rhythm to launch the movement and, in the binary rhythm itself, playing the off-beat and syncopation, which give motion its *force*.

This brings us to the notion of *energy* as ultimate reality, stuff of the universe, which for our contemporaries, makes the symbiosis between flux and corpuscle, between matter and spirit. One recognizes here one of the great ideas of Pierre Teilhard de Chardin who, in an anti-materialistic dialectic reversal, established the pre-existence of spirit over matter. I discovered that the socialist leader Jean Jaurès was already maintaining, at the end of the last century, that matter is "imbued with thought, or rather that it is mere thought itself, obscure and confused, and looking for its path."[38] Nevertheless, we saw that Black-African mythology is more finely differentiated, placing as it does, against the God-Spirit, the primordial placenta: *matter.*

Nothing bears witness to the fact that energy is the stuff of the universe better than *behavior,* which is the *re-action* of the existent to its environment. Not even the behavior of living matter, but of that matter which, at first sight, seems inert, dead, like the ninety-two basic elements that physicists have catalogued. The latter teach us that the quasi-totality of the universe is constituted by "stellar matter", which is to say very small atomic nuclei composed of protons and electrons, "sexed" in terms of negative and positive, or male and female corpuscles, as in Black-African cosmogony. On a higher level, according to Louis de Broglie the atom "would be comparable to a miniature solar system shaped out of electrons playing the part of planets and gravitating... around a central positively charged sun."[39] Niels Bohr would present us with a more complex system, as we know. Ultimately, reality would present itself as "energy grains" of which each is, at the same time, flux and corpuscle and which become matter-inertia or spirit-motion, depending on their avatars. Yet what is most remarkable is not the movements of the grains of energy, but the fact that one cannot foresee them with certainty at that microscopic level, although it is possible to work out some probability; for, like living individuals, these corpuscles react to their surroundings:

they have a behavior – the product of the *inter-actions* between the grains of energy, or the existents. As Jacques Rueff writes,

> These interactions vary in accordance with the nature of the order they generate. Our antropomorphic interpretation of the universe always invests them with the characteristics of *forces of attraction* that lie at the basis of our explanatory theories of the physical world. These forces bear various names . . . exchange forces within the nucleus; electric or electromagnetic forces within the atom, tropisms, appetencies or appetites in an animal being, the *will* in the thinking being. In every case, they may be considered . . . the true cement of existence.[40] (my italics).

This text is characteristic, in the first place of this tendency of the contemporary mind to reintroduce *unity* in the universe and life, despite the often contradictory explanations provided by scholars and thinkers. Also, from the atomic nucleus of stellar matter to the human brain, spirit has been discovered *under* the stuff, indeed *as* the stuff of the universe: everything becomes force, because it is progressive *consciousness* and will. As in Black-African philosophy and its pan-psyche. In the end, the cement, or better, the driving force that is at the same time the reality of the universe, is the *structure*, which is to say, the network of interactions that relate between themselves grains of existence within the individual, individuals in our global society, suns and planets in the universe. At the end of Jacques Rueff's analysis, this vast network appears to us as a binary system, or better, a system of complementary elements based on union, that is to say, on love, which completes and enriches by allowing for being-more, as Teilhard de Chardin wished. Black-Africans do not say anything different, as we saw, especially as to the role and action of human beings in and on the world.

Thus, Black-African thought gives almost the same answers to the fundamental question, the question of epistemology, as contemporary thought, even though it does not always use the same means. For the latter, as the former, refers itself to the human being.

I know that since the era between the two world wars, we have been hearing about a "new Humanism", which the neo-Thomist Jacques Maritain has contributed to render fashionable with his work whose title is suggestive: *Integral Humanism*.[41] Actually, modern Humanism did not just happen yesterday. It was born, in Europe, on the ruins of the Revolution of 1789. From Hegel to Teilhard de Chardin, a twofold lineage of thinkers – atheists and believers – have founded it, some by challenging metaphysics, and the others, more often, by creating a new one. I will only mention, here, Nietzsche, Marx and Lenin, Bergson and Kierkegaard, Husserl and Heidegger, Sartre and my compatriot Berger.[42] Modern Humanism, founded on the converging thought of all these philosophers, can be summarized as follows: *the human being making him – or her – self through the world and making the world.*

As paleontologists and ethnologists have shown, it is by relying *on* nature and by making use *of* the surrounding nature, by re-acting to it, that humanity came out of animality. However, Hegel, then Marx and Engels, were the first to present humanity as a product of its generic activity. I am referring you to Engels' *Dialectic of Nature* and to a posthumous work by Marx, entitled *Alienated Labor*.[43] Pierre Teilhard de Chardin, himself a paleontologist, took up and reinforced this thesis. But this is not the whole story. "Man, some say, is that being through which all existents are revealed, he is the revealer of things." Unlike Gaetan Picon, I do not see this "formula" as being "ambiguous."[44] Already in *Alienated Labor*, Marx explained that it is our senses, educated by the hand and the brain, which enrich nature – which has thereby become "a part of human consciousness." Marx's successors – I am thinking of Husserl and Heidegger, but also of Sartre and Teilhard de Chardin – can be credited for insisting on the virtues of the *spoken word* – that Marx and Engels had mentioned under the name "language," by the way – as founding, or more accurately perhaps, as revealing, coinciding with the being.

I will not insist on the convergence existing between contemporary Humanism and, in the guise of myth, Black-African Humanism: both have the same conception of the role, as of the genesis, of human beings. *Nommo*, the Man-Word, does not create, but helps creation; *Nommo* does not create being, but reveals it. Through religion, morals, and art.

I do not need to insist either on the *religious fact*, which is a given of contemporary world. The trials of certain Soviet writers are the best proof that *Holy Russia* is not dead. The Second Vatican Council, in which the Third World, and Black Africa in particular, have played a significant role of humanization, was the best way to defend the divine, transcendental character of religion against the too logical and too juridical interpretations of those European theologians who are inclined to put religion into formulas, into capsules.

No need, finally, to insist on the humanization of contemporary morals. There too, the evolution of the Catholic Church is characteristic since, in the Third World for instance, it gives primacy to the spirit of productivity over the spirit of poverty, and to charity over chastity. It is significant that last year, in that Eastern Africa where the first humans arose, Pope Paul VI spoke highly of Negritude.

But it is still with art, the expansion of which coincides with the entry of Europe and America into a civilization of leisure, that the convergence between the two humanisms turns into a symbiosis. We all know well enough, nowadays, how the artists of the Paris School – painters, then sculptors, met with Black Art at the beginning of the century and worked on assimilating its virtues, as the European musicians, in turn, enriched themselves with Black music through the American detour. And we would not be complete if we did not mention the general influence exerted by the studies of ethnologists who specialized in the civilizations of Asia, America and Africa. Now among these, Black-African civilization is, indisputably, the most remote from the European model.

After having read my article on "Black-African Esthetics" in the journal *Diogène*,[45] the painter Soulages told me, by way of commentary: "It is the very aesthetics of the twentieth century." I could say, in turn, that the aesthetics of the Paris School expresses, in modern terms, Black-African aesthetics. I was convinced of it even more while reading last month, in the Parisian weekly journal *L'Express*, an article by Pierre Schneider, which is significantly entitled, "Matisse, the Painter of Emotion."[46] The article has retained my attention because Matisse was, along with Picasso, the greatest painter of the Paris School; because Schneider is the organizer of the biggest show ever of Matisse's works – painting, sculpture, drawing –, which is currently being held at the Grand Palais; but above all, because the traits that have been retained as characteristic of Matissian art are the very traits of Black art.

And, in the first place, its *utility* as a technique of essentialization: of participation in vital force. "I would like it to be useful," said Matisse about his work. And also: "the proper characteristic of modern art is to participate in our life." As Pierre Schneider underlines, "The essential was," for Matisse, who insisted on color, that through it, "he had found the old emotional ground of human beings." I would like to stop on the notion of *emotion*, which I have made the cornerstone of Negritude in the past, through the following formula – for which some people have blamed me: "emotion is Black as reason is Greek." Of course, I was schematizing, but the truth of the idea remains. I explained it in my lecture to the *Second Congress of Black Artists and Writers*,[47] starting with the definition that Sartre gives in his *Outline for a Theory of Emotions*: "a sudden fall of consciousness in the world of magic."[48] I know, there is a physical, animal reaction to emotion, but in the end, it is actually a consciousness disorder, which comes down from the world of visible and clear things to that of invisible and confused things, or from the world of static appearances to that of dynamic realities: from the world of the eye-reason to that of the embrace-reason. Schneider is indeed very well aware of that, since he writes: "The art that is founded on intelligence identifies things; the art that is founded on emotion identifies itself to things. The work of art is no longer a discourse on a subject, but a dialogue with it. Imitation gives place to participation." *Participation*, the keyword of Negritude.

It is the power of emotion and the will to participation that explain Matisse's renunciation of the techniques of classical painting born from the Renaissance, and his adoption of this then very special style that I can only qualify as "Negro." Modern painting abandons "gradations, models, shadows, perspective, everything that allows for the illusion of space, volume and weight"[49]: the illusion of objective truth. He therefore abandons visual realism in order to create a subjective painting, born out of emotion and producing, not pleasure for the mind, but joy – often solemn, even anguished – for the soul. He thus simplifies forms, which is to say drawing, to substitute for it colors – albeit flat colors. As in Black-African painting-sculpture, whose essential characteristic, once again, is to be *rhythmical.*

As we said, it is not a matter of representing this reality of the Renaissance, where everything is a distinct object, where each element of the object is placed next to the other, separate and different; rather, it is a matter of *re-creating* the world of internal reality, where everything is linked to everything, where everything participates in everything in an identificatory similitude or in a complementary difference. It is a matter of rendering the ultimate reality of the universe, which is the *inter-action* of vital forces: *rhythm*. This is why Matisse simplifies drawing and color to make them more powerful. At the same time, repetition and opposition of the lines (straight and curved) and colors (in flat shades) give the painting its analogical images and rhythms: its rhythmical images, by which I define poetry. These are the anaphoras and chiasmas, alliterations and assonances of a word, the parallelisms and asymmetries that we noticed in Black-African poetry. With this difference, however, that the "thought figures" of Classical painting completely give way to "language figures." Paradoxically, that painting which tends toward abstraction is, for this very reason, the most *emotive*.

Like Black art and Celtic art, whose lineage in abstraction can be explained solely by their moving power. For by employing rhythmical signs that work as symbol-images, instead of photography-images, one has substituted a world of feeling-ideas for a world of objects; for a world of intelligible evidence, a world of forces that are obscure, yet fecund: *creative.*

Conclusion

If I have compared Negritude to contemporary Humanism, it was, as you can guess, to arrive at a positive conclusion. We had already started to formulate this proposition in the Latin Quarter, during the years before the Second World War: we, the Negritude militants. It was not, it is not a matter of racism, but of pan-human Humanism which, as such, is directed toward all races, all continents, but in the first place to White Europeans and to Black-Africans who, because they are the most remote, are also the most complementary as civilizations. We know that colonization is a universal phenomenon which, besides its negative aspects, has some positive aspects. Especially since, from the advent of *Homo Sapiens*, when people meet they fight, but they do not annihilate each other: they cross-breed. And above all: they cross-breed their civilizations. This is the most important thing, for the only true culture is that of the *Soul.*

Today, thanks to the perfecting and multiplication of the means of communication, the world is contracting and human beings are drawn closer. If the old process had kept going, the result would have been a general exchange of blood, ideas and techniques. Now it indeed seems that on the one hand, biological mixing – the least important – happens naturally, even in the United-States, even in South Africa, despite numerous prohibitions; on the other hand, however, it seems that cultural mixing – which started at the beginning of the century – is on its way to being bridled by opposing imperialisms, each of which wants to impose their particular civilization as the "universal civilization." We, Negritude militants, have had the opportunity to discuss that issue with the *European Society for Culture.* It was in Rome, before 1960, the year in which many African countries became independent. It gave our thesis its true dimension, which is cultural. This thesis is the following: in no way should Europe impose its civilization on the world, as "universal civilization," even though we are the first to recognize the fecund power of some of its values, such as the spirit of method and organization, where rationality means efficiency. But all of us together – all continents, races and nations – should build the *Civilization of the Universal*, to which each particular civilization will bring its most creative, because most complementary, values.

The civilization of the twenty-first century – that today's civilization is preparing – will certainly be *over-industrial*, that is technological. It will be either *Humanism* or *Barbarism*, depending on whether the peoples of the Third World, and among them the Black peoples, will have contributed to it. Like Plato, Aristotle, the founder of European rationalism, gave priority to intuitive reason over discursive reason, all the while associating both. One forgets that too easily.

Notes

1 In English in the original. – trans.
2 In English in the original. – trans.
3 March 23, 1970.
4 Jean-Paul Sartre, "Orphée Noir", Preface to *Anthologie de la nouvelle poésie nègre et malgache de langue française*, edited by L. S. Senghor, (Paris: Presses Universitaires de France), p. xv; trans. "Black Orpheus" (chapter 7, page 119, this volume).
5 Erica Simon, *Reveil national et culture populaire en Scandinavie*, Paris: PUF, 1960.
6 "Orphée noir", p. xiv; trans. "Black Orpheus" (chapter 7, page 118, this volume.) – Ed.
7 Marcel Griaule, *Dieu d'eau. Entretiens avec Ogotemmeli*, (Paris: Fayard, 1948); trans. Ralph Butler, *Conversations with Ogotemmeli*, (Oxford: Oxford University Press, 1965). Also Geneviève Calame-Griaule, *Ethnologie et language. La parole chez les Dogon*, (Paris: Gallimard, 1965), pp. 93–103.
8 I mean by "existent" (*existant*), that which is alive, whereas "being" (*étant*) must be understood in its more general sense as a contingent element of *Being* (*Être*).
9 Alfred Croiset and Maurice Croiset, *Manuel d'histoire de la littérature grecque*, (Paris: Albert Fontemoing, 1900), p. 221; trans. George F. Heffelbower, *An Abridged History of Greek Literature*, (New York: Macmillan, 1904), p. 153. Trans. modified.
10 Alexis Kagamé, *La Philosophie bantu-rwandaise de l'être*, (Bruxelles: Académie royale des sciences coloniales, 1956).
11 Jahnheiz Jahn, *Muntu. Umrisse der neoafrikanischen Kultur*, (Dusseldorf-Cologne: Eugen Diedrichs, 1958); trans. Marjorie Grene, *Muntu. An Outline of the New African Culture*, (New York: Grove Press, 1961). Senghor cites the French translation: *Muntu, l'homme africain et le culture néo-africaine*, (Paris: Seuil, 1988).
12 Jahn, *Muntu*, (Paris), pp. 111–14. [Jahn, *Muntu*, pp. 104–8; English trans. *Muntu*, pp. 99–104. In subsequent notes the French edition will be cited first, followed by the German original and then the English translation. –Ed.]
13 Placide Tempels, *La philosophie bantoue*, translated from the Dutch by A. Rubbens, (*Présence Africaine*, 1949), p. 35; trans. A. Colin, *Bantu Philosophy*, (*Présence Africaine*, 1953), p. 35.
14 Geneviève Calame-Griaule, *Ethnologie et Language*, pp. 32–48.
15 Quoted by Louis-Vincent Thomas in "*Pour un programme d'études théoriques des religions et d'un humanisme africains*", (*Présence Africaine*, deuxième trimestre, 1961), p. 68.
16 Engelbert Mveng, *Les Sources grecques de l'histoire négro-africaine*. [This appears to be his thesis at the University of Lille from 1970. Republished by Présence Africaine (Paris) in 1972. –Ed.]
17 The last Congress of Africanist pre-historians, held in AddisAbaba, fixes this emergence at about 5,500,000 years before Christ.
18 Cf. preceding note.
19 "L' Afrique Equatoriale: Une Etape de l'Histoire de l'Humanité" in *Cahiers des Explorateurs*, Paris, December 1967.
20 Louis-Vincent Thomas, "Pour un programme d'études théoriques des religions", p. 61.
21 Cf. Geneviève Calame-Griaule, *Ethnologie et language*, pp. 48–57.
22 Camara Laye, *L'enfant noir*, (Paris: Plon, 1953); trans. James Kirkup, *The Dark Child*, (New York: Noonday Press, 1954).
23 In Senegal, young men call the beautiful young woman *baxai*, which is to say "goodness."
24 Cf. Geneviève Calame-Griaule, *Ethnologie et language*, chap. IV, "Physiologie de la fécondité par la parole", pp. 74–80.

25 The *New Negro* is the title of a famous anthology edited by Alain Locke (New York: Albert and Charles Buni, 1925). It included contributions by Zora Neale Hurston, Corntee Cullen, Claude McKay, Langston Hugues, James Weldon Johnson, E. Franklin Frazier, and W. E. B Du Bois. –Ed.

26 "Orphée noir", *Anthologie de la nouvelle poésie*, p. xv; trans. "Black Orpheus" (chapter 7, p. 119, this volume).

27 Senghor refers to the publication of Henri Bergson, *Essai sur les données immédiates de la conscience*, (Paris: Félix Alcan, 1889); trans. F. L. Pogson, *Time and Free Will: An Essay on the Immediate Data of Consciousness*, (New York: Macmillan, 1910) and Paul Claudel, *Tête d'or*, (New Haven: Yale University Press, 1919). –Ed.

28 Jacques Rueff, *Les Dieux et les rois*, (Paris: Hachette, 1968); trans. George Robinson and Roger Glémet, *The Gods and the Kings*, (New York: Macmillan, 1973).

29 "D'un style de l'esprit contemporain", which is the introduction to an anthology entitled, *Panorama des idées contemporaines*, (Paris: Gallimard, 1957).

30 "Je suis un nègre". Arthur Rimbaud, "Mauvais sang", *Une saison en enfer* in *Selected Verse*, ed. Oliver Bernard (Harmondsworth: Penguin, 1962), p. 308. –Ed.

31 Jahn, *Muntu*, (Paris), p. 105. [*Muntu*, p. 100; English trans., p. 96. –Ed.]

32 Gaetan Picon, *op. cit.*, p. 30.

33 Cf. Georges Gusdorf, *La parole*, (Paris: Presses Universitaires de France, 1953); trans. Paul T. Brockelman, *Speaking*, (Evanston: Northwestern University Press, 1965).

34 The quotations from Martin Heidegger are from "Logos" in *Vorträge und Aufsätze*, (Pfullingen: Neske, 1954), pp. 224–8; trans. D. F. Krell and F. A. Capuzzi, *Early Greek Thinking*, (New York: Harper and Row, 1975), pp. 74–7. Senghor uses the French translation by André Preau found in Pierre Trotignon's *Heidegger, sa vie, son oeuvre*, (Paris: Presses Universitaires de France, 1965), pp. 118–20. –Ed.

35 The quotations are from M. Heidegger, *Einführung in die Metaphysik*, (Tübingen: Max Nierreyer, 1953), pp. 130–31; trans. Ralph Manheim, *An Introduction to Metaphysics*, (New Haven, Yale University Press, 1959), pp. 171–2. Senghor used the translation by G. Khan reprinted by Trotignon, pp. 120–1.

36 Quoted by Pierre Trotignon in his *Heidegger, sa vie, son oeuvre*, p. 112 and p. 113.

37 *Les Dieux et les rois*, p. 313; trans, *The Gods and the Kings*, p. 246.

38 Quoted by Henri Guillemin in *L'arrière pensée de Jaurès*, (Paris: Gallimard, 1966), p. 22; after "La Dépèche de Toulouse", June 25, 1891.

39 Louis de Broglie, *Matière et lumière*, (Paris: Albin Michel, 1937), p. 75; trans. W. M. Johnston, *Matter and Light*, (New York: Norton, 1939), p. 71. Quoted by Rueff, *Les Dieux et les rois*, pp. 16–17; trans. *The Gods and the Kings*, p. 8.

40 Jacques Rueff, *Les Dieux et les rois*, p. 31; trans. *The Gods and the Kings*, pp. 19–20. Trans. Modified.

41 Jacques Maritain, *Humanisme intégral*, (Paris: Fernand Aubier, 1936); trans. Joseph W. Evans, *Integral Humanism*, (New York: Charles Scribner, 1968). –Ed.

42 Inventor of *Prospective*, the French-Senegalese mixed race Gaston Berger was born in Saint-Louis in Senegal at the end of the nineteenth century.

43 *La Revue socialiste*, Paris, 1947, p. 161. ["Die entfremdete Arbeit", in Karl Marx and Friedrich Engels, *Werke. Ergänzungsband*, pt. 1, (Berlin: Dietz, 1974), p. 515; trans. Rodney Livingstone and Gregor Benton, *Early Writings*, (Harmondsworth: Penguin, 1975), p. 327. –Ed.]

44 *Op. cit.*, 34

45 "L'esthétique négro-africaine", October 1956; trans. Elaine Halperin, "African-Negro Aesthetics", *Diogene* 18, Winter 1956, 23–38. Reprinted in *Liberté I* (Paris: Seuil, 1964), pp. 202–17.

46 April 20–26, 1970, pp. 44–7.

47 The lecture, entitled *Constitutive Elements for a Civilization of Black-African Inspiration*, was published by Présence Africaine publishers. Reprinted in *Liberté I*, pp. 252–86. [See especially, p. 260. Senghor introduced the formula in "Ce que l'homme noir apporte" in 1939. Reprinted *ibid.*, p. 24. –Ed.]

48 Jean-Paul Sartre, *Esquisse d'une théorie des émotions*, (Paris: Hermann, second ed., 1948), p. 49; trans. Philip Mairet, *Sketch for a Theory of Emotions*, (London: Methuen, 1962), p. 90. –Ed.

49 Pierre Schneider, *op. cit.*, p. 45

PART V

FANON AND THE PHENOMENOLOGY OF RACE

9

FANON, MERLEAU-PONTY AND THE DIFFERENCE OF PHENOMENOLOGY

Jeremy Weate

> *... but people who cannot suffer can never grow up, can never discover who they are. That man who is forced each day to snatch his manhood, his identity, out of the fire of human cruelty that rages to destroy it knows, if he survives his effort, and even if he does not survive it, something about himself and human life that no school on earth – and, indeed, no church – can teach. He achieves his own authority, and that is unshakeable. This is because, in order to save his life, he is forced to look beneath appearances, to take nothing for granted, to hear the meaning behind the words. If one is continually surviving the worst that life can bring, one eventually ceases to be controlled by a fear of what life can bring; whatever it brings must be borne.*
>
> James Baldwin *The Fire Next Time*

One of the most abiding criticisms of phenomenology in both latent and manifest form in recent philosophical discourse is that it must install itself on the basis of the repression of difference. Phenomenology across its authors is assumed to involve a fundamental ground or unity which engenders meaningful activity in the world. That which appears, the phenomenon, is violated by metaphysical over-generalization, "Sameness" or "presence" in the hands of phenomenologists, according to their critics, and this whether the epistemic frame is transcendental or somatic.[1]

The problem with such criticism is that it encourages a non-experiential notion of thought. Metaphysics or ontology then becomes a matter for "thinking," to which any experiential or lived dimension would be derivative or secondary. In the eighties, this reductionism developed a semiological-textual armature, chiefly through the influence of deconstruction in the States. What is interesting in the post-structuralist approach to "thinking difference" is that its relation to lived experience is never entirely disavowed. As with Heidegger and Levinas in earlier years, phenomenology is suppressed or sublated in the development of theory, but never entirely rejected. We remain unclear about the relations between the body, experience and thought.[2]

No wonder then that philosophy has been slow to participate in the burgeoning field of "race studies," and its various offshoots, including the more recent development of "whiteness" as a category of academic critique.[3] I will argue that whilst there *are* problems lurking in the assumptions phenomenology makes about its ground, these problems are not fatal to its future. As recent feminist thinkers have discovered, on the contrary, an encounter with phenomenology, particularly the thought of Maurice Merleau-Ponty, is *needed* today in order to re-establish a relation between lived experience and thought.[4] In order to challenge a universalist approach to phenomenology and open up a philosophy of race, I shall display one of the profoundest critiques of phenomenology offered this century, that of Frantz Fanon in his paper *The Lived Experience of the Black.* It has been said that Fanon is not "a terribly sophisticated phenomenologist" – well, I am not sure whether sophistication ought to be a virtue of this discipline.[5] As I shall show, in fact Fanon's critique of phenomenology quickly exposes the core of its problematic relation to difference. Fanon's text therefore in my view provides a corrective to phenomenology, at the same time as showing how the theorization of lived experience that is its source can reveal the key issues at work between agency, history and the world, and perhaps most fundamentally, the possibilities for justice.

★

Fanon's most significant philosophical influence is often taken to be the existential phenomenology of Sartre. In particular, the connection has often been made that Fanon's thought is closely connected to issues of authenticity and bad-faith and the power of being-for-others.[6] Whilst Sartre's shadow is undoubtedly cast across many pages of a text such as *Black Skin, White Masks*, it is important to register that Fanon was also engaged in a dialogue with Merleau-Ponty.[7] I will claim that Merleau-Ponty's inclusive notion of "world" is both the point of criticism for Fanon and the source of the construction of his ideal of "disalienation."[8] Only by looking at the implicit dialogue between Sartre and Merleau-Ponty that Fanon enacts will we be able to comprehend Fanon's politics of difference. As Fanon's method in *Black Skin, White Masks* is in part phenomenological, an excursus into the chapter entitled *The Lived Experience of the Black*, and an examination of the final chapter, *En guise de conclusion*, will lead to a radical phenomenology of difference. It will also lead to a reformulated genealogy of political ideals, grounded in a phenomenology of the body.

It is not difficult to show how *The Lived Experience of the Black* involves a dialogue with Merleau-Ponty. The most obvious references are given in the first few pages of the text, with Fanon's substitution of Merleau-Ponty's notion of "corporeal schema" (schéma corporel) first of all for the "schéma historico-racial" and secondly in terms of the "schéma épidermique racial." Put briefly, the corporeal schema in Merleau-Ponty's work refers to the body's agency and its work in relating to and disclosing the historical world. At all stages in his oeuvre, Merleau-Ponty espouses a pre-dualistic ontology which affirms the reproductive synergy between body and world. He writes,

> We grasp external space through our bodily situation. A "corporeal or postural schema" gives us at every moment a global, practical, and implicit notion of the relation between our body and things, of our hold on them. A system of possible movements, or "motor projects," radiates from us to our environment. Our body is not in space like things; it inhabits or haunts space. It applies itself to space like a hand to an instrument, and when

> we wish to move about we do not move the body as we move an object. We transport it without instruments as if by magic, since it is ours and because through it we have direct access to space. For us the body [. . .] is our expression in the world, the visible form of our intentions.[9]

The corporeal schema lies *between* the body and the world, as that which engenders communication between one and the other. This does not imply an exchange between two independently subsisting entities suspended from temporality. Rather, this communication, which Merleau-Ponty elsewhere describes as "more ancient than thought" ("plus vieille que la pensée")[10] is the moment where body and world reorder each other according to a "perpetual contribution"[11] of reciprocal transfer. Being "embedded" within a cultural-historical horizon therefore means, in Merleau-Pontyan terms, that that horizon itself is open to be altered, transformed or disrupted. For example, no one could separate the history of the guitar from its players. Somebody comes along, "learns" the guitar and manipulates it as never before, and the history of guitar music is altered. With fingers and stance, their body communicates with the guitar through a pre-thetic schema that opens up the parameters of possibility (and therefore the history) of the instrument,[12] at the same time as transforming the player's life. Moreover, even those who will not change the history of guitar music themselves are liable to be "altered" as their practice develops and that music communicates itself through their increasingly expressive being.

Ultimately, Merleau-Ponty's concept of the corporeal schema reveals the relation between agency, freedom and temporality. For Merleau-Ponty, the corporeal capacity of the body allows for a "communication" with the expressive patternings of the cultural traditions to which it belongs or has attached itself. Within the interplay between body and world prior to intellectual representation, the possibility of the creative inflection between both engenders a corporealized conception of freedom. The body is "free" to the extent that it can participate in the transformation of its expressive horizons. As with the guitar player, this conception of freedom entails a fundamental relation to the historical: being free involves the body's capacity through expression to transfigure (and be transfigured by) what is given as history. In this way, Merleau-Ponty's notion of the corporeal schema leads implicitly to a conception of history as characterized essentially by *difference*. Each moment of a culture's transfer across time through the agency of bodies is at the same time the site of its own differentiation. Moreover, there is therefore no "originary" moment to any culture: every culture that attempts to assert its sameness across time has to repress the difference at work in its origin in every present. Although there is some ambiguity in Merleau-Ponty's thought here, it is on the whole the case that he posits this relation between agency and historical freedom as a condition of *habituation*. In other words, it is a matter of habit and inhabitation that we perpetually contribute to the differentiation of our historical world (our "habitus"), from one moment's action to the next.

We are now in a position to begin to explain Fanon's substitution of terms. In *The Lived Experience of the Black*, Fanon's opening argument is that a phenomenology of blackness cannot be understood in the context of the "Black among his own."[13] It is only in the encounter with whiteness and more specifically the white imagination that an analysis of the experience of skin difference, of being the black other, can be undertaken. For Fanon at home in the Antillean setting of Martinique, the coercion and internalization of racial inferiority could not be encountered as a form of experience. Before entering the "white world," Fanon was content with "an intellectual comprehension of these tensions."[14] It was only after Fanon moved to Paris that he began to be aware of the preintellectualist dynamics of the interracial encounter. With the first explicit reference to Merleau-Ponty's terminology, Fanon writes,

> In the white world the man of color faces difficulties in the elaboration of his bodily schema.[15]

Fanon proceeds to explicate Merleau-Ponty's notion of corporeal schema in the following paragraph. He ends the paragraph with the summary statement,

> A slow construction of my self as a body in the midst of a spatial and temporal world, such seems to be the schema. It is not imposed on me; rather, it is a definitive structuring of the self and the world – definitive because in this way an effective dialectic is settled between my body and the world.[16]

Fanon clearly concurs initially with Merleau-Ponty's insight that the self and the world are constructed through the work of the *schéma corporel*. However, his detour through phenomenology is adopted in order to theorize the interracial encounter of black bodies in the west. It immediately becomes clear that in this case Merleau-Ponty's terminology is inadequate,

> Below the corporeal schema I created a historico-racial one. The elements that I used were provided to me not by "residual sensations and perceptions primarily of a tactile, vestibular, kinesthetic, and visual order," but by the other, the White, who has woven me out of a thousand details, anecdotes and stories.[17]

The move announced here against the primordial unity of the perceived world in Merleau-Ponty's phenomenology is dramatic. Fanon is suggesting that Merleau-Ponty's conception of the corporeal schema, hitherto the iteractive locus of the reciprocal emergence of self and world, is undercut or undermined in the case of the black subject in Europe. Rather than ascribing to an inclusive conception of the field of corporeal communication, Fanon points to a fundamental asymmetry between blacks and whites and their active relation to "the world" in Europe. In the interracial encounter, the White is able to participate in the schematization of the world, whilst the Black may not, for his skin difference closes down the possibility of free agency. A white *mythos* inserts itself between the black body and its self-image, becoming the "elements used" in a reflexive understanding of black subjectivity. In contesting the terms of Merleau-Ponty's account of bodily freedom, Fanon provides a genealogy of the existential *unfreedom* of the black body in the racialized encounter. His account in *The Lived Experience of the Black* operates as a non-linear narrative, a scrambled descent into hell with ever more entrenched levels of alienation and the black body-in-pain in operation. Fanon introduces his piece as "the fragments put together by another self." I shall now highlight aspects of the schizoid path of this descent.

Fanon sets up the historico-racial schema by way of a simple narrative which recurs as a fragmented refrain throughout the rest of the essay. It is the experience of a white child saying to his mother on a train, "Tiens, un nègre!" ("Look, a Negro!") This is the overture to alienation for the black subject. To begin, the experience is taken lightly. "Look, a Negro!" It was true. I was amused."[18] This amusement is annulled as the child continues badgering his mother, this time adding to the expression of the gaze a component of fear. The fear of the child is read as the outcome of all that Fanon's skin represents. The child is no longer merely pointing to the skin difference as a form of naive wonder at a rare site – the curiosity of seeing (perhaps for the first time close up) a black human being. The child, this allegedly pre-coding type, has in actual fact already imbibed various presuppositions beyond the simple physicality of skin difference. That is, the black skin is already operating as a kind of metonym for the child, representing a specific imaginary-historical construction of otherness.

> I could not be amused anymore because I already knew of the legends, the stories, history, and especially, the *historicity* I learned from Jaspers. Then the corporeal schema collapsed, assailed at various points, yielding to a racial-epidermal schema.[19]

The ontological violation of the train episode is therefore given a more dramatic context because of the gaze being expressed by a *child*. The power of the gaze described resides in its demonstration that racist attitudes in Europe have permeated to the level of the "innocent." More significantly still, the careful reader will have noted that this last passage marks a subtle but important slippage, from the "historico-racial" schema to the "racial-epidermal schema." The passage from the corporeal schema to the "historico-racial" schema is intended to reveal that Merleau-Ponty's claim in favor of free historical agency on the part of able-bodied beings *tout court* is false. How then is this further passage from the historico-racial to the racial-epidermal schema to be understood? In my view, the slippage is Fanon's attempt to proved a *genealogy* of racial essentialism. To begin with, his analysis closely resembles the Sartrean model for alienation:

> I existed in triplicate: I was occupying space. I moved toward the other . . . and the evanescent other, hostile yet not opaque, transparent, absent, disappeared. Nausea . . .[20]

Here Fanon reproduces Sartre's threefold model of the subject in relation to others. The subject is first of all an outlook upon the world, the locus of perception, a *pour soi*. In encountering the other, the subject is forced however to acknowledge a view of itself from the outside, as a contingent difference within the world, as an "other." The subject therefore becomes aware of its "being-for-others." This tension between a subjective and an objective account of the subject's embodiment must be resolved, for as it stands the two views are opposed. As is well known, for Sartre this resolution, the dream of a *for itself in-itself* is a futile one.[21] The "double consciousness" schism between being experienced as an other in relation to one's own interior experience can only lead to the unresolved *third* modality of nausea and abjection. The "occupation of space" therefore refers to the moment of being-for-others, when the body begins to lose its internally constituted freedom and is reduced to a lump presence through exteriorization. Fanon's response, that of "moving towards the other," is the response of refusing the abjection of physical reductionism by attempting to adopt the constitutive agency of the other – hence the *movement* towards the other. The other's rejection then appears in the form of a non-recognition, a fading-away. The black subject can neither accept an internally derived body-image nor the exterior view, at the same time as being refused the final possibility of adopting the exterior view as a form of agency in-itself. The resulting despair and sickness is not left alone however, for there is still the existential framework of a caricatured history:

> I was all at once responsible for my body, for my race, for my ancestors. I ran an objective gaze over myself, discovering my blackness, my ethnic characteristics; and then I was deafened by cannibalism, intellectual deficiency, fetishism, racial defects, slave-ships, and above all, above all else, "Sho' good Banania."[22]

The gaze of the child is the domino-effect, which, with the experience of nausea, leads to a questioning of bodily freedom and the paralysis of agency. Instead of the body being located in the present of a "communication more ancient than thought," of being the site of a possible inflection of the cultural givens of bodily patternings, the black "subject" experiences his own skin as the metonym for a parodic primitivism. In contrast to an autonomous relation to the reproductive inflection of history which Merleau-Ponty's corporeal schema suggests, history is cast upon the black subject in the moment of despair as a being-for-others. Black skin is indissoluly connected to a history constructed by a white imaginary. The black subject finds himself no longer in the present of possible transformation, but thrown back into a past that was never his own. Fanon writes, "The Negro, however sincere, is the slave of the past."[23] Fanon therefore is showing that he is in strong agreement with Merleau-Ponty's insight that freedom is the freedom to inflect the world, and to enter into a corporeal dialogue with historical grounds. But Fanon's point is that this freedom is expressed to the black subject in the form of a *denial*. As Fanon's analysis of his own experience shows, the politics of exclusion embodied in the child's gaze disables the corporeal schema. This disabling is at the same time an alienation of the subject from the possibility of historical freedom in the present.

It is at this juncture that we can understand more fully the grounds for the slippage between the historico-racial schema and the epidermal schema. The former moment marks the inauguration of being *pour soi* succumbing to the European framework of being for others. The body image of the black subject is spliced asunder by historical means: an autonomously constructed self-image is thwarted by a fantastical parody of history. The entrance into Europe of black subjects is at the same time a movement into an all-encompassing frame of historical reference that black agency can do little to resist. The second moment, that of the *racial-epidermal* schema, occupies a later stage in psychosomatic disintegration and alienation. Instead of remaining an *historical* ascription of identity (albeit a false one supplied by a white mythos), the schema becomes "naturalized" as a *condition* of skin. The epidermal marks the stage where historical construction and contingency is effaced and replaced with the facticity of flesh. The colour of skin now appears to be intrinsically significant. With the outset of epidermalization, we are at the edge of being-for-others sedimenting into an essence, a "fact" of blackness. Fanon is therefore demonstrating that essentialism is a discourse derived from a perversive repression of history. By marking the two stages of the "historico-racial" and then the "racial-epidermal", he is therefore contesting the view that essentialism, and in particular black essentialism, is grounded in a biological problematic. For Fanon, the essentialization of blackness is the product of a concealed perversion of history. It is only once this concealment is consolidated (through epidermalization) that questions concerning the *biological* ground of race arise. The distinction he makes between two stages of schematization or epistemic enframing therefore allow biologistic discourses around race to be seen as phenomena derivative upon a prior perversion of history that is subsequently concealed.

Although it may sound initially a strange suggestion, in the midst of Fanon's painful genealogy of alienation and essentialism, I find it hard to resist detecting the emergent dynamics of hope. In a similar manner to Foucault's investigations into the birth of disciplinarity in modernity being at once implacable *and* contingent, Fanon's narrative of alienation marks the path of what has been done and can therefore be *undone*. As I understand it, the function of a genealogical history is to expose the ideology of historical logic and necessity as the reified legitimation of force. If a genealogical undercurrent to Fanon's text gathers plausibility, then its facility is to expose the processes of black alienation in order to prepare the ground for their *unravelling*. Fanon's hope then is that there is no necessity or inevitability in the corporeal schema ceding to the racial-epidermal schema. However, within *The Lived Experience of the Black*, this subterranean movement of resistance is masked to an extent by Fanon's desire to remain faithful to the profound sense of hopeless alienation at work in the black existential situation.

For instance, later in the essay, this sentiment is expressed succinctly in two words, "Too late."[24] From this mournful shibboleth everything that pertains to Fanon's analysis of existential dread unfolds. The black subject enters the arena of interpersonal encounters in the colonial situation with his or her history already constructed and given. The already given history, the parodic primitivism most powerfully represented by cannibalism, is the form of the denial of ascribing historical agency to the black subject. "Everything has been foreseen, discovered, proven, taken advantage of. My nervous hands rein in nothing; the vein is exhausted. Too late!"[25] Given a temporal expression, nausea renders impossible the simplest bodily gesture. Heidegger's elementary criteria for being-in-the-world, the categories of being "ready-to-hand" (*Vor-handen*) and "present-at-hand" (*Zu-handen*) are denied. At the brink of the decomposition of self and world, all Fanon's hands can do is shake. The limit point of this incapacitated alienation comes when Fanon finally acquiesces to the onslaught of the alienating gaze and *internalizes* it. At two points in his essay Fanon describes this moment with acute force,

> On that day, disoriented and incapable of being outside with the other, the White who unmercifully imprisoned me, I took myself far away, very far away indeed from my being-there, thus making myself an object.[26]

> I sit down at the fire and I discover my livery.[27]

Here, the white imaginary perspective intrudes to the extent that it becomes a self-inflicted inferiorization. Again however, in the midst of despair, the flower of hope appears. For Fanon is clear that the black subject is not merely an unwilling victim in the procession towards incapacitated alienation. There is then a *complicity* at work in the reification of a parodic and inferiorized black body-image. As Fanon writes later in the *Black Skin, White Masks*, "I have ceaselessly striven to show the Negro man that in a sense he makes himself abnormal."[28] The black subject mimics the white gaze, and in a panopticon-like manner, the white other no longer needs to be there.

⋆

Fanon's analysis of black *Erlebnis* under colonialism and imperialism clearly deeply problematizes orthodox phenomenology, and in particular the thought of Merleau-Ponty. The equality that Merleau-Ponty assumed exists across all able-bodied beings is nullified and rendered naïve by the black experience. In *The Lived Experience of the Black*, Fanon pushes this critique further, in the direction of problematizing a more fundamental category of western thought – ontology itself:

> When one has admitted once and for all that ontology leaves existence aside, one sees why it does not allow for understanding the being of the Black. It is not a question of the Black being black anymore, but rather of his being black opposite the White.[29]

For Fanon, the encounter between "being" and difference leads to the dehiscence of ontology itself. Fanon repeats the Levinasian move here of construing ontology as the field of the Same.[30] Ontology is therefore revealed as a strategy of legitimation for the repression of autonomous difference. More particularly, for Fanon, ontology conceals the work of the white mythos in *constructing* the image of blackness which black people in his view have subsequently adopted in a reflexive comprehension of "black being."

Undoubtedly, Fanon is correct in asserting the violence wrought by ontology and its phenomenological variant in the repression and concealment of intrinsic difference. It is less certain however that any subsequent appeals to either a specific form of embodied experience or to hope can do without them. What is required is less a rejection of ontology and phenomenology outright and more a critique of the means to which they have been put. My argument is then that any assertion of the *difference* of black lived experience cannot be undertaken without recourse to the terms of a phenomenological ontology. This is partially acknowledged in the conclusion to *Black Skin, White Masks*, where Fanon writes, "I am a part of Being to the degree that I go beyond it."[31] Far from a phenomenological ontology necessarily demarcating (however unconsciously) the community of being that excludes or represses difference, the demand is that ontology itself is rethought (the implicit suggestion of Fanon here) as *differential*. Ontology would therefore mark the boundary of the same and the other. In an older terminology, ontology is re-cast as involving *transcendence within immanence*.[32] In this way "being" as a unified ontological category can no longer cash out in epistemological terms as the *a priori* given conditionals for experience. The phenomenon is not disclosed on the basis of the assumption of a unified transcendental ground. As we shall see, on the contrary, being is deferred and reconstituted as the form of the ideal, and the conditions of possibility for experience are pluralized. Within the present, ontology would always therefore involve difference – the interplay of immanence and transcendence. What alternatives are there to this solution? If a phenomenological ontology were delegitimated by the experience of difference, difference itself would be rendered impossible to thinking – nothing would be available to thought (save perhaps different strategies of immanence or different forms of will to power). The phenomenon of difference must be therefore understood as that which defers (and deters) being. But this argument moves far too quickly. What needs to be accounted for first of all in any phenomenological ontology of difference is the possibility of maintaining the difference of lived experience.

One of the sharpest commentators on the differences of experience that result from different forms of embodiment is James Baldwin. In a short essay called "Stranger in the Village," he recounts his experiences staying in a Swiss village. Towards the end of the piece, he considers the hypothetical differences between himself and the villagers in terms of varying interpretations of a work of architecture:

> The cathedral at Chartres, I have said, says something to the people of this village which it cannot say to me; but it is important to understand that this cathedral says something to me which it cannot say to them. Perhaps they are struck by the power of the spires, the glory of the windows; but they have known God, after all, longer than I have known him, and in a different way, and I am terrified by the slippery bottomless well to be found in the crypt, down which heretics were hurled to death, and by the obscene, inescapable gargoyles jutting out of the stone and seeming to say that God and the devil can never be divorced.[33]

Although the cathedral is situated within a common temporal horizon between villagers and Baldwin, the difference of embodiment divides the way in which it is revealed to both as an experiential/imaginary construct. Hence, a common horizon of terms fragments into different worlds of experience. In this way, everything that reveals itself in the world is liable to double readings across embodied difference (of race, class, gender, sexuality...). Works of art, places, stories, traditions are all liable to be fragmented by contestive interpretations. As these counter-interpretations themselves are revealed in the face of the normative view, they therefore tend to reflect the forces of exclusion back to the subject of the experience. In this way, counter-interpretations repeat the pain of marginality. As Fanon writes, on the last page of *The Lived Experience of the Black*,

> Impossible to go to the movies without running into myself. I wait for myself. At the interval, and right before the movie starts, I wait for myself. Those in front of me look at me, spy on me, wait for me. A Negro groom is going to appear. My heart turns my head.[34]

With these experiences of difference and the "pain of interpretations" in mind, we are now in a position to work through the problem of expressing a desire for a community of being without violating difference. In *The Lived Experience of the Black*, Fanon expresses this desire as follows,

> All I wanted was to be a man among other men. I had wanted to arrive smooth and young in a world that was ours, that together we would have erected.[35]

For Fanon, this redemption from the gaze is articulated in terms of a transformative historicality, outlined forcefully in the final chapter of *Black Skin, White Masks, En guise de conclusion.* Freedom for Fanon is first of all freedom from the weight of the past,

> The problem considered here is one of time. Those Negroes and white men will be disalienated who refuse to let themselves be sealed away in the materialized Tower of the Past.[36]

Instead of being mesmerized by the past, the present is attended to as the site of possible transformation and disalienation. The weight of history has therefore to be dismissed. "I will not make myself the man of any past. I do not want to exalt the past at the expense of my present and of my future."[37] The only past that is legitimate for the purposes of freedom is a *universal* past. "I am a man, and what I have to recapture is the whole past of the world."[38] In a series of passionate pronouncements, Fanon reiterates this desire for an unburdened universality, grounded in the present of agency:

> I am not a prisoner of history. I should not seek there for the meaning of my destiny.[39]
>
> In the world through which I travel, I am endlessly creating myself.[40]
>
> I am not the slave of the Slavery that dehumanized my ancestors.[41]
>
> I am my own foundation.[42]

Here then, Fanon argues that the present is the site of a potential rupture of what is given to have occurred: the unbearable *weight* of historical being. Fanon's redemption from the past involves not responding or *reacting* to it. Freedom for Fanon involves the active inflection of the "now," rather than a reactive valorization or reproduction of what has been given. History, as the framework of cultural origins (and therefore projections), is denied.

In these terms, it is not possible to avoid parallels with the account of the relations between history, agency and freedom found in Merleau-Ponty's *Phenomenology of Perception*, in particular with the latter's notion of a pre-personal communication between the body and its habitus opening up the moment of freedom and the denial of fixed historical origins. Fanon transcends a locked Sartrean dialectical logic by relativizing history within the terms of an active present. Fanon's "endless recreation of himself," his existence as his own foundation, are the echo of Merleau-Ponty's "resumption at every moment" of the "perpetual contribution of his bodily being."[43] In both philosophers, rather than a mere moment within the dialectical process, freedom is a function of the present, as the site of a possible transformation of the given. In such a manner, the linearity of the past is broken, and the future is opened to difference, the difference of a transcendence of the same, participating in being by going beyond it.

There is however an important, if subtle difference between the two versions of historical freedom. For Merleau-Ponty, as we have seen, the possibility of active inflection in and of the present is given with the ease of a "perpetual contribution."

It would seem that the present is the site of rupture of the given's linearity, and that this rupture is guaranteed merely by the motility of the agent, as a matter of habit. In contrast, Fanon's freedom from the past involves a great deal more effort and resolve. For Fanon, transformation of the present requires something like a critical resistance to the dominating episteme – an active denial of the mythos that intervenes in the formation of body-images. Without that, black subjectivity in particular is threatened with the weight of a past which disavows and disables the possibility of transforming the present. Once again, this weight cannot simply be off-loaded or deflected through a sort of ontological judo – the structures of complicity and internalization must be negotiated and worked through as stages on the way to an autonomously grounded differentiation. In contrast, the lack of a critical resistance amongst those who approximate to the norm in Europe (white, male, straight, able-bodied) results in a complicit reproduction of the framework that privileges them through the ease of their actions. In this light, Merleau-Ponty's reflections on the body's relation to freedom risk being blind to the aporias of difference. Fanon's critique of phenomenology teaches us that the universal is the end of the struggle, not that which precedes it. *Black Skin White Masks* ends with the most solemn of vows to a vigilancy of the corporeal,

> My final prayer:
> O my body, make of me always a man who questions![44]

As a result of my presentation of the encounter between Merleau-Ponty and Fanon, the phenomenological ontology of difference introduced above can now be clarified. Being, operating as a unified given (Merleau-Ponty's "one single world"), is incompatible with an agonistic hermeneutics engendered by bodily difference. As a temporo-historical horizon, being conventionally discloses difference only through the disjunctive movement of *time*, not through the difference of bodies.[45] Thus, in the case of Baldwin's cathedral, there would be no way of accounting for differences in the way the building is experienced or imagined, or rather, any such explanation would not be respected as of philosophical merit. Against this, through the characterization of ontology under development, each present becomes differentiated by different forms of embodiment, as the phenomena disclosed in that present are in turn revealed differently according to corporeal variation. Through our bodies, we belong to relatively different worlds, with different forms of visibility and invisibility, history and value being thereby disclosed. The merging of these worlds through encounters of difference leads inevitably to contested comprehensions of the phenomenon. Being therefore must, in order to maintain this phenomenological plurality and not *repress* it, re-situate itself as a *spatio-temporal* horizon, or rather as the ideal. What is is what is to come. As Fanon says, we are indeed a part of being to the degree that we go beyond it. Being, as the possibility of (comm)unity, becomes the form of the ideal. Moreover, precisely because it cannot be given and does not function as the *a priori*, being is therefore an *ethical* ideal – it is the ideal of a community that is yet to exist and yet *ought* to exist, as the fulfillment of transcendence within immanence. In contrast, the extent to which a unified world is imposed as the episteme of the present marks the extent to which difference itself will be violated. The ethics of community is therefore the inverse of the repression of difference. In order to maintain this difference (and strive for community), it behooves us as participants in difference to be mindful of the ever-present possibility of a conflict of interpretations. Although the potentials of the present for inflectional agency have been stressed until now, it must be stated that this community has an inescapably *futural* dimension. The project of a community of difference, between those who have nothing in common, is a project that comes *after* experience. Community is unveiled *a posteriori*. It is only therefore possible to affirm a community that is forever "yet to come."[46] Any community of being is therefore a project, an openly processual entity forever cast into the future as ongoing work.

How can we begin to work towards this community of being? On what basis can *communication* between different beings begin? In what way does this analysis bear upon relations between others in the present of agency? If the imaginary framework of being-for-others (most sharply represented by Fanon's child on the train) is refused, what is now to take its place across difference? Here, I can offer no more than a suggestion, an allusion to what may turn out to be a "new humanism:" we communicate with and move towards the other by dint of recognizing both their capacity and our own for *suffering*.[47] Fanon's *The Lived Experience of the Black* exemplifies this first step; as a testimony to affliction and psychic fragmentation it communicates the desire for community across difference. At the limit, although the other may look different, speak a language we do not understand, participate in rituals and practice that obey a different rationality to our own, regard the objects and artifacts in our world through a somatic lens that we cannot comprehend – we move toward each other through a common sentience and a shared capacity to suffer. In this sense, the grounds for hope lie where cultural juxtaposition is at its most vehement: in the contemporary metropolis. Richard Sennett ends his magisterial work on the fleshy history of the western city in this way,

> Lurking in the civic problems of a multi-cultural city is the moral difficulty of arousing sympathy for those who are Other. And this can only occur, I believe, by understanding why bodily pain requires a place in which it can be acknowledged, and in which its transcendent origins become visible. Such pain has a trajectory in human experience. It disorients and makes incomplete the self, defeats the desire for coherence; the body accepting pain is ready to become a civic body, sensible to the pain of another person, pains present together on the street, at last endurable – even though, in a diverse world, each person cannot explain what he or she is feeling, who he or she is, to the other.[48]

In this paper I have argued that Merleau-Ponty's phenomenology of the body risks privileging a relation between freedom, agency and historicality that ultimately violates the embodiment of difference such as that interposed by race. Fanon's *The Lived Experience of the Black* and the example drawn from Baldwin display forcefully how difference denies the possibility of an already given community and commonality between human subjects. However, as I have argued throughout, Fanon's critique does not by necessity condemn Merleau-Ponty's phenomenology to a violent ontology of the Same. Rather, Fanon's critique has been used to begin to develop an ontology of difference that lies as the hidden soil of Merleau-Ponty's text. Despite Fanon's strong reservations over the legitimacy of "ontology," I have argued that only on its terms can emancipatory strategies be thought through. The "communication more ancient than thought" of the *Phenomenology of Perception* in particular provides the most powerful and resourceful way of thinking embodied free agency grounded in the difference of the present. Only on the basis of a conceptual schema itself present in Merleau-Ponty's work can Fanon's critique result in a productive phenomenology of difference which repositions community as the Ideal, the deferred universal, and not the given.[49] As I have suggested, the work towards this community begins by allowing for the communication of pain across difference in this present. Thus, a critical awareness of embodied differences between the subject and the horizons of its being does not seek to denounce or renounce justice, community and a "new humanism" for the sake of irreducibility or a voluntaristic will-to-power. Rather, the phenomenologists' dream of uncovering a pre-thetic community is shown finally to be the goal of those who seek with vigilance to question their bodies in the present.

Notes

1 Among the key critical texts are Levinas' "Meaning and Sense" (in *Emmanuel Levinas: Basic Philosophical Writings*, Indiana University Press, 1996), Heidegger's "My Way to Phenomenology" (in *On Time and Being*, Harper and Row, 1972), and of course Derrida's early reading of Husserl, *Speech and Phenomena*, (Northwestern University Press, 1973).

2 See M. C. Dillon's book *Semiological Reductionism: A Critique of the Deconstructionist Movement in Postmodern Thought*, State University of New York Press, 1995.

3 The two key authors inaugurating this are Toni Morrison, specifically her text *Playing in the Dark: Whiteness and the Literary Imagination*, Picador, 1990 and the work of David Roediger.

4 For example in the work of Elizabeth Grosz in *Volatile Bodies*, Indiana University Press, 1994 and Gail Weiss *Body Images: Embodiment as Intercorporeality*, Routledge, 1999.

5 David Macey, "Fanon, phenomenology, race" p. 10 in *Radical Philosophy* no. 95 May/June 1999. Macey's impoverished comprehension of phenomenology leaves him searching for a biographical explanation as to why Fanon adopted its framework.

6 This is the tendency of Lewis R. Gordon's interpretation. See his book, *Fanon and the Crisis of European Man*, Routledge, 1995.

7 Gordon's book acknowledges the influence of Merleau-Ponty on Fanon, without developing the nature of the dialogue in depth. See p. 14. Also, in his essay "Fanon's Body of Black Experience" (in *Fanon: A Critical Reader*, Blackwell, 1996). Ronald A. T. Judy spends the first page discussing Markmann's problematic translation of the fifth chapter's title, including mentioning Robert's tracing of l'expérience vécue to Merleau-Ponty's translation of *Erlebnis*, as a prelude to relating Fanon's text to Hegel's concept of experience.

8 Merleau-Ponty writes, "...we must learn to find the communication between one consciousness and another in one and the same world. In reality, the other is not shut up inside my perspective of the world, because this perspective itself has no definite limits, because it slips spontaneously into the other's, and because both are brought together in the one single world in which we all participate as anonymous subjects of perception" (*Phenomenology of Perception*, Routledge, 1962, p. 253).

9 "An Unpublished Text by Maurice Merleau-Ponty: *A Prospectus of His Work*" in *The Primacy of Perception*, Northwestern University Press, 1964, p. 5.

10 *Phenomenology of Perception*, p. 254; *Phénoménologie de la Perception*, Editions Gallimard, 1990, p. 294.

11 *Phenomenology of Perception*, Ibid.

12 Contenders along the way include Charlie Christian, Wes Montgomery, Django Reinhardt, Jimmy Hendrix and Derek Bailey.
13 *The Lived Experience of the Black*, p. 184, this volume.
14 Ibid. p. 185.
15 Ibid. p. 185.
16 Ibid. p. 185.
17 Ibid. p. 185.
18 Ibid. p. 185.
19 Ibid. p. 185.
20 Ibid. p. 185.
21 In *Being and Nothingness*, Sartre writes, "Everything happens therefore as if the in-itself and the for-itself were presented in a state of disintegration in relation to an ideal synthesis. Not that the integration has ever *taken place* but on the contrary precisely because it is always indicated and always impossible." (Sartre, 1958: 623).
22 *The Lived Experience of the Black*, pp. 185–6, this volume.
23 *Black Skin, White Masks*, Pluto Press, London, 1986, p. 225.
24 *The Lived Experience of the Black*, p. 190, this volume.
25 Ibid. p. 190.
26 Ibid. p. 186.
27 Ibid. p. 186.
28 *Black Skin, White Masks*, p. 225.
29 Ibid. p. 1.
30 Levinas writes, "Western philosophy has most often been an ontology: a reduction of the other to the same by interposition of a middle and neutral term that ensures the comprehension of being." *Totality and Infinity*, Duquene University Press, 1969, p. 43.
31 *Black Skin, White Masks*, p. 229.
32 This argument for a reformulation of ontology embracing difference is developed at length in my PhD thesis, *Phenomenology and Difference: the Body, Architecture and Race*, Warwick University, 1998.
33 James Baldwin, "Stranger in the Village" in *The Price of the Ticket*, Michael Joseph Ltd., 1985, p. 89.
34 *The Lived Experience of the Black*, p. 200, this volume.
35 Ibid. p. 186.
36 *Black Skin, White Masks*, p. 226.
37 Ibid. p. 226.
38 Ibid. p. 226.
39 Ibid. p. 229.
40 Ibid. p. 229.
41 Ibid. p. 230.
42 Ibid. p. 231.
43 *Phenomenology of Perception*, p. 254.
44 *Black Skin, White Masks*, p. 232.
45 This is in broad terms Heidegger's characterization of the relation between Being or the *Es gibt* and difference in *On Time and Being*, Harper and Row, 1972.
46 Through different means, I concur finally with a Derridean logic.
47 See Robert Bernasconi, "Casting the Slough: Fanon's New Humanism for a New Humanity" in *Fanon: A Critical Reader*. As an alternative to a humanism engendered by internal violence (the view subsequently favoured by Fanon), what is being suggested here is a humanism grounded in injustice and the body-in-pain of the other.

48 Richard Sennett, *Flesh and Stone: The Body and the City in Western Civilization*, Faber and Faber, 1994, p. 376.

49 Here, I must echo Lewis Gordon's cautionary note in *Fanon and the Crisis of European Man*, "... it is not our intent to continue the long tradition of treating the thoughts of black philosophers as derivative of white ones" (p. 14). I have only sought to show *parallels* in the opening towards strategies of emancipation, not lines of causality.

10

THE LIVED EXPERIENCE OF THE BLACK

Frantz Fanon

"Dirty nigger!" or simply, "Look, a Negro!"

I came into the world, anxious to see things give off a meaning, my soul filled with the desire to be at the origin of the world, and I discovered myself an object among other objects.

Locked up in this crushing objecthood, I turned beseechingly to the other. His liberating gaze, creeping over my body which was thereby suddenly smoothed out, gives me back a lightness that I had thought lost and, by removing me from the world, gives me back to the world. But over there, right when I was reaching the other side, I stumble, and through his movements, attitudes and gaze, the other fixes me, just like a dye is used to fix a chemical solution. I lost my temper and demanded an explanation... But nothing came. I exploded. Here are the fragments put together by another self.

As long as the Black is with his own, he will not have to experience his being for the other, except on the occasion of minor internal conflicts. There is of course the moment of the "Being-for-others", of which Hegel speaks, but ontology is unrealizable in a colonized and civilized society. It seems that this fact has not sufficiently retained the attention of those who have written about the question. There is an impurity in the *Weltanschauung* of a colonized people, a defect that forbids any ontological explanation. It might be objected that that it is the case for every individual, but it would merely cover up a fundamental problem. When one has admitted once and for all that ontology leaves existence aside, one sees why it does not allow for understanding the being of the Black. It is not a question of the Black being black anymore, but rather, of his being black opposite the White. Some will take it on themselves to remind us that this situation works both ways. We say that it is false. The Black does not have any ontological resistance in the eyes of the White. Overnight, Negroes have had to situate themselves with regard to two frames of reference. Their metaphysics, or, less pretentiously, their customs and the instances to which they referred, were suppressed because they were found to be in contradiction with a civilization that they did not know anything about and that was impressive to them.

In the twentieth century, the Black among his own does not know the moment at which his inferiority passes through the other... Undoubtedly, now and then I have talked about the black problem with friends, or more rarely with Black Americans. Together we protested and affirmed the equality of all men before the world. In the Antilles, there also was this little gap between the light-skinned (*békaille*), the mulatto (*mulataille*), and the negro (*négraille*). But we contented ourselves with an intellectual comprehension of these tensions. In fact, it was not tragic. But then...

Then we came to have to confront the white gaze. An unusual weight burdened us. The genuine world was challenging our due. In the white world, the man of color faces difficulties in the elaboration of his bodily schema. Knowledge of the body is a merely negating activity. It is knowledge in the third-person mode. The body is surrounded by an uncertainty that is certain. I know that if I want to smoke, I will have to reach out my right arm and take hold of the pack lying at the other end of the table. Since the matches are in the left drawer, however, I shall have to lean back slightly. And I perform all these movements not out of habit, but out of an implicit knowledge. A slow construction of my self as a body in the midst of a spatial and temporal world, such seems to be the schema. It is not imposed on me; rather, it is a definitive structuring of the self and the world – definitive because in this way an effective dialectic is settled between my body and the world.

For several years, laboratories have wanted to produce a serum for denegrification; with all the seriousness in the world, laboratories have rinsed their test tubes, checked their scales and embarked on researches that will allow the unfortunate Negroes to whiten themselves and rid themselves of that corporeal curse. Below the corporeal schema, I created a historico-racial one. The elements I used were provided to me not by "residual sensations and perceptions of a primarily tactile, vestibular, kinesthetic, and visual order,"[1] but by the other, the White, who has woven me out of a thousand details, anecdotes and stories. I believed I would have to construct a physiological self, to balance space, to localize sensations, and here I was being called on for a supplement.

"Look, a Negro!" It was an external stimulus that flicked over me fleetingly. I gave the ghost of a smile.

"Look, a Negro!" It was true. I was amused.

"Look, a Negro!" The circle was drawing tighter. I was openly amused.

"Mommy, look at the Negro, I'm afraid!" Afraid! Afraid! Here they were starting to fear me. I wanted to laugh until I choked, but I had become unable to.

I could not be amused anymore because I already knew of the legends, the stories, history, and especially, the historicity I learned from Jaspers. Then the corporeal schema collapsed, assailed at various points, yielding to a racial epidermal schema. In the train it was not a matter of knowing my body in the third-person mode anymore, but as a threefold person. In the train, instead of one seat, I was granted two, three seats. Already I was not being amused anymore. It was not that I was discovering feverish coordinates in the world. I existed in triplicate: I was occupying space. I moved towards the other... And the evanescent other, hostile yet not opaque, transparent, absent, disappeared. Nausea...

I was all at once responsible for my body, responsible for my race, for my ancestors. I ran an objective gaze over myself, discovering my blackness, my ethnic characteristics, and then I was deafened by cannibalism, intellectual deficiency, fetishism, racial defects, slave-ships, and above all, above all else, "Sho' good Banania."

On that day, disoriented and incapable of being outside with the other, the White who unmercifully imprisoned me, I took myself far away, very far away indeed from my being-there, thus making myself an object. What else could it be for me but an excision, an amputation, a hemorrhage that congealed black blood all over my body? However, I did not want this revision, this thematization. All I wanted was to be a man among other men. I had wanted to arrive smooth and young in a world of ours, that together we would have erected.

But I rejected all emotional tetanization. I wanted to be a man, only a man. Some identified me with my enslaved and lynched ancestors: I decided to take it on. It was through the universal plane of the intellect that I understood this inner kinship – I was the grandson of slaves just as President Lebrun was the grandson of share-cropping feudal peasants. At bottom, the distress was vanishing quickly.

In America, Negroes are set apart. In South America, Negroes are whipped in the streets, and the Negro strikers are machine-gunned. In West Africa, the Negro is a beast. And here, right next to me, my schoolfriend at the university, a native of Algeria, tells me: "As long as the Arabs are treated as men like us, no solution will be possible."

"You see, my dear, color prejudice is something I don't know anything about... But of course, come in, sir, there is no color prejudice with us... Certainly, Negroes are men like us... It is not because they are black that they are less intelligent than we are... I had a Senegalese mate in the army, who was very smart..."

Where shall I put myself? Or, if you prefer, where shall I bury myself?

"A Martinican, a native of 'our' old colonies."

Where shall I hide?

"Look at the Negro!... Mommy, a Negro! Hush, he is going to get mad... Pay no attention, sir, he doesn't know that you are as civilized as we are..."

My body was coming back to me flattened out, disjointed, destroyed, mourning on that white winter day. The Negro is a beast, the Negro is evil, the Negro is mischievous, the Negro is ugly; look, a Negro, it is cold outside, the Negro is shaking because he is cold, the boy is shaking because he is afraid of the Negro, the Negro is shaking with cold, that cold that goes through your bones, the handsome boy is shaking because he thinks the Negro is shaking with anger, the white boy throws himself into his mother's arms: Mommy, the Negro is going to eat me.

All around me the Whites; above, the sky tears at its navel, the earth grinds under my feet, and a white song, white. All this whiteness that is burning me up...

I sit down by the fire and I discover my livery. I had never seen it before. It is definitely ugly. I stop here, for who will tell me what beauty is?

Where shall I bury myself now? I felt an easily recognizable rush of blood rising from the countless facets of my being. I was about to get angry. The fire had died long ago, and again, the Negro was shaking.

"Look at this Negro, how handsome he is!..."

"The handsome Negro shits on you, madam!"

Shame adorned her face. Finally I was freed from my rumination. All at once I was realizing two things: I was identifying my enemies and I was provoking uproar. Everything I could wish for. Now the fun could begin.

With the battlefield marked out, I joined the struggle.

What? Whereas I was forgetting, forgiving and wanting only to love, my message was thrown back at me like a slap in the face. The white world, the only honorable one, was excluding me from all participation. One expects a man to behave like a man. I was expected to behave like a Black man – or at least a Negro. I was hailing the world, and the world cut me off from my enthusiasm. I was told to confine myself, to shrink.

I would show them! I had warned them, though. Slavery? No one ever mentioned it anymore: a bad memory. My alleged inferiority? A hoax that could only be laughed at. I would forget everything, but on condition that the world did not dodge my blows anymore. I had sharp teeth to try out. I could feel they were robust. Besides...

What? While I was the one with every reason for hating, for detesting, I was the one who was being rejected? When I should have been begged, implored, I was being denied all recognition? I decided, since it was impossible for me to start from an *inborn complex*, to affirm myself as BLACK. Since the other was reluctant to recognize (*reconnaître*) me, there was only one solution: to make myself known (*connaître*).

In *Anti-Semite and Jew*, Jean-Paul Sartre writes: "They (the Jews) have allowed themselves to be poisoned by a certain representation that others have of them, and they live in fear that their acts might conform to it. Thus, we may say... that their behavior is perpetually over-determined from the inside."[2]

However, the Jew's Jewishness can stay unknown. He is not wholly what he is. One hopes, one waits. His actions and behavior ultimately decide. He is White, and apart from some rather debatable features, he can sometimes pass unnoticed. He belongs to a race that since the beginning of time has never known cannibalism. What an idea to eat one's father, anyway! All right then, just don't be a Negro. Of course, the Jews are being bullied. Rather, they are pursued, exterminated, incinerated, but these are merely little family difficulties. The Jew is disliked from the moment he is tracked down. But with me everything takes on a *new* face. I am given no chance. I am over-determined from the outside. I am the slave, not of an "idea" that others have of me, but of my appearing.

I come slowly into the world, now resigned to no longer aspire to my own emergence. I creep my way through. And already I am being dissected under the white gaze, the only true gaze. I am fixed. Having adjusted their microtome, they objectively make cuts in my reality and the innumerable autotoxic lashes suddenly throw me away, bound hand and foot. I am being laid bare. I can feel, I can see in the white gaze that it is not a new man who is coming in, but a new type of man, a new kind – why, a Negro!

I slip into corners, picking up with my long antennae the proving ground scattered over the surface of things – the Negro's linen smells of Negro – the Negro's teeth are white – the Negro's feet are big – the Negro's broad chest – I slip into corners, I stay silent, I strive for anonymity and oblivion. Look, I will accept everything, as long as no one notices me anymore!

"Here, I want you to meet my Black friend... Aimé Césaire, a Black man, a university professor... Marian Anderson, the best Negro singer... Doctor Cobb, who invented white blood, is a Negro... Here, say hello to my friend from Martinique (be careful, he's extremely thin-skinned)..."

Shame. Shame and self-contempt. Nausea. A psychic rigidity that demolishes the senile walls of naiveté.

When people like me, they tell me it is in spite of my color. When they hate me, they point out it is not because of my color – in this case, precisely, where I would have preferred it to be for this reason. I would avoid the inscription of a host of little animalcules that can only disturb the calm of my consciousness. Either way, I am the boorish prisoner of an infernal circle.

I turn away from these scrutineers of the impending deluge and I cling to my brothers, Negroes like myself. To my horror they, too, reject me. *They* are almost white. Besides, they are each going to marry a white woman. They will have light-brown children . . . Who knows, little by little, perhaps . . .

I had been dreaming . . .

"You see, sir, I am one of the most Negro-loving people in Lyon."

The evidence was there, relentless. My blackness was there, dense and incontrovertible. And it was tormenting me, pursuing me, upsetting me, angering me . . .

Negroes are savages, idiots, illiterate. But for my part, I knew that in my own case, these claims were false. There was a myth of the Negro that had to be destroyed at all costs. It was some time since a Negro priest was a surprise. We had doctors, professors, statesmen . . . Granted, even though these cases persisted in seeming strange. "We have a Senegalese history teacher. He is very smart . . . Our doctor is Black. He is very gentle."

It was the Negro teacher, the Negro doctor; I was beginning to become frail, I was quaking at the slightest alarm. For example, I knew that if the doctor made a mistake, it would finish him and all those who came after him. Indeed, what could one expect from a Negro doctor? While everything was going well, he was praised to the skies, but look out, no blunders allowed at any price! The Black physician can never be sure how close he is to disrepute. I'm telling you, I was walled in: I was given no credit for my polite manners, my literary knowledge, or my understanding of the quantum theory. I craved, I demanded explanations. Having stumbled over the bolt of the world, I started to strike back. Gently, as if speaking to a child, they told me of the existence of an opinion that was held by certain people, yet, they always added, "We must hope it will soon disappear." What was it? Color prejudice.

> It is nothing more than the unreasoning hatred of one race for another, the contempt of the stronger and richer peoples for those whom they consider inferior to themselves, and the bitter resentment of those who are kept in subjection and are so frequently insulted. As color is the most obvious outward manifestation of race it has been made the criterion by which men are judged, irrespective of their social or educational achievements. The light-skinned races have come to despise all those of a darker color, and the dark-skinned peoples no longer accept without protest the inferior position to which they have been relegated.[3]

I had read it right. It was hate; I was hated, detested, despised, not by my close neighbor or my maternal cousin, but by a whole race. I was exposed to something irrational. Psychoanalysts say that there is nothing more traumatizing for a young child than to be confronted with rationality. I would say, for my part, that for a man whose only weapon is reason, there is nothing more likely to cause neurosis than to be confronted with irrationality.

I felt knife blades grow within me. I decided to defend myself. As a good tactician, I was determined to rationalize the world and show the White man that he was wrong.

Jean-Paul Sartre says that in the Jew, there is "a sort of impassioned imperialism of reason; for he wishes not only to convince others that he is right; his goal is to persuade them that there is an absolute and unconditioned value to rationalism. He feels himself to be a missionary of the universal; against the universalism of the Catholic religion, from which he is excluded, he asserts the 'catholicity' of the rational, an instrument by which to attain to the truth and establish a spiritual bond among men."[4]

And, the author adds, that although there may have been Jews who have made intuition into the fundamental category, in the Kantian sense, of their philosophy, "it has no resemblance to the Pascalian subtlety of spirit, and it is this latter – unanswerable, emotional, based on a thousand imperceptible perceptions – which to the Jew seems his worst enemy. As for Bergson, his philosophy offers the curious appearance of an anti-intellectualist doctrine conceived entirely by the most rational and most critical of intelligences. It is through argument that he establishes the existence of pure duration, of philosophic intuition; and this very intuition, which discovers duration, or life, is universal, since anyone may practice it, and it leads toward the universal, since its objects can be named and conceived."[5]

I eagerly set to cataloguing and investigating the setting. As times improved, the Catholic religion justified and then condemned slavery and discrimination. But by measuring all of it in terms of the notion of human dignity, prejudice had been smashed. After much reticence, scientists had granted that the Negro was a human being; *in vivo* and *in vitro*, the Negro was revealed to be analogous to the White: they have the same morphology, the same histology. Reason was guaranteed victory on every level. I returned to the meetings. But I had to come down a peg.

Victory was playing cat and mouse; it was scoffing at me. As the saying goes, when I am there, it is not, when it is there, I am no longer. We agreed about the idea: the Negro is a human being. That is to say, the less firmly convinced added, his heart is on the left, just like ours. But the Whites remained intractable on certain issues. The Whites did not want intimacy between the races at any price, for as we know, "crossings between widely different races can lower the physical and mental level ... Until we have more definite knowledge of the effect of race-crossings, we shall certainly do best to avoid crossings between widely different races."[6]

As for me, I would certainly know how to react. In a sense, if I had to define myself, I would say that I am one who waits; I examine the surroundings, I interpret everything in terms of my discoveries, I have become sensory.

At the beginning of the history that others have made for me, the base of cannibalism is fully conspicuous so that I may remember it. Some pointed out on my chromosomes several more or less thick genes that represented cannibalism. Next to the *sex-linked*, they had now discovered the *racial-linked*.[7] This science is a disgrace!

But I understand this "psychological mechanism" for, as everybody knows, it is a merely psychological mechanism. Two centuries ago I was lost to humanity, I was a slave forever. Then some men came, who declared that it had all been going on for too long. My tenacity did the rest; I was rescued from the civilizing deluge. I came forward...

Too late. Everything has been foreseen, discovered, proven, taken advantage of. My nervous hands rein in nothing; the vein is exhausted. Too late! But still, I want to understand.

Ever since the time that someone declared that he had arrived too late and everything had been said, it seems that there has been nostalgia for the past. Could it be that lost paradise of origins, of which Otto Rank speaks? How many such men, fixed, it seems, to the uterus of the world, have consecrated their lives to deciphering the Delphic Oracles or done everything they could to rediscover Ulysses' journey! The pan-idealists seek to prove the existence of a soul in animals by using the following argument: a dog lies down on its master's tomb until it starves to death. We owe Janet the proof that dogs, unlike men, are simply unable to liquidate the past. We speak of Greek greatness, says Artaud; yet, he adds, if the modern masses cannot understand Aeschylus' *Choephoroi* any longer, it is Aeschylus who is at fault. It is in the name of tradition that the anti-Semites put value on their "point of view." It is in the name of tradition, of this long past history, of this blood tie with Pascal and Descartes that the Jews are told, "you don't have a place within the community." Recently I heard one of these good Frenchman, in the train I was sitting in, say "As long as the true French virtues continue, the race is safe! At the present time, National Unity must be made a reality. No more internal struggles! Confront the foreigners (and turning toward my corner), whoever they are." (It should be said in his defense that he stank of cheap wine; if he had been up to it, he would have told me that my emancipated-slave blood could not possibly be stirred by the names of Villon or Taine.)

A shame!

The Jew and I: not content to racialize myself, by a happy turn of fate I was humanizing myself. I rejoined the Jew, my brother in misery.

A shame!

At first sight, it might seem surprising that the anti-Semite's struggle should be related to the Negrophobe's. Our philosophy teacher, an Antillean, reminded us one day: "Whenever you hear anyone insult the Jews, listen up, because they are speaking about you." And we thought he was universally right – meaning thereby that I was answerable, in my body and my soul, for the destiny reserved for my brother. Since then I have understood that he simply meant that an anti-Semite is necessarily a Negrophobe.

You come too late, much too late. There will always be a – white – world between you and us... It is impossible for the other to wipe out the past once and for all. In the face of this affective anchylosis of the Whites, it is understandable that I could have decided to utter my Negro cry. Little by little, throwing pseudopodia here and there, I was secreting a race, and that race was staggering under the weight of a fundamental element. What was it? *Rhythm*! Listen to Senghor, our bard:

> It is the most sensitive and the least material of things. It is the vital element "par excellence". It is the first condition and the sign of Art, as breath is the sign of life; breath, which quickens or slows down, becomes even or spasmodic depending on the tension in the being, the degree and the quality of emotion. Such is rhythm primordially

> in its purity, such is it in the masterpieces of Negro art, especially in its sculpture. It is constituted from a theme – the sculptural form – set in opposition to a sister theme, as inhalation is to exhalation, and that is repeated. It is not symmetry that gives rise to monotony; rhythm is alive, it is free... Thus it is that rhythm affects what is least intellectual in us, and does so despotically, to let us penetrate the spirituality of objects; and that attitude of surrender which is ours, is itself rhythmic.[8]

Had I read that correctly? I reread it with redoubled attention. From the other side of the White world, a fairy-like Negro culture was saluting me. Negro sculpture! I began to blush with pride. Was this salvation?

I had rationalized the world and the world had rejected me in the name of color prejudice. Since no agreement was possible on the level of reason, I threw myself back toward irrationality. On condition that the White Man be more irrational than I was. For the sake of the cause, I had adopted the regressive method, but the fact remained that it was a foreign weapon. Here I am, at home; I am constructed from the irrational; I wale in the irrational. Up to the neck in the irrational. And now my voice vibrates!

> Those who invented neither gunpowder nor the compass
> Those who never knew how to subdue steam or electricity
> Those who explored neither the seas nor the sky
> But they know the remotest corners of the country of suffering
> Those whose only journeys have been uprootings
> Those who have softened in kneeling
> Those who have been domesticated and Christianized
> Those who have been inoculated with bastardization...

Yes, all of these are my brothers – a "rough brotherhood" clings to us in like manner. Having asserted the minor thesis, I am hailing something else overboard.

> ...But those without whom the earth would not be the earth
> Protuberance so much the more fruitful than
> the desert land
> even more the land
> Silo where is stored and ripened that which
> On earth is most from the earth
> My negritude is not a stone, its deafness
> hurled against the clamor of the day
> My negritude is not a drop of lifeless water
> over the dead eye of the earth
> My negritude is neither a tower nor a cathedral
> It dives into the red flesh of the soil
> It dives into the scorching flesh of the sky
> It perforates the opaque despondency of its upright patience.[9]

Eia! The tom-tom jabbers out the cosmic message. The Negro alone is able to convey it, to decipher its meaning, its scope. Riding the world, my vigorous heels against the flanks of the world, I glare at the neck of the world, as the sacrificer glares between the eyes of his victim.

But they surrender, enraptured, to the essence of all things,
ignorant of the surfaces but enraptured by the movement of all things
heedless to subduing but playing the game of the world
truly the oldest sons of the world
porous to all the breaths of the world
fraternal site of all the breaths of the world
undrained bed of all the waters of the world
spark of the sacred fire of the World
flesh of the flesh of the world throbbing with the very movement of the world![10]

Blood! Blood! . . . Birth! Dizziness of becoming! Three-quarters swallowed by the daze of the day, I felt myself redden with blood. The arteries of the world, overturned, extracted, uprooted, had turned toward me and impregnated me.

"Blood! Blood! All our blood moved by the male heart of the sun."[11]

Sacrifice was a middle term between creation and myself – I was going back, not to origins anymore, but to the Origin. However, rhythm – the Earth-Mother love, that mystic and carnal marriage of the group to the cosmos – had to be distrusted.

In *La Vie Sexuelle en Afrique Noire*, a work rich in observations, De Pédrals implies that whatever field is under investigation, there is always in Africa a certain magico-social structure. And he adds, one finds all these elements again, on a still greater scale, in the realm of secret societies. Indeed, to the extent that the circumcised, the cut, operated on during adolescence, under penalty of death must not divulge to the uninitiated what they have been subjected to, and to the extent that initiation to a secret society always calls for acts of *sacred love*, there is a basis from which to conclude that circumcision and the rites it exemplifies constitute minor secret societies.[12]

I walk on white spikes. Sheets of water threaten my fiery soul. In the face of these rites, I redouble my attention. Black Magic! Orgies, the sabbath, pagan ceremonies, gris-gris. Coitus is an occasion to invoke the gods of the clan. It is a sacred, pure, absolute act fostering the intervention of invisible forces. What is one to think of all these manifestations, initiations and operations? From all sides the obscenity of dances and proposals come to mind. Close to me this song echoes:

Before our hearts were very hot
Now they are cold
All we dream of now is Love
Returning to the village
When we will meet up with a giant phallus
Ah! how then we will make good loving
For our sex will be dry and clean.[13]

The ground, which just now was still a subdued charger, begins to laugh. Are these nymphomaniacs virgins? Black magic, primitive mentality, animism, animal eroticism, it all floods back to me. All of this is typical of peoples who have not followed the evolution of humanity. This is what one could call, if one likes, discount humanity. Having reached this point, I hesitated to get involved. The stars became aggressive. I had to make a choice. What am I saying, I did not have a choice . . .

Yes, we (the Negro) are backward, plain, free in our behavior. For to us the body is not the opposite of what you call the mind. We are in the world. Long live the couple formed by Man and Earth! Indeed, our men of letters were helping me convince you; your white civilization disregards our wealth in sensitivity. Listen:

> Emotive sensitivity. *Emotion is Negro as reason is Greek.*[14] Water that every puff ripples? Exposed soul battered by the winds, soul whose fruit often drops before it is ripe? Yes, in a way Negroes today are richer *in gifts than in works*[15]. But the tree plunges its roots into the earth. The river runs deep, bearing its precious grains of gold-dust. And the African-American poet, Langston Hughes, sings:
>
> I've known rivers
> Ancient dusky rivers
>
> My soul has grown deep like the rivers.[16]
>
> The very nature of emotion, of the Negro's sensitivity, on the other hand, explains the latter's attitude toward the object he perceives with such essential violence. It is a surrender that becomes need, an active attitude of communion, indeed of identification, however negligible the action – I was almost going to say the personality – of the object. Let us keep in mind this word: rhythmic attitude.[17]

Here is the Negro rehabilitated, "standing at the bar," governing the world by his intuition, the Negro rediscovered, gathered together, claimed, taken up, and he is a Negro – no, he is not a Negro but the Negro, stirring the fertile antennae of the world, standing in the foreground of the world, sprinkling the world with his poetic power, "porous to all the breaths of the world." I embrace the world! I am the world! The Whites never understood this magical substitution. The Whites want the world; they want it for themselves alone. They consider themselves the predestined masters of the world. They enslave it. They set up an appropriative relationship between the world and themselves. Yet there are some values that are mine alone. Like a sorcerer, I robbed the Whites of a certain world, forever lost to them. On that day, they must have felt a shock in return for something they could not identify, being so little used to such reactions. For beyond the objective world of fields and banana-trees or rubber-trees, I had delicately brought the real world into being. The essence of the world was my asset. A relation of coexistence was being established between the world and me. I had recovered the primordial One. My "resonant hands" were devouring the hysterical gorge of the world. The white man had the painful feeling that I was escaping from him, that I was taking something away with me. He searched my pockets. He thrust probes into the least determined of my circumvolutions. Everywhere he found only what he already knew. Now it was obvious that I held a secret. I was interrogated; turning away with an air of mystery, I murmured:

> Tokowaly, my uncle, do you remember the nights long gone

When my head weighted heavy on your patient shoulders
or when
Holding my hand your hand led me through shadows and signs
The fields are flowers of glowworms, stars settle on the weeds, on the trees
Silence is everywhere
Only the scents of the bush hum, swarms of reddish bees that are heard above the crickets' highpitched vibrations,
And muffled tom-toms, the breathing of the night in the distance,
You, Tokowaly, you hear the inaudible, and you explain to me the signs of the ancestors in the marine serenity of the constellations,
The bull, the scorpion, the leopard, the elephant and the friendly fish.
And the milky pomp of the Spirits in the tan-colored sky that never ends.
But now comes the intelligence of the goddess Moon, and now the veils of darkness fall away.
Night of Africa, my black night, mystical and bright, black and brilliant.[18]

I was making myself the poet of the world. The Whites had discovered a poetry that had nothing poetic about it. The soul of the White Man was corrupted and, as a friend who taught in the United States told me, "Over against the Whites, the Negroes are a form of insurance on humanity. When the Whites feel they have become too mechanized, they turn towards the men of color and ask them for a little human nourishment." At last I was being recognized: I was no longer nothing.

I soon had to come down a peg. Disconnected only for a moment, the White man explained to me that genetically speaking, I represented a stage of evolution: "Your qualities have been exhausted by us. We have had earth mystics as you will never know them. Look into our history and you will see how far this fusion has gone." I then had the sense that I was repeating a cycle. My originality was being wrung from me. For a long time I was crying, and then I went back to living again. But I was haunted by a series of destructive clichés: the Negro's *sui generis* smell . . . the *sui generis* good-heartedness of the Negro . . . *the sui generis* naivete of the Negro . . .

I had tried to flee through the side, but the Whites had thrown themselves on me and cut off my left flank. I was surveying the limits of my essence; without a doubt, it was fairly meagre. It was at this point that I made my most extraordinary discovery. Properly speaking, this discovery was a rediscovery.

I rummaged dizzily through black antiquity. What I discovered there took my breath away. In his book *The Abolition of Slavery*, Schoelcher presented us with decisive arguments. Since then Frobenius, Westermann, Delafosse – all of them white – have joined the chorus: Ségou and Djenné, cities of more than a hundred thousand people; someone talks of learned Black men (doctors of theology who were going to Mecca to interpret the Koran). Once all that was brought to light, inwards exposed, I was able to rediscover a valid historical category. The Whites had been mistaken; I was not a primitive, no more than I was a half-man; I belonged to a race that, two thousand years ago, was already working on gold and silver. And then there was something else, something that the Whites could not understand. Listen:

What sort of men were these, then, who for centuries had been torn away from their countries, their gods and their families with unparalleled savagery?

> Gentle men, polite, courteous, without doubt superior to their torturers – that bunch of adventurers who smashed, violated and insulted Africa in order to plunder her more thoroughly.
>
> They knew how to erect houses, administrate empires, build cities, cultivate fields, melt ore, weave cotton, forge steel.
>
> Their religion was beautiful, formed from mysterious connections with the founder of the city. Their customs were gracious, founded on solidarity, kindness, and respect for the old.
>
> No coercion, but only mutual help, the joy of living, a discipline freely consented to.
>
> Order – Intensity – Poetry and freedom.
>
> From the contented individual to the almost fabulous chief, an unbroken chain of understanding and trust. No science? Maybe, but they had, to protect them from fear, great myths in which the finest observation and the boldest imagination were balanced and founded each other. No art? They had their magnificent sculpture, in which, in accordance with the obsessive laws of rhythm, human emotion never exploded so fiercely as when it organized the great surfaces of a material summoned to capture, in order to redistribute, the most secret forces of the universe...[19]

> ...Monuments in the very heart of Africa? Schools? Hospitals? No bourgeois of the twentieth century, no Durand, Smith, or Brown, suspects that such things existed in Africa before the Europeans came...
>
> ...Schoelcher reports their existence following Caillé, Mollien, and the Cander brothers. However, he nowhere mentions that when the Portuguese landed on the banks of Congo in 1498, they found a rich and flourishing state there, and that the Court of Ambas was dressed in silk and brocade. Nevertheless, he knows that Africa developed on its own a juridical concept of the state, and he suspects, in the midst of an imperialist age, that, after all, the European civilization is merely one civilization among others – and not the most kind.[20]

I put the White back in his place; emboldened, I jostled him and told him straight to his face, "adapt yourself to me, I won't adapt to anyone." I giggled uncontrollably. The White, I could see, was grumbling. His reaction time prolonged itself indefinitely... I had won. I was rejoicing.

"Lay aside your history, your investigations of the past, and try to tune up to our rhythm. In a society like ours, industrialized to the extreme, pervaded by science, there is no longer room for your sensitivity. One must be tough to be allowed to live. It is no longer a matter of playing the world's game, but rather of subjugating it with integers and atoms. Of course," I would be told, "from time to time, when we get tired of life in our buildings, we will come to you as we do to our children... innocent... surprised... spontaneous. We will come to you as we would to the childhood of the world. You are so genuine in your life – so frivolous, that is. Let us drop for a little while our formal and polite civilization, and let us bend to those heads, those delightfully expressive faces. In a sense, you reconcile us to ourselves."

Thus, they were opposing my irrationality with their rationality, and my rationality with the "true rationality." Every hand I played was a losing hand. I tested my lineage. I conducted a complete audit of my illness. I wanted to be typically Negro, but that was no longer possible. I wanted to be white, but that was laughable. And when I tried, on the level of ideas and intellectual activity, to claim my negritude, it was snatched from me. I was clearly shown that my attempt was a mere moment in the dialectic:

> But there is something more serious: the Negro, as we have said, creates for himself an anti-racist racism. He wishes in no way to rule over the world: he desires the abolition of ethnic privileges, wherever they come from; he asserts his solidarity with the oppressed of every color. Thus the subjective, existential, ethnic notion of negritude "passes," as Hegel says, into the objective, positive, and precise notion of *proletariat.* Senghor says, "For Césaire, the 'White' symbolizes Capital, just as the Negro symbolizes work... Over and beyond the black-skinned men of his race, he sings about the world-wide proletariat struggle."
>
> It is easy to say, not so easy to think. And, it is certainly not just by accident that the most ardent cantors of negritude are also Marxist militants.
>
> Nevertheless, the notion of race does not mix with the notion of class: the former is concrete and particular; the latter, universal and abstract; one belongs to what Jaspers calls comprehension, and the other to intellection; the first is the product of a psycho-biological syncretism, and the other is a methodical construction starting with experience. In fact, negritude appears as the minor moment of a dialectical progression: the theoretical and practical affirmation of the white supremacy is the thesis; the position of negritude as an antithetical value is the moment of negativity. But this negative moment is not sufficient in itself and these Blacks who use it know this perfectly well; they know that it aims at preparing the synthesis or realization of the human in a raceless society. Thus Negritude is for destroying itself, it is a passage and not an outcome, a means and not an ultimate end.[21]

When I read this page, I felt like I was being robbed of my last chance. I said to my friends, "The generation of young Black poets has just suffered a fatal blow." We had been seeking help from a friend of the colored peoples, and this friend had not found anything better to do than show the relativity of their action. For once, this born Hegelian had forgotten that consciousness needs to lose itself in the night of the absolute, the only condition able to attain to self-consciousness. Against rationalism, he was forgetting the negative side, and this negativity draws its value from a quasi-substantial absoluteness. Consciousness, when committed to experience, does not know and must not know the essences and determinations of its being. In insisting on *saying* the orientation of my action, the author was making himself guilty of an epistemological error.

Black Orpheus marks an epoch in the intellectualization of Black existing. And Sartre's error was not only to attempt to go to the source of the source, but also, in a certain way, to dry up this source:

> Will the source of Poetry run dry? Or in spite of everything else will the great black river color the sea into which it flows? It does not matter: each era has its poetry; in each era, circumstances of history elect a nation, a race, a class to take up the torch, by creating situations that can be expressed or that can go beyond themselves only through poetry; sometimes the poetic *élan* coincides with the revolutionary *élan*, and sometimes they diverge. Let us greet today the historic chance that will permit Blacks to "shout out the great Negro cry so hard, that the foundations will be shaken."[22]

There you have it, I am not the one who creates a meaning for myself, but the meaning was already there, pre-existing and waiting for me. It is not with my bad

Negro wretchedness, my bad Negro teeth, my bad Negro hunger, that I will model a torch I can set on fire in order to burn down the world, but the torch was there already, waiting for that historic opportunity.

As far as consciousness is concerned, the Black consciousness is given as an absolute density, as if filled with itself, a stage prior to any crack, or any abolition of the self by desire. Jean-Paul Sartre, in this work, has destroyed Black enthusiasm. To historical becoming, the unforeseeable should have been opposed. I felt the need to lose myself absolutely in my negritude. Some day, perhaps, in the heart of that unhappy romanticism . . .

But *I needed* not to know. This struggle, this come down had to wear a look of completeness. Nothing is more unpleasant than the sentence, "You'll change, my son; I too, when I was young, you will see, everything passes away."

The dialectic that introduces necessity into the cornerstone of my freedom expels me from myself. It shatters my non-reflective position. Still in terms of consciousness, the black consciousness is immanent to itself. I am not the potentiality of something, I am wholly what I am. I do not have to look for the universal. No probabilities have any place in my breast. My Negro consciousness does not hold itself out as a lack. It *is*. It sticks to itself.

But, some will say, your statements betray a misunderstanding of the historical process. For evidence, listen to this:

> Africa I have kept your memory Africa
> you are within me
> Like the splinter in the wound
> like a guardian fetish at the center of the village
> make me the stone of your sling
> my mouth the lips of your cut
> my knees the broken columns of your abasement
> AND YET
> I want to be of your race alone
> peasant workers of all countries . . .
> . . . white worker in Detroit black peon in Alabama
> innumerable people of the capitalist galleys
> destiny drills us shoulder to shoulder
> and abjuring the ancient evil spells of blood taboos
> we trample down the ruins of our solitudes.
> If the torrent is a frontier
> we will snatch from the ravine its inexhaustible
> tail
> If the Sierra is a frontier
> we will crush the jaws of volcanoes
> affirming the Cordilleras
> and the plain will be the esplanade of dawn
> where we regroup our forces torn
> by the ruse of our masters
> As contradiction among character traits
> is resolved in the harmony of the face
> we proclaim the unity of the suffering

and the revolt
of all peoples all over the face of the earth
and we stir the mortar of brotherly times
in the dust of idols.[23]

Precisely, we will reply, the Negro experience is ambiguous, for there is not *one* Negro, but *several* Negroes. See the difference, for instance, with this other poem:

The White killed my father
For my father was proud
The White raped my mother
For my mother was beautiful
The White bent my brother under the sun of the roads
For my brother was strong
Then the White turned toward me
His hands red with blood
Black spat his scorn to my face
And in his master's voice:
"Hey boy, a basin, a towel, water."[24]

And this other one:

My brother with teeth that sparkle at the compliments of hypocrites
My brother with gold-rimmed glasses
Over your eyes turned blue by the Master's words
My poor brother in smoking jacket with its silk lapels
Squealing and murmuring and swaggering through the parlors of Condescension
We pity you
The sun of your country is no more than a shadow
On your composed because civilized face
And the hut of your grandmother
Brings blushes to cheeks made white by years of humiliation and *Mea Culpa*
But when satiated with loud and empty words
Like the load that overcomes your shoulders
You will trample down the bitter and red soil of Africa
These words of anguish will then put rhythm into your anxious steps
I feel so lonely, so lonely here![25]

From time to time, one felt like stopping. To express the real is an arduous task. Yet when one is determined to express existence, one runs the risk of finding only the non-existent. What is certain is that at the very moment when I was attempting to grasp my being, Sartre, who remains the Other, shatters my illusions by naming me. Although I tell him:

My negritude is neither a tower nor a cathedral
It dives into the red flesh of the soil
It dives into the scorching flesh of the sky
It perforates the opaque despondency of its own upright patience . . .[26]

While I am shouting that, in the paroxysm of life and fury, he reminds me that my Negritude is a mere minor moment. In truth, in truth I tell you, my shoulders have slid away from the structure of the world, my feet have stopped feeling the caress of the soil. Deprived of a Negro past, deprived of a Negro future, it was impossible for me to exist my Negrohood. Not yet White, no longer wholly Black, I was damned. Jean-Paul Sartre forgot that the Negro suffers in his body differently than the White.[27] Between the White and myself, there is an irrevocable relation of transascendence.[28]

But the constancy of my love has been overlooked. I define myself as an absolute tension of opening. And I grab this Negritude and, with tears in my eyes, I reconstruct its mechanism. What had been shattered to pieces is rebuilt, erected by my hands, these intuitive vines.

My outcry grew more violent: I am a Negro, I am a Negro, I am a Negro . . .

And there is my poor brother, living his neurosis to the extreme and finding himself paralyzed[29]:

THE NEGRO: I can't, madam.
LIZZIE: What?
THE NEGRO: I can't shoot at the Whites,
LIZZIE: Really? *They*[30] are not going to put themselves out!
THE NEGRO: They are Whites, madam.
LIZZIE: So what? Just because they are white they got a right to bleed you like a pig?
THE NEGRO: They are Whites.[31]

A feeling of inferiority? No, a feeling of non-existence. Sin is Negro as virtue is white. All those Whites together, gun in hand, cannot be wrong. I am guilty. I don't know of what, but I can feel that I am a poor wretch.

THE NEGRO: That's the way it is, ma'am. That's always the way it is with the Whites.
LIZZIE: You too, you feel guilty?
THE NEGRO: Yes, ma'am.[32]

It is Bigger Thomas, who is afraid, terribly afraid. He is afraid, but afraid of what? Of himself. One does not yet know who he is, but he knows that fear will inhabit the world once the world knows. And once the world knows, the world always expects something from the Negro. He is afraid that the world will know, he is afraid of the fear that the world would feel if the world knew. Like that old woman, who begged me on her knees to tie her down to her bed:

"I can feel at every instant, doctor, this thing that takes hold of me."

"What thing?"

"The desire to kill myself. Tie me down, I'm afraid."

In the end, Bigger Thomas acts. In order to put an end to the tension, he acts, he responds to the world's expectations.[33]

It is like the character in *If He Hollers, Let Him Go*,[34] who does precisely what he didn't want to do. That fat blond who is always in his way, flinching, sensual, an offer, open, fearing (wishing) to be raped, in the end becomes his mistress. The Negro is a toy between the White's hands; so, in order to break from this infernal circle, he explodes it. Impossible to go to the movies without running into myself. I wait for myself. At the interval, and right before the movie starts, I wait for myself. Those in front of me look at me, spy on me, wait for me. A Negro groom is going to appear. My heart turns my head.

The crippled veteran of the Pacific war tells my brother: "resign yourself to your color as I got used to my stump; we are both casualties."[35]

However, with all my being, I refuse this amputation. I feel like a soul as wide as the world, a truly deep soul, as deep as the deepest river; my chest has the power to expand infinitely. I am a don and I am advised to accept the humility of the crippled... Yesterday, opening my eyes to the world, I saw the sky turn upon itself through and through. I tried to rise, but the disemboweled silence flooded back towards me, its wings paralyzed. Irresponsible, straddling Nothingness and Infinity, I began to weep.

Notes

1 Jean Lhermitte, *L'image de notre corps*, (Paris: Editions de la Nouvelle Revue Critique, 1939), p. 17.

2 Jean-Paul Sartre, *Réflexions sur la question juive*, (Paris: Paul Morihien, 1946), p. 146–7; trans. George E. Becker, *Anti-Semite and Jew*, (New York: Schocken, 1976), p. 95 Trans. modified.

3 Sir Alan Burns, *Color Prejudice*, London: Allen and Unwin, 1948), p. 16.

4 *Réflexions sur la question juive*, pp. 146–7; trans. *Anti-Semite and Jew*, (New York: Grove Press, 1960), pp. 112–13.

5 *Réflexions sur la question juive*, pp. 149–50; trans. *Anti-Semite and Jew*, p. 115.

6 Jon Alfred Mjoen, "Harmonic and Disharmonic Race-crossings", The Second International Congress of Eugenics (1921). *Eugenics in Race and State* (Baltimore: Williams and Wilkins, 1923), vol. II, p. 60, quoted by Sir Alan Burns, *op. cit*, p. 120.

7 Italicized phrases in English in the original – Trans.

8 "Ce que l'homme noir apporte", in *L'Homme de Couleur*, (Paris: Plon, 1939), pp. 309–10.

9 Aimé Césaire, *Cahiers d'un Retour au Pays Natal*, (Paris: Bordas, 1947), pp. 77–8

10 Ibid, p. 78.

11 Ibid, p. 79.

12 Denis-Pierre De Pédrals, *La vie sexuelle en Afrique noire*, (Paris: Payot, 1950), p. 83.

13 A. M. Vergiat, *Les rites secrets des primitifs de L'Oubangui*, (Paris: Payot, 1951), p. 96. [Fanon's reference corrected – Ed.]

14 My italics – F.F

15 My italics – F.F

16 Langston Hughes, "The Negro Speaks of Rivers" in Arnold Rampersad, ed. *The Collected Poems of Langston Hughes*, (New York: Alfred A. Knopf, 1994), p. 23. – Ed.

17 Senghor, "Ce que l'homme noir apporte", 295.

18 Senghor, ["Que m'accompagnent Koras et Balafong"], *Chants d'Ombre*, (Paris: Editions du Seuil, 1945).

19 Aimé Césaire, ["Victor Schoelcher et l'abolition de l'esclavage"], *Esclavage et colonisation*, (Paris: Presses Universitaires de France, 1948), p. 7.

20 Ibid, p. 8.

21 Jean-Paul Sartre, "Orphée noir", in *Anthologie de la nouvelle poésie nègre et malgache*, (Paris: Presses Universitaires de France, 1948), p. xl–xli; trans. "Black Orpheus" (chapter 7, p. 137, this volume).

22 "Orphée noir", p. xliv; trans. "Black Orpheus" (chapter 7, p. 139, this volume)
23 Jacques Roumain, ["Bois d'Ebène", Prélude], *Anthologie de la nouvelle poésie nègre et malgache*, pp. 116–18.
24 David Diop, ["Trois poèmes", *Le Temps du Martyre*], Ibid, p. 174.
25 David Diop, "Le Renégat".
26 Aimé Césaire, *Cahier d'un retour au pays natal*, p. 78 – Ed.
27 Even though Sartre's studies on the existence of the other are accurate (to the extent, let us recall, that *Being and Nothingness* describes an alienated consciousness), their application to a Negro consciousness proves fallacious. That is because the White is not only the Other, but also the master, whether real or imaginary.
28 In Jean Wahl's sense of the word. See *Existence humaine et transcendence*, (Neuchatel: La Baconnière, 1944).
29 *Je suis un Nègre*. (French title of Mark Robson's film *Home of the Brave*).
30 Translator's italics.
31 J-P Sartre, *La Putain Respectueuse*, (Paris: Gallimard, 1947), p. 71; trans. Lionel Abel, *No Exit and Three Other Plays* (New York: Vintage, 1984), p. 271. Trans. modified.
32 *La Putain Respectueuse*, p. 76; trans. *No Exit* p. 272.
33 Richard Wright, *Native Son*, (New York: Harper, 1940).
34 Chester Himes, *If He Hollers, Let him Go*, (Garden City: Doubleday, 1945).
35 *Home of the Brave*.

PART VI

DUMONT AND THE STRUCTURALIST ANALYSIS OF RACE

11

IS THERE A STRUCTURALIST ANALYSIS OF RACISM?

On Louis Dumont's Philosophy of Hierarchy

Kamala Visweswaran

Introduction

Much has been written of the racial theory produced in the nineteenth century. And part of the story anthropologists have told themselves about the origin of their discipline at the end of this century centers on its role in discrediting the racial theories of the time, largely through the efforts of Franz Boas (Stocking, 1968, 1974). The Boasian critique of evolutionary racism, coupled with a form of functionalist ethnographic particularism was part of what established the modern anthropological paradigm of cultural relativism. This paradigm, and in particular, Boas's insistence that culture was more important than race, became so much an international worldview that the UNESCO Statements on Race would not have been possible without it (Visweswaran, 1998).

By the 1960s, when an anthropological structuralism was ascendant, its primary theorist, Claude Levi-Strauss, saw little reason to depart from the Boasian position on race. The question of why structuralism resurfaces at the height of the anti-colonial era, when the yoke of racial domination was challenged by claims to national self-determination, has itself never been adequately addressed. However, if there was a structuralist attempt to analyze racism, it can be found not in Levi-Strauss's writing, but in the work of Louis Dumont. In Dumont's work, we find the attempt to apply the linguistic structuralism of parts and wholes to the analysis of *holisms*, the ideological forms that establish different types of society.

No one who has read Louis Dumont's profound, but disturbing account of the Indian caste system, can forget that he raises the fundamental question of a comparative, and therefore universal (as opposed to general) sociology. Yet Dumont is uninterested in whether certain forms of social phenomena are universal. He is rather more concerned with the principles of sociological engagement – a first-order assertion that our values are but particular instances of a universal. In order to understand the truth of another social system, he argued, we must first understand the principles of our own. In some ways ahead of his time, Dumont was one of the first to articulate a radical self-reflexive anthropology, and this is what he meant when he asserted that "social anthropology is comparative at heart even when it is not explicitly so" (1977, p. 3).

First published in French in 1966, with the English translation arriving in the Anglophone academy four years later, *Homo Hierarchicus* was met with instant protest and controversy (Berreman, 1971; Khare, 1971a; Leach, 1971a; Kolenda, 1973; Marriot, 1969, 1976; Tambiah, 1972; Yalman, 1969) and was the subject of two review symposiums in *Contributions to Indian Sociology* (Madan, 1971; Berreman, 1971; Das and Uberoi, 1971; Heesterman, 1971; Kantowsky, 1971; Leach, 1971b; Khare, 1971b; Singer, 1971; Von Furer-Haimendorf, 1971) and the *Journal of Asian Studies* (Richards and Nichols, 1976; Barnett et al., 1976; Kolenda, 1976). In these critiques, Dumont, who claimed to have isolated the principle of equality that characterized Western society from the principle of hierarchy that distinguished the social systems of Asia, was frequently taken to task for being less the ethnographer than Indologist for his reliance upon classical Hindu texts rather than observed sociological reality to make his argument.[1] I do not wish to quarrel with these assessments of Dumont's work, as much of the criticism was sound. I wish only to note that, if the criticism of *Homo Hierarchicus* has stood the test of time, so too, has the text itself. It continues to be read, debated, and indeed, is clearly a major site of engagement for South Asia specialists, as a second spate of critiques reveals (Srinivas, 1984; Appadurai, 1986; 1992; Dirks, 1992).

Though many demand the text for its "intellectualism" or "idealism," in the storm of criticism that erupted over *Homo Hierarchicus*, few paid attention to Dumont's philosophical orientation, or even addressed his attempt to say something about the question of inequality in modern democratic society.[2] Rarer still was the reviewer who took account of Dumont's adaptation of Max Weber's earlier comparative sociology. In many ways, Weber's *Religion of India* is clearly the inspiration for *Homo Hierarchicus*[3] – Dumont actually reviewed the English translation of the *Religion of India* in 1962 – and *Homo Hierarchicus* can be read as Dumont's attempt to systematize and build upon Weber's understanding of the relationship of caste to Hinduism. Thus, to the extent that Dumont's project was flawed by a certain ideational emphasis, so too was Weber's earlier notion of ideal type (though no anthropologist criticizes Weber's *Protestant Ethic* or his *Religion of India* with nearly the same fervor). Indeed, the astute reader of Dumont's work knows that *Homo Hierarchicus* was all along part of Dumont's larger comparative project and must be read alongside the later collection of essays *From Mandeville to Marx: The Genesis and Triumph of Economic Ideology*, which Dumont once lightheartedly called "Homo Aequalis" (1977: vii).

Here I want to argue that sustained attention to Dumont's early (1960) essay, "Caste, Racism and 'Stratification' Reflections of a Social Anthropologist," (CRS) is not only overdue, but teaches us something invaluable about the limits of structural analysis confronted with the phenomena of racism or fascism. Although CRS preceded the publication of *Homo Hierarchicus* by six years and laid the groundwork for most of Dumont's later argumentation, most readers, unless they were South Asianists, would not have known of the essay until it was republished as an appendix to the first (1970) and second revised (1980) English editions of *Homo Hierarchicus*. Therefore, my discussion will first touch on the major elements of

Dumont's argument in *Homo Hierarchicus*, his dispute with the so-called "social stratificationists," and finally upon his central claims about racism in "Caste, Racism and 'Stratification'."

I The Structural Analysis of Hierarchy

Homo Hierarchicus represents Dumont's attempt at a structural analysis of both the whole (caste system) and holism (as ideology). The analysis of ideology is quite central to Dumont's project in *Homo Hierarchicus*. He asserts that, "Any concrete, localized, whole, when actually observed, is found to be decisively oriented by its ideology," which he takes to be a "system of ideas and values" (p. 36–7). But it is only in relation to a totality that the "ideology takes on its true social significance" (1980, p. 38). Thus, "... the whole should not be seen by starting from the notion of element, in terms of which it would be known through the number and nature of the constituent elements, but by starting from the notion of the 'system' in terms of which certain fixed principles govern the arrangement of fluid and fluctuating 'elements'" (1980, p. 34). That is, hierarchy can only be understood with reference to the caste system as a whole, not with reference to its elements, particular castes.

Dumont says further that the elements by which a system is composed are not essences in and of themselves, but have meaning only in relation to each other. Thus, "A phoneme has only the characteristics that oppose it to other phonemes, it is not some thing but only the other of others, thanks to which it signifies something" (1980, p. 40). For Dumont, structure is "when the interdependence of elements of a system is so great that 'they disappear without residue if an inventory is made of the relations between them; a system of relations, in short, not a system of elements" (ibid). This system of relations is what Dumont calls the "ideology" of "holism." For this reason, "while in our society the reference is to the elements, in (Indian) society it is to the whole" (1980, p. 41). For Dumont, then, the "whole" constitutes both method and object of his analysis.

Dumont elaborates upon some of the central tenets of structuralist thought by picking up on Levi-Strauss's notion of the "distinctive opposition," (1980, p. 41) to argue that in India the fundamental opposition is between the pure and impure; it is this opposition that underlies hierarchy (1980, p. 43). Hierarchy itself can be defined as the "principle by which the elements of the whole are ranked in relation to the whole" (1980, p. 66) or "the attribution of rank to each element in relation to the whole" (1980, p. 91).

Yet *Homo Hierarchicus* relies principally upon a separation of status from power to advance the structuralist argument. Thus, "Hierarchy certainly involves gradation, but is neither power nor authority" (1980, p. 65). Hierarchy is rather "the principle by which the elements of a whole are ranked in relation to the whole" (1980, p. 66). For Dumont, it is religion which provides the correct view of the whole. Hierarchy can thereby be isolated as "purely a matter of religious values," and since it rests upon the opposition between the pure and impure, which is a religious opposition, "it tells us nothing about the place of power in society" (1980, p. 66).

To support his argument, Dumont turns to the theory of the Varnas,[4] which he claims also distinguishes between the temporal authority of the King (or Kshatriya) and the spiritual authority of the Priest (or Brahman). Since kings have lost their religious prerogatives and cannot themselves perform rites or ceremonies, power (in theory) is ultimately subordinate to priesthood, though on a day-to-day level, "priesthood submits to power" (1980, p. 71–2). Dumont summarizes:

> It is correct to say that the opposition between pure and impure is a religious, even a ritualistic, matter. For this ideal type of hierarchy to emerge it was necessary that the mixture of status and power ordinarily encountered (everywhere else?) should be separated, but this was not enough: for pure hierarchy to develop without hindrance it was also necessary that power should be absolutely inferior to status. These are the two conditions we find fulfilled early on, in the relationship between Brahman and Kshatriya. (1980, p. 74)

In other words, the warrior or King who holds secular power is subordinate to the priest who holds higher sacral status.

Much has been written of Dumont's separation of power from status. Indeed, the very convergence of status with power forms one of the major critiques of Dumont's work. Dumont's response to his critics (Dumont, 1971) – that he has focused upon the notion of an *ideal type* – has understandably never satisfied them. Yet, in CRS, Dumont made it clear that the notion of status he was working with was essentially a Weberian one: "the disjunction of power and status illustrates perfectly Weber's analytical distinction; its interest for comparison is great, for it presents in unmixed form, it realizes an 'ideal type'" (1980, p. 260). Thus, the value of Dumont's ideal typic picture of India lay *in the comparison*. A fair assessment of Dumont's project, then – one that evaluates it according to the terms of argument he himself set out – requires some attention to the form of society to which India is being compared.

II Toward a Self-reflexive Social Anthropology

Dumont's sociology is an avowedly reflexive one. The first page of the text declares that "caste has something to teach us about ourselves" (1980, p. 1) but warns that because the "caste system is so different from our own social system" the reader may "condemn outright anything which departs from it" (pp. 1–2). Yet it is precisely because Indian society is so different from "our own" that the comparison is fruitful. Difference thus represents both the danger and promise of analysis.

Homo Hierarchicus rests upon a philosophical distinction between what Dumont terms "holism" and "individualism." Yet he goes further to claim that "The principle of equality and the principle of hierarchy are facts..." (1980, p. 3) which distinguish Western from Asian societies. Throughout the introduction to *Homo Hierarchicus*, Dumont muses upon the premises of egalitarianism and individualism in the thought of Rousseau and de Toqueville to understand how "The fusion of equality and identity has become established at the level of common sense." We are therefore unable to separate our own identities from egalitarian ideology and hence are unable to understand the principles of other complex societies. In other words, the egalitarianism of western observers is itself a kind of "sociocentrism" – at best a blindness, and at worst, a willful refusal to understand India on its own terms. Dumont concludes "our modern denial of hierarchy is what chiefly hinders us in understanding the caste system" (1980, p. 20).

Dumont argues that our misunderstanding of hierarchy stems from conflating it with the realm of power; of seeing hierarchy as being synonymous with social stratification. The social stratificationist bias results in part from seeing caste and social class as "phenomena of the same nature" (1980, p. 36). Dumont accepts that hierarchy exists elsewhere, but not in the "ideal" form found in India. But since it exists elsewhere as a "residual" effect of egalitarianism, it represents a contradiction, is therefore "unthinkable" and in its contaminated form is called "social stratification."

> We find for example, in modern societies a residue of hierarchy in the form of social inequalities, but as hierarchy as such is condemned and unthinkable, we find that this residue is currently designated by an expression that evokes inanimate nature and thus presents the phenomenon as devoid of human meaning, incomprehensible: we call it "social stratification." (1977, p. 11–12)

For Dumont, the comparison between India and Western society had to yield pure antinomy or difference. But since comparison between the two forms of society inevitably revealed significant similarity – hierarchy – Dumont had to account for hierarchy in an otherwise "egalitarian" society. And so we arrive at the question of race and Dumont's troubling contention that racism in the West results from the attempt of democratic or egalitarian society to eliminate difference. This is the central argument of Dumont's essay, "Caste, Racism and 'Stratification'."

III The Problem of Racism in Democratic Society: The Caste School of Race Relations

CRS, as noted earlier, fully anticipated the major themes of *Homo Hierarchicus*. First published in French in 1960 in the *Cahiers Internationaux de Sociologie*, it appeared in English in *Contributions to Indian Sociology* in 1961. In this essay, Dumont begins with the question of whether it is possible to speak of castes outside of India and asks more specifically whether the term can be applied "to the division between Whites and Negroes in the Southern states" of the US (1980, p. 247). With hindsight, we not only know that Dumont's answer will be "no," but why.

It is important to recognize, however, that Dumont's question was prompted by the arguments of the "caste school of race relations" which posed an equivalence between caste and race, and more particularly, between casteism and racism. Interestingly, both Dumont and the theorists of the caste school of race relations seemed to have had the same problem in mind – the relationship of caste society to race – but offered divergent conclusions about that relationship.

Emerging as a byproduct of the Chicago School of Sociology, the lineage of the race as caste argument is conventionally traced to Lloyd Warner's arrival at Chicago and the publication of his (1936) article, "American Caste and Class" in the *American Journal of Sociology*. In fact, however, Robert Park's race relations theory also relied upon an understanding of caste.[5] And in a 1928 article, Park held that "race prejudice in the Southern States is caste prejudice" (1928, p. 11). Warner also drew substantially upon Alfred Kroeber's (1930) article on caste in the *Encyclopedia of the Social Sciences* which asserted that "Castes . . . are a special form of social classes, which in tendency at least are present in each society" (1930, p. 254).

These definitional articles were followed by a series of ethnographies of the US South undertaken by sociologists and black anthropologists such as Allison Davis and St. Clair Drake. John Dollard's (1937) *Caste and Class in a Southern Town* and B. G. Gallagher's (1938) *American Caste and the Negro College* preceded the anthropologist Hortense Powdermaker's (1939) *After Freedom*, which avoided the term "caste" and attempted to assert the question of social class. Allison Davis and Burleigh and Mary Gardner's (1941) *Deep South*, however, returned to the "color-caste" system of the South, becoming the paradigmatic study for Gunnar Myrdal's sweeping (1944) *American Dilemma*. In 1945, St. Clair Drake and Horace Cayton's (1945) *Black Metropolis* asked more cautiously whether the caste system of *Deep South* "was present elsewhere in the United States, particularly in the northern cities where there are large concentrations of Negro populations" (1993, p. 775). *Deep South*, of course, was completed under Warner's supervision, with acknowledgments to Drake and Dollard; *Black Metropolis* was dedicated to Robert Park.

All of these works drew from Warner's (and therefore Kroeber's) ubiquitous definition of caste. In other words, most of this work did not reference the Indian situation, but simply asserted, rather than established, caste as the best way to understand US race relations (a point made by the black sociologist Oliver Cox, who contested the formulations of the caste school of race relations). Dollard for example wrote,

> Caste is often seen as a barrier to social contact or, at least, to some forms of social contact. It defines a superior and inferior group and regulates the behavior of members in each group. . . . the caste idea seems to be a barrier to legitimate descent. A union of members of the two castes may not have a legitimate child. (1937, p. 63)

Gallagher asserted simply that,

> The caste in which one is kept is determined by his external racial characteristics, and it is presumed that an individual cannot leave the caste into which he is born. . . . Caste is determined by birth; it may not change. Class is determined by 'family' and by economic circumstance; it may change. (1938, p. 71–2)

By the time the *American Dilemma* appeared in 1944, caste was applied to US race relations not because the comparison to India held, but because "class" and "race" seemed inadequate to the task of understanding US society. As Myrdal put it,

> The term 'race' is . . . inappropriate in a scientific inquiry since it has biological and genetic connotations which . . . run parallel to widely spread racial beliefs. The . . . term 'class' is impractical and confusing . . . since it is generally used to refer to a non-rigid status group from which an individual member can rise or fall. . . . We need a term to distinguish the large and systematic type of social differentiation from the small and spotty type and have . . . used the term caste. (1944: 667)

When *Caste, Class and Race* was published in 1948, Oliver Cromwell Cox had taken exception to the liberal, "race as caste" school and re-entered the (secondary) Indological scholarship on India to establish that caste was unique to India in order to advance a materialist argument for the class basis of US race relations. Accusing Myrdal of writing a "powerful piece of propaganda against the status quo," he charged "if the 'race problem' in the United States is pre-eminently a moral question, it must naturally be resolved by moral means, and this conclusion is precisely the social illusion which the ruling political class has sought to produce" (1948, p. 538).

Cox felt that "caste" had been so objectified as a concept that race relations in the Southern states were made to appear as a natural form of social organization. "The idea of a 'type of society' obscures the actual pathological racial antagonism, leaving some diffused impression that it is socially right, even as the caste system in India is right" (1948, p. 544). Cox here seems to distinguish between a morally "right" Indian caste system and a racial system based on pathological antagonism, Cox's critique of the caste school of race relations is later reincorporated by Dumont in his essay as justification for an Indological reading of the caste system.[6]

In CRS, Dumont considers Kroeber's definition of caste as an extreme form of social class (1980, p. 248–9) only to dismiss it in short order. This is in part because Weber's distinction between class and 'strand' or status group, with caste occupying the extreme case of a status group (1980, p. 249–51), is more useful for him. Though Weber's notion of power differs from Dumont's, Weber's statement "the general place of 'classes' is in the economic order, the place of 'status groups' is within the social order" (Weber, 1946, p. 194) was easily assimilated into Dumont's distinction between (economic) power and (social) status. It is important to note, however, that Dumont seems to have ignored several points in Weber's *Religion of India* where the analogy of the Indian caste system to race relations in the US South is positively considered (1958, pp. 30, 40, 42–3). At one point Weber even refers to segregated Jim Crow trains as "caste coaches" (1958, p. 30). Similarly, in the section on "Ethnic Segregation and Caste" in Weber's essay "Class, Status and Party," forms of segregation are clearly seen to be caste-like (1946, p. 188–9).

Dumont then turns to the "social stratificationists," who he says, "introduce that value-charged word hierarchy" into the study of social classes without understanding the meaning of hierarchy. Here Dumont advances the formulation that will be the backbone of *Homo Hierarchicus*: "It is necessary to distinguish between two very different things: the scale of statuses (called 'religious') which I name hierarchy and which is absolutely distinct from the fact of power; and the distribution of power, economic and political, which is very important in practice, but is distinct from, and subordinate to, hierarchy" (1980, p. 259).

In *Homo Hierarchicus*, Dumont argued that a misunderstanding of hierarchy is what made it possible to understand a "serious and unexpected consequence of egalitarianism:"

> In a universe in which men are conceived no longer as hierarchically ranked in various social or cultural species, but as essentially equal and identical, the difference of nature and status between communities is sometimes reasserted in a disastrous way; it is then conceived as preceding from somatic characteristics – which is racism. (1980, p. 16)

Since racism is a modern phenomenon, Dumont reasoned that

> racism fulfills an old function under a new form. It is as if it were representing in an egalitarian society a resurgence of what was differently and more directly and naturally expressed in a hierarchical society. Make distinction illegitimate and you get discrimination; suppress the former modes of distinction and you have a racist ideology (1980, p. 262).

Implicit here is an almost evolutionary view of hierarchical societies being the originary ones against which egalitarian societies fashion themselves. Hierarchy is naturalized by Dumont as he poses it as a universal means of conceptualizing difference in contrast to that "disastrous" somaticization of difference which is racism.

Perhaps surprisingly, Dumont's argument about the residual nature of racism occupies one scant paragraph in the last five pages of CRS. The argument can be isolated into four distinct propositions (1980, p. 263):

1 Racial discrimination succeeded the slavery of the Negro people once the latter was abolished.
2 The distinction between master and slave was succeeded by the discrimination between White against Black.
3 Racism appears because "the essence of the distinction (between master and slave) was juridical; by suppressing it the transformation of its racial attribute into racist substance was encouraged."
4 If things had been otherwise, the distinction itself would have been overcome.

Dumont's fourth proposition is tautological, and need not concern us. However, the first proposition warrants further attention. Here Dumont seems to rely too much on Hannah Arendt's contention in "Race Thinking Before Racism" that "race thinking, with its roots deep in the 18th century, emerged simultaneously in all Western countries during the 19th century" (1958, p. 158). Arendt seemed to have further suggested that "in America and England, where people had to solve a problem of living together after the abolition of slavery," (1958, p. 177) racism emerged as a part of this vacuum. While it is true that some of the most virulent forms of racism emerged in the wake of abolitionism, that does not mean there were not forms of racism justifying slavery *before* its abolition. And while slavery existed in the classical world and was not necessarily racialized, by the middle of the sixteenth century in Europe, there was considerable evidence to suggest the development of what St. Clair Drake called "racial slavery" and corresponding racist ideologies to justify it (Drake, 1990, p. 227–303).

New world slavery in particular was founded upon and justified by racial ideologies of inferiority. With regard to Dumont's second proposition then, the terms "white" and "black" did not succeed the distinction between master and slave, but were rather so synonymous that the freed Black was presumed a slave until proven otherwise.

As for the third proposition, if we accept that the distinction between master and slave was founded upon the distinction between white and black in the Southern US, then the distinction was not purely juridical, as Dumont would have it, but socially founded. It is thus not surprising that racial discrimination persisted after the formal end of slavery because slavery was not merely a legal or economic institution, but a social one. Racial discrimination therefore took other forms than slavery, and caste was one of those forms. As Drake puts it, "After the abolition of slavery in the 19th century, the White racism that had buttressed racial slavery did not disappear but became the ideology supporting color-caste systems and systems of color-class with non-whites at the bottom" (1990, p. 302). Drake's formulation here echoes various proponents of the caste as race school. Dollard for example argued that, "Caste has replaced slavery as a means of maintaining the essence of the old status order in the South" (1937, p. 62)

Ignoring Myrdal's definition of race as caste, Dumont somewhat paradoxically based his hypothesis upon a passage from Myrdal's *The American Dilemma, The Negro Problem and Modern Democracy.* According to Myrdal, the philosophy of the Enlightenment sought to minimize innate differences, holding that the "natural rights of man" rested upon a biological egalitarianism. (We will ignore for the moment, the first constitution of the US which explicitly prohibited citizenship for those who were not white and not men.) Thus,

> the dogma of racial inequality may, in a sense, be regarded as a strange fruit of the Enlightenment. . . . The race dogma is nearly the only way out for a people so moralistically egalitarian, if it is not prepared to live up to its faith. A nation less fervently committed to democracy could probably live happily in a caste system . . . race prejudice is, in a sense, a function (a perversion) of egalitarianism. (Myrdal, 1944, p. 89 in Dumont 1980, p. 264).

Dumont wonders whether the "mere recall of the egalitarian ideal" is effective in the fight against racism. Quite polemically he asserts,

> It would be better to prevent the passage from the moral principle of equality to the notion that all men are identical. One feels sure that equality can, in our day, be combined with the recognition of differences, so long as such differences are morally neutral. People must be provided with the means of conceptualizing differences.

Clearly, for Dumont, hierarchy was the means of conceptualizing difference.

It is hard to follow Dumont here. People do conceptualize difference (all the time); why hierarchy should be a better way of conceptualizing difference is unclear. At another point in his argument, Dumont himself seems to think that "the diffusion of pluralistic notions of culture and society, affording a counterweight and setting bounds to individualism, is the obvious thing" (1980, p. 265).

In an essay written after *Homo Hierarchicus*, "A Comparative Approach to Modern Ideology and to the Place Within it of Economic Thought" Dumont responded again to his critics,

> I never said, as some seemed to believe, that hierarchy is better than equality, or in the present instance that slavery is preferable to racism. I say only that facts of this kind show that ideology has the power to transform social reality only between certain limits and that when we ignore those limits we produce the contrary of what was desired. (1977, p. 12)

Yet he insists, as he did in CRS and *Homo Hierarchicus* that "the abolition of slavery also gave rise after a short period of time to racism." Dumont calls this, "a spectacular example of the involuntary consequences of equalitarianism" (1977, p. 12).

In "A Comparative Approach to Modern Ideology," Dumont also addresses the case of Nazism, which he defines, not as an instance of racist ideology, but of totalitarianism. Although he is concerned to show how totalitarian society is not a form of holism (as in the Indian case) his account of the emergence of violence is parallel to that for the US South. There he is concerned with distinguishing false notions of hierarchy from the "pure" form in India. In a similar vein, fascism provides the test case for him to distinguish false notions of holism from the pure form in India. He says, "as the totalitarian regime constrains its subjects most radically, it appears to oppose individualism in the current meaning of the term, so the analyst is faced with a contradiction." To solve the contradiction, he says, involves a recognition that totalitarianism lies within modern ideology, not outside of it. Thus, "totalitarianism results from *the attempt, in a society where individualism is deeply rooted and predominant, to subordinate it to the primacy of the society as a whole*" (1977: 12). As it combines conflicting values unknowingly, its "ferocious stress on the social whole" results in violence.

Here again, Dumont leaves us on unsatisfactory ground. Since democratic society and fascist society face similar (though opposite) contradictions: egalitarianism confronted with difference on the one hand; extreme individualism confronted by the subordination to a whole, on the other, it is not clear why the one results in racism and the other in fascism. In fact racism frequently does rely upon and produce sociopolitical violence, and part of what made a "social whole" available for the exercise of fascist violence was the articulation of racial difference. But in fact the heart of the difference lies not between the caste system and racism or fascism (which can then be made interchangeable and seen as similar, though divergent phenomena) but between the caste system or slavery and nazism. As Uday Mehta puts it,

> The Hindu caste system and slavery were at a minimum predicated on an exploitative conception of social and economic order, and in which, therefore, the systematic extermination of those exploited would have been antithetical to that order. In contrast, Nazism was directed precisely to such an extermination. (1997, p. 235)

In the end, what Dumont's argument on racism and fascism reveal are the limits of the structural analysis of the whole coupled with a Weberian ideal type. If power cannot be separated from status, Dumont's analyses of racism and fascism perhaps show more quickly the limits of his thinking than two decades of critique by South Asia area specialists. Still, we might profitably ask why the comparative nature of Dumont's reflections on racism and democratic society have been ignored so long. It is almost as if the study of modern India could not exist without the critique of Dumont's work, while an increasingly empiricist sociology could well afford to ignore it.

Notes

1 The exceptions were Das and Uberoi (1971) and Das (1977) who did not dispute Dumont's Indological focus, but declaimed the lack of method of his Indology.

2 Reviews by Yalman (1969), Barnett et al. (1976), Berreman (1971) and Tambiah (1972) are the exceptions here.

3 Marriot (1969) and Yalman (1969) tag the Weberian influence as one among many; Leach (1971b) and Kantowsky (1971) point to the introduction to *The Protestant Ethic and the Spirit of Capitalism* as the source of Weberian influence on Dumont though the introduction to the *Protestant Ethics* establishes a fraught comparison between "Occident" and "Orient" and Weber frequently uses India as an example of oriental or "Eastern" civilization, his systematic attempt to understand the region is reserved for *The Religion of India.*

4 The four varnas, in order are: Brahmin (priest), Kshatriya (king, warrior), Vaisya (trader, merchant), Sudra (craftsmen). "Untouchables" (alternately called "harijans" or "dalits") are seen to be outside the varnic order.

5 In India, the caste is determined by birth, and it is distinguished by a characteristic trait: the persons of one caste can live with, eat with, and marry only individuals of the same caste. In Europe it is not only birth, but circumstances and education which determine the entrance of an individual into a caste; to marry, to frequent, to invite to the same table only people of the same caste, exist practically in Europe as in India . . . We all live in a confined circle, where we find our friends, our guests, our sons – and daughter-in-law. (Park and Burgess 1924, p. 205–6).

6 At the same time, Gerald Berreman, a former civil rights activist in the US South, worked from his ethnographic experience in the Himalayas to make a case for "Caste in India and the United States," arguing against Dumont and Cox.

Bibliography

Appadurai, A. 1986: Is Homo Hierarchicus? *American Ethnologist*, 13 (4), 745–61.

——1992: Putting Hierarchy in its Place. In George Marcus (ed.), *Rereading Cultural Anthropology*, Duke University Press, 34–47.

Arendt, H. 1958: Race-Thinking Before Racism. In H. Arendt *The Origins of Totalitarianism*, N.Y: Meridian Books, 158–84.

Barnett, S., Fruzetti, L. and Ostor, A. 1976: Hierarchy Purified: notes on Dumont and His Critics. *Journal of Asian Studies*, 35 (4), 627–46.

——1960: Caste in India and the United States. American Journal of Sociology, 66, 120–7 Reprinted in G. Berreman (ed.) 1979: *Caste and Other Inequities*, Delhi: Folklore Institute, 1–13.

Berreman, G. 1971: The Brahminical View of Caste. *Contributions to Indian Sociology* (n.s.), 5, 18–25. Reprinted in G. Berreman (ed.), 1979: *Caste and Other Inequities*, Delhi: Folklore Institute, 155–63.

Collins, S. 1989: Louis Dumont and the Study of Religion. *Religious Studies Review*, 15(1), January, 14–20.

Cox, O. C. 1948: *Caste, Class and Race*. N. Y: Monthly Review Press.

—— 1961: Berreman's Caste in India and the United States. *American Journal of Sociology*, 66, 510–12. Reprinted in G. Berreman (ed.) 1979: *Caste and Other Inequities*, Delhi: Folklore Institute, 14–16.

Das, V. 1977: *Structure and Cognition*. Delhi: OUP.

Das, V. and Uberoi, J. S. 1971: The Elementary Structure of Caste. *Contributions to Indian Sociology*, 5, 33–43.

Davis, K. 1981: Caste, Class, and Stratification. In K. Davis (ed.), *Human Society*, Delhi: Surjeet, 364–91.

Davis, A., Gardner, B. B. and Gardner, M. R. 1941: *Deep South*. University of Chicago Press.

Dirks, N. 1992: Castes of Mind. Representations, 37, 56–78.

Dollard, J. 1937. *Caste and Class in a Southern Town*. New Haven: Yale University Press. Revised edition: 1945.

Drake, St. C. 1990: *Black Folk Here and There*, vol. II. Los Angeles: Center for Afro-American Studies.

—— and Cayton, H. 1945: *Black Metropolis*. University of Chicago Press.

Dumont, L. 1960: Caste, Racisme et "Stratification". *Cahiers Internationaux de Sociologie*, 29, 91–112.

—— 1971: On Putative Hierarchy and Some Allergies to It. *Contributions to Indian Sociology*, 5, 58–78.

—— 1977: A Comparative Approach to Modern Ideology and the Place within it of Economic Thought. In L. Dumont (ed.), *From Mandeville to Marx*, University of Chicago Press, 3–32.

—— 1980: *Homo Hierarchicus*, 2nd rev. ed. University of Chicago Press. (First edition published in 1970.)

—— 1986: The Totalitarian Disease: Individualism and Racism in Adolf Hitler's Representations. In L. Dumont (ed.), *Essays on Individualism: Modern Ideology in Anthropological Perspective*, University of Chicago Press, 149–79.

Gallagher, B. G. 1938: *American Caste and the Negro College*. NY: Columbia University Press.

Heesterman, J. C. 1971: Priesthood and Brahminism. *Contributions to Indian Sociology*, 5, 43–7.

Kantowsky, D. 1971: The Problem of Sponsored Change. *Contributions to Indian Sociology*, 5, 47–50.

Khare, R. S. 1971a: Encompassing and Encompassed: A Deductive Theory of the Caste System. *Journal of Asian Studies*, 30, 859–68.

—— 1971b: A Theory of Pure Hierarchy. *Contributions to Indian Sociology*, 5, 27–33.

Kolenda, P. 1973: Review of Homo Hierarchicus. *Journal of the American Oriental Society*, 93 (1), 121–4.

—— 1976: Seven Kinds of Hierarchy in Homo Hierarchicus. *Journal of Asian Studies*, 35 (4), 581–96.

Kroeber, A. 1930: Caste. In E. R. A. Seligman and A. Johnson (eds), *Encyclopedia of the Social Sciences*, vol. III, 254–7.

Leach, E. 1971a: Hierarchical Man: Louis Dumont and His Critics. *South Asian Review*, 4 (3), 233–7.

—— 1971b: Espirit in Homo Hierarchicus. *Contributions to Indian Sociology* (n.s.), 5, 14–23.

Madan, T. N. 1971: On the Nature of Caste in India: A Review Symposium on Louis Dumont's Homo Hierarchicus. *Contributions to Indian Sociology* (n.s.), 5, 1–13.

Marriot, McK. 1969: Review of Homo Hierarchicus. *American Anthropologist*, 71, 1166–75.
—— 1976: Correspondence "Interpreting Indian Society: A Monistic Alternative to Dumont's Dualism". *Journal of Asian Studies*, 36 (1), 189–95.
Mehta, U. 1997: The Essential Ambiguities of Race and Racism. *Political Power and Social Theory*, 11, 235–46.
Myrdal, G. 1944: *An American Dilemma: The Negro Problem and Modern Democracy*. NY: Harper and Brothers.
Park, R. E. 1928: The Bases of Race Prejudice. *Annals of the American Academy of Political and Social Sciences*. CXL (Nov. 1928): 11–20.
Park, R. E. and Burgess, E. W. 1924: *Introduction to the Science of Sociology*. University of Chicago Press.
Powdermaker, H. 1939: *After Freedom*. NY: Viking.
Richards, J. F. and Nichols, R. W. 1976: Symposium of the Contribution of Louis Dumont: Introduction. *Journal of Asian Studies*. 35(4): 579–80.
Singer, M. 1971: Modernization or Traditionalization. *Contributions to Indian Society*, 5, 50–7.
Srinivas, M. N. 1984: Some reflections of the Nature of Caste Hierarchy. *Contributions to Indian Sociology*, 18 (2), 151–67.
Stocking, G. 1968: *Race, Culture and Evolution: Essays in the History of Anthropology*. University of Chicago Press.
Stocking, G. (ed.) 1974: *A Franz Boas Reader: The Shaping of American Anthropology, 1883–1911*. Midway reprint. University of Chicago Press.
Tambiah, S. J. 1972: Review of Homo Hierarchicus. *American Anthropologist*, 74 (4), 832–5.
Visweswaran, K. 1998: Race and the Culture of Anthropology. *American Anthropologist*, 100 (1), 1–14.
Von Furer-Haimendorf, C. 1971: Tribes and Hindu Society. *Contributions to Indian Society*, 5, 24–7.
Warner, L. 1936: American Caste and Class. *American Journal of Sociology*, XLII (2), 234–7.
Weber, M. 1946: Class, Status and Party. In H. H. Gerth and C. Wright Mills (eds), *From Max Weber*, NY: Oxford, 180–95.
—— 1958: *The Religion of India*. NY: Free Press.
Yalman, N. 1969: De Toqueville in India: An Essay on the Caste System. *Man* (n.s.), 4, 123–31.

12

CASTE, RACISM AND "STRATIFICATION" REFLECTIONS OF A SOCIAL ANTHROPOLOGIST*

Louis Dumont

In a recent article Professor Raymond Aron writes about sociology: "what there exists of a critical, comparative, pluralist theory is slight".[1] This in indeed the feeling one has when, after studying the caste system in India, one turns to comparing it with other social systems and to seeing, in particular, how it has been accommodated within the theory of "social stratification" as developed in America. To begin with, the problem can be put in very simple terms: is it permissible, or is it not, to speak of "castes" outside India? More particularly, may the term be applied to the division between Whites and Negroes in the southern states of the United States of America? To this question a positive answer has been given by some American sociologists[2] – in accordance with the common use of the word – while most anthropologists with Indian experience would probably answer it in the negative.[3] Ideally, this question might appear as a matter of mere terminological choice: either we accept the former alternative and adopt a very broad definition, and as a result we may have to distinguish sub types, as some authors who have opposed the "racial caste" (USA) to the "cultural caste" (India); or we refuse any extension of the term and apply it exclusively to the Indian type precisely defined, and in this case other terms will be necessary to designate the other types. But in actual fact, a certain usage has been established, and perhaps it is only by criticizing its already manifest implications that a way can be opened to a better comparative view. I shall, therefore, begin by criticizing the usage which predominates in America in the hope of showing how social anthropology can assist sociology in this matter. Two aspects will particularly require attention: what idea the authors in question have formed of the Indian system, and which place they give to the concept of "caste" in relation to neighbouring concepts such as "class" and to the broad heading of "social stratification" under which they often group such facts. Thereafter I shall tentatively outline the framework of a true comparison.

A Caste as an Extreme Case of Class: Kroeber

A definition of caste given by Kroeber is rightly regarded as classical, for the whole sociological trend with which I am concerned here links up with it.

In his article on "Caste" in the *Encyclopoedia of Social Sciences* (Vol. iii, 1930, 254b–257a), he enumerates the characteristics of caste (endogamy, heredity, relative rank) and goes on to say: "*Castes, therefore, are a special form of social classes*, which in tendency at least are present in every society. Castes differ from social classes, however, in that they have emerged into social consciousness to the point that custom and law attempt their rigid and permanent separation from one another. *Social classes are the generic soil from which caste systems have at various times and places independently grown up* . . ." (my italics).

By "caste systems" he means in what follows, apart from India, medieval Europe and medieval Japan. He implicitly admits, however, that the last two cases are imperfect: either the caste organization extends to only a part of the society, or, as in the Japanese "quasi-caste system", the division of labour and the integration with religion remain vague.

For us, the essential point here is that "caste" is considered as an extreme case of "class". Why? Probably in the first place because of the "universality of anthropology", as Lloyd Warner says while accepting Kroeber's definition.[4] In the second place, because "caste" is at once rigid and relatively rare, whereas "class" is more flexible, vaguer and relatively very widespread. But the problem is only deferred, for in such a perspective it should be necessary to define "class", which is much more difficult than to define "caste". Never mind, "class", after all, is familiar to us, while "caste" is strange. . . . We are landed at the core of the socio-centricity within which the whole school of authors under discussion develops. Actually, if one were prepared to make light of the relative frequency with which the supposed "class" occurs, and if one were solely concerned with conceptual clarity, the terms could just as well be reversed, and one could start from the Indian caste system, which offers in a clear and crystalline form what is elsewhere diluted and blurred in many ways. The definition quoted reduces a society's consciousness of itself to an epiphenomenon – although some importance is attached to it: "They have emerged into social consciousness." The case shows that to do this is to condemn oneself to obscurity.

B Distinction between Caste, Estate, and Class

The oneness of the human species, however, does not demand the arbitrary reduction of diversity to unity, it only demands that it should be possible to pass from one particularity to another, and that no effort should be spared in order to elaborate a common language in which each particularity can be adequately described. The first step to that end consists in recognizing differences.

Before Kroeber gave his definition, Max Weber had made an absolute distinction between "class" and *Stand*, "status-group", or "estate" in the sense of pre-revolutionary

France – as between economy on the one hand and "honour" and "social intercourse" on the other.[5] His definition of class as an economic group has been criticized, but it has the merit of not being too vague. Allowing that social classes as commonly referred to in our societies have these two aspects, the analytical distinction is none the less indispensable from a comparative point of view, as we shall see. In Max Weber as in Kroeber, caste represents an extreme case; but this time it is the status-group which becomes a caste when its separation is secured not only through convention and laws, but also ritually (impurity through contact). Is this transition from status-group to caste conceived as genetic or only logical? One notes in passing that, in the passage of *Wirtschaft und Gesellschaft* which I have in view here, Weber thinks that individual castes develop some measure of distinct cults and gods – a mistake of Western common sense which believes that whatever can be distinguished must be different. Into the genesis of caste, Weber introduces a second component, namely a reputedly ethnic difference. From this point of view, castes would be closed communities (*Gemeinschaften*), endogamous and believing their members to be of the same blood, which would put themselves in society (*vergesellschaftet*) one with the other. On the whole, caste would be the outcome of a conjunction between status-group and ethnic community. At this juncture a difficulty appears. For it seems that Weber maintains the difference between *Gesellschaft* and *Gemeinschaft*: on the one hand the *Vergesellschaftung* of a reputedly ethnic group, a "Paria people", tolerated only for the indispensable economic services it performs, like the Jews in medieval Europe, on the other the *Gemeinschaft* made up of status-groups or, in the extreme case, of castes. If I am not mistaken, the difficulty emerges in the concluding sentence, which has to reconcile the two by means of an artificial transition from the one to the other: "Eine umgreifende *Vergesellschaftung* die ethnisch geschiedenen Gemeinschaften zu einem spezifischen, politischen *Gemeinschaftshandeln* zusammenschliesst" (my italics), or, freely translated, "the *societalization* of ethnically distinct communities embraces them to the point of uniting them, on the level of political action, in a *community* of a new kind". The particular group then acknowledges a hierarchy of honour and at the same time its ethnic difference becomes a difference of function (warriors, priests, etc.). However remarkable the conjunction here achieved between hierarchy, ethnic difference and division of labour may be, one may wonder whether Weber's failure is not due to the fact that to a hierarchical view he added "ethnic" considerations through which he wanted to link up widespread ideas on the racial origin of the caste system with the exceptional situation of certain minority communities like Jews or Gypsies in Western societies.

What remains is the distinction, as analytical as one could wish, between economic group and status-group. In the latter category, one can then distinguish more clearly, as Sorokin did,[6] between "order" or "estate" and caste. As an instance, the clergy in prerevolutionary France did not renew itself from within, it was an open "estate".

C "Caste" in the USA

At first sight there is a paradox in the works of the two most notable authors who have applied the term "caste" to the separation between White and Negroes in the USA.

While their purpose is to oppose the "colour line" to class distinctions, they both accept the idea that caste is a particular and extreme form of class, not a distinct phenomenon. We have seen that Lloyd Warner accepts Kroeber's idea of continuity; however he immediately insists, as early as his article of 1936, that whilst Whites and Negroes make up two "castes", the two groups are stratified into classes according to a common principle, so that the Negroes of the upper class are superior from the point of view of class to the small Whites, while at the same time being inferior to them from the point of view of "caste".[7] Gunnar Myrdal also states that "caste may thus in a sense be viewed as the extreme form of absolutely rigid class", in this sense "caste" constitutes "a harsh deviation from the ordinary American social structure and the American Creed".[8] The expression "*harsh* deviation" is necessary here to correct the idea of continuity posited in the preceding sentence. In other words, the supposed essential identity between class and caste appears to be rooted in the fact that, once equality is accepted as the norm, any form of inequality appears to be the same as any other because of their common deviation from the norm. We shall see presently that this is fully conscious, elaborately justified in Myrdal. But if, from the standpoint of comparative sociology, one purports to describe these forms of inequality in themselves and if, moreover, one finds that many societies have a norm of inequality, then the presumed unity between class on the one hand and the American form of discrimination on the other becomes meaningless, as our authors themselves sufficiently witness.

The use of the term "caste" for the American situation is justified by our two authors in very different ways. For Myrdal, the choice of a term is a purely practical matter. One should take a word of common usage – and not try to escape from the value judgments implicit in such a choice. Of the three available terms, "class" is not suitable, "race" would give an objective appearance to subjective justifications and prejudices, so there remains only "caste" which is already used in this sense, and which can be used, in a monographic manner, without any obligation to consider how far it means the same thing in India and in the USA[9] In point of fact, the pejorative coloration of the word by no means displeases Myrdal. While the word "race" embodies a false justification, the word "caste" carries a condemnation. This is in accordance with American values as defined by the author in the following pages. The American ideology is egalitarian to the extreme. The "American Creed" demands free competition, which from the point of view of social stratification represents a combination of two basic norms, equality and liberty, but accepts inequality as a result of competition.[10] From this one deduces the "meaning" of differences of social status in this particular country, one conceives classes as the "results of the restriction of free competition", while "caste", with its draconian limitations of free competition, directly negates the American Creed, creates a contradiction in the conscience of every White, survives only because of a whole system of prejudices, and should disappear altogether.

All this is fine, and the militant attitude in which Gunnar Myrdal sees the sole possibility of true objectivity could hardly be more solidly based. In particular, he has the merit of showing that it is in relation to values (a relation not expressed by Kroeber and Warner) that the assumed continuity of class and caste can be best understood. But was it really necessary in all this to use the word "caste" without scientific guarantee?[11] Would the argument have lost in efficacy if it had been expressed only in terms of "discrimination", "segregation", etc.? Even if it had, ought one to risk obscuring comparison in order to promote action? Gunnar Myrdal does not care for comparison. Further, does he not eschew comparative theory, in so far as he achieves his objectivity only when he can personally share the values of the society he is studying?

Unlike Myrdal, Lloyd Warner thinks that "caste" can be used of the Southern USA in the same sense as it is used of India. This is seen from a "comparative study" by Warner and Allison Davis,[12] in which the results of their American study are summarized, "caste" defined, and two or three pages devoted to the Indian side. This Indian summary, though based on good authors, is not very convincing. The variability of the system in time and space is insisted upon to the point of stating that: "It is not correct to speak of an Indian caste system since there is a variety of systems there."

In general, caste here is conceived as a variety of class, differing from it in that it forbids mobility either up or down. The central argument runs as follows: in the Southern States, in addition to the disabilities imposed upon the Negroes and the impossibility for them to "pass", there is between Whites and Negroes neither marriage nor commensality; the same is true in India between different castes. It is the same kind of social phenomenon. "Therefore, for the comparative sociologist and social anthropologist they are forms of behaviour which must have the same term applied to them" (p. 233).

This formula has the virtue of stating the problem clearly, so that if we do not agree with Warner we can easily say why. A first reason, which might receive ready acceptance, is that under the label of "behaviour pattern" or "social phenomena" Warner confuses two different things, namely a collection of particular features (endogamy, mobility and commensality prohibition, etc.) and a whole social system, "caste" in the case of India obviously meaning "the caste system". It is not asked whether the sum of the features under consideration is enough (to the exclusion of all the features left out of consideration) to define the social system: in fact there is no question of a system but only of a certain number of features of the Indian caste system which, according to the author, would be sufficient to define the system. There is really here a *choice* which there is no necessity to follow.[13]

Let me try to indicate the reasons against the proposed choice. It is generally admitted, at any rate in social anthropology, that particular features must be seen in their relations with other particular features. There follows, to my mind, a radical consequence – that a particular feature, if taken not in itself but in its concrete position within a system (what is sometimes called its "function"), can have a totally different meaning according to the position it occupies. That is to say, from a sociological standpoint it is *actually different*. Thus as regards the endogamy of a group: it is not sufficient to say that the group is "closed", for this very closure is perhaps not, sociologically speaking, the same thing in all cases; in itself it is the same thing, but in itself it is simply not a sociological fact, as it is not, in the first place, a conscious fact. One is led inevitably to the ideology, overlooked in the behaviouristic sociology of Warner and others, which implicitly posits that, among the particular features to be seen in relation to each other, ideological features do not have the same status as the others. Nevertheless a great part of the effort of Durkheim (and of Max Weber as well) bore on the necessity of recognizing in them the same objectivity as in other aspects of social life. Of course this is not to claim that ideology is necessarily the ultimate reality of social facts and delivers their "explanation", but only that it is the condition of their existence.

The case of endogamy shows very clearly how social facts are distorted through a certain approach. Warner and Allison treat it as a fact of behaviour and not as a fact of values. As such it would be the same as the factual endogamy of a tribe having no prejudice against intermarriage with another tribe, but which given circumstances alone prevent from practising it. If, on the contrary, endogamy is a fact of values, we are not justified in separating it in the analysis from other facts of values, and particularly – though not solely – from the justifications of it the people give. It is only by neglecting this that racial discrimination and the caste system can be confused. But, one might say, is it not possible that analysis may reveal a close kinship between social facts outwardly similar and ideologically different? The possibility can be readily admitted, but only to insist the more vigorously that we are as yet very far indeed from having reached that point, and that the task for the moment is to take social facts as they are given, without imposing upon them a discrimination scientifically as unwarrantable as is, in American society, the discrimination which these authors attack. The main point is that the refusal to allow their legitimate place to facts of consciousness makes true sociological comparison impossible, because it carries with it a sociocentric attitude. In order to see one's own society from without, one must become conscious of its values and their implications. Difficult as this always is, it becomes impossible if values are neglected. This is confirmed here from the fact that, in Warner's conceptual scheme, the continuity between class and caste proceeds, as we have seen, from an unsuspected relation to the egalitarian norm, whilst it is presented as a matter of behaviour.

The criticism of the "Caste School of Race Relations" has been remarkably carried out by Oliver C. Cox.[14] From the same sources as Warner, Cox, with admirable insight, has evolved a picture of the caste system which is infinitely truer than that with which Warner was satisfied. It is true that one cannot everywhere agree with Cox, but we must remember that he was working at second and even at third hand (for instance from Bouglé). Even the limits of Cox's understanding show up precisely our most rooted Western prejudices. He is insufficient mainly in what regards the religious moorings of the system (purity and impurity); because for the Westerner society exists independently of religion and he hardly imagines that it could be otherwise. On the other hand, Cox sees that one should not speak of the individual caste but of the system (pp. 3–4), and that it is not a matter of racial ideology: "... Although the individual is born heir to his caste, his identification with it is assumed to be based upon some sort of psychological and moral heritage which does not go back to any fundamental somatic determinant" (p. 5).

Elsewhere he writes (p. 14): "Social inequality is the keynote of the system ... there is a fundamental creed or presumption (of inequality) ... antithesis of the Stoic doctrine of human equality. ... " We see here how Cox strikes on important and incontrovertible points whenever he wishes to emphasize the difference between India and America. I will not enlarge on his criticism of Warner and his school; we have already seen that he makes the essential point: the Indian system is a coherent social system based on the principle of inequality, while the American "colour bar" contradicts the egalitarian system within which it occurs and of which it is a kind of disease.[15]

The use of the word "caste" to designate American racial segregation has led some authors, in an effort to recognize at the same time the ideological difference, to make a secondary distinction. Already in 1937 John Dollard was writing: "American caste is pinned not to cultural but to biological factors."[16] In 1941, in an article called "Intermarriage in Caste Society" in which he was considering, besides India, the Natchez and the society of the Southern United States, Kingsley Davis asked: how is marriage between different units possible in these societies, while stratification into castes is closely dependent on caste endogamy? His answer was, in the main, that a distinction must be made between a "racial caste system" in which hybrids present an acute problem, and a "non-racial caste system" where this is not so. In India, hypergamy as defined by Blunt for the north of India, i.e. marriage between a man of an upper subcaste and a woman of a lower subcaste within the same caste can be understood in particular as a factor of "vertical solidarity" and as allowing for the exchange of prestige in return for goods (p. 386). (The last point actually marks an essential aspect of true hypergamy, in which the status or prestige of the husband as well as the sons is not affected by the relatively inferior status of the wife or mother.) Another difference between the two kinds of "caste systems" is that the "racial" systems rather oppose two groups only, whereas the other systems distinguish a great number of "strata". Finally, K. Davis remarks that the hypothesis of the racial origin of the Indian caste system is not proven and that at any rate it is not racial today (n. 22). It is strange that all this did not lead Davis to reflect upon the inappropriateness of using the same word to denote so widely different facts. For him caste, whatever its content may be, is "an extreme form of stratification", as for others it was an extreme case of class. This brings us to the question of the nature of this category of "stratification".

D "Social Stratification"

Though the expression deserves attention in view of the proliferation of studies published under this title in the United States and the theoretical discussions to which it has given rise, it does not in effect introduce anything new on the point with which we are here concerned. We meet again the same attitude of mind we have already encountered, but here it runs up against difficulties. As Pfautz acknowledges in his critical bibliography of works published between 1945 and 1952, it is essentially a matter of "class".[17] However, Weber's distinction has made its way in the world: one can distinguish types of social stratification according to whether the basis of inequality is power, or prestige, or a combination of both, and classes are usually conceived of as implying a hierarchy of power (political as well as economic), castes and "estates" a hierarchy of prestige (pp. 392–3). One notes however that the community studies of Warner and others conclude that the status hierarchy is a matter of prestige and not of power. Let us stress here the use of the word "hierarchy", which appears to be introduced in order to allow different species to be distinguished within the genus "stratification". But here are two strikingly different concepts: should the quasi-geological impassibility suggested by the latter give way to the consideration of values?

A theoretical controversy in the columns of the *American Sociological Review* is very interesting for the light it throws on the preoccupations and implicit postulates of some sociologists.[18] The starting-point was an article published in 1945 by Kingsley Davis and Wilbert E. Moore. Davis had, three years earlier, given basic definitions for the study of stratification (*status*, *stratum*, etc.). Here the authors raised the question of the "function" of stratification. How is it that such palpable inequalities as those referred to under the name of social classes are encountered in a society whose acknowledged norm is equality? Davis and Moore formulate the hypothesis that it is the result of a mechanism comparable to that of the market: inequality of rewards is necessary in a differentiated society in order that the more difficult or important occupations, those demanding a long training in special skills or involving heavy responsibilities, can be effectively carried out. Buckley objected that Davis and Moore had confused true stratification and pure and simple differentiation: the problem of stratification is not, or is not only, one of knowing how individuals potentially equal at the start find themselves in unequal positions ("achieved inequality"), but of discovering how inequality is maintained, since terms like stratum or stratification are generally taken as implying permanent, hereditary, "ascribed" inequality. In a rejoinder to Buckley, Davis admitted the difference of points of view; he added that the critic's animosity seemed to him to be directed against the attempt to explain inequality functionally. In my opinion, Davis was right in raising the question of inequality; he was wrong, as Buckley seems to imply, in raising it where inequality is weakest instead of tackling it where it is strongest and most articulate. But in so doing he remained within the tradition we have observed here, which always implicitly refers itself to equality as the norm, as this controversy and the very use of the term "inequality" show.

In a recent article Dennis H. Wrong sums up the debate. He points out the limitations of Davis's and Moore's theory and quotes from a work of the former a passage which again shows his pursuit of the functional necessity of stratification, as illustrated for instance by the fact that sweepers tend to have an inferior status in all societies (he is thinking of India).[19] In the end, Wrong asks for studies on certain relations between the egalitarian ideal and other aspects of society, such as the undesirable consequences of extreme equality or mobility (p. 780). It appears that equality and inequality are considered here as opposite tendencies to be studied on the functional level. Referring to the Utopians, Wrong recalls the difficulty of "making the leap from history into freedom" (p. 775).

Something has happened then in this branch of American sociology. With the multiplication of studies on social classes, one has been led to introduce values and that value-charged word, "hierarchy"; one has been led to search for the functions (and dysfunctions) of what our societies valorize as well as of what they do not valorize ("in-equality") and which had been called for that reason by a neutral and even pejorative term, "stratification". What is in fact set against the egalitarian norm is not, as the term suggests, a kind of residue, a precipitate, a geological legacy, but actual forces, factors or functions. These are negated by the norm, but they nevertheless exist; to express them, the term "stratification" is altogether inadequate. Nelson N. Foote wrote in a preface to a series of studies: "The dialectical theme of American history... has been a counterpoint of the principles of hierarchy and equality."[20] The "problem" of social classes, or of "social stratification" as it appears to our sociologists springs from the contradiction between the egalitarian ideal, accepted by all these scholars as by the society to which they belong, and an array of facts showing that difference, differentiation, tends even among us to assume a hierarchical aspect, and to become permanent or hereditary inequality, or discrimination. As Raymond Aron says: "At the heart of the problem of classes I perceive the antinomy between the fact of differentiation and the ideal of equality."[21] There are here realities which are made obscure to us by the fact that our values and the forms of our consciousness reject or ignore them. (This is probably still more so for Americans.) In order to understand them better, it is advantageous to turn to those societies which on the contrary approve and emphasize them. In so doing we shall move from "stratification" to hierarchy.

E Hierarchy in India

It is impossible to describe the caste system in detail here. Rather, after briefly recalling its main features, I shall isolate more or less arbitarily the aspect which concerns us. Bouglé's definition can be the starting-point: the society is divided into a large number of permanent groups which are at once specialized, hierarchized and separated (in matter of marriage, food, physical contact) in relation to each other.[22] It is sufficient to add that the common basis of these three features is the opposition of pure and impure, an opposition of a hierarchical nature which implies separation and, on the professional level, specialization of the occupations relevant to the opposition; that this basic opposition can segment itself without limit; finally, if one likes, that the conceptual reality of the system lies in this opposition, and not in the groups which it opposes – this accounts for the structural character of these groups, caste and subcaste being the same thing seen from different points of view.

It has been acknowledged that hierarchy is thus rendered perfectly univocal in principle.[23] Unfortunately, there has sometimes been a tendency to obscure the issue by speaking of not only religious (or "ritual") status, but also "secular" (or "social") status based upon power, wealth, etc. which Indians would also take into consideration. Naturally Indians do not confuse a rich man with a poor man but, as specialists seem to become increasingly aware, it is necessary to distinguish between two very different things: the scale of statuses (called "religious") which I name hierarchy and which is absolutely distinct from the fact of power; and the distribution of power, economic and political, which is very important in practice but is distinct from, and subordinate to, hierarchy. It will be asked then how power and hierarchy are related to each other. Precisely, Indian society answers this question in a very explicit manner.[24] Hierarchy culminates in the Brahman, or priest; it is the Brahman who consecrates the king's power, which otherwise depends entirely on force (this results from the dichotomy). From very early times, the relationships between Brahman and king or Kshatriya are fixed. While the Brahman is spiritually or absolutely supreme, he is materially dependent; whilst the king is materially the master, he is spiritually subordinate. A similar relation distinguishes one from the other the two superior "human ends", *dharma* (action conforming to) universal order and *artha* (action conforming to) selfish interest, which are also hierarchized in such a way that the latter is legitimate only within the limits set by the former. Again, the theory of the *gift* made to Brahmans, a pre-eminently meritorious action, can be regarded as establishing a means of transformation of material goods into values (*cf.* hypergamy, mentioned above, p. 248: one gets prestige from the gift of a girl to superiors).

This disjunction of power and status illustrates perfectly Weber's analytical distinction; its interest for comparison is great, for it presents an unmixed form, it realizes an "ideal type". Two features stand out: first, in India, any totality is expressed in the form of a hierarchical enumeration of its components (thus of the state or kingdom for example), hierarchy marks the conceptual integration of a whole, it is, so to say, its intellectual cement. Secondly, if we are to generalize, it can be supposed that hierarchy, in the sense that we are using the word here, and in accord with its etymology, never attaches itself to power as such, but always to religious functions, because religion is the form that the universally true assumes in these societies. For example, when the king has the supreme rank, as is generally the case, it is very likely not by reason of his power but by reason of the religious nature of his function. From the point of view of rank at any rate, it is the opposite to what one most often supposes, namely that power is the essential which then attracts to itself religious dignities or finds in them support and justification.

One may see in the hierarchical principle, as it appears in India in its pure state, a fundamental feature of complex societies other than our own, and a principle of their unity; not their material, but their conceptual or symbolic unity. That is the essential "function" of hierarchy: it expresses the unity of such a society whilst connecting it to what appears to it to be universal, namely a conception of the cosmic order, whether or not it includes a God, or a king as mediator. If one likes, hierarchy integrates the society by reference to its values. Apart from the general reluctance which searching for social functions at this level is likely to encounter, it will be objected that there are societies without hierarchy, or else societies in which hierarchy does not play the part described above. It is true for example that tribes, while they are not entirely devoid of inequalities, may have neither a king nor, say, a secret society with successive grades. But that applies to relatively simple societies, with few people, and where the division of labour is little developed.

F The Modern Revolution

There remain the societies of the modern Western type, which go so far as to inscribe the principle of equality in their constitutions. It is indeed true that, if values and not behaviour alone are considered, a profound gap has to be acknowledged between the two kinds. What has happened? Is it possible to take a simple view of it? The societies of the past, most societies, have believed themselves to be based in the order of things, natural as well as social; they thought they were copying or designing their very conventions after the principles of life and the world. Modern society wants to be "rational", to break away from nature in order to set up an autonomous human order. To that end, it is enough to take the true measure of man and from it deduce the human order. No gap between the ideal and the real: like an engineer's blueprint, the representation will create the actuality. At this point society, the old mediator between man in his particularity and nature, disappears. There are but human individuals, and the problem is how to make them all fit together. Man will now draw from himself an order which is sure to satisfy him. As the source of this rationality, Hobbes posits not an ideal, always open to question, but the most general passion, the common generator of human actions, the most assured human reality. The individual becomes the measure of all things, the source of all "rationality"; the egalitarian principle is the outcome of this attitude, for it conforms to reason, being the simplest view of the matter, while it most directly negates the old hierarchies.[25]

As against the societies which believed themselves to be natural, here is the society which wants itself to be rational. Whilst the "natural" society was hierarchized, finding its rationality in setting itself as a whole within a vaster whole, and was unaware of the "individual", the "rational" society on the other hand, recognizing only the individual, i.e. seeing universality, or reason, only in the particular man, places itself under the standard of equality and is unaware of itself as a hierarchized whole. In a sense, the "leap from history into freedom" has already been made, and we live in a realized Utopia.

Between these two types which it is convenient to contrast directly, there should probably be located an intermediary type, in which nature and convention are distinguished and social conventions are susceptible of being judged by reference to an ideal model accessible to reason alone. But whatever may be the transitions which make for the evolution of the second type from the first, it is in the modern revolution which separates the two types, really the two leaves of the same diptych, that the central problem of comparative sociology most probably lies: how can we describe in the same language two "choices" so diametrically opposed to each other, how can we take into account at once the revolution in values which has transformed modern societies as well as the "unity of anthropology"? Certainly this cannot be done by refusing to acknowledge the change and reducing everything to "behaviour", nor by extending the obscurity from one side to the other, as we should by talking of "social stratification" in general. But we remark that where one of the leaves of the diptych is obscure and blurred, the other is clear and distinct; use can be made of what is conscious in one of the two types of society in order to decipher what is not conscious in the other.

G From Hierarchy to Discrimination

One can attempt, in broad terms, to apply this comparative perspective to the American racist phenomenon. It is obvious on the one hand that society did not completely cease to be society, as a hierarchized whole, on the day it willed itself to be simply a collection of individuals. In particular, the tendency to make hierarchical distinctions continued. On the other hand, racism is more often than not understood to be a modern phenomenon. (Economic causes of its emergence have sometimes been sought, whilst much closer and more probable ideological connections were neglected.) The simplest hypothesis therefore is to assume that racism fulfils an old function under a new form. It is as if it were representing in an egalitarian society a resurgence of what was differently and more directly and naturally expressed in a hierarchical society. Make distinction illegitimate, and you get discrimination; suppress the former modes of distinction and you have a racist ideology. Can this view be made more precise and confirmed? Societies of the past knew a hierarchy of status bringing with it privileges and disabilities, amongst others the total juridical disability of slavery. Now the history of the United States tells us just this, that racial discrimination succeeded the slavery of the Negro people once the latter was abolished. (One is tempted to wonder why this all important transition has not been more systematically studied, from a sociological point of view, than it seems to have been, but perhaps one's ignorance is the answer.[26]) The distinction between master and slave was succeeded by discrimination by White against Black. To ask why racism appears is already to have in part answered the question: the essence of the distinction was juridical; by suppressing it the transformation of its racial attribute into racist substance was encouraged. For things to have been otherwise the distinction itself should have been overcome.

In general, racism certainly has more complex roots. Besides the internal difference of status, traditional societies knew an external difference, itself coloured by hierarchy, between the "we" and the others. It was normally social and cultural. For the Greeks as for others, foreigners were barbarians, strangers to the civilization and society of the "we"; for that reason they could be enslaved. In the modern Western world not only are citizens free and equal before the law, but a transition develops, at least in popular mentality, from the moral principle of equality to the belief in the basic identity of all men, because they are no longer taken as samples of a culture, a society or a social group, but as *individuals* existing in and for themselves.[27] In other words, the recognition of a cultural difference can no longer ethnocentrically justify inequality. But it is observed that in certain circumstances, which it would be necessary to describe, a hierarchical difference continues to be posited, which is this time attached to somatic characteristics, physiognomy, colour of the skin, "blood". No doubt, these were at all times marks of distinction, but they have now become the essence of it. How is this to be explained? It is perhaps apposite to recall that we are heirs to a dualistic religion and philosophy: the distinction between matter and spirit, body and soul, permeates our entire culture and especially the popular mentality. Everything looks as if the egalitarian-identitarian mentality was situated within this dualism, as if once equality and identity bear on the individual *souls*, distinction could only be effected with regard to the *bodies*. What is more, discrimination is collective, it is as if only physical characteristics were essentially collective where everything mental tends to be primarily individual. (Thus mental differences are attributed to physical types). Is this far-fetched? It is only emphasizing the Christian ancestry of modern individualism and egalitarianism: the individual has only fellow-men (even his enemies are considered, not only as objects, but also as subjects), and he believes in the fundamental equality of all men taken severally; at the same time, for him, the collective inferiority of a category of men, when it is in his interest to state it, is expressed and justified in terms of what physically differentiates them from himself and people of his group. To sum up, the proclamation of equality has burst asunder a mode of distinction centred upon the social, but in which physical, cultural and social characteristics were indiscriminately mixed. To reaffirm inequality, the underlying dualism demanded that physical characteristics be brought to the fore. While in India heredity is an attribute of status, the racist attributes status to "race".

All this may be regarded as an arbitrary view of the abstract intellect. Yet, the hypothesis is confirmed at least in part in Myrdal's work. Dealing with the American facts, this author discovers a close connection between egalitarianism and racism. To begin with, he notes in the philosophy of the enlightenment the tendency to minimize innate differences; then, generally everywhere and especially in America, the essentially moral doctrine of the "natural rights" of man rests on a biological egalitarianism: all men are "created equal". The period 1830–1860 sees the development of an ideology for the defence of slavery: slavery being condemned in the name of natural equality, its champions argue against this the doctrine of the inequality of races; later the argument is used to justify discrimination, which becomes established from the moment when, about 1877, the North gives up enforcing assimilation. The author's conclusions are worth pondering upon: "The dogma of racial inequality may, in a sense, be regarded as a strange fruit of the Enlightenment. . . . The race dogma is nearly the only way out for a people so moralistically egalitarian, if it is not prepared to live up to its faith. A nation less fervently committed to democracy could probably live happily in a caste system . . . race prejudice is, in a sense, a function (a perversion) of egalitarianism".[28]

If this is so, it is permissible to doubt whether, in the fight against racism in general, the mere recall of the egalitarian ideal, however solemn it may be, and even though accompanied by a scientific criticism of racist prejudices, will be really efficient. It would be better to prevent the passage from the moral principle of equality to the notion that all men are identical. One feels sure that equality can, in our day, be combined with the recognition of differences, so long as such differences are morally neutral. People must be provided with the means for conceptualizing differences. The diffusion of the pluralistic notions of culture, society, etc., affording a counterweight and setting bounds to individualism, is the obvious thing.[29] Finally, if the tendency to hierarchize still exists, if the affirmation of the modern ideal is not sufficient to make it disappear but, on the contrary, by a complicated mechanism, can on occasion make it ferocious and morbid, the antagonisms and interests which exploit it should not be lost sight of – but this is beyond our subject.

Cutting short here the attempt to define racism comparatively, I should like to recall, albeit too briefly, a structural relation which is essential to the possible developments of comparison. Equality and hierarchy are not, in fact, opposed to each other in the mechanical way which the exclusive consideration of values might lead one to suppose: the pole of the opposition which is not valorized is none the less present, each implies the other and is supported by it. Talcott Parsons draws attention, at the very beginning of his study, to the fact that distinction of statuses carries with it and presupposes equality within each status (*op. cit.*, p. 1). Conversely, where equality is affirmed, it is within a group which is hierarchized in relation to others, as in the Greek cities or, in the modern world, in British democracy and imperialism, the latter being tinged with hierarchy (e.g., incipient racism in India in the second half of the nineteenth century).[30] It is this structural relation that the egalitarian ideal tends to destroy, the result of its action being what is most often studied under the name of "social stratification". In the first place the relation is inverted: equality contains inequalities instead of being contained in a hierarchy. In the second place a whole series of transformations happen which can perhaps be summarized by saying that hierarchy is repressed, made non-conscious: it is replaced by a manifold network of inequalities, matters of fact instead of right, of quantity and gradualness instead of quality and discontinuity. Hence, in part, the well-known difficulty of defining social classes.

H Conclusion

To conclude in general terms, comparative sociology requires concepts which take into account the values that different societies have, so to speak, chosen for themselves. A consequence of this choice of values is that certain aspects of social reality are clearly and consciously elaborated, whilst others are left in the dark. In order to express what a given society does not express, the sociologist cannot invent concepts, for when he attempts to do so he only manages, as in the case of "social stratification", to translate in a way at once pretentious and obscure the prejudices of his own society. He must therefore have recourse to societies which have expressed those same aspects. A general theory of "inequality", if it is deemed necessary, must be centred upon those societies which give it a meaning and not upon those which, while presenting certain forms of it, have chosen to disavow it. It must be a theory of hierarchy in its valorized, or simple and direct forms, as well as in its non-valorized or devalorized, or complex, hybrid, covert forms. (Let us note, following Talcott Parsons,[31] that such a theory is only one particular way of considering the total social system.) In so doing one will of course in no way impose upon one society the values of another, but only endeavour to set mutually "in perspective"[32] the various types of societies. One will try to see each society in the light not only of itself but of the others. From the point of view of social anthropology at any rate, this appears to be not only the formula for an objective comparison, but even the condition for understanding each particular society.

Notes

* This is an English version of a paper first published in French in *Cahiers Internationaux de Sociologie*, Paris XXIX, 1960, pp. 91–112. The text is taken from *Contributions to Indian Sociology*, V, 1961. The following reflections have sprung mainly from the preparation of an article on "caste" for the *Vocabulary of Social Sciences* (Unesco). The question of the proximate extensions of the term "caste", for instance to societies of South-East Asia, is left out. Only a remote extension is considered which appears to require that sociological and anthropological approaches be confronted, even if in a somewhat hasty and temporary manner.

1 Raymond Aron, "Science et conscience de la société", *European Journal of Sociology*, I, 1, 1960, p. 29.

2 The tendency, which its only systematic opponent, O. C. Cox, has called "the Caste School of Race Relations", seems to have won the day. Another, more moderate, tendency consists in applying the word "caste" to USA in a monographic manner, without comparative prejudice (Myrdal, etc., see below). The dictionaries give, besides the proper sense of the

word, the extended meaning, e.g., *Shorter Oxford English Dictionary, s.v.*: "3. *fig.* A class who keep themselves socially distinct, or inherit exclusive privileges 1807." [The French text has here a reference to Littré instead of O.S.D.]

3 Yet, among recent authors who are familiar with the Indian system, a sociologist working in Ceylon insists on the fundamental difference between India and US (Bryce Ryan, *Caste in Modern Ceylon*, New Brunswick, N.J., 1953, p. 18, note), while F. G. Bailey asserts *a priori* that this comparison must take place under the word "caste" (*Contributions*, III, p. 90). Morris Carstairs is less categorical, but he accepts, with Kroeber's definition (below), the American usage, because of its advantages as compared with "race" (*The Twice-Born*, London, 1957, p. 23). Much earlier an Indian author, Ketkar, insisted on a hierarchical division of American society based on race and occupation, and he enumerated ten groups (based in fact on the country of origin). He did not use the word "caste" but he underlined with some relish the features which in his view were reminiscent of the Indian system. (Shridar V. Ketkar, *The History of Caste in India*, I, Ithaca, N.Y., 1909, pp. 100 n., 102 n., 115 n. 5.) The general question has recently been discussed in: E. R. Leach (ed.), *Aspects of Caste in South India, Ceylon and N.-W. Pakistan*, Cambridge, 1960 (Cambridge Papers in Social Anthropology, No. 2), notably p. 5.

4 W. Lloyd Warner (Dir.), *Deep South, A Social Anthropological Study of Caste and Class*, Chicago, *c.* 1941, ed. 1946, p. 9. B. S. Ghurye's position is close to that of Kroeber: well marked status groups are common in Indo-European cultures; comparatively, the Indian caste system represents only an extreme case (untouchability, etc.), see *Caste and Race in India*, New York, 1932, pp. 140, 142.

5 Max Weber, *Wirtschaft und Gesellschaft*, II, pp. 635–7. Discussed by Cox, *Caste, Class and Race*, p. 287, and: "Max Weber on Social Stratification", *American Sociological Review*, II, 1950, pp. 223–7; cf. also Hans Gerth, "Max Weber vs. Oliver C. Cox", *American Sociological Review*, ibid., pp. 557–8 (as regards Jews and castes).

6 Pitrim A. Sorokin, *Society, Culture and Personality, Their Structure and Dynamics*, New York, *c.* 1947, p. 259 (the "order" or "estate" as a "diluted caste", *cf.* what has been said above about class and caste). Max Weber distinguishes between open and closed status groups (*Ges. Aufs. z. Religionssoziologie*, II, ed. 1923, pp. 41–2). It is to be noted that a recent work recognizes two fundamental types of "social stratification", the caste type which comprises "orders" or "estates", and the open class type, related respectively to the poles of Talcott Parsons' alternative of particularism-universalism (Bernard Barber, *Social Stratification, A Comparative Analysis of Structure and Process*, New York, 1957).

7 W. Lloyd Warner, "American Caste and Class", *American Journal of Sociology*, XLII, 1936, pp. 234–7.

8 Gunnar Myrdal, *An American Dilemma, The Negro Problem and Modern Democracy* (with the assistance of Richard Sterner and Arnold Rose), New York and London, *c.* 1944, p. 675; also p. 668: "The scientifically important difference between the terms 'caste' and 'class' as we are using them is, from this point of view, *a relatively large difference in freedom of movement between groups*" (his italics). Same justification for the use of the term (practical reasons, not indicating identity with the Indian facts), in Westie and Westie, *American Journal of Sociology*, LXIII, 1957–1958, p. 192, n. 5.

9 *Op. cit.*, pp. 667–8. In a footnote, Myrdal takes up an objection made in particular by Charles S. Johnson: the word "caste" connotes an invariable and stable system in which the tensions and frictions which characterize the relations between Whites and Blacks in the United States are not found; he replies that he does not believe that a caste system having such characteristics exists anywhere (pp. 1374–5, n. 2) and says earlier (p. 668) that Hindu society today does not show that "stable equilibrium" that American sociologists, observing from a distance, have been inclined to attribute to it. We see here some trace of the

egalitarian Creed. The author has, since, had first-hand experience of India and one wonders whether he would maintain this today, whether, even, he would continue to use the word "caste" for American phenomena.

10 Ibid., pp. 670–1. There is here an interesting judgment on the Lloyd Warner school: according to Myrdal, one must take account of the extreme egalitarianism in the "popular national theory" in order to understand both the tendency among these authors to exaggerate the rigidity of distinctions of class and caste in America, and the interest aroused by their works, which has been greater than their strictly scientific novelty.

11 It is a little surprising to find, next to the ideas here summarized, a rather narrow idea of the place of concepts in science: "Concepts are our created instruments and have no other form of reality than in our usage. Their purpose is to help make our thinking clear and our observations accurate" (p. 667).

12 W. Lloyd Warner and Allison Davis, "A Comparative Study of American Caste", in Edgar T. Thomson, ed., *Race Relations and the Race Problem*, Durham, North Car., 1939, pp. 219–45; for India see pp. 229–32.

13 The operation of this choice is clear in principle: the caste system of India has been characterized by only those of its traits that it is thought may be found in America, where however they do not constitute a complete system but only part of a system which is called a class-and-caste system.

14 Oliver, C. Cox, "Race and Caste, A Distinction", *American Journal of Sociology*, 1944–1945, pp. 306–8, and above all *Caste, Class and Race, A Study in Social Dynamics*, New York, 1918, to which the reference in the text relate.

15 Cox's thesis appears to have had little effect. Sorokin however refers to his article and takes a similar position: the relation between Blacks and Whites has some of the elements of relations between castes but it differs fundamentally (*op. cit.*, p. 258, n. 12).

16 John Dollard, *Caste and Class in a Southern Town*, New York, *c.* 1937, ed. 1940, p. 64; Kingsley Davis, "Intermarriage in Caste Society", *American Anthropologist*, XLIII, 1941, pp. 376–95.

17 Harold W. Pfautz, "The Current Literature on Social Stratification, Critique and Bibliography", *American Journal of Sociology*, LVIII, 1953, pp. 391–418. The theory of stratification is approached, not starting from class, but from an absolutely general point of view, by Talcott Parsons in "A Revised Theoretical Approach to the Theory of Social Stratification" (R. Bendix and S. M. Lipset, eds., *Class, Status and Power, A Reader in Social Stratification*, Blencoe, III., 1953). While it adopts the same label, the work is outside the current here criticized; the general conception (*in fine*) removes the habitual implications of the word. The argument proceeds from values and the hierarchy which necessarily results from them. The conceptual framework is that of the general theory.

18 Kingley Davis, "A Conceptual Analysis of Stratification", *American Sociological Review*, VII, 1942, pp. 309–21; K. Davis and Wilbert E. Moore, "Some Principles of Stratification", *A.S.R.*, 10, 1945, pp. 242–9; W. Buckley, "Social Stratification and Social Differentiation", *A.S.R.*, 23, 1958, pp. 369–75; K. Davis, "A Reply to Buckley", *A.S.R.*, 24, 1959, p. 82; Dennis H. Wrong, *A.S.R.*, 24, pp. 772–82. Reference will be found in the articles of Buckley and Wrong to other articles not used here.

19 I was unfortunately unable to consult during the preparation of this article Kingsley Davis's book, *Human Society*, New York, 1949, quoted by Wrong, and which would have been of particular interest since the author was concerned with India at that time (*cf. The Population of India and Pakistan*, Princeton, 1951).

20 Nelson N. Foote, "Destratification and Restratification", Editorial Foreword, *American Journal of Sociology*, LVIII, 1953, pp. 325–6.

21 *European Journal of Sociology*, I, 1, 1960, p. 14.

22 Célestin Bouglé, *Essais sur le régime des castes*, Paris, 1908, p. 4. The English translation of Bouglé's thesis, and a commentary on his book together with that of Hocart, which poses the problem of power, is in *Contributions*, II, 1958.

23 Talcott Parsons, *loc. cit.*

24 What follows is summarized from my chapter on the conception of Kingship in ancient India, to appear in L. Renou and J. Filliozat, *L'Inde Classique*, III.

25 On Hobbes and the artificial society, "rational" in the sense of being devised according to the reality of man (the individual) and not inspired by an ideal order, *cf.* Léo Strauss, *Natural Right and History*, Chicago, 1953, Chapter 5; Élie Halévy, *La formation du radicalisme philosophique*, 3 vols., Paris, 1901–1904 I, pp. 3, 41, 53, 90; III, pp. 347–8, etc.

26 *Cf.* Gunnar Myrdal, ibid., p. 581 ff., the "Jim Crow Laws", etc. The reaction to the abolition of slavery was not immediate but developed slowly. Discrimination appears as simple separation under the slogan "separate but equal". For the period before the civil war also, Myrdal gives a succinct history, but the analysis, apparently, remains to be done. It promises to be fruitful, see for example the declarations of Jefferson and Lincoln (*cf. Times Literary Supplement*, July 22, 1960, pp. 457–8, according to J. W. Schulte-Nordholt, *The People That Walk in Darkness*, London, Burke 1960). Recent articles by P. L. Van der Berghe partly satisfy my wish. *Cf.* the last one: "Apartheid, une interprétation sociologique de la ségrégation raciale", *Cahiers internationaux de sociologie*, XXVIII, nouv. sér., 7[e]année, 1960, pp. 47–56. According to this author, segregation has replaced etiquette as mode of social distance. The change would correspond to the movement from slavery to racism.

27 The fact that the transition from "equality" to "identity" operates chiefly at the level of popular mentality makes it more difficult to seize on than if it were present in the great authors. I propose nevertheless to study elsewhere more closely this particular complementarity between egalitarianism and racism.

28 Gunnar Myrdal, ibid., pp. 83 ff., the quotations are from p. 89. Myrdal also takes account of the development of the biological view of man: *Homo sapiens* as a species in the animal world; *cf.* also p. 591: "The persistent preoccupation with sex and marriage in the rationalization . . . is, to this extent, an irrational escape on the part of the whites from voicing an open demand for difference in social status . . . for its own sake."

29 *Cf.* Claude Lévi-Strauss, *Race et histoire*, UNESCO, *c.* 1952.

30 Machiavelli observes that a "republic" which wishes to extend its empire and not remain small and stagnant, should like Rome confide the defence of liberty to the people and not, like Sparta and Venice, to the great. (*Discourses on the First Decade of T. Livy*, I, chapters V–VI.)

31 *Cf.* n. 17.

32 E. E. Evans-Pritchard, *Social Anthropology*, London, 1951, p. 129.

PART VII

THE POLITICS OF RACE

13

RACE, MULTICULTURALISM AND DEMOCRACY

Robert Gooding-Williams*

Introduction

In this paper I bring into conversation two debates pertaining to identities in the contemporary United States. The first of these is a debate about race and the second a debate about multiculturalism. The debate about race has been prompted by the proposition that, as ordinarily conceptualized by most Americans, biological racial identities do not exist. This view is sometimes associated with the claim that historians and social scientists should expunge talk of race and racial identities from their vocabularies, a proposal that often is rejected by those who would defend a social constructionist account of racial identities. The debate about multiculturalism is less well focused, but generally concerns the justification of multicultural educational practices in the context of a so-called "politics of recognition." A central question, here, is whether multiculturalism should be embraced for the reason that it advances the self-esteem of individuals belonging to socially oppressed groups by enabling them to discover the reflection or representation of their identities in a reformed canon.[1]

Part 1 of the paper engages the first debate by addressing an important skeptical reply to the claim that racial identities are social constructs. Focusing in particular on black identity, I answer Walter Benn Michaels's objection that a non biological and social constructionist account of American racial identities is not possible because the practice of racial classification in America involves the idea that racial passing is possible.

Having met Michael's objection, I proceed in Part 2 to detail a social constructionist view of black identity that builds on the work of Anna Stubblefield and Anthony Appiah. Here, I suggest that black identities have both a third-person and a first-person dimension. I also explore some of the implications of my interpretation of black identity, focusing in particular on the issues of racial authenticity, African–American identity, and mixed race identity.

In Part 3 of the paper I shift my attention to multiculturalism and, specifically, to a version of Afrocentrism often associated with multiculturalism. In particular, I argue that Molefi Asante's notion of Afrocentric "re-centering" suggests a model of multicultural education that, because it rests on a questionable understanding of African–American identity, should be rejected. In addition, I propose that in rejecting Asante's Afrocentrism we should decline to exchange it for the embrace of an anti-Afrocentric nationalism of the sort that Arthur M. Schlesinger, Jr. articulates in *The Disuniting of America*. Despite their differences, Schlesinger and Asante each promotes an identity politics that makes identity into a form of kitsch.

Neither Afrocentric, nor dependent on an argument from self-esteem, my defense of multicultural education in the fourth part of this essay rests on a normative claim about the point of public education in a democratic society. In elaborating that defense, I employ my social constructionist concept of black identity to show that multiculturalism in contemporary America should be race conscious. More exactly, I argue for endorsing race conscious multiculturalism as a pedagogical and research program for disseminating a "cultural capital" that fosters the capacity for democratic deliberation in contemporary America.[2]

Finally, in the fifth and concluding part of the paper, I summarize my argument for multiculturalism by recurring to W. E. B. Du Bois's seminal turn-of-the-century reflections on the nature and point of a politics of recognition.

1 Meeting the Skeptical Objection

Let me begin by stipulating that, by "racialism", I mean a brand of nineteenth-century biological essentialism according to which "there are heritable characteristics, possessed by members of our species, which allow us to divide them into a small set of races, in such a way that all members of those races share certain traits and tendencies with each other that they do not share with members of any other race."[3] The racialist thesis that having a racial identity is a matter of embodying a biological racial "essence" or "type" is now widely regarded to be false due to post-Darwinian developments in population genetics.[4] Here, I mention this thesis, because it plays a central role in Walter Benn Michaels's critique of the social constructionist approach to racial identity. To be sure, Michaels does not deny that racialism is false. Rather his point is that a prior commitment to racial essentialism is implicit in any social constructionist account of American racial identities that acknowledges the possibility of racial passing. In Michaels's view, it is not possible to give a social constructionist account of American racial identities that acknowledges this possibility but is not parasitic on the assumption that biological racial essences exist.

Michaels begins his criticism of social constructionism by reviewing Michael Omi's and Howard Winant's influential attempt to develop a theory of racial formations that conceptualizes racial identity "without biology."[5] His critique concentrates not on Omi and Winant, however, but

1 on the 1985 Louisiana Fourth Circuit Court of Appeals' ruling that "Susie Phipps, 'who had always thought she was white, had lived as white, and had twice married as white, 'was not in fact white because her parents . . . had thought of themselves and of her as 'colored' "[6] and

2 on some remarks that Adrian Piper makes in her essay, "Passing for White, Passing for Black."

According to Piper

> [w]hat joins me to other blacks . . . and other blacks to another, is not a set of shared physical characteristics. Rather it is the shared experience of being visually or cognitively *identified* as black by a white racist society, and the punitive and damaging effects of that identification.[7]

Michaels responds to the Louisiana court ruling and to Piper's remarks as follows:

> This is the Louisiana standard: if you're *perceived* as black, you are black. [emphasis added] But Piper's account of her own experience makes the incoherence of this standard even more obvious than it is in the Phipps case. For Piper describes herself as so light skinned that she is constantly being treated as if she were white. She is thus made to feel that she is passing for white, and since passing for white seems to her "a really authentically shameful thing to do" . . . she is led into strenuous efforts to identify herself as a black. But what consequences must these efforts have for her nonbiological definition of racial identity? The point of the definition is that being black means being identified by a white racist society as black. On what grounds, then, can someone who is *not* identified by that society as black be said to be black?
>
> Piper makes this dilemma even clearer by going on to remark that she has "white friends who fit the prevailing stereotype of a black person" and thus have "experiences" "similar" to ones that make blacks black . . . If they really do have such experiences, what can she mean by calling these friends "white"? That they can be white even if they are treated as black; that she can be black even if she is treated as white – these facts are tributes to, not critiques of, racial essentialism. The very idea of passing – whether it takes the form of looking like you belong to a different race or of acting like you belong to a different race – requires an understanding of race as something separate from the way you look and act. If race really were nothing but culture, that is, if race were nothing but a distinctive array of beliefs and practices, then, of course, there could be no passing, since to believe and practices, then, of course, there could be no passing, since to believe and practice what the members of any race believed and practiced would, by definition, make you a member of that race.[8]

For Michaels, Piper's suggestion that black identity is a matter of being classified and thus identified as black makes explicit the social constructionist account of racial identity that is implicit in the Louisiana Court of Appeals ruling. As I read him, the argument he adduces in criticism of both Piper and the court can be reconstructed as follows:

1 Premise: If racial identities in America can be coherently conceptualized as social constructs, absent the assumption that biological racial essences exist, then it is not true that the practice of racial classification in America permits the possibility of passing.

2 Premise: The practice of racial classification in America permits the possibility of passing.

3 Conclusion: It is not true that racial identities in America can be coherently conceptualized as social constructs, absent the assumption that biological racial essences exist.

Thus construed, Michaels's argument is valid. It is unsound, however, because the first premise is false. This premise is false, because it is a conditional whose antecedent is true and consequent false. In other words, racial identities in America can be coherently conceptualized as social constructs, absent the assumption that biological racial essences exist, even though the practice of racial classification in America permits the possibility of passing.

We can begin to see why Michaels's argument is unsound by noting a confusion that animates his reading of Piper in the second passage I cite. For Michaels, Piper's suggestion that race is "nothing but culture" amounts to the claim that someone is black if, and only if, she subscribes to certain beliefs and participates in certain practices. More exactly, he reads Piper as defining black racial identity with reference to the idea of a culture that is common to and only to persons who have been designated as black. But this is precisely what she does *not* do. On the contrary, her approach is to conceptualize black identity with reference to a practice of racial classification to which blacks have been subjected by American society. Black identity is a consequence of *that* practice, Piper implies, and not of the beliefs and practices which are shared by or distinctive to the people whom that practice designates as black. Socially constructed racial identities *are* cultural phenomena (in this sense, race *is* culture), but, *pace* Michaels, two individuals can have the same socially constructed racial identity (e.g., both can be socially constructed as black) without having what an anthropologist would call "a common culture."[9]

Michael's response to Piper in the first passage I cite is more to the point, though finally flawed. Given Piper's view of black racial identity, he asks, how can it make sense to say that blacks who pass for white are not white, or that whites who pass for black are not black? Michaels is prompted to raise these questions, I think, because he ignores a significant part of Piper's conception of black racial identity. Where Piper sees the American practice of racial classification as incorporating both visual *and cognitive* identifications, Michaels pays attention only to visual identifications, that is, to the *perception* of individuals as black ("[I]f you're *perceived* as black," Michaels writes, "you are black"). Piper's reference to cognitive identification is meant, I assume, to flag the fact that the American practice of racial classification involves criteria entailing that someone perceived to be white can be black and that someone perceived to be black can be white. For Piper, then, someone who would not be classified as black on the basis of visual criteria could still *be black* because Americans' conventional (though not universal) adherence to the one-drop rule *cognitively* identifies her as black.[10] For Michaels, of course, the thought that such a person could exist is contradictory and incoherent. Because Michaels understands racial classification with reference only to visual criteria, he equates not being perceived to be black with not being classified as black. He believes, then, that Piper contradicts herself in allowing that there exist persons (e.g., blacks passing as white) who, though they are not perceived to be black, are classified as black. The appearance of contradiction disappears, I have been arguing, if one bears in mind the distinction between visual and cognitive identification. Similarly, for Piper, there is no contradiction in claiming that someone classified as white could be perceived to be black and have experiences "similar" to those whom the American practice of racial classification counts as black.

Racial identities in America can be coherently conceptualized as social constructs, absent the assumption that biological racial essences exist, even though the American practice of racial classification permits the possibility of passing. Piper shows that this is so by offering a noncontradictory, social constructionist account of racial identities that, without presupposing the existence of racial essences, acknowledges that passing can occur. In treating black identity as the product of a rule-governed social practice of racial classification, Piper interprets it as a social construct.[11] Needless to say, she *does not* assert that being black amounts to satisfying the false and often pernicious notions of black identity that historically have informed the American practice of racial classification. She does not claim, for example, that to be black is to be psychologically indisposed to hard work or to be by innate constitution intellectually inferior to whites. Neither does she propose, explicitly or otherwise, that black identity is a consequence of satisfying the one-drop rule or of embodying a biological racial essence. Rather Piper suggests that black identity is an effect of being *designated as black* by a practice of racial classification that has adhered to the one-drop rule through much of this century[12] and promoted the belief that racial essences exist. In her view, being black is a matter of being classified as black by a particular practice of racial classification; it is not a function of satisfying all the odd rules and beliefs that have animated that practice.[13]

2 On Being a Black Person

Thus far, my elaboration of a view that Piper only sketches has focused on defending that view from Michaels's critique. Here, however, I would like to shift ground. In particular, I would like to complicate Piper's conception of black identity by drawing a distinction between being black and being a black person. Piper, I wish to say, defines a necessary but not a sufficient condition of being a black person. Even if one considers her point that being black not only involves being identified as black, but, additionally, the negative effects of being thus identified, it seems clear that her stated "definition" of black identity expresses a third-person perspective intended to highlight the objectification of blacks *as blacks* by a racist society.[14] Anna Stubblefield's and Anthony Appiah's recent treatments of racial identity point in a similar direction when, in keeping with Piper's nominalist intuitions, they propose that racial identities result from criteria governed practices of racial classification through the application of racial labels.[15] In explaining the concept of a black person I aim to enrich this perspective with a first-person point of view that notes the ways in which individuals classified as black contribute to the construction of their racial identities. Following Appiah, I draw on Ian Hacking's essay, "Making Up People,"[16] to discuss the "identifications"[17] by which black people shape their projects in light of the racial labelings and classifications to which they have been subjected.

Hacking's central idea is a view he calls "dynamic nominalism." Dynamic nominalism, he says, is the

> doctrine . . . that numerous kinds of human beings and human acts come into being hand in hand with our invention of the categories labeling them . . . it contends that our spheres of possibility, and hence our selves, are to some extent made up by our naming and what that entails.[18]

To be sure, Hacking is not proposing here that the sheer utterance or inscription of newly invented names suffices in itself to cause the existence of the human beings named. Rather his point is that our sense of ourselves and of the possibilities existing for us is, to a significant degree, a function of the descriptions we have available to us to conceptualize our intended actions and prospective lives. "What is curious about human action," Hacking remarks "is that by and large what I am deliberately doing depends on the possibilities of description . . . [h]ence if new modes of description come into being, new possibilities of action come into being in consequence."[19]

Hacking's dynamic nominalism helps to explain the concept of a black person because it provides a means of conceptualizing the contributions individuals make to the construction of their racial identities. In effect, it suggests that individuals classified as black become black persons just in case they begin to act in the world under a description of themselves as racially black. As I have previously suggested, being black – that is, being racially classified as black – is a necessary but not a sufficient condition of being a black person. One becomes a black person only if

1 one begins to identify (to classify) *oneself* as black and
2 one begins to make choices, to formulate plans, to express concerns, etc., in light of one's identification of oneself as black.

Though this way of explaining the concept of a black person may seem a bit abstract, it is best understood as a philosopher's gloss on the sort of experience which is described time and again in the letters and literature of black persons. Consider, for example, the scene of visiting-card exchanges which Du Bois describes near the beginning of *The Souls of Black Folk*. Only after his card is refused, "peremptorily, with a glance," does it dawn on Du Bois that he "was different from the others."[20] Only then, moreover, does Du Bois begin to live his life in light of the fact that he has been classified as racially black and different, recognizing possibilities and making choices that he could not have recognized or made before, including, for example, the choice to prove his racial worth by competing with his white schoolmates: "But they should not keep their prizes, I said; some, all, I would wrest from them."[21] Or consider the reflections of James Weldon Johnson's protagonist in *The Autobiography of an Ex-Coloured Man* as he recalls the experience of having been labeled one "fateful day at school" for the first time as a "nigger" and then as "coloured":

> I have often lived through that hour, that day, that week, in which was wrought the miracle of my transition from one world into another; for I did indeed pass into another world. From that time I looked out through other eyes, my thoughts were coloured, my

> words dictated, my actions limited by one dominating, all pervading idea which constantly increased its force and weight until I finally realized in it a great, tangible fact.
>
> And this is the dwarfing, warping, distorting influence which operates upon each and every coloured man in the United States. He is forced to take his outlook on all things, not from the point of view of a citizen, or a man, or even a human being, but from the point of view of a *coloured* man.[22]

For Du Bois and Johnson's protagonist alike, a new world of new possibilities and impossibilities is born when acts of objectifying racial classification move them to understand themselves, to formulate aspirations, and to plan the future courses of their lives under descriptions of themselves as black, or coloured. By acting under these descriptions, both individuals actively contribute to the construction of their identities as black persons. Johnson's ex-coloured man is a particularly interesting example of a black person who *becomes* a black person at a memorable moment in his life, for he is the sort of black person who learns to pass for white in the new world into which he passes.

Elsewhere I have argued that Du Bois, notwithstanding his insight into the social construction of black persons, errs in *The Souls of Black Folk* in supposing in an Hegelian vein that a single "folk spirit" or "social mind" pervades the lives of black Americans. I have also suggested that Du Bois himself speaks persuasively against this supposition by highlighting (in *Souls*) the multiple minds and sensibilities and modes of self-understanding that polyphonically characterize black identity in America. It would be a mistake, of course, to think that a rejection of the Du Boisian idea of a collective black *Geist*, along with the older notion of a biological black racial essence, entails a rejection of the view that one can speak of black identity in general terms. Generally speaking, to be black (in America) is, simply, to be subject to a practice of racial classification that counts one as black. Corresponding to being black, however, are numerous ways of being a black person; that is, numerous ways of interpreting and assigning significance to being black.[23] In some cases, the significance one assigns to being black in identifying oneself as black bears centrally on one's view of oneself. In other cases, it does not. It should be noted, moreover, that many of the most politically salient modes of being a black person involve the assignment of a *collective* significance to being black, a fact to which I will return in my discussion of race conscious multiculturalism.

Let me conclude my explanation of the concept of a black person by sketching a few of its consequences for our thinking about racial authenticity, African–American identity, and mixed race identity.

Racial authenticity

The distinction between *being authentically a black person* and *being inauthentically a black person* makes no sense in my view, since one becomes a black person by, and only by, acting under certain descriptions. In other words, I postulate no black personhood *apart* from a black person's actions to which she or he could be true or untrue in the performance of those actions.[24] Put a bit differently, I do not suppose that, prior to the performance of discursively shaped actions, there exist black selves or persons that such actions could authentically or inauthentically express.[25] It would be a mistake, then, to assert that some black persons are more authentic in their black personhood than others.

The putative distinction between *being authentically black* and *being inauthentically black* requires separate consideration, given that I differentiate between being black and being a black person. In considering this distinction, it is useful to note the affinity between my notion of being black and Sartre's notion of being a Jew. According to Sartre, the anti-Semite creates the Jew by identifying him *as a Jew.* To be a Jew, Sartre proclaims, "is to be thrown into – *to be abandoned to* – the situation of a Jew."[26] Sartre posits a distinction between authentic and inauthentic Jews. I doubt the usefulness of this distinction, because I see no clearly defined criteria for distinguishing authentic choices and behaviors – said to express "a true and lucid consciousness of [one's] situation" – from the types of choices and behaviors (e.g., the Jewish rationalist's universalism) that Sartre, somewhat arbitrarily, brands as inauthentic.[27] For the same reason, I doubt the value of the distinction between being authentically black and being inauthentically black. What criteria could one persuasively invoke for distinguishing between existentially lucid and less-than-lucid responses to the fact that one has been thrown into a world shaped by a practice of racial classification classifying one as black? Even supposing that one could clearly define some such criteria, it would remain to be shown that they provided a basis for identifying some specific *types* of behavior as inauthentic.[28]

African–American identity

On my account, being African–American is coextensive neither with being black nor with being a black person. Being African–American is being a native-born American who is black – who is, in other words, racially classified as black – and who typically is a black person. Yet the class of blacks and black persons in America also includes West Indian, Nigerian, Eritrean, Ghanaian, and other individuals who are not African–Americans. As I shall argue in the next part of this paper, African–American identity is culturally complex. Yet it would be false to claim that a commitment to the perpetuation of cultural forms associated with African–Americans is either a necessary or a sufficient condition of being a black person in America. As is well known, there exist black persons in America who are not committed to the perpetuation of any of these cultural forms and many non-blacks – and thus non-black persons – who are devoted to jazz and who take delight in the art of signifying.

Mixed race identity

A few words, finally, about the politics of mixed race identity, which actively contests America's traditional practice of racial classification. Advocates of a mixed race identity, though still classified as black by that practice, deliberately decline to live in the world as black persons. Refusing to act under descriptions of themselves as black, they act, instead, under descriptions of themselves as racially mixed. One could still say of these individuals that they *are in fact black*, meaning simply that, regardless of their self-descriptions, they remain subject to a practice of racial classification that, to the extent that it is still governed by the one-drop rule, counts them as black. Yet claims of this sort will seem increasingly odd as the politics of mixed race gathers steam, if only because an essential element of that politics is its repudiation of the one-drop rule. (Such claims will seem odd in just the way that it would have seemed odd to say to Susie Guillory Phipps, in the face of *her* challenge to the one-drop rule, that she was in fact black in virtue of the rule.) The politics of mixed race disturbs the current conventions of racial classification with an eye to enacting and making pervasive a new convention providing social space for the appearance of dynamic nominalist "mixed race persons."[29]

3 Multiculturalism and Kitsch

In the third part of this essay I turn my attention to multiculturalism, which I view as both an educational and a political project. In particular, I proffer a critique of the educational program implicit in Molefi Asante's Afrocentrism. I then proceed to a critical analysis of Arthur Schlesinger, Jr.'s explicitly anti-Afrocentric American nationalism.

My critique of Afrocentrism has some affinity to Anthony Appiah's repeated attack on what he describes, borrowing a term from Paulin Hountondji, as Afrocentrism's "unanimist" idea of Africa. By "unanimism" Appiah has in mind the view "that Africa is culturally homogeneous – the belief that there is some central body of folk philosophy that is shared by black Africans quite generally."[30] Against this view, he insists on "the extraordinary diversity of Africa's peoples and its cultures," remarking that it is "surely preposterous to suppose that there is a single African culture, shared by everyone from the civilizations of the Upper Nile thousands of years ago to the thousand or so language-zones of contemporary Africa."[31] Afrocentrists embrace a simplistic vision of Africa, Appiah argues, and so obscure the radically heterogeneous character of Africa's cultural life. Here, I likewise take issue with Afrocentrism's yearning for simplicity, though not as regards its idea of Africa; rather my focus will be Afrocentrism's conception of African-American identity.

In "Racism, Consciousness, and Afrocentricity," Asante identifies himself as African-American and remarks that "a precondition of [his] fullness, a necessary and natural part of [his] maturity [has been] the commitment to be who [he is], to be Afrocentric."[32] "One becomes Afrocentric," Asante continues, by:

> exploring connections, visiting the quiet places, and remaining connected. The furious pace of our dislocation, mislocation, displacement, off-centeredness, and marginalization, often brought on by the incredible conspiracy of the Eurocentric architecton, drives us further and further away from ourselves, reinforcing us in our dislocation and affirming us in our out-of-placeness. In such a situation, in the fringes of the European experience, pushed away from the center, we swirl around lost looking for place, for location.

> Afrocentricity is the active centering of the African in subject place in our historical landscape. This has always been my search; it has been a quest for sanity. Therefore, it was unthinkable for me to entertain ideas of living in the margins, being in the periphery of someone else's historical and cultural experiences. My aim was more fundamental, basic, the essential quality of being normal, uncomplicated. By being normal, I do not reject the other; I embrace that which I truly know, i.e., jazz, blues, railroads, Obatala, roots, hoodoo, soul, rhythms, sweet mommas, Dunbar and Hughes, Sanchez, Mari Evans, and Charles Fuller, and so on, in ways that I do not know the products of the other, i.e., country music, mistletoe, Valhalla, Wotan, pale blonds, Frost and Mailer. *I recognize these products as part of my experience in the large but they do not impact on me in the same way as those which seem to grow from the soil of my ancestors.* With my own products I can walk confidently toward the future knowing full well that I can grasp whatever else is out there because my own center is secured.[33] (emphasis mine)

Eurocentrism, on this account, has alienated and de-centered the African–American subject, driving him further and further away from himself and leaving him lost and without sanity at the periphery of Europe's historical and cultural experience. The aim of an Afrocentric re-centering and, Asante suggests, re-education of the African–American subject is an identity whose defining quality, essence and foundation is a state of being that is normal and uncomplicated. One can become "normal" and "uncomplicated," he proposes, by embracing what one *truly* knows. At first this suggestion might seem to present a problem, since what the African–American subject *appears* to know is the contents of an experience that has been *complicated* by the integration of African and European elements, of jazz and country music, of sweet mommas and pale blonds. Yet we soon discover that what the African–American subject apparently knows is a good deal more than what he truly knows, since what he truly knows is simply those elements in his experience that express his African heritage. On what basis, however, can this subject claim to know truly the African elements in his experience but *not* the European elements? Asante's answer is that the former, unlike the latter, *seem to grow from the soil of the African–American subject's ancestors*.

Although there is much to object to in Asante's argument, the issue on which I should like to focus is his rhetorical resolution of what he admits to be the phenomenological complexity of African–American experience. Asante's African–American experience is complicated, not only because it involves his African and European heritages alike, but because his African heritage harbors complexities that he does not explicitly acknowledge, e.g., its inseparability from things European in the example of the railroads, and its patchwork combination of the originally African Obatala and the orginally African–American jazz. The complexity Asante addresses he quickly disowns by appropriating the rhetoric of organic, biological growth. In other words, it is the figure of plant-like connectedness to an ancestral soil that provides Asante the epistemological vehicle he requires to bifurcate his experience into what he truly and does not truly know. Here, the effect of his language is to resurrect the specter of the nineteenth-century racial sciences and their view that cultural identities express biological racial essences.[34] For Asante, the naturalizing rhetoric of biological growth is a simplifying rhetoric by which he dissociates himself from what he (putatively) fails truly to know in order to represent himself as the normal, uncomplicated and secure product of a specifically Afrocentric *Bildung*.

I can summarize my reading of Asante's rhetoric by identifying it as the rhetoric of kitsch. According to Karsten Harries, kitsch in modern art is the art of a realism that "[u]nlike most modern art, which betrays the precariousness of its project... seems sure of itself. Kitsch pretends to be in possession of an adequate image of man."[35] Asante speaks the language of kitsch because he invokes the imagery of fixed biological identity to construct a putatively adequate image of African–American cultural identity. His language successfully secures a "normal" and normalizing vision of that identity by obscuring the hybrid, complex and multidimensional character of African–American life and experience.[36] We can think of Afrocentrism as an Afro-kitsch, because it sacrifices a skeptical sensibility – a sense that African–Americans are much too complicated culturally to be reduced to whitewashed (or better, "blackwashed") images of unambiguous self-possession – to the sentimental impulse to see them sure of themselves, striding "confidently" toward the future.[37] What African–American novelist Charles Johnson says of the Negritude movement – that "[l]ike fascist art in Germany... Negritude – all Kitsch – is a retreat from ambiguity" – can just as well be said of Asante's program for the Afrocentric re-education and re-centering of African–American subjects.[38]

If African–American identities are complicated, this is (in part) because they have been constituted not only by African–American cultures and societies, but, likewise, by a perpetual dialogue and violent engagement with the larger society to which they belong.[39] It is important to remember, moreover, that the converse is true of the identities of Americans who are not African–Americans. As Albert Murray puts the point, "American culture, even in its most rigidly segregated precincts, is patently and irrevocably composite. It is, regardless of all the hysterical protestations of those who would have it otherwise, incontestably mulatto."[40] Ralph Ellison makes a similar point when he remarks that "most American whites are culturally part Negro American without even realizing it."[41] In a more humorous vein, Ellison notes that the American language "began by merging the sounds of many tongues, brought together in the struggle of diverse regions. And whether it is admitted or not, much of the sound of that language is derived from the timbre of the African voice and the listening habits of the African ear. So there is a de'z and do'z of slave speech sounding beneath our most polished Harvard accents, and if there is such a thing as a Yale accent, there is a Negro wail in it – doubtlessly introduced there by Old Yalie John C. Calhoun, who probably got it from his mammy."[42]

It is a significant and valuable feature of Arthur Schlesinger, Jr.'s *The Disuniting of America* that it acknowledges the mulatto character of American culture that Murray and Ellison were once at such pains to stress. "Historically and culturally," Schlesinger writes, "this republic has had an Anglo-Saxon base; but from the start that base has been modified, enriched, and reconstituted by transfusions from other continents and civilizations. The movement from exclusion to inclusion causes a constant revision in the texture of our culture. The ethnic transfusions affect all aspects of American life – our politics, our literature, our music, our painting, our movies, our cuisine, our customs, our dreams. Black Americans in particular have influenced the ever-changing national culture in many ways. They have been here for centuries..."[43] Still,

Schlesinger is not happy with contemporary American culture, as he fears that the differences animating its perpetually changing mosaic of multiple and heterogeneous hybridities may tear it apart: "If the republic now turns away from Washington's old goal of "one people," he worries, "what is its future? – disintegration of the national community, apartheid, Balkanization, tribalization?"[44]

Schlesinger would fend off the threat of "Balkanization" and "tribalization" by having all Americans, despite their differences, affirm a "democratic faith" in certain common and unifying "political ideals."[45] These "ideals of democracy and human rights," which Schlesinger, following Myrdal, calls the "American Creed," "transcend ethnic, religious and political lines."[46] They are the stuff of an "overarching political commitment" that Schlesinger believes can provide "the solvent that will prevent differences from escalating into antagonism and hatred."[47] Reminiscent of Asante, whose educational proposals for strengthing the self-esteem of black students he harshly criticizes, Schlesinger's search for a solvent bespeaks a desire to dissolve the complications he associates with hybridity and difference. But where Asante seeks his solvent in a rhetoric of ancestral soil and biological growth, Schlesinger finds his in a fantastical vision of ideals that, to his mind, have a well-defined content and meaning that transcend the group-based disagreements of a complex and quarrelsome American society. No less than Asante's rhetoric Schlesinger's vision is a kind of kitsch, precisely because its figure of a semantically fixed and stable creed abstracts from the ambiguities and, especially, the conflicts of interpretation that have historically constituted Americans' engagement with political ideals. The creed, and the laws Schlesinger thinks embody it – e.g., the antidiscrimination laws yielded by the civil rights movement – are not transparent in their meaning and admit of multiple and contradictory readings reflecting the various ways Americans understand themselves.[48] Schlesinger's flight from difference cannot escape difference, because difference reproduces itself in the contest over the disputed meanings of unifying democratic ideals. Granting that these ideals are in some sense constitutive of democracy, their precise content and scope remains ever open to democratic debate.[49]

I can summarize my critique of Schlesinger by saying that he only partially acknowledges what Michael Walzer aptly depicts as the doubly hyphenated character of American identities. "[I]t is not the case that Irish–Americans, say, are culturally Irish and politically American," writes Walzer, "[r]ather, they are culturally Irish–American and politically Irish–American. Their culture has been significantly influenced by American culture; their politics is still, both in style and substance, significantly ethnic."[50] Schlesinger, though he admits and indeed insists on the American–Irish and American–African hybridity of Irish–American and African–American *ethnic* identities, still romances the prospect of an American political identity that has been purified of ethnic and racial difference, and hence cleansed of struggles over the meanings of political ideals. Somewhat like the Afrocentrist who yearns for a simple and normal African–American identity – and so refuses to embrace the cultural hybridity of African–American lives – Schlesinger yearns for a simple and normal American political identity.[51] In both cases, identity is fashioned as a safe and placid home, free of ambiguity, contradiction, and conflict.[52]

4 Race Conscious Multiculturalism

In the fourth part of this paper I defend a version of multiculturalism that avoids the kitsch of Afro-and other ethno-centrisms, as well as the kitsch of a political nationalism that eschews difference. In particular, I make the case that multicultural education in contemporary America should be race conscious.

I begin with the assumption that fostering the capacity for democratic deliberation is a central aim of public education in a democratic society.[53] I also follow a number of contemporary political theorists in supposing that democratic deliberation is a form of public reasoning geared towards adducing considerations that all parties to a given deliberation can find compelling.[54] On this view, successful deliberation requires that co-deliberators cultivate a mutual understanding of the differences in conviction that divide them, so that they can formulate reasons (say, for implementing or not implementing a proposed policy) that will be generally acceptable despite those differences.[55] In the words of one theorist, "[d]eliberation encourages people with conflicting perspectives to understand each other's point of view, to minimize their moral disagreements, and to search for common ground."[56]

Lorenzo Simpson usefully glosses the pursuit of mutual understanding when he writes that it requires

> a "reversibility of perspectives," not in the sense of my collapsing into you or you into me, but in the sense that I try to understand – but not necessarily agree with – what you take your life to be about and you do the same for me . . . [i]n such a . . . mutual understanding you may come to alter the way in which you understand yourself and I . . . may find that listening to you leads me to alter my self-understanding.[57]

According to Simpson, the search for common ground need not leave us with the convictions with which we began. On the contrary, the process of democratic deliberation can be a source of self-transformation that enriches one's view of the issues at hand and even alters one's conception of the demands of social justice.[58]

In multicultural America, multicultural public education is a good that promotes mutual understanding across cultural differences, thereby fostering and strengthening citizens' capacities for democratic deliberation. In essence, multicultural education is a form of pedagogy whereby students study the histories and cultures of differently cultured fellow citizens, many of whose identities have a composite, multicultural character. More exactly, it is a form of cross-cultural hermeneutical dialogue, and therefore a way of entering into conversation with those histories and cultures.[59] By disseminating the cultural capital of cross-cultural knowledge, multicultural education can cultivate citizens' abilities to "reverse perspectives." By facilitating mutual understanding, it can help them to shape shared vocabularies for understanding their moral and cultural identities and for finding common ground in their deliberations.[60]

By strengthening a student's ability to reverse perspectives, multicultural education may bolster her disposition to engage the self-understandings of differently cultured others, even if the particulars of her multicultural education have not involved an engagement with the cultures of precisely *those* others (consider, e.g., someone whose multicultural education has included courses in Asian–American literatures, but who knows nothing of American Latino subcultures). Acquiring a know-how and a feel for cross-cultural hermeneutical conversation is likely to reinforce a student's inclination to understand and learn from the self-interpretations of cultural "others," in just the way that the cultivation of an athletic skill (e.g. the ability to "head" a soccer ball) tends to reinforce one's inclination to participate in the sports for which having that skill is an advantage (e.g. playing soccer). In the case of multicultural education, one cultivates a skill which is motivationally conducive to the sort of mutual understanding that is critical to the flourishing of deliberative democracy in a multicultural society.[61]

Let me summarize my argument so far. In contrast to Schlesinger, who yearns for a society in which the understanding of key political ideals remains immune from deliberative debate animated by cultural and other group differences, I have been suggesting that deliberative debate of this sort is an appropriate medium for seeking and forging common grounds and ideals. I have also been arguing

1 that a commitment to deliberative democracy in multicultural America entails a commitment to promoting the mutual understanding of differences through cross-cultural dialogue and
2 that such a commitment justifies the institution of multicultural education.

The promotion of mutual understanding avoids Schlesinger's and Asante's kitsch, because it is not predicated on an imperative to preserve an uncomplicated national or ethnic identity in the face of cultural and social complexity. Indeed, the ideal of mutual understanding invites *increasing* complexity by suggesting that cross-cultural educational insights, since they can effect changes in the self-understandings of persons who have benefitted from a multicultural education, may alter and further complicate those persons' identities, perhaps making them *more* multicultural. In what follows, I further explore the implications of this ideal by proposing that a commitment to deliberative democracy in multicultural America justifies a form of multicultural education that is, specifically, *race conscious*.

Multicultural education in America should be race conscious, because the mutual understanding of differences in America is impossible absent attention to race. As regards cross-cultural conversations with specifically African–American *cultures*[62], this is perhaps obvious. To be sure, my claim here *is not* that these cultures are somehow reducible to black Americans' reactions to racial classification, or to the slavery and racism that have attended that classification. As Ralph Ellison once asked, "can a people . . . live and develop for over three hundred years simply by *reacting?*"[63] Still, it seems to me incontrovertible that any cross-cultural inquiry into African–American cultures will have to address the largely racialized character of African–Americans' self-understandings; that is, it will have to investigate the ways in which African–Americans, in describing themselves as black, have coped with racial classification and racial oppression, thereby modifying the character of African–American life, art, and politics. African–American cultures, notwithstanding their past and present diversity, have been and continue to be inflected by meanings and self-understandings that *black persons* have assigned to being black in a society that has been shaped by black slavery and antiblack racism. Because racism, the legacies of slavery, and black personhood cut across the cultural differences distinguishing African–Americans, cross-cultural education that engages the complexity of African–American cultures will *almost always* attend to the meanings that black persons, mindful of the slave past and of antiblack racism, ascribe to being black.

Let me develop this point by highlighting the role that the concept of a black person, like that of subjective gender identity, can play in historical inquiry. Using the latter concept, Joan Scott has shown how nineteenth-century French seamstresses, acting under descriptions of themselves as *women*, established a "distinctively feminine work identity" that significantly shaped their political actions. Similarly, Robin D. G. Kelley has argued that "[r]ace, particularly a sense of 'blackness,' . . . figures prominently in the collective identities of black working people." In effect, he implies that the concept of a black person – that is, of someone black who acts in the world under a description of himself as black – can make a valuable contribution to the historian's study of America's black working class, a point that he later bears out in his discussion of the African–Americans who fought in Spain with the Abraham Lincoln Brigade "out of their concern for *black people*."[64] Kelley's work is relevent to my argument, because it offers an indication of the sort of race conscious insight that ought to inform American multicultural education. To be precise, it suggests that students' cross-cultural study of African–American working class cultures should focus, in part, on the ways in which the racialized self-understandings of black persons have informed and continue to inform those cultures.

Kelley's example stresses the *collective* significance that working class black persons have assigned to being black. This is significant, in my view, for I suspect that race conscious multiculturalism will enhance nonblacks capacity to find deliberative common ground with blacks – a ground that at times seems sorely to be missing from American public life (as, for example, in discussions of the million man march and of the "not guilty" verdict in the O. J. Simpson criminal trial) – just to the extent that it emphasizes African–American views of and debates about being black that develop the insight that black identity is a collective predicament. In the same vein, one could easily envision a race conscious multicultural curriculum that investigated African–American history and political thought with the explicit aim of making sense of such views and debates.

Consider, for example, the view held by many (though not all) African–Americans that the (comparatively) low, average socioeconomic status of African–Americans, because it is due to the cumulative effects of racial slavery and antiblack racism, is an injustice for which African–Americans deserve compensation. Some white Americans will dismiss this assertion of injustice, largely because they are "reluctant to see the present social plight of blacks as the result of American slavery."[65] Still, were these whites to learn something of American racial slavery and of its impact on African–American life, they could begin to see that the argument for reparations is plausible and begin to share with the African–Americans who advance that argument a common moral ground for further deliberations. In other words, through the study of African–American social history, they could begin to acknowledge the cogency of the considerations in light of which many African–American black persons, in reflecting on that history, have insisted that being black in America involves collective injustice.

Supposing that they augmented this study with inquiry into the central themes of African–American political thought[66] (as it has evolved, say, from the writings of Martin Delaney to those of Martin King), they could enlarge the common ground by beginning to recognize the range and force of African–American perspectives on other race-related issues.

It would be a mistake, of course, to think that multiculturalism needs to be race conscious only when addressing the self-understandings of black persons or, by analogy, the self-understandings of racially classified but non-black "persons of color." America is also a nation of racially classified whites and white persons; and white personhood, we know, cuts across ethnic lines. Again, by analogy to blacks who become black persons, whites who become white persons let their descriptions of themselves as white matter to the ways in which they live their lives. David Roediger's work on the racial formation of Irish–American workers is relevant here, as it provides a model for historical inquiry that illuminates the social construction and ethnic cultural significance of white racial identities.[67] Also important, in this context, is Toni Morrison's book, *Playing in the Dark*. Reflecting on the nature of American literature, Morrison writes:

> that cultural identities are formed and informed by a nation's literature, and . . . what seemed to be on the "mind" of the literature of the United States was the self-conscious construction of the American as a new white man. Emerson's call for this new man in "The American Scholar" indicates the deliberateness of the construction, the conscious necessity for establishing the difference. But the writers who responded to this call, accepting or rejecting it, did not look solely to Europe to establish a reference for difference. There was a very theatrical difference underfoot. Writers were able to celebrate and deplore an identity already existing or rapidly taking a form that was elaborated through racial difference. That difference provided a huge payout of sign, symbol, and agency in the process of organizing, separating, and consolidating identity . . .[68]

For Morrison, reading American writers after Emerson (e.g., Poe and Twain) is a matter of engaging complicated constructions of white racial identities implicated in a racial ideology ("American Africanism" is Morrison's phrase) that assigns multiple meanings to the African presence in America. Self-consciously constructing a literature in light of descriptions of themselves as white, the "founding writers of young America" were white persons (in my sense of the term) for whom the figure of the black African became a "staging ground and arena for the elaboration of the quintessential American identity."[69] For my purposes, Morrison's short study is valuable, because it affords some excellent examples of the ways multicultural inquiry can explore the cultural construction of white racial identities and their connection to the promotion of racial ideologies. In America, multicultural education cannot avoid race, because socially constructed racial identites – those of black persons and white persons alike – come into view no matter what class or ethnic perspective one occupies in cross-cultural deliberations. And while one ought not to conflate multiculturalism with struggles against racism and economic injustice, or promote it as a substitute for such struggles, multicultural education, by being race conscious, can contribute to an understanding of the issues posed by these struggles.[70]

Conclusion: The Politics of Recognition

Let me conclude this essay by returning to Du Bois.

In 1897, Du Bois sketched his position on the question of cultural recognition in a paper he entitled "The Conservation of Races." In this essay, he argued that each race has a cultural or "spiritual" message for humanity, although some races, the Negro race among them, have yet fully to deliver themselves of their messages. Among the central themes of "The Conservation of Races" is Du Bois's effort to exhort his fellow Negroes, especially his fellow American Negroes, to act in concert to cultivate and bring to fruition the Negro's message for humanity. Here, however, I wish only to emphasize Du Bois's guiding assumption in this essay that recognizing the cultural worth of a race's spiritual message is a matter of seeing that that message has something to say to all human beings. In 1897, then, Du Bois conceptualized cultural recognition as the predication of universal value.[71]

In *The Souls of Black Folk*, published just six years after "The Conservation of Races," Du Bois develops a somewhat different notion of recognition; not recognition as the predication of universal value, but what I shall call "self-recognition." The self of self-recognition is not, for the Hegelian Du Bois, the self taken by itself, but the self conceived as socially mediated. For Du Bois, then, self-recognition is a form of cultural recognition that entails seeing one's own cultural identity in connection to the cultural identities of the other members of one's community. Where self-recognition is frustrated by racial prejudice, Du Bois proposes, the likely outcome is social tragedy.[72]

The emergence in Du Bois's writing of a second conception of cultural recognition marks a distinction that continues to play a role in debates about the politics of recognition. Charles Taylor, for example, in his influential essay on that topic, explicitly conceptualizes cultural recognition as the predication of universal value. For Taylor, one's hermeneutic engagement with cultures not one's own should be guided by the defeasible presumption that "all human cultures that have animated whole societies over some considerable stretch of time have something important to say to all human beings."[73] Now compare Taylor's understanding of recognition to the one Susan Wolf propounds in her critique of Taylor. According to Wolf,

> [t]he politics of recognition urges us not just to make efforts to recognize the other more actively and accurately – to recognize those people and those cultures that occupy the world in addition to ourselves – it urges us to take a closer, less selective look at who is sharing our cities, the libraries, the schools we call our own. There is nothing wrong with allotting a special place in the curriculum for the study of our history, our literature, our culture. But if we are to study our culture, we had better recognize who we, as a community, are.[74]

Here, like the Du Bois of *Souls*, Wolf concerns herself with *self*-recognition, suggesting that one aim of multicultural education is a knowledge of one's community in its multifaceted complexity. Recognizing who *we* are, as distinct from recognizing that *they* have something valuable to say, is the critical element in her interpretation of the politics of recognition.

Now it is clear, I hope, that the conception of the politics of recognition which I have been defending is Wolf's "self-recognition" conception. Recognition, as I conceive it, is recognition gained through multicultural education oriented towards mutual understanding. Thus understood, recognition is, as it was for Du Bois, a matter of seeing one's cultural identity in connection to the cultural identities of other members of one's community. Sometimes this will involve seeing more clearly the point of the needs-interpretations of others; and sometimes it will lead to criticism and debate about the validity of those needs-interpretations. On still other occasions, recognition will move us to change our views of ourselves, or to see that our sense of what matters to us brings our culturally hybrid selves closer to culturally hybrid others than we ever expected. Whatever the case may be, the pursuit of socially mediated self-recognition is important to advancing the goal of deliberative democracy in America. "America's dilemma," Ronald Takaki reminds us, "has been our resistance to ourselves – our denial of our immensely varied selves."[75]

Notes

* For helpful comments on earlier drafts of this paper I wish to thank Alexander George, Andy Parker, Jan Dizard, Amrita Basu, Mark Kesselman, Preston King, Stanley Fish, Gary Watson, Georgia Warnke, Paul Stern, David Wills, Anna Stubblefield, Tom Wartenberg, Jyl Gentzler, Iris Young, Donald Morrison, Nancy Gilson, Starry Schor, Judith Butler, George Kateb, Lorenzo Simpson, Michael Hardimon, Tom McCarthy, and Sara Gooding-Williams. I am also grateful to the Columbia University Seminar in Social and Political Thought, to Princeton University's University Center for Human Values, and to the Yale Political Theory Workshop for opportunities to present this paper.

1 See Henry Louis Gates, Jr., *Loose Canons* (Oxford: Oxford University Press, 1992), p. 35.
2 This way of formulating my argument draws inspiration from John Guillory's excellent discussion of the current canon wars in his *Cultural Capital: The Problem of Literary Canon Formation* (Chicago: University of Chicago Press), pp. 38–55.
3 Kwame Anthony Appiah, *In My Father's House: Africa in the Philosophy of Culture* (New York: Oxford University Press, 1992), p. 13. For Appiah's more detailed discussion of racialism, see his "Racisms" in David Goldberg, ed. *Anatomy of Racism* (Minneapolis: University of Minnesota Press, 1990) and [the two separate essays by] K. Anthony Appiah and Amy Gutmann, *Color Conscious* (Princeton: Princeton University Press), pp. 54–6.
4 On the population geneticist's conception of races as breeding populations, see Ernst Mayr, "Typological versus Population Thinking," in E. Mayr, ed. *Evolution and the Diversity of Life* (Cambridge: Harvard University Press, 1975), pp. 26–9, and Richard Goldsby, *Race and Races* (New York: MacMillian, 1971).
5 See Michael Omi and Howard Winant, *Racial Formation in the United States* (New York: Routledge, 1986), p. 90 and Walter Benn Michaels, "The No-Drop Rule," *Critical Inquiry* 20 (Summer 1994), p. 90.
6 Ibid., p. 764.
7 Adrian Piper, "Passing for White, Passing for Black," *Transition* 58 (1992), pp. 30–1.
8 Michaels, "The No-Drop Rule," pp. 767–8.
9 Appiah makes a similar point in *Color Conscious*, pp. 85–90.

10 See Piper, "Passing for White, Passing for Black," pp. 18–19.

11 Here, I do not take up the important question of what it is that makes a practice of racial classification a practice of *racial* classification. The problem, here, is to identify the concepts and beliefs that distinguish practices of racial classification from other practices of social classification (e.g., practices of gender identification). This is *not* a question that Omi and Winant take up in either the first or the revised edition of *Racial Formation in the United States*. Nor does Winant take up the issue in his recent book, *Racial Conditions* (Minneapolis: University of Minnesota Press, 1994). Robert Miles does address the issue in his *Racism* ((New York: Routledge, 1989), pp. 74–5), but it is not obvious to me that his notion of ritualization suffices to capture all the practices of social identification which we are inclined to call "racial" (e.g., racial identification in Brazil, which proceeds on the basis of principles very different than those which obtain in the United States). In the final analysis, there may be no adequate general concept of practices of racial identification. Still, there may be significant family resemblances (in Wittgenstein's sense) between these different practices.

12 Only in the twentieth-century does the one-drop rule become the dominant rule of racial classification in the United States. Indeed, in much of the nineteenth century, it finds itself in competition with a rule that defines mulattoes as other than black. For a detailed recounting of the social and political history of the one-drop rule and of black and white challenges to the rule, see F. James Davis, *Who Is Black* (University Park: Pennsylvania University Press, 1991). See, also, David Hollinger, *PostEthnic America* (New York: Basic Books, 1995), pp. 32, 44–5.

13 If, for Piper, being black were a function, say, of satisfying the one-drop rule, then she would be committed to the view that, even in the absence of a practice of racial classification wherein the rule found application (explicitly or implicitly), America would still contain its share of black folk. On my reconstruction of her position, this is a view she rejects.

14 This is not to deny that the bulk of Piper's powerful autobiographical essay deftly expresses her own "first-person" perspective.

15 See Anna Stubblefield, "Racial Identity and Non-Essentialism about Race," *Social Theory and Practice*, 21 (3) (Fall 1995) and Anthony Appiah, *Color Conscious*, pp. 76–83.

16 See Ian Hacking, "Making Up People," in Thomas C. Heller, Morton Sosna, and David Wellbery, eds. *Reconstructing Individualism*, (Stanford: Stanford University Press, 1986), pp. 222–36.

17 By "identification," Appiah means "the process through which an individual intentionally shapes her projects – including her plans for her own life and her conception of the good – by reference to available labels, available identities." See *Color Conscious*, p. 78.

18 See Hacking, "Making Up People," p. 236.

19 Ibid., p. 231.

20 W. E. B. Du Bois, *The Souls of Black Folk*, ed. David W. Blight and Robert Gooding-Williams (New York: Bedford Books, 1997), p. 38.

21 Ibid.

22 James Weldon Johnson, *The Autobiography of an Ex-Colored Man* (New York: Vintage, 1989), pp. 20–1.

23 The position I sketch here is consistent, I think, with Stuart Hall's well known remarks regarding the "end of the innocent notion of the essential black subject." "What is at issue," Hall argues, "is the extraordinary diversity of subject positions, social experiences, and cultural identities which compose the category 'black'." On my account, this diversity is in part a function of the numerous ways in which one can be a "black person." See Stuart Hall, "New Ethnicities," in James Donald and Ali Rattansi, eds. *"Race", Culture and Difference*, (Thousand Oaks: Sage Publications, 1992), p. 254.

24 In other words, I do not subscribe to the sort of philosophical realism that, as Appiah puts it, "seems inherent in the ways questions of authenticity are normally posed." See Appiah, *Color Conscious*, p. 96.

25 By "discursively shaped" I mean, simply, description-shaped. For a similar approach to the topic of gender identity, see Judith Butler, *Gender Trouble* (New York: Routledge, 1990).

26 Jean-Paul Sartre, *Anti-Semite and Jew*, trans. George Becker, with an introduction by Michael Walzer (New York: Schocken, 1995), p. 89.

27 Ibid., pp. 90, 111.

28 For a more detailed critique of Sartre's remarks about inauthentic Jews and about Jewish identity in general, see Michael Walzer's introduction to the edition of *Anti-Semite and Jew* cited above.

29 It is important to see that the politics of mixed race is, ambiguously, a politics of disturbance *and* enactment. To the extent that it aims to institute a new order of racial classification conventions that still relies on a principle of descent (mixed race identity is, after all, a function of the racial identities of one's parents), I find it difficult to see in this politics, as does David Hollinger, a "fundamental challenge to the authority of descent-defined categories." See David Hollinger, *PostEthnic America*, p. 165. For an interesting argument to the effect that the very heart of democratic politics is an ambiguous tension between disturbance and enactment see William E. Connolly, *The Ethos of Pluralization* (Ithaca: Cornell University Press, 1995), pp. 75–104.

30 Appiah, *In My Father's House*, p. 24.

31 Ibid. See also Kwame Anthony Appiah, "Europe Upside Down: Fallacies of the New Afrocentrism," *SAPINA Newsletter* V (January–June 1993): 5. Appiah makes a similar point in the context of his critique of Afrocentrism in his "Afrocentrism, 'Difference,' Role Models and the Construction of Race," *Salmagundi* 104–5 (Fall 1994–Winter 1995), pp. 93–4.

32 Molefi Kete Asante, "Racism, Consciousness, and Afrocentricity," in Gerald Early ed. *Lure and Loathing: Essays on Race, Identity, and the Ambivalence of Assimilation* (New York: Penguin, 1993), p. 142.

33 Asante, "Racism, Consciousness, and Afrocentricity," pp. 142–3.

34 For a good discussion of the theoretical commitments of the nineteenth century racial sciences, see Michael Banton, *Racial Theories* (Cambridge: Cambridge University Press, 1987), chapter 2.

35 Karsten Harries, *The Meaning of Modern Art* (Evanston: Northwestern University Press, 1968), p. 149.

36 The production of normalizing norms and images of African–American identity is at staple of African–American cultural nationalism. On this point, see William L. Van DeBurg, *New Day in Babylon: The Black Power Movement and American Culture 1965–1975* (Chicago: University of Chicago Press, 1992), pp. 170ff.

37 Manthia Diawara has also interpreted Afrocentricity as Afro-kitsch in his "Afro-Kitsch," in Gina Dent, ed., *Black Popular Culture*, (Dia Center for the Arts, 1992), pp. 285–91.

38 Charles Johnson, *Being and Race: Black Writing since 1970* (Bloomington: Indiana University Press, 1988), p. 20. Eve Sedgwick has suggested, if I read her correctly, that kitsch-attribution is a supercilious gesture expressing an attitude of "self-exemption or cynicism but nothing much more interesting than that." Harries's and Johnson's use of the term "kitsch" seem to me to be exempt from this criticism in that it relies on a clearly stated concept of kitsch (kitsch as a retreat from ambiguity) rather than on the haughty pretension simply to be able to "recognize kitsch when [one] sees it" (see Eve Kosofsky Sedgwick, *Epistemology of the Closet* (Berkeley: University of California Press, 1990), pp. 155–6). For a more recent and equally persuasive critique of the ideology of "negritude," see Tsenay

Serequeberhan, *The Hermeneutics of African Philosophy* (New York: Routledge, 1994), pp. 42–53. For a critique of Afrocentric education that differs from (but is complementary to) the one offered here, see Amy Gutmann, "Challenges to multiculturalism in democratic education," in Robert K. Fullinwider, ed. *Public Education In A Multicultural Society*, (Cambridge: Cambridge University Press, 1996), pp. 158–9.

39 Appiah makes a similar point in his "Identity, Authenticity, Survival: Multicultural Societies and Social Reproduction," in Amy Guttman, ed. *Multiculturalism: Examining the Politics of Recognition*, Gutmann (Princeton: Princeton University Press, 1994), pp. 154–5.

40 Albert Murray, *The Omni-Americans* (New York: Vintage, 1983), p. 22.

41 Ralph Ellison, *Going to the Territory* (New York: Vintage, 1987), p. 108. Murray's and Ellison's central point is that American identities are *multicultural*. For a recent sounding of a similar theme that stresses the multicultural or "mélange" character of modern identities generally, see Jeremy Waldron, "Multiculturalism and Mélange" in Robert K. Fullinwider, ed. *Public Education in a Multicultural Society*, (Cambridge: Cambridge University Press, 1996), pp. 90–118. For a recent discussion of the hybrid and syncretic character of African–American and other "black Atlantic" cultures, see Paul Gilroy, *The Black Atlantic: Double Consciousness and Modernity* (Cambridge: Harvard University Press, 1993), chapter 3.

42 Ellison, *Going to the Territory*, pp. 108–9.

43 Arthur M. Schlesinger, Jr., *The Disuniting of America: Reflections on a Multicultural Society* (New York: W. W. Norton, 1992), p. 135.

44 Ibid., p. 118.

45 Ibid., pp. 135–6.

46 Ibid., pp. 27, 118.

47 Ibid., p. 135.

48 On the ambiguities built into antidiscrimination legislation, see Kimberlé Williams Crenshaw, "Race, Reform, and Retrenchment: Transformation and Legitimation in Antidiscrimination Law," *Harvard Law Review* 101 (May 1988), pp. 1341–6.

49 For more on this point, and on the hermeneutic circle that characterizes democratic debate about basic rights and liberties, see Seyla Benhabib, "Toward a Deliberative Model of Democratic Legitimacy," in Seyla Benhabib, ed. *Democracy and Difference: Contesting the Boundaries of the Political*, (Princeton: Princeton University Press, 1996), pp. 77–80. See, in the same volume, Chantel Mouffe, "Democracy, Power, and the 'Political'," p. 254. Also see Amy Gutmann, "Challenges of multiculturalism in democratic education," pp. 168–9.

50 Michael Walzer, "What Does It Mean to Be an 'American'?," *Social Research* 57 (Fall 1990), p. 612.

51 For clear-sighted resistance to kitsch conceptions of American identity of the sort that Schlesinger's position represents, see Thomas L. Dumm's letter to Laurie Anderson in the first chapter of his *united states* (Ithaca: Cornell University Press, 1994) and Anne Norton's "Engendering Another American Identity" in Frederick M. Dolan and Thomas L. Dumm, eds. *Rhetorical Republic: Governing Representations in American Politics*, (Amherst: University of Massachusetts Press, 1993), pp. 125–42.

52 Here, I mean to suggest that both Asante's Afrocentrism and Schlesinger's nationalism exemplify what Bonnie Honig has recently called "the politics of home." See Bonnie Honig, "Difference, Dilemmas, and the Politics of Home," in Seyla Benhabib, ed. *Democracy and Difference: Contesting the Boundaries of the Political*, (Princeton: Princton University Press, 1996), pp. 257–77.

53 Following Amy Gutmann, I use public education to refer to "all publically subsidized and publically accredited institutions that satisfy a mandatory schooling requirement, whether they are actually controlled by public or private organizations." This includes publically

accredited private schools. See Amy Gutmann, "Challenges of multiculturalism in democratic education," p. 176, fn. 1

54 See, for example, Joshua Cohen, "Procedure and Substance in Deliberative Democracy," in Seyla Benhabib, ed. *Democracy and Difference: Contesting the Boundaries of the Political*, (Princeton: Princeton University Press, 1996), pp. 95–119; Amy Gutmann and Dennis Thompson, *Democracy and Disagreement* (Cambridge: Harvard University Press, 1996), especially chapter 2; and Seyla Benhabib, "Toward a Deliberative Model of Democratic Legitimacy."

55 Joshua Cohen is especially clear on this point: "In an idealized deliberative setting, it will not do simply to advance reasons that one takes to be true or compelling: such considerations may be rejected by others who are themselves reasonable. One must instead find reasons that are compelling to others, acknowledging those others as equals, aware that they have alternative reasonable commitments and knowing something about the kinds of commitments that they are likely to have." See Joshua Cohen, "Procedure and Substance in Deliberative Democracy," p. 100.

56 Amy Gutmann, "The Challenge of Multiculturalism in Political Ethics," *Philosophy and Public Affairs* 22 (Summer 1993), p. 199.

57 Lorenzo C. Simpson, "Community and Difference: Reflections In the Wake of Rodney King," in C. C. Gould and R. S. Cohen, eds. *Artifacts, Representations and Social Practice* (Netherlands: Kluwer Academic Publishers, 1994), pp. 531–2. Here, it is important to note that, for Simpson, "reversing perspectives" does not entail that one be able literally to put oneself in the position of the other; or that one find a way to live the history she has lived; or even that one be able adequately to imagine her perspective as one's own – none of which possibilities are *real* possibilities according to Iris Young. On the contrary, he seems to have in mind precisely the sort of listening and learning "across differences" that Young endorses. In this essay, I use the idea of reversing perspectives as Simpson uses it. For Young's discussion of this issue, see her "Asymmetrical Reciprocity: On Moral Respect, Wonder and Enlarged Thought," *Constellations* 3 (January 1997), pp. 340–63.

58 Iris Young makes a similar point in her essay "Difference as a Resource for Democratic Communication," in J. Bohman and W. Rehg eds. *Deliberative Democracy: Essays on Reason and Politics* (Cambridge, MA: MIT Press, 1997), pp. 383–406.

59 Here, I follow Gadamer in allowing that one can enter into dialogue, not only with persons, but with narratives and other forms of written expression.

60 See Lorenzo Simpson, "Community and Difference," pp. 532–3.

61 For a related argument that, from a somewhat different perspective, raises the question of the connection between multicultural education and democratic citizenship, see Janet Farrell Smith, "A Critique of Adversarial Discourse: Gender as an Aspect of Cultural Difference," in Lawrence Foster and Patricia Herzog, eds., *Contemporary Philosophical Perspectives on Pluralism and Multiculturalism* (Amherst: University of Massachusetts Press, 1994), pp. 59–82.

62 Here, I mean to flag that fact that, like Anthony Appiah, I remain skeptical of the view that there is a single culture shared in common by all African-Americans. On this point, see Appiah's recent contribution to Appiah and Gutmann, *Color Conscious*. See, also, Bernard Boxill, *Blacks and Social Justice* (Totowa, New Jersey: Rowman and Alenheld, 1984), p. 178.

63 Ralph Ellison, "An American Dilemma: A Review" in R. Ellison, ed., *Shadow and Act* (New York: Vintage, 1972), p. 315.

64 See Joan Wallach Scott, *Gender and the Politics of History* (New York: Columbia University Press, 1988), pp. 44, 104, and Robin D. G. Kelley, *Race Rebels* (New York: The Free Press), pp. 4–5, 104.

65 Bill E. Lawson, "Moral Discourse and Slavery," in Howard McGary and Bill E. Lawson, eds., *Between Slavery and Freedom: Philosophy and American Slavery*, (Bloomington: Indiana University Press, 1992), p. 85.

66 For a brief but excellent introduction to the central themes of African American political thought, see Bernard Boxill, "Two Traditions in African American Political Philosophy," *The Philosophical Forum* 24 (Fall–Spring 1992–93), pp. 119–35.

67 See David Roediger, *The Wages of Whiteness: Race and the Making of the American Working Class* (London: Verso, 1991).

68 Toni Morrison, *Playing in the Dark: Whiteness and the Literary Imagination* (Cambridge: Harvard University Press, 1992), p. 39.

69 Ibid., pp. 44, 51. See also, in this vein, Karen Sánchez-Eppler, *Touching Liberty* (Berkeley: University of California Press, 1993), especially her chapter on Walt Whitman.

70 For an insightful and valuable discussion of the differences and possible connections between multiculturalism and antiracism, see Lawrence Blum, "Multiculturalism, Racial Injustice, and Community: Reflections on Charles Taylor's 'Politics of Recognition,'" in Lawrence Foster and Patricia Herzog, eds., *Contemporary Philosophical Perspectives on Pluralism and Multiculturalism* (Amherst: University of Massachusetts Press, 1994), pp. 175–205. On the dangers of letting the promotion of multiculturalism substitute for struggles against racism and other forms of social injustice, see Hazel Carby, "The Multicultural Wars," *Radical History* 54 (Fall 1992), pp. 10–11, as well as her unpublished paper "Cultural Integration/Political Apartheid" delivered at the December 2nd and 3rd "Brown at Forty" conference held at Amherst College. For a related critique of an identity politics that "caresses the better-off female, gay, and/or minority self while consigning its working class sisters and brothers to their 'richly' deserved misery," see Micaela di Leonardo, "White Ethnicities, Identity Politics, and Baby Bear's Chair," *Social Text* 41 (Winter 1994), pp. 165–91.

71 For the full text of "The Conservation of Races" see chapter 4, p. 84–91 this volume.

72 I explore the relation between recognition and tragedy in *Souls* in chapter three of an unpublished manuscript, *Recognizing Race: Du Boisian Meditations on Black Identity in America*. A short version of this chapter appears under the title "Du Bois's Counter-Sublime," *Massachusetts Review* 35 (Summer 1994), pp. 202–24. See also the editors' introduction to the Bedford Books edition of *The Souls of Black Folk* cited in fn. 20.

73. Charles Taylor, "The Politics of Recognition," in Amy Gutmann, ed., *Multiculturalism: Examining the Politics of Recognition*, (Princeton: Princeton University Press, 1994), p. 66.

74 Susan Wolk, "Comment," in Amy Gutmann, ed., *Multiculturalism: Examining the Politics of Recognition*, (Princeton: Princeton University Press, 1994), p. 85.

75 Ronald Takaki, *A Different Mirror: A History of Multicultural America* (Boston: Little, Brown, and Co., 1993), p. 427.

14

CONVERSATIONAL BREAK: A REPLY TO ROBERT GOODING-WILLIAMS

Judith Butler

I am especially pleased to be responding to Robert Gooding-Williams essay, and to continue this dialogue, one that we have been having for at least 15 years. I'm not one to engage the confessional mode, but it seems relevant to the argument at hand here, one that has everything to do with the possibility of dialogue within multiculturalism, to review for a moment my professional friendship with Gooding-Williams: it raises some of the very points that are thematically pursued in his paper.

Although he was slightly ahead of me in graduate school, we both studied philosophy at Yale in the early 80s, and for the most part I remember that we debated about Hegel and Nietzsche and about which part of the Frankfurt School was more to our liking, and I suppose as well that there was between us an assumption that hermeneutics remained an important and hopeful conception of philosophy: a notion of thinking as conversation seemed crucial to us both. At that time, I read feminist theory and taught it, but on the side. And Gooding-Williams read widely in cultural theory, including works on race, but that also did not appear in the classes that we took, in the papers that we wrote or, indeed, in the dissertations that we finally completed. It was only some years later that we both found ourselves teaching parallel courses at different universities on gender and race, and I remember well the excitement of moving between a philosophical tradition that we knew and engaging a cultural and political set of texts pertaining to the question of identity. Gooding-Williams explored in Du Bois, for instance, the appropriation and revision of Hegel's view of reciprocal recognition, and I offered a theory of gender performance that remained indebted to a phenomenological notion of constituting acts. We were, as it were, both in the philosophical canon and yet strangely outside of it at the same time.

I tell this story to give you some sense of the reasons for my rather profound and abiding sense of identification with him, but also to explain the occasion in which I invoke the "we" in something of the sense that he proposes toward the end of his paper. But I also offer this context to raise some questions about what this identification consists in, and how identification more generally relates to questions of race, multiculturalism, and the task of hermeneutical conversation that he raises in his excellent essay. Indeed, I have just sought to give a narrative in which I offer some insight into who "we" are, who after all go back a long way, indeed, were born within a mile of each other. That mile is the stretch of Cleveland, Ohio around West 105th street in which for a time the black middle class lived not far from the Jewish middle class, where much of Cleveland's artworld exists, where my synagogue was, where Bob's father taught, where beautiful brick homes lined the streets, a stretch that is now plagued by poverty, populated with poor and working-class blacks, and where Jews arrive and leave from the hospital and the synagogue in great haste, and integration is a lost dream.

There is much, then, that binds us together, and there is much, from the start, that separates us. The question, I suppose, has to do with how we come to think that separation, and whether the hermeneutical solution that Bob proposes is enough to help us with this difficulty. Indeed, the more general philosophical problem might be understood as the problem of identification in politics (Lacoue-Labarthe suggests that identification is the central question of the political) and, more specifically, whether identification does not require a constitutive difference between those who are said to identify with one another.

At the very close of his essay, Gooding-Williams asks us to replace the we–they framework that governs some ethical reflections on the problem of multicultural understanding with a more expansive and internally fractious notion of the "we;" thus the ethical problem posed by multiculturalism is not, strictly speaking, that of coming to understand the Other, but, rather, of revising and expanding an understanding of who "we" are. I take this to be an important point, not only for the reasons that Susan Wolf points out in her response to Charles Taylor, but also for those who think that by appropriating a Levinasian view of the ineffability of the Other that multicultural understanding might be significantly advanced. After all, what does it mean to continue to conceive of the Other as radically Other, as beyond the reach of reason, as some Levinasians maintain? Does such a casting of alterity beyond the domain of the thinkable not reconstitute the radically alien character of "the other," and continue to cover over the ways in which the "other" may well be more properly a constitutive part of the self than first appears. If one takes the argument that Gooding-Williams advances, namely, that contemporary culture is itself syncretic, if not hybrid, then the very distinction between self and other appears not only arbitrary, but belated and imposed, deflecting from the kind of inquiry that interrogates the complex cultural sources of the self that multiculturalism demands of us.

There are of course ways of realizing that the other is part of the self which simply reinstate of colonizing notion of the self in which every moment of alterity is recast as an always already internal feature of the self, a situation in which no confrontation with difference, and no transformation in light of that confrontation is demanded or undergone.

Gooding-Williams proposes that we revise and expand the "we" and come to understand that black culture is not foreign to mainstream culture, but constitutes it essentially. Here he seems to be in favor of a certain conception of cultural hybridity. And he is also is right, in my view, to continue the critique of Charles Taylor, who uses the notion of "our culture" and "their culture" as if they are sociological givens, without ever inquiring into what composes those cultures and the appearance of their external difference to one another. His essay on multiculturalism does not include the question of whether such "cultures" are composed in ways that make them radically inextricable from one another.

If we accept Gooding-Williams thesis that the putative "alterity" of black culture needs to be rethought as part of the mainstream American culture, which it seems imperative to do, ought we then to do away fully with the notion of the "they" and with the problem of alterity that it poses? How do we continue to emphasize the problem of exclusion and marginalization if we begin with the heuristic that black culture is not a minority culture, but part of the majority from the start? What does Gooding-Williams think of those critiques of the category of the "we," such as Gayatri Chakravorty Spivak's, in which its invocations can work in the service of a suppression, in which the very expansion of the "we" constitutes an imperialist gesture whereby cultural differences are subordinated precisely through the strategy of an ever-expansive "inclusion"? *Is there a way to distinguish between the revision and expansion of the "we" that avows the ways in which cultural alterity is part of the majoritarian "self," as it were, without that very revision and expansion becoming a new form of domination?*

The quasi-religious invocation of alterity that the Levinasian view supports seems to be the extreme alternative to the project that seeks to redefine the problem of alterity as a problem of the constitutive cultural complexity of the self. Is there a way to navigate between these two views?

Gooding-Williams not only understands mainstream US culture to be an irreducible multiplicity of cultures, but he also insists that "black culture" is not unitary, and that it must be thought in terms of its complex cultural articulations. He defends his view through recourse to a specific version of social constructionism. And yet, the definitions he offers seem not fully to accord with the view of a multiplicitous black identity that he also wants to affirm.

Gooding-Williams defines black identity, for instance, as the "the effect of a rule-governed social practice of racial classification," and uses this definition to clarify the sense of social construction that he means to defend. He distinguishes, with Stuart Hall, black identity from an African–American identity, and points out that there are several historical and cultural contexts for blackness in the United States that are not necessarily the same as that denoted by African–American. He names Afro-Caribbean and Latin American routes of descent, as well as African origins that are not mediated by the institution of exported slavery, and in this respect, Gooding-Williams insists in general on a non-unitary character of blackness.

My question then is this: how is it that an internally complex and non-unitary notion of blackness is the *singular* "effect of a rule-governed social practice of racial classification?" In other words, *does not a non-unitary conception of blackness require a non-unitary conception of a rule-governed social practice of racial classification?* Is "race" the effect of a single such social practice, and is that social practice always that of racial *classification*, one that can be traced to a distinct periodization within European history? Are there less official and less overt forms of racial construction that are not reducible to such schemes of racial classification or that cannot be traced back to them historically? In particular, I am reminded of the problem with Sartre's view in *Anti-Semite and Jew* that the Jew is one who has been called a Jew, constructed as a Jew within the terms of anti-semitism. Is not the Jew also something other than what the anti-semite says the Jew is? Is not the black something other than what racialist forms of race classification "say" that the black is? Are there not traditions and communities that produce their own social and cultural values that are "black" but not in the *same* sense that a racial classification scheme deems someone to be black?

The next two questions follow from the last, and they have to do with conceiving race as an "effect." At times, Gooding-Williams seems to claim that race is produced as a result of such classificatory schemes, but he also adds that "one becomes black only if one begins to identify as black [and] one begins to make choices, to formulate plans, to express concerns in light of one's identification of oneself as black." *What is the theory of identification at work in such a formulation?* In other words, what does it mean to make such an identification? Some psychoanalytic accounts of identification argue that identification is never fully complete and never fully successful, and that this failure constitutive of identification is precisely what distinguishes it from identity. Can the identification with blackness that Gooding-Williams mentions ever be complete? And if one must identify with blackness to be black, what is the blackness with which one identifies? Is it prior to the identification, or is it, in some sense, also its result? Is the blackness with which one identifies a cultural value or norm? Is it an idealization or, indeed, a fantasy of some sort? To what extent does the process of identification postulate the very norm that then functions as the model it seeks to approximate?

If efforts to make such identifications are never fully successful, is the failure to identify that results from every such effort a significant one? In other words, does the failure to achieve the norm of identity not itself expose the incommensurability between the norm and any of its embodiments, and does the exposure of that incommensurability not open up possibilities for a rearticulation of the norm itself? What is Gooding-Williams's view on the distinction between identity and identification? Is there some significant use to be made of identification, as Stuart Hall suggests, as it is appropriated from psychoanalysis for the purposes of social theory? If identification only becomes possible when identity is not fully achieved, and identification requires an insuperable difference or incommensurability between the one who identifies and that with which identification is made, then is identification a prerequisite for identity, or is it rather the internal limit of any possible identity? If identification undermines identity in this sense, then it would seem that, in a sense that Fanon clearly understood, it is not possible to "be" black and, indeed, not possible to "be" white either.[1]

Moreover, if race is not only an "effect" of a classificatory scheme, but also, as Gooding-Williams suggests, a mode of choice and indeed, a choice of identification, how is race to be understood as both produced by social norms and voluntaristically engaged? The demand for a theory that accounts for race as an effect that is at once lived and transformed in the course of its being lived suggests a move away from those mechanistically formulated versions of social construction to one in which norms are understood to have a revisable temporality. Indeed, it is unclear to me that Gooding-Williams wants finally to stay with the notion of race as as "effect" if he also wants to make room for an agential construction of race. Does the very meaning of race change as its status as "effect of a social practice of classification" is altered, that is, as the "effect" becomes taken up and transformed as a result of that appropriation? For "race" to become a sign of agency and cultural self-affirmation, its historicity must not be fully constrained from its putatively classificatory origins, the possibilities for its meanings must exceed the original purposes for which it was designed. I would expect Gooding-Williams to accept this basically Nietzschean view that such terms form a "sign-chain" in which the original purposes for which they are devised are sometimes reversed and superseded by subsequent usages.

Finally, then, I have a question about the hermeneutical dimension of Gooding-Williams' normative views concerning the future of multicultural understanding. Gooding-Williams puts forth a view of cultural dialogue that involves the self-transformation of those who engage in such a dialogue. But for there to be dialogue, does there not have to be a certain notion of distance, one that cannot be overcome through the revision and rearticulation of the "we"? In other words, does the dialogic form of hermeneutical self-understanding and self-transformation that Gooding-Williams proposes not require a subject and its Other? That I identify with you does not mean that I am the same as you, or that I think that the analogies between us make our experiences radically interchangeable with one another. But it does give me the chance to speak to you and to hear you, a chance that may be as much conditioned by what separates us as by any common set of presuppositions we might have. Is it not the case that what divides two interlocutors may be as necessary to the possibility of conversation than what implicitly binds them together? Does the hermeneutical view stress the existence of common presuppositions to such a degree that it domesticates the differences that animate conversation, predicating the notion of conversation that it promotes on that very domestication? Here I am not only referring to differences that are necessarily enabling of conversation, but those that impeded and stop conversation as well (indeed, a multicultural conversation might well have to run into such breaks and ruptures in order to enter into radical reflection on the presuppositions that foreclose conversation from the start). What place is there within the hermeneutical dialogue for the expression of such a difference that produces a break in common understanding or "epistemic rupture" to use Gayatri Chakravorty Spivak's term? Such ruptures are significant, challenging, galvanizing, even necessary in order to call the racial presuppositions of conversation into question, in order to force a revaluation of an abiding schema of understanding that has exclusionary or marginalizing moves built into it. One of the reasons that multicultural conversation often seems so difficult is that it often turns on such moments, ones that can quickly become paralyzing, tempting the "rational" speaker back into his or her own linguistic stable. But the risk of such conversation may well be in leaving available schema of rationality behind or, at least, forcing them into radical transformation. From the point of view that seeks to resist this encounter, the "break" in question looks like irrationalism, but it is only the exposure of the contingent limits of an available rationality scheme. Or still others who resist that important rupture will understand this epistemic hiatus as a permanent obstruction to dialogue. But this break can operate as a violent inauguration of a new understanding as well, one that must break with dialogue in order to begin it again. Importing this sort of violence into the hermeneutic scheme may well allow us to develop a view that prizes the "we" as a condition and effect of dialogue without sacrificing the mobilizing force of difference.

Note

1 See Frantz Fanon, *Black Skin, White Masks*, (New York: Grove Press), 1967, pp. 223–32.

Part VIII

THE PHENOMENOLOGY OF RACIAL EMBODIMENT

15

TOWARD A PHENOMENOLOGY OF RACIAL EMBODIMENT[1]

Linda Martín Alcoff

When one realizes the indeterminacy of racial categories, their fluid borders and cultural variety, it is often tempting to adopt a nominalism about race, that race is no more real than phlogiston or witchcraft. In this essay I resist this conclusion primarily on phenomenological grounds. Race is real, certainly more real than phlogiston, though like witchcraft its "reality" is internal to certain schemas of social ontology that are themselves dependent on social practice and, moreover, the current reality of race is certainly capable of radical transformation and perhaps eradication. My focus, however, will not be on the possible future permutations of racializing practices but on the intense present reality of race. I will explore reasons for the current confusion about race, consider various approaches to knowledge about race, and venture a preliminary phenomenological account of racial identity as it is lived in the body of various racialized subjects at a given cultural moment. Only when we come to be very clear about how race is lived, in its multiple manifestations, only when we can come to appreciate its often hidden epistemic effects and its power over collective imaginations of public space, can we entertain even the remote possibility of its eventual transformation.

I

Contemporary confusions about race can be directly traced to the historical emergence of the present concept. Recently, the West (meaning Anglo-European cultures) has been credited with originating the idea of race, in the era of early modernism and even more specifically in the era that Foucault called the Classical episteme.[2] In this era, Foucault suggests, the newly emerging sciences understood knowledge primarily as a practice of ordering and classifying on the basis of essential differences.[3] Race-making also had a strong historical as well as conceptual relationship with mapmaking, in which the expanding geographical areas that came to be known by Europeans were given order and intelligibility in part through their association with racial types. The ordering and labeling of natural terrain, the classifying of natural types, and the typologies of "natural races" thus emerged simultaneously and were no doubt motivated by European anxiety about the suddenly increased size and diversity of their world. This diversity could come to be both known and neutralized through the formulation of an ordering system. There is a wonderful moment in the 1993 film, "Map of the Human Heart," in which an Inuit man asks a white engineer who has come to northern Canada to map the region, "Why are you making maps?" Without hesitation, the white man responds "They will be very accurate." To map or not map a region was a question beyond the circumference of European discourse. Similarly out of bounds was the question of ranking or not ranking diversity.

Arguing via Foucault, both Cornell West and David Theo Goldberg have attempted genealogies of modern racism that link the western fetishistic practices of classification, the forming of tables, and the consequent primacy of the visible with the creation of metaphysical and moral hierarchies between racialized categories of human beings.[4] Given this genesis, the concept of race and of racial difference emerged as that which is visible, classifiable, and morally salient. West argues that the application of natural history techniques to the study of the human species yields a comparative analysis "based on visible, especially physical, characteristics . . . [which] permit one to discern identity and difference, equality and inequality, beauty and ugliness among animals and human bodies."[5] In our own materialist society, where science trumps religion and where cultural rituals – whether religious, patriotic, or familial – must increasingly revolve around the exchange of material commodities in order to retain their significance, what is true is what is visible. Secular, commodity-driven society is dominated by the realm of the visible. In such a context, visible differences operate as powerful determinants over social interaction.

However, in the early modern period, the juxtaposition of these classification practices with an emerging liberal ideology espousing universalism produced a confused and contradictory account of race, from which I believe Western discourses as well as Western "common knowledge," in a Gramscian sense, is still suffering today. Visible difference is still the route to classification and therefore knowledge, and yet visible difference threatens the liberal universalistic concepts of truth and justice by invoking the specter of relativism. Classification systems can attempt to contain this threat and impede relativism by enclosing the entirety of difference within a taxonomy organized by a single logic, such as a table of I.Q. test scores grouped by race. Ranking differences thus works to nullify relativism and protect universalism. But the resultant juxtaposition between universalist legitimation narratives that deny or trivialize difference (one might think of Habermas, here, or Rawls) and the detailed taxonomies of physical, moral, and intellectual human difference (as, for example, in the recent best-selling book, *The Bell Curve*) is one of the greatest antinomies of modernism.[6]

The new development of critical race studies has begun to erode most of the theoretical props for racial hierarchies in academic discourses. Today the naturalistic classification systems which would reify human variability into moral categories and the Eurocentric teleologies which would excuse, if not justify, colonialism have been largely exposed as specious. And the realm of the visible, or what is taken as self-evidently visible (which is how the ideology of racism naturalizes racial designation), is recognized as the product of a specific form of perceptual practice, rather than the natural result of human sight. Anti-essentialisms have corroded the sense of visible difference as the "sign" of a deeper, more fundamental difference, a difference in behavioral disposition, in moral and rational capacity, or in cultural achievement. Moreover, there is a newly emerging biological consensus that race is a myth, that the term corresponds to no significant biological category, and that no existing racial classifications correlate in useful ways to gene frequencies, clinal variations or any significant human biological difference.[7]

However, at the same time, and in a striking parallel to the earlier modernist contradictions regarding the significance of race, in the very midst of our contemporary skepticism toward race as a natural kind stands the compelling social reality that race, or racialized identities have as much political, sociological, and economic salience as they ever had. As Goldberg puts it, liberal Western societies today maintain a paradoxical position whereby "Race is irrelevant, but all is race."[8] The legitimacy and moral relevance of racial concepts is officially denied even while race continues to determine job prospects, career possibilities, available places to live, potential friends and lovers, reactions from police, credence from jurors, and the amount of credibility one is given by one's students. Race may not correlate with clinal variations, but it persistently correlates with a statistically overwhelming significance in wage levels, unemployment levels, poverty levels, and the likelihood of incarceration. As of 1992, black and Latino men working full-time in the US earned an average of 68% of what white men earned, while black and Latina women earned 59%. As of 1995, Latino and black unemployment rates were more than double that of whites.[9]

But for those still working within a Liberal framework, the devastating sociological reality of race is but an artificial overlay on more fundamental constituents of the self. The specificity of culturally embedded and marked bodies is routinely set aside in projects that aim toward a general analysis. Even for some post-structuralists, because race is a contingent construction, the epiphenomena of essentialist discourses, it is ultimately without any more explanatory power or epistemological relevance than on the Liberal view. Thus, for all our critical innovations in understanding the vagaries of racist domination and the conceptual apparatus that yields racism, too many today remain stuck in the modernist paradox that race is determinant of a great deal of social reality, even while our scientists, policy makers and philosophers would have us deny its existence.

No wonder, then, that we are confused about what to do with the category of race. Naturalistic approaches to the "real" – in which conceptual frameworks are thought to be determined by nature herself – cannot make sense of the cultural variety, recent history, and biological invalidity of race, though there are some positions that endeavor to define race in this way nonetheless. Universalistic political systems in which justice is predicated on sameness cannot help but view racial consciousness with consternation and dismay. Thus, within the modern episteme, the continued use of racial categories leads inevitably to paradox.

II

Contemporary race theory has endeavored to transcend the paradoxes of classical liberalism and to address explicitly the implicit ideologies of race. On the questions of the status of the category race and whether racial identity should be continued, this recent body of work falls out into three basic positions:

1 Race is not real, principally because recent science has invalidated race as a salient or even meaningful biological category. It is the biological meaning of racial concepts that have led to racism. Therefore, the use of racial concepts should be avoided in order to be metaphysically accurate as well as to further an anti-racist agenda.
2 Race is always politically salient and always the most important element of identity. Members of racial groups share a set of characteristics, a set of political interests, and a historical destiny. Current racial identities are stable across history.
3 Race is socially constructed, historically malleable, culturally contextual, and produced through learned perceptual practice. Whether or not it is valid to use racial concepts, and whether or not their use will have positive or negative political effects, depends on the context.

The first position – what I will call a nominalism about race – fails to capture the multiple meanings of race and assumes incorrectly that race can only refer to biology. It also falsely assumes on the basis of a commitment to semantic realism and an over-inflation of the importance of science that racial concepts can have no possible referent and thus no valid meaning. It naively assumes that an end to the use of racial concepts will solve (or contribute toward solving) the current enormous sociological and economic determinism of racialized identities, before we try to understand the ways in which beliefs and practices of racialization have informed every political theory, every conceptual framework, and every metanarrative, at least in the West.

The second position – what I will call an essentialism about race – fails to capture the fluidity and open-endedness of racial meanings. It wrongly assumes that racial identities are obvious and easily demarcated, that racialized groupings are homogeneous, and that ancestry is all-determining. It operates on a mistaken notion of what cultures are, as if they are merely the developing expression of an originary logic rather than the effect of negotiations from multiple sources. And it promotes the futile mission of opposing the tide of global hybridization.

The third position – what I will call a contextualism about race – is clearly the best option both politically and as a metaphysical description.[10] It can acknowledge the current devastating reality of race while holding open the possibility that present-day racial formations may change significantly or perhaps wither away. It provides a better explanation for the variety of racial beliefs and practices across cultures, and thus acknowledges the contingency and uncertainty of racial identities and boundaries. One can hold without contradiction that racialized identities are produced, sustained, and sometimes transformed through social beliefs and practices and yet that race is real, as real as anything else in lived experience, with operative effects in the social world.

Contextualist approaches come in two forms: objectivist and subjectivist. Objectivist approaches attempt a definition of race general enough to be applicable across a variety of contexts even while recognizing that context will determine the specific content and political valence given to a racial concept. These approaches start with sociological facts, census categories and their transformations, and the history of racializations to develop an account of how race organizes social relations. Sanjek, for example, defines race as "the framework of ranked categories segmenting the human population that was developed by western Europeans following their global expansion in the 1400's."[11] Most of the current debates over race concern only objective definitions of race and racial identity.

However, objectivist approaches to race that chart its impact in the public domain sometimes hinder an appreciation for the everydayness of racial experience. Objectivist approaches that define race by invoking metanarratives of historical experience, cultural traditions, or processes of colonization and that take a third-person perspective can be inattentive to the micro-interactions in which racialization operates, is reproduced and sometimes resignified. In contrast, subjectivist approaches which begin from the lived experience of racialization can reveal how race is constitutive of bodily experience, subjectivity, judgment, and epistemic relationships. Such descriptions can then justify the claim that one's designated race is a constitutive element of fundamental, everyday embodied existence and social interaction.

Omi and Winant offer an account of race that attempts to include both the macro-level and the micro-level of social relations. The macro-level consists of economic, political and cultural structures, or "sites," in which the formation and management of racial collectivities occur, and thus is what I am calling an objectivist account. The micro-level consists of the micro-processes by which individual identities are formed.[12] In regard to the micro-level, they claim that "One of the first things we notice about people when we meet them (along with their sex) is their race."[13] They also develop a description of "racial etiquette" as:

> a set of interpretive codes and racial meanings which operate in the interactions of daily life. Rules shaped by our perception of race in a comprehensively racial society determine the "presentation of self," distinction of status, and appropriate modes of conduct.[14]

Although Omi and Winant don't pursue this approach much further, it is a productive way to explore how race operates pre-consciously on spoken and unspoken interaction, gesture, affect, and stance, and in this way producing what I am calling a subjectivist account. Greetings, handshakes, proximity, tone of voice, all reveal the effects of racial awareness, the presumption of superiority *vis-à-vis* the other, or the protective defenses against the possibility of racism and misrecognition.[15] I will argue that Merleau-Ponty's concept of the habitual body – a default position the body assumes in various commonly experienced circumstances that integrates and unifies our movements – could be useful here to understand how individuals fall into race-conscious habitual postures in cross-racial encounters.[16] Merleau-Ponty is mainly discussing motor habits of perception and movement used in performing various operations such as driving or typing, but the concept can easily be applied to postural attitudes and modes of perception taken in interactions with others whose identities are marked by gender, race, age, and so on. Following Fanon, Gordon, and Weiss, I will also argue that racialization structures the visual sphere and the imaginary self, and can block the development of coherent body-images.[17]

Subjectivist and objectivist approaches to understanding race are not mutually exclusive, and I agree with Omi and Winant that a full account would need to encompass both. But it seems to me that although subjectivist approaches have important advantages in accounting for how race works, they have been underdeveloped in the recent theoretical literature, even while there are many first-person memoirs and rich descriptions of racial experience that might be tapped for theoretical analysis.

A possible reason for the hesitancy one might have in going in this direction is a fear that phenomenological description will naturalize or fetishize racial experiences. This can happen when descriptions of felt experience begin to operate as *explanations* of felt experience, as if the experience itself is fully self-presenting. For example, if one believes that human beings group perceptual objects under concepts as the natural result of our need to cope with the blooming, buzzing variety of perceptual experience, then one might be led to think that racial categories are the understandable result of the need to group and categorize. In other words, racism is the unfortunate but inevitable result of human cognitive processes. Phenomenological descriptions that detail the overwhelming salience of racializations for given individuals would then be seen as support for such a belief.

Against this, I will argue that although racial classification does operate on the basis of perceptual difference, it is also the case that, as Merleau-Ponty argues, perception represents sedimented contextual knowledges. So the process by which human bodies are differentiated and categorized by type is a process preceded by racism, rather than one that causes and thus "explains" racism as a natural result. Such an account is compatible with Hegel's view that conflict arises from our parallel desires rather than our "innate" differences, a view that has many advantages it seems to me.

However, I would not want to say, as some nominalists seem almost to say, that racialization has only an arbitrary connection to the realm of the visible. Visual differences are "real" differences, and by that very fact they are especially valuable for the naturalizing ideologies of racism. But there is no perception of the visible that is not already imbued with value. And the body itself is a dynamic material domain, not just because it can be "seen" differently, but because the materiality of the body itself is, as Grosz puts it, volatile: "It is not simply that the body is represented in a variety of ways according to historical, social, and cultural exigencies while it remains basically the same; these factors actively produce the body of a determinate type."[18]

In what follows, then, I will pursue a subjectivist approach that relies on Merleau-Ponty's non-foundationalist account of lived experience. A phenomenological approach can render our tacit knowledge about racial embodiment explicit. Despite the fact that, at least until recently, it appears generally to be the case that most whites did not consciously "feel white," there were gestural and perceptual practices correlated to racial identity and a tacit but substantive racialized subjectivity. Other groups in the US have often been very conscious of the ways in which racial categories affected experience and presentations of self, but some of their knowledge about race is also tacit and carried in the body.

By drawing from tacit knowledge about racial identity, subjectivist approaches also, I would argue, operate from a different epistemology or justificatory strategy, and one that can make productive use of Gramsci's account of "common sense" or everyday consciousness discernible in practices, rather than a self-consciousness achieved through reflection. Common sense is made up of that which seems obviously true and enjoys consensus or near consensus. Despite its felt naturalness, however, common sense is formed, not as a false consciousness is imposed from above, but by the sediment of past historical beliefs and practices of a given society or culture.[19] If we apply this account to a racial common sense, we would not understand it as the imposition of ideology, but as part of the backdrop of practical consciousness, circulating, as Foucault would say, from the bottom up as well as from the top down. Racial knowledges exist at the site of common sense. Effectively in agreement with this Foucauldian approach, Omi and Winant also argue that racialization should not be understood as simply an imposition; for example, they suggest that racial "etiquette is not mere universal adherence to the dominant group's rules, but a more dynamic combination of these rules with the values and beliefs of subordinated groups."[20] They emphasize that a subordinate group can play a role in shaping racial formations through the particular patterns of resistance taken up.

The epistemically relevant point here is that the *source* of racializations, or at least one important source, is in the micro-processes of subjective existence. I would add to this, however, the obvious point that racial common sense varies both across and within racial groups, and the differences we find are likely to be significant. In any case, it has largely been an uninterrogated white common sense, albeit in all its internal variety, that has dominated the public discourse and theoretical analysis about race in the United States.

III

Here is Jack Kerouac, the iconized white Beat prophet, writing in his journal in 1949, describing a late evening walk through the black and Mexican neighborhoods of Denver:

> I stopped at a little shack where a man sold hot, red chili in paper containers. I bought some and ate it strolling in the dark, mysterious streets. I wished I was a Negro, a Denver Mexican, or even a Jap, anything but a white man disillusioned by the best in his own "white" world. (And all my life I had white ambitions!)[21]

Kerouac with this passage is characteristically ahead of his time. Kerouac was aware of the racialized others, whom he recognizes in their unified non-whiteness, but unlike many other whites (at least, Northern whites), he was also aware of his own whiteness and able to articulate the contours of its segregated subjective life in his comment that even ambitions have a racial identity. He is disillusioned with the pretensions of white culture, and out of this disillusionment he senses the arbitrariness of his dominant status, which makes it impossible for him to rest easy with it or relax in it. And thus he longs to escape it.

This felt disjuncture for Kerouac between his white body (or his non-nonwhiteness) and his sense of having a nonwhite sensibility operates in the very postural model of the body, a concept introduced by Sir Henry Head to name that nonlinguistic imaginary position of the body in the world and its imagined relation to its environment and to other bodies.[22] Kerouac pictured himself as outside "white society" or positioned on its margins. He thought of himself as having the aesthetic sensibility and temporal orientation of the other-than-white, in his irreverent cynicism toward the white world's self-presentations and declared intentions. In a different diary entry, he said that "the best the 'white world' has to offer [is] not enough ecstasy for me, not enough life, joy, kicks, music; not enough night."[23] Who is this "me" whose ability to appreciate and to desire joy, kicks, music, and life exceeds the white world? Who is it indeed whose virility and capacity for feeling is larger than the sallow, impotent blandness the white world can afford? It can only be a non-white, though Kerouac here relies precisely on the white world's own projection of "too much emotion" outside of itself, outside of white identity. In other words, even in his "nonwhite" sensibility, he operates from within a white schema of signification (a paradox that can also beset nonwhite bodies).

Kerouac's nonwhite postural body image, though, is pierced by the experience of walking through these "dark" streets, encountering the "real" other in the flesh, which then prompts him to recognize the incoherence between his own felt body-image – the one he surely felt in upper class white society – and the body-image now induced by the alienation he felt in what for him were foreign neighborhoods. Returning to the entry where he described his Denver walk, we find him say:

> I was so sad – in the violet dark, strolling – wishing I could exchange worlds with the happy, true-minded, ecstatic Negroes of America . . . How I yearned to be transformed into an Eddy, a Neal, a jazz musician, a nigger, a construction worker, a softball pitcher, anything in these wild, dark humming streets of Denver night – anything but myself so pale and unhappy, so dim.[24]

Fanon suggested that for black people in the colonial world, it was Sartre's third ontological dimension of bodily experience that dominates, that is, the consciousness of one's body as a body-for-others.[25] Kerouac experiences this in the nonwhite Denver neighborhoods, where the third dimension comes to dominate his own preferred body-image, to render his postural model incoherent, leading him to a melancholic resignation of his "paleness."

Notice also that in these passages Kerouac juxtaposes, perhaps unconsciously, reiterations of the darkness and mystery of his surroundings with a characterization of "Negroes" as open, fully readable, transparent. What is "dark" to him is not their nature or state of mind, which he presumes to fully know, but their *ability* to be happy and true-minded. This capacity has escaped him, and he hasn't a clue about how to retrieve it. He is not satisfied with the level of ecstasy available in the white world; and yet he cannot discover how to access the affect he perceives here. He yearns to be "anything but myself so pale and unhappy, so dim." Just as ambitions are racialized, so too are *his* melancholia and *their* happiness.

Fanon also suggested that racism and colonialism create significant challenges for the creation of an equilibrium in one's body image, an equilibrium achieved, as Weiss helpfully explains, through reconciling one's own " 'tactile, vestibular, kinesthetic, and visual' experiences with the structure imposed by this historico-racial schema, a structure that provides the 'racial parameters' within which the corporeal schema is supposed to fit."[26] The near-incommensurability between first person experience and historico-racial schema disenables equilibrium and creates what Fanon calls a "corporeal malediction." Kerouac, coming from the other side of the colonial equation, must have experienced this corporeal malediction as well. His desire to be transformed into an "Eddy," etc. etc., is a desire to resolve the disequilibrium induced by conflicting first and third person dimensions of the body, in favor of the first. I would suggest that today, more and more whites are experiencing a similar disequilibrium, as they come to perceive the racial parameters that structure whiteness differently in different communities – white and nonwhite – and may find that none of these can be made coherent with their own preferred body or postural image.

Because race works through the domain of the visible, the experience of race is predicated first and foremost on the perception of race, a perception whose specific mode is a learned ability. Merleau-Ponty says of perception:

> Perception is not a science of the world, it is not even an act, a deliberate taking up of a position; it is the background from which all acts stand out, and is presupposed by them. The world is not an object such that I have in my possession the law of its making; it is the natural setting of, and field for, all my thoughts and all my explicit perceptions . . . man is in the world, and only in the world does he know himself.[27]

If race is a structure of contemporary perception, then it helps constitute the necessary background from which I know myself. It makes up a part of what appears to me as the natural setting of all my thoughts. The perceptual practices involved in racializations are then tacit, almost hidden from view, and thus almost immune from critical reflection. Merleau-Ponty goes on: ". . . perception is, not presumed true, but defined as access to truth."[28] Inside such a system, perception cannot then be the object of analysis itself. Thus, Kerouac could "see" with immediacy the character of nonwhite lives and nonwhite emotional subjectivity. And yet the mechanism of that act of perceiving itself could not be seen, and thus could not be seen by him as also racialized.

Perceptual practices can be organized, like bodily movements used to perform various operations, into integrated units that become habitual. In the following passage Merleau-Ponty explains his idea of perceptual habits through the example of a blind man's use of a stick to find objects:

> It would appear in this case that perception is always a reading off from the same sensory data, but constantly accelerated, and operating with ever more attenuated signals. But habit does not *consist* in interpreting the pressures of the stick on the hand as indications of certain positions of the stick, and these as signs of an external object, since it *relieves us of the necessity* of doing so.[29]

In other words, the overt act of interpretation itself is skipped in an attenuated process of perceptual knowing. He goes on to contrast this account with a more positivist approach:

> Intellectualism cannot conceive any passage from the perspective to the thing itself, or from sign to significance otherwise than as an interpretation, an apperception, a cognitive intention . . . But this analysis distorts both the sign and the meaning: it separates out, by a process of objectification of both, the sense-content, which is already "pregnant" with a

> meaning, and the invariant core . . . it conceals the organic relationship between subject and world, the active transcendence of consciousness, the momentum which carries it into a thing and into a world by means of its organs and instruments. The analysis of motor habit as an extension of existence leads on, then, to an analysis of perceptual habit as the coming into possession of a world . . . In the gaze we have at our disposal a natural instrument analogous to the blind man's stick.[30]

This account would explain both why racializing attributions are nearly impossible to discern and why they are resistant to alteration or erasure. Our experience of habitual perceptions is so attenuated as to skip the stage of conscious interpretation and intent. Indeed, interpretation is the wrong word here: we are simply perceiving. And the traditional pre-Hegelian modernist account of perception, what I called above "positivism", blocks our appreciation of this. It is just such a modernist account that would explain why it is commonly believed that for one to be a racist one must be able to access in their consciousness some racist belief, and that if introspection fails to produce such a belief then one is simply not racist. A fear of African–Americans or a condescension toward Latinos is seen as simple perception of the real, justified by the nature of things in themselves without need of an interpretive intermediary of historico-cultural schemas of meaning.

If interpretation by this account is inseparable from perception, at least in certain cases, why would not such a view lead only to pessimism about altering the perceptual habits of racializations? Here I would think that the multiple schemas operating in many if not most social spaces today would mitigate against an absolute determinism and thus pessimism. Perceptual practices are dynamic even when congealed into habit, and that dynamism can be activated by the existence of multiple forms of the gaze in various cultural productions and by the challenge of contradictory perceptions. To put it simply, people are capable of change. Merleau-Ponty's analysis helps to provide a more accurate understanding of where – i.e. at what level of experience – that change needs to occur.

Phenomenological descriptions of racial identity can reveal a differentiation or distribution of felt connectedness to others. Kerouac's sadness is prompted by his lack of felt connection, a connection he may have anticipated when initiating his walk through the black and Mexican Denver neighborhoods, but one that does not present itself. However, felt connection is a complex issue, undetermined solely by phenotype. The felt connectedness to visibly similar others may produce either flight or empathic identification or other possible dispositions.

Compare Kerouac's perceptions with the autobiographical confession that dramatically opens Richard Rodriguez's book, *Days of Obligation*:

> I used to stare at the Indian in the mirror. The wide nostrils, the thick lips. Starring Paul Muni as Benito Juarez. Such a long face – such a long nose – sculpted by indifferent, blunt thumbs, and of such common clay. No one in my family had a face as dark or as Indian as mine. My face could not portray the ambition I brought to it.[31]

Here there is actually little contrast with Kerouac's account: Rodriguez echoes the racialization of ambition, in which his desire to be a writer and a public intellectual in the United States cannot be associated with an "Indian" face. In an earlier memoir, he recounts how as an adolescent he tried to shave the darkness off his skin in a fit of agonized frustration.[32] Like Kerouac again, Rodriguez wants to escape, and he experiences racial identity as a cage constraining his future, his aspirations; also like Kerouac he experiences it as somehow at odds with his felt subjectivity. His postural body-image is internally incoherent, and Rodriguez struggles persistently against the racial parameters that Fanon says characterizes colonized consciousness. Where Kerouac foregoes white ambition and yet resigns himself to whiteness, Rodriguez pursues white ambitions and in this way seeks to escape his visible identity and to repudiate his felt connection with visibly similar others.

Rodriguez recounts a conversation he had with an American Indian student when he was teaching at Berkeley.

> "You're not Indian, you're Mexican," he said. "You wouldn't understand."
> He meant I was cut. Diluted.
> Understand what?
> He meant I was not an Indian in America. He meant he was an enemy of the history that had otherwise created me . . . I saw his face – his refusal to consort with the living – as the face of a dead man.[33]

Rodriguez experiences Mexican identity as necessarily hybridized, "cut," "diluted." He projects onto his interlocutor the belief that Mexican identity is a deformed identity, when in actuality the man simply said "You are Mexican and not Indian," counter-posing two identities rather than an identity and a dilution of identity. Yet Rodriguez's projection is of course overdetermined by the denigration of mixed identities, particularly mixed racial identities, that is a painful feature of many, though not all, societies. The mixed person, unless she or he declares in her self-representation as well as her everyday practices to be identified with one group or another, feels rejection from every group, and is ready to be slighted on an everyday basis for presuming an unjustified association. She is constantly on trial, and unable to claim epistemic authority to speak as or to represent.[34] Rodriguez experiences a doubled hybridity: the hybridity of a Mexican–American educated and enculturated in an Anglo environment, and the hybridity of *Latinidad* itself, between *indigenismo* and *conquistador*.

Rodriguez deflects this denigration by demarcating his hybrid world into neatly mapped spaces and urging their segregation. He argues that Spanish, the mother tongue, the female tongue, is proper to the private sphere, and should be spoken only at home for bilingual Latinos in the United States. He characterizes English as the public language, the language of social intercourse, the language for intervening in politics, and thus a language clearly coded masculine. English is justifiably normative because its universality is simply inevitable, Rodriguez argues. Thus he has been an important public critic of bilingual education programs and any policy that might have the effect of incorrectly merging what should be carefully sequestered realms of discourse.

Rodriguez also construes his own white ambitions – to master English and assimilate in a public Anglo world – as representing life. Life moves forward, it adapts, it transforms and in this way survives. Assimilation to an Anglo world is life; the resistance to this is an embrace of death. Thus he sees the man's face in the cafeteria as the face of a dead man. Unlike Kerouac on this point, Rodriguez does not romanticize the nonwhite racial Other, which is a form of love Lewis Gordon aptly likens to pet loving.[35] By incorporating aspects of an Anglo identity, and pursuing an identity based on the metanarrative of "American" progress and cultural development, Rodriguez perceives himself as choosing life. He further describes his interlocutor in the conversation already quoted as a "moody brave," and

> a near-somnambulist, beautiful in an off-putting way, but interesting, too, because I never saw him without the current issue of *The New York Review of Books* under his arm, which I took as an advertisement of ambition.[36]

For Rodriguez, ambition can *only* be white; there is no conception of an ambition beyond or apart from intercourse in a dominant Anglo world. In the description just given, Rodriguez associates the man's physical appearance with distance: it is off-putting despite its beauty. Racial difference is often experienced as a distancing without regard to spatial proximity. Yet Rodriguez has hopes for the possibility of a relationship, of the man being included in Rodriguez's own wider frame of reference, by his possession of a journal that signifies a transcendence of the physical mark. Anglo identity is again associated with the public, the realm of ambition, of action in a social world, where Indian identity remains on the body, pulling against ambition, social intercourse, even, Rodriguez says, life itself. Thus, he sees the man as a near-somnambulist, a man poised between the life embodied in the *New York Review of Books* and the death of a historical dreamworld.

No less than Kerouac, Rodriguez reads others and himself through visible signs on the body, reading his "long nose sculpted by indifferent, blunt thumbs" as "incapable of portraying" his ambition. I would argue that this mediation through the visible, working on both the inside and the outside, both on the way we read ourselves and the way others read us, is what is unique to racialized identities as against ethnic and cultural identities. The criteria thought to determine racial identity have ranged from ancestry, experience, self-understanding, to habits and practices, yet these sources are coded through visible inscriptions on the body. The processes by which racial identities are produced work through the shapes and shades of human morphology, the size and shape of the nose, the breadth of the cheekbones, the texture of hair, and the intensity of pigment, and these subordinate other markers such as dress, customs, and practices. And the visual registry thus produced has been correlated with rational capacity, epistemic reliability, moral condition, and, of course, aesthetic status. Rodriguez has learned this visual registry in its dominant white form, and thus he moves back and forth between exploring its racism[37] and adopting it as his own perspective, letting it dominate his body-image almost as a perceptual habit-body, or habit of perception.

"Visibility is a trap," says Foucault.[38] He explains: "Hence the major effect of the Panopticon: to induce in the inmate a state of conscious and permanent visibility that assures the automatic functioning of power."[39] What could be more permanently visible than that which is inscribed on the body itself?

Racialized identities that are not visible create fear and consternation. In the film *Europa, Europa* the young, closeted Jewish hero is chosen by his teacher to model Aryan facial features before a classroom of boys. His teacher has ironically but terrifyingly gotten it wrong, ironically in mistaking his Jewish student as a paradigm of Aryan looks, but terrifyingly in bringing the boy to the front of the class for inspection. Despite the teacher's mistake, the modeling nonetheless conveys the importance of visibility within the Nazi regime. Jews *had* to be visible, and thus were measured carefully, from nose to ear, and navel to penis, in the attempt to establish a reliable and perceptible means of identification.

Similar to the Jews, the Irish were a racialized group internal to Europe until this century. Gibbons quotes the following passage in which a first time English visitor to Ireland records his observations:

> I am haunted by the human chimpanzees I saw along that hundred miles of horrible country... But to see white chimpanzees was dreadful; if they were black, one would not feel it so much, but their skins, except where tanned by exposure, are as white as ours...[40]

The observer in this passage experienced a disequilibrium in his corporeal self-image prompted by finding his own features in the degraded Other.

Clearly, one source of the importance of visibility for racialized identities is the need to manage and segregate populations and to catch individuals who trespass beyond their rightful bounds. But there is another reason for the importance of visibility, a reason I would argue is as significant as the first, and this is that visible difference naturalizes racial meanings. Merleau-Ponty claims that "When we speak of the flesh of the visible, we do not mean to do anthropology, to describe a world covered over with our own projections."[41] In other words, the visible is not merely an epiphenomenon of culture, and thus precisely lies its value for racialization. We may need to be trained to pick out some features over others as the most salient to identity, but those features nonetheless have a material reality. This is why both Kerouac and Rodriguez experience racial identity as impossible to alter: Kerouac cannot "become Negro" no matter how much he would like to, and Rodriguez can only fail to shave off the darkness of his skin. Locating race in the visible thus produces the experience that racial identity is immutable.

This is why race *must* work through the visible markers on the body, even if those markers are *made* visible through learned processes. Visible difference, which is materially present even if its meanings are not, can be used to signify or provide purported access to a subjectivity through observable, "natural" attributes, to provide a window on the interiority of the self – thus making it possible for a Kerouac to confidently assume an ability to perceive directly ecstasy and true-mindedness, knowing nothing more about the individuals that surrounded him than the color of their skin.

In some cases, the perceptual habits are so strong and so unnoticed that visible difference is deployed in every encounter. In other situations, the deployment of visible difference can be dependent on the presence of other elements to become salient or all-determining. For an example of such a situation, I will relate a case I discussed with a philosophy graduate student with whom I regularly converse about issues in the classroom. White undergraduates walking into an introductory philosophy course in upstate New York might not expect an Asian instructor, but after an initial surprise the students appeared to feel at ease in the class as he (I'll call him "John") discussed Descartes and Leibniz and patiently explained to struggling undergraduates how to follow an argument in early modern texts. John himself then began to relax in the classroom, interacting without self-consciousness with a largely white class. His postural body image was at those moments normative, familiar, trustworthy. Despite the hierarchy between students and teacher, there seemed to be little or no racial distancing in their interactions.

However, at a certain point in the semester, John introduced the subject of race into the course through an assigned reading on the cognitive dimensions of racism. This topic had a visceral effect on classroom dynamics. Previously open-faced students lowered their eyes and declined to participate in discussion. John felt a different texture of perception, as if he were being watched or observed from a distance. His previously felt normativity eroded, and with it his teaching confidence. It was not that before he had thought of himself as white, but that he had imagined *and experienced* himself as normative, accepted, recognized as an instructor capable of leading students toward greater understanding. Now he was reminded, forcibly, that his body image self was unstable and contingent, and that his racialized identity was uppermost in the minds of white students who suddenly developed a skeptical attitude toward his analysis and imparted it in a manner they had not been confident enough to develop before.

I have actually experienced this scenario many times myself, if I raise the issue of race, cultural imperialism, the US invasion of Panama, or sometimes issues of sexism in classes not focussed on these topics, and other colleagues of mine who are African-American or Latino have described similar classroom experiences. Such an experience, as Eduardo Mendieta has suggested, is as if one finds oneself in the world ahead of oneself, the space one occupies as already occupied. One's lived self is effectively dislodged when an already outlined but very different self appears to be operating in the same exact location.

Fanon argues that the "Negro, because of his body, impedes the closing of the postural schema for the white man."[42] But this seems not to be the case until something that seems to be a "nonwhite subjectivity" is made apparent. Before a nonwhite Professor assigns an article on race, white students' postural body image can remain intact, unchallenged. The teachers' otherness at this stage can be subsumed under a number of non-threatening categories, from servant, to assimilated other who demonstrably accepts a white world-view as the truth, and so on. The students do not perceive the teachers' recognition of them as challenging in any way. At the point where race enters the classroom as a theme, and especially as a theme introduced by a nonwhite, their confidence and ease about how the teacher is perceiving them begins to erode, creating a break between first and third person perspective. Only then is their postural schema disrupted. Disequilibrium for whites is not an inevitable result of the presence of racial others, even in a historico-racial schema of white supremacy, though it may be a potential disruption that the body appreciates and which puts it in the mode of watchfulness.

For a nonwhite called back from a normative postural image to a racialized "epidermal schema" as Fanon put it, the habit-body one falls into at such moments, I would suggest, is protective, defensive. Double layers of self-awareness must interrogate the likely meanings that will be attributed to every utterance, gesture, action one takes. The available options of interaction seem closed down to two: combative resistance without hope of persuasion, or an attempt to return to the category of non-threatening other, perhaps through the place of the not-really-other. Neither can yield a true relationship or dialogue; both are options already given within the white dominant racial structure. No original move can be recognized.

When I was much younger, I remember finding out with a shock that a white lover, my first serious relationship, had pursued me because I was Latina, which no doubt stimulated his vision of exoticism. Our first encounters, our first dates, which I had naively believed were dominated by a powerful emotional and intellectual connection, were experienced by him as a crossing over to the forbidden, to the Other in that reified, racializing sense.[43] I felt incredulity, and then humiliation, trying to imagine myself as he saw me, replaying my gestures and actions, reflecting back even on the clothes I wore, all in an attempt to discern the signs he may have picked up, to see myself as he must have seen me. I felt caught in that moment, finding myself occupying a position already occupied, incapable of mutual interaction.

There is a visual registry operating in social relations which is socially constructed, historically evolving, and culturally variegated but nonetheless powerfully determinant over individual experience. And, for that reason, it also powerfully mediates body image and the postural model of the body. Racial self-awareness has its own habit-body, created by individual responses to racism, to challenges from racial others, and so on. The existence of multiple historico-racial schemas produces a disequilibrium that cannot easily be solved in multiracial democratic spaces, i.e. where no side is completely silenced. Racial identity, then, permeates our being in the world, our being-with-others, and our consciousness of our self as a being-for-others.

Phenomenological descriptions such as the ones I have discussed here operate uncomfortably to reactivate racist perception and experience. One might worry that such descriptions will have consolidating effects by repeating, even explaining, the process of racist attribution, suggesting its depth and impermeability. But the reactivations produced by critical phenomenological description don't simply repeat the racializing perception but can reorient the positionality of consciousness. Unveiling the steps that are now attenuated and habitual will force a recognition of one's agency in reconfiguring a postural body image or a habitual perception. Noticing the way in which meanings are located on the body has at least the potential to disrupt the current racializing processes.

If racism is manifest at the level of perception itself and in the very domain of visibility, then an amelioration of racism would be apparent in the world we perceive as visible. A reduction of racism will affect perception itself, as well as comportment, body image, and so on. Toward this, our first task, it seems to me, is to make visible the practices of visibility itself, to outline the background from which our knowledge of others and of ourselves appears in relief. From there we may be able to alter the associated meanings ascribed to visible difference.

Notes

1 I would like to thank Robert Bernasconi and William Wilkerson for their very helpful critical comments on this paper. Numerous discussions that I had with Raul Vargas, David Kim, Eduardo Mendieta, Paula Moya, Michael Hames-Garcia, Tom McKay, Paul Taylor,

Simon Critchley, Elizabeth Grosz, and Lewis Gordon had a significant effect on the formulation of the arguments below. The discussions of bodily experience in Lewis Gordon's *Bad Faith and Antiblack Racism* (Humanities, 1995) and Elizabeth Grosz's *Volatile Bodies* (Indiana, 1994) inspired my analysis here, and the publication of Gail Weiss's excellent book *Body Images* (Routledge, 1998) after I began work on this paper caused me to rethink many points.

2 On the origin of race as an idea, see Michael Omi and Howard Winant, *Racial Formations in the United States: From the 1960s to the 1980s* (New York: Routledge, 1986), pp. 58–9; Steven Gregory and Roger Sanjek, eds., *Race*, (New Brunswick: Rutgers University Press, 1994), p. 2. See also Emmanuel Eze, ed., *Race and the Enlightenment* (Cambridge, MA: Blackwell, 1997).

3 Michel Foucault, *The Order of Things: An Archaeology of the Human Sciences* (New York: Random House, 1970, 1994).

4 David Theo Goldberg, *Racist Cultures: Philosophy and the Politics of Meaning* (Oxford: Basil Blackwell, 1993); Cornell West *Prophesy Deliverance!* (Philadelphia: Westminster Press, 1982).

5 West, p. 55.

6 The widespread popularity of *The Bell Curve* thesis, which classifies and ranks intellectual ability by racial identity, and assumes a single standard of intelligence, is proof that vestiges of the classical episteme remain in place today. See Richard J. Herrnstein and Charles Murray *The Bell Curve: Intelligence and Class Structure in American Life* (New York: Free Press, 1994).

7 On these points, see Frank B. Livingstone "On the Nonexistence of Human Races," in *The Racial Economy of Science: Toward a Democratic Future* ed. by Sandra Harding (Bloomington: Indiana University Press, 1993), pp. 133–41. Harding explains that a cline is "a continuous gradation over space in the form of a frequency of a trait." (p. 133) Livingstone argues that the differences in gene frequency among populations can be adequately explained without any reference to race.

8 Goldberg, p. 6.

9 For more statistics on racial disparities, see Andrew Hacker *Two Nations: Black and White, Separate, Hostile Unequal* expanded edition, (New York: Ballantine, 1995).

10 I prefer contextualism to social constructionism because of the wide misuse and misunderstandings too often prevalent with the use of the second term. Social constructionism is sometimes interpreted along the lines of an idealism in which total agency is given to individual actors, as if we can construct new identities out of whole cloth. I hope that contextualism will convey the idea that what race *is* is dependent on context.

11 Sanjek, p. 1.

12 Omi and Winant, pp. 66–7.

13 Omi and Winant, p. 62.

14 Omi and Winant, p. 62.

15 Mixed race people who are not easily categorizable by visible markers create unease precisely because one doesn't know how to act or talk with them. All of these practices change enormously across cultures; for example, in Latin America mixed race persons do not create a cognitive crisis because they are the norm. There, racial identity is determined along a continuum of color without sharp borders.

16 See Maurice Merleau-Ponty, *Phenomenology of Perception* translated by Colin Smith (New Jersey: The Humanities Praise), esp. Part One. See also the elucidation of this concept in Gail Weiss *Body Images: Embodiment as Intercorporeality* (New York: Routledge, 1998), chapter one.

17 Frantz Fanon, *Black Skin, White Masks* translated by Charles Lam Markmann (New York, Grove Press, 1967); Lewis Gordon, *Bad Faith and Antiblack Racism* (Atlantic Highlands, New Jersey: Humanities Press, 1995); Weiss, *Body Images*, esp. pp. 26–33. See also Elizabeth Grosz, *Volatile Bodies: Toward a Corporeal Feminism* (Bloomington: Indiana University Press, 1994) for an excellent explanation and development of the concept of body image, esp. chapters 3 and 4.
18 Grosz, *Volatile Bodies*, p. x.
19 See Antonio Gramsci, *Selections from the Prison Notebooks*, in Q. Hoare and G. N. Smith, eds. (London: Lawrence and Wishart, 1971).
20 Omi and Winant, p. 62.
21 Jack Kerouac, "On the Road Again," unpublished journals, *The New Yorker* June 22 and 29, 1998, p. 56.
22 See Grosz, pp. 64–9; and Weiss, pp. 7–9.
23 Kerouac, p. 56.
24 Kerouac, p. 56.
25 Fanon, chapters 5 and 7.
26 Weiss, p. 27.
27 Merleau-Ponty, p. x–xi.
28 Merleau-Ponty, p. xvi.
29 Merleau-Ponty, p. 152 (emphasis in original).
30 Merleau-Ponty, pp. 152–3.
31 Rodriguez, *Days of Obligation: An Argument with my Mexican Father*, (New York: Viking Books, 1992), p. 1.
32 Rodriguez, *Hunger of Memory* (New York: Bantam, 1983), p. 124.
33 Rodriguez, *Days of Obligation*, p. 5.
34 Danzy Senna's novel *Caucasia* (New York: Penguin, 1998) powerfully describes this particular form of alienation.
35 Lewis Gordon, *Bad Faith and Antiblack Racism*, p. 117 ff. Gordon argues that romanticizing and exoticizing racial others (as in "I just *love* black people") is like animal loving in that it seeks an object that has consciousness without judgement, that can know it is loved but be incapable of understanding or judging the one who loves.
36 Rodriguez, *Days of Obligation*, pp. 4–5.
37 There are numerous insightful analyses of racism in *Days of Obligation*; see esp. chapter one.
38 Michel Foucault, *Discipline and Punish: The Birth of the Prison* translated by Alan Sheridan (New York: Random House, 1979), p. 200.
39 Foucault, *Discipline and Punish* p. 201.
40 From L. Gibbons, "Race Against Time, Racial Discourse and Irish History," *Oxford Literary Review* 13 (1–2): pp. 95–117; quoted in Ania Loomba *Colonialism/Postcolonialism* (London: Routledge, 1998), p. 109.
41 Merleau-Ponty, *The Visible and the Invisible* trans. by Alphonso Lingis (Evanston, Ill.: Northwestern University Press, 1968), p. 136. Emphasis added.
42 Fanon, *Black Skin, White Masks*, p. 160. Quoted in Weiss, p. 28.
43 I learned this because he has written a novel based on his experience of our relationship.

16

THE INVISIBILITY OF RACIAL MINORITIES IN THE PUBLIC REALM OF APPEARANCES

Robert Bernasconi

During the strike that preceded the assassination of Martin Luther King Jr., the sanitation workers of Memphis and their African–American supporters paraded with posters that read, "I AM A MAN." This was not only a labor dispute in which the right of public employees to strike against a city was in question, but was also, given the historical context and especially the racial identity of most of the sanitation workers, immediately recognized as an important chapter in the Civil Rights Movement. There were signs that read "JOBS JOBS JOBS," "UNIONIZATION FOR THE SANITATION WORKERS," and "JUSTICE AND EQUALITY FOR ALL MEN." But most signs read simply "I AM A MAN" and the photographs of scores of Black protesters holding these signs provide the abiding image of the strike. They wanted economic justice and recognition of their union, but contemporary accounts record that more than anything else they wanted to be "recognized" for themselves.[1]

Even when Whites have not gone to the extreme of explicitly denying the humanity of Blacks, they have frequently found numerous ways, institutional and personal, in which to demean Blacks. The need to declare one's humanity arises as a response to this kind of racism. Beyond the appeal to civil rights due to someone as a citizen, there is also, at least since their recognition in the eighteenth century, the appeal to human rights due to a person on the basis of their humanity. Human rights stand as a testimony to the power of the universal. They have given the oppressed of the world a new basis on which to protest discrimination based on the particularities of class, sex, nationality, religion, or race. Human Rights are widely acknowledged as providing a standard that transcends national and cultural boundaries. But does universality offer an adequate defense against racism? Does the appeal to the universal provide a means for overcoming discrimination against groups on the basis of racial differences? Or is racism thereby being addressed by a cosmopolitanism that keeps White privilege intact?

A recent example may serve to clarify what is at stake. During the 1996 election campaign the opponents of affirmative action liked to quote Martin Luther King's "I

Have a Dream" speech with its vision of a land where everyone would "not be judged by the color of their skin but by the content of their character."[2] Policies that made explicit use of racial designations were said to be discriminatory. Meanwhile, the opponents of affirmative action chose to ignore King's support for such programs under the heading of "compensatory or preferential treatment." King had written:

> It is impossible to create a formula for the future which does not take into account that our society has been doing something special *against* the Negro for hundreds of years. How then can he be absorbed into the mainstream of American life if we do not do something special *for* him now, in order to balance the equation and equip him to compete on a just and equal basis?[3]

This attempt to enlist Martin Luther King's support against affirmative action is part of a disingenuous attempt to deny minorities a political identity, while leaving in place the legacy of the racial oppression they have suffered in the name of that identity. This could not be more different from the call of the Memphis sanitation workers, which was a call for justice, respect, and recognition, but not a call for homogenization.

Within the universal order of humanity there is a question about the political status to be accorded to solidarity based on gender, race, linguistic grouping, class, nationality, and so on. Are these divisions merely divisive? Is their value at best only strategic? Or do these differences have positive value so that appeals to cosmopolitanism or to global identity must be looked upon with suspicion? In this essay I focus on racial difference, with particular attention to anti-Black racism among Whites in contemporary America, but the issues are larger. Fanon wrote, "I wanted to be a man, nothing but a man."[4] His book, *Black Skin, White Masks*, shows that racism cannot be overcome without addressing the effects of racism. But Fanon's formulation, like the quotation from Martin Luther King in the previous paragraph, now strikes us as insensitive to issues of sexual difference, inviting Sojourner Truth's response: "Ar'n't I a woman?"[5] In the face of overlapping identities and a tendency to experience identities as more tyrannical than liberating, there is a temptation to want to employ singularity and abstract humanism as the main resources in the battle against discrimination. But this is to overlook the need for identities that offer a sense of community, that inspire loyalty, and that promote a common interest, especially among members of an oppressed group.

There is much still to be learned about how and why the classification of people into races took hold at the end of the eighteenth century and was quickly regarded as obvious.[6] At almost exactly the same time that the concept of race was given precision, the American Declaration of Independence proclaimed human equality. Since the Enlightenment one of the great political puzzles has been the combination of cosmopolitan ideals and racist practices. One does not see an initial failure to meet a new higher set of standards, so much as a series of appalling blindspots in the application of the noble and profound statements of human dignity that are the hallmark of the period. Declarations of universal rights were authored and pronounced by people who were apparently oblivious of whole classes of people to whom those rights nominally applied, but to whom hardly anyone thought to apply them: the poor, women, nonWhites, and, above all, poor, nonWhite, women.[7]

Take slavery, for example. There were few European voices against the slavery of Blacks until the last half of the eighteenth century. That is why one rarely finds justifications or defenses of this form of slavery until that time. The institution did not raise moral problems. It was somehow taken for granted, so long as it was contained within certain parameters that limited slavery to nonWhites and, although this proviso had to be dropped under pressure from the missionaries, to non-Christians. The puzzle is that, when the principle of the equality of all human beings was enunciated by the American colonists, they failed to apply it to the Black slaves in their midst. For a society of slaveowners under the rule of a colonial power to demand liberation from "slavery" for themselves at the same time that they themselves relied for their prosperity on an especially brutal system of slavery was nothing new in the history of morals. What was new was the universal language that they brought to their cause while at the same time apparently being oblivious of its real meaning.

One can say that this contradiction is evidence of brazen hypocrisy, although that would not explain why they insisted on postulating the universal principles that produced the contradiction. One can refer to racism, although that is to name the problem rather than to explain it. One can construct a philosophy of history that would attempt to resolve the contradiction by postulating that, against such deep-seated prejudice, the principle had first to be stated almost unwittingly long before its full application could be envisaged. But this philosophy of history, predicated on progress, would have to explain whether the broadening of the principle's application was the only way for history to resolve the contradiction inherent in the founding documents. The particularly virulent form of racism produced in the United States in the late nineteenth century, in which the very humanity of Blacks was questioned, can also be understood as an attempt at resolving the contradiction.[8] However, the focus of this paper is not the history of the contradiction between the principle and the practice, but the underlying phenomenological truth that racial difference, as what is most visible, is within the public realm rendered invisible to the extent that the dominant group succeeds in overlooking a minority, denying its members their place in the sun.[9]

What does it tell us about the nature of the political realm that those who are most visible phenomenally for the dominant group, can nevertheless at the same time be rendered invisible within the public realm of appearances? In referring to the public realm of appearances, I am alluding to Hannah Arendt's notion that in the public or political sphere appearance constitutes reality, albeit without underwriting the precise terms in which she insists on a division between the public and the private.[10] I have addressed elsewhere what I regard to be the systemic failure of Hannah Arendt's phenomenological conception of politics to accommodate an appreciation of the issues raised by race in American society and I will not rehearse that analysis here.[11] However, I refer to her here to make the point that the political realm is the realm of appearances and that, because appearances can be manipulated, reality can also be manipulated. Furthermore, it is sufficient that race be visible, in the sense that racial identities be marked with sufficient clarity, either physiognomically or by dress code, to give rise to a consistent system of identifications, for its political reality to be secure.

Only philosophers with an impoverished conception of perception could imagine that the category of race, let alone racism itself, could be contested by exposing the distinction between the phenomenal appearance of certain physical characteristics and what is said to lie "behind" that appearance once the appearance has been isolated.[12] The problem is that within a racialized society to see skin color is to see someone as of another race with all that entails. However unjustified the stereotypes may be, they are part of the political reality. To that extent, racism has made race "real" without making it true. As Tshembe explains to the American journalist, Charlie Morris, in Lorraine Hansberry's play *Les Blancs*, race once invented takes on a reality of its own: "it is pointless to pretend it doesn't *exist* – merely because it is a *lie*!"[13] The fact that we now reject the racial science that taught previous generations to treat race as an indicator of character and even of moral worth does not mean that the stereotypes that are deeply embedded in popular culture and that are reinforced by the media can be broken by pointing out that they are unjustified. It is not just with reference to skin color that people are judged by appearances. Sexism often operates in the same way. Nothing is to be gained by pretending that racism and sexism can be eradicated by the introduction of a few skillfully chosen distinctions and the policing of ordinary language to ensure that these distinctions are respected. Rather, we must try to understand better the process by which society sustains, in this case, racism.

Those who are most invisible in the public realm, in the sense of being powerless, mute, and deprived of human rights, are often most visible to those who disempower them, silence them, and exploit them. During segregation in the United States, Whites as a class never lacked the capacity to see the Blacks that waited on their tables, did their yard work, and passed them on the sidewalks. Their invisibility was in some sense deliberate or, at least, programmed. As Ralph Ellison wrote in *Invisible Man*, describing the experience of a Black man in a White society, "I am invisible, understand, simply because people refuse to see me."[14] It has not been necessary for Whites to look Blacks in the face because Blacks were taught to divert their gaze. bell hooks has described this process in the following terms:

> One mark of oppression was that black folks were compelled to assume the mantle of invisibility, to erase all traces of their subjectivity during slavery and the long years of racial apartheid, so that they would be better, less threatening servants. An effective strategy of white supremacist terror and dehumanization during slavery centered around white control of the black gaze.[15]

This practice was so striking that Sartre remarked on the phenomenon in a newspaper article published after only his first visit to the United States: "if by chance their eyes meet yours, it seems to you that they do not see you and it is better for them and you that you pretend not to have noticed them."[16] The refusal of Whites to see Blacks was predicated on the fact that they knew who was there to be seen and sought to control them by choosing not to see them. That is to say, Whites saw Blacks without seeing them. How was this possible? In no small measure by controlling the Black gaze, so that Whites did not experience themselves as they were seen by Blacks.[17]

Prejudice wants to make those against whom it is directed disappear. It wants to exterminate them but usually has to satisfy itself with hiding them away. It turns them into outcasts. Christians expelled the Jews or forced the Jews to live in ghettos. Whites today produce the same effect by staying in the suburbs and refusing to go downtown for fear that they would have to share the sidewalk with Blacks who might return their gaze. In this context to exaggerate one's difference as Jew or Black is to make a gesture of defiance. But if the prejudiced find this threatening, they are even more threatened by the possibility of being fooled, as when they mistake a foe for a friend. Thus Jews were obliged to wear a yellow badge as a sign of their Jewishness. This was so there would be no mistake, which was to admit that otherwise a Jew could be mistaken for a Gentile. The pressure on Jews to assimilate highlights racism at the point where the demand to assimilate seems to have succeeded. That is why the persecution directed against the Marranos is regarded as one of the original instances of modern racism.[18] Fear of failing to identify those from whom one differentiated oneself led racial scientists in Nazi Germany to instruct people on how to identify the distinctive features of each race.[19] The visibility of Blackness in a "White world" – that space carved out by Whites for themselves – gave anti-Black racism a unique self-confidence. And yet one of the historical obsessions of anti-Black racism in the United States has been the fear that there are Blacks who can pass as White. This problem is of racism's own making. Because Whites in the United States have for much of their history been concerned with their own racial purity, they operated a "one-drop" rule that produced a class of people for whom passing was an option. Such people looked White but were counted as Black. To the members of this racialized society their "appearance" belied their "reality," not because skin color did not mean something, but because their skin color was a misleading indicator of how society classified them. When, as in Nella Larsen's *Passing*, a White man found that his apparently White wife in fact counted as Black, that man did not conclude that the idea of racial essence was false.[20] So far as he was concerned, it was not his idea of race that had deceived him but his wife, because he now saw her as Black, something that, in this case, he had already seen – hence his use of "Nig" as a nickname for her – but which at the same time he had refused to see. Racism wants to make its targets disappear, but it does not want them to disappear into anonymity. It wants to see them without seeing them. It wants to identify its targets unambiguously without having to face them.

This is accomplished in part by controlling how Blacks are made to appear. In slavery times, Whites saw Blacks as slaves: freed Blacks had to be able to prove their status. Furthermore, under slavery, Blacks were supposed to appear happy; under segregation, submissive; and today the stereotypes are manipulated in the form of images of the welfare queen, the teenage mother, the gang member, and the drug addict. As a result of the construction of these stereotypes that are disseminated through the media and through hearsay, many Whites are threatened simply by the sight of a young Black man. If he is not already known to us, the stereotype intervenes. We Whites have trouble seeing past the stereotype as if it formed a layer of invisibility. It is a case of seeing without seeing.

It is not that Blacks are invisible to Whites. On one diagnosis that means that their humanity is invisible to those Whites who are nevertheless most aware of them. Given that there can be few racists left, if any, who deny the biological humanity of Blacks, this raises the question of how modern-day racists express a belief in the equality of all human beings and at the same time treat Blacks as inferior. This blatant contradiction is in part sustained by the persistence of stereotypes. How do the stereotypes hold sway even among people who know better? One can begin to address this problem by noting what it is one does and does not see. One does not in the standard case see another human being as simply that, another human being. If one did, it would not have been necessary for the Memphis sanitation workers to line the street with their signs that read: "I AM A MAN." In a racialized society, everyone is seen in terms of the racial categories of the moment. Today they are seen *as* Black, White, Hispanic or Asian. This is so prevalent that there are times in such a society when it seems that it is impossible for an audience to follow an anecdote or a news story until the racial identity of the protagonists has been established: "Was he Black or White?" Within the context of racism, particularity intervenes between universality and singularity. This analysis is what leads to the widespread claim that if one could only look beyond the particularity of race, class, gender, and so on, then one would encounter a person in his or her singularity and there would be no obstacle against arriving at the universal designation "human" in terms of which all are equal.

Levinas must be counted among those who have claimed that the "as" structure, according to which the individual is given to perception as being of a certain type, lends itself to racism:

> It is evident that it is in the knowledge of the other (*autrui*) as a simple individual – individual of a genus, a class, or a race – that peace with the other (*autrui*) turns into hatred; it is the approach of the other as "such and such a type."[21]

Not surprisingly, given the problems that his treatment of the feminine had already raised for him, Levinas did not say whether the sex of the individual should also be included in those characteristics that need to be overlooked for the encounter with the Other to take place. Nevertheless, although he said in an interview that to encounter the Other it is best not to notice the color of his or her eyes, one should beware jumping to the conclusion that Levinas offered this as a practical proposal, still less as an injunction.[22] Although Levinas is not always read this way, it seems to me that he construes singularity not as a phenomenon that can be unveiled, but as an enigma. That is to say, it is "up to me" to retain its exorbitant meaning.[23] Singularity interrupts the system of social identity that inevitably returns or, more precisely, always remains intact. To see someone in his or her singularity would not be unlike addressing them in their singularity in what Levinas calls "saying" (*le dire*).[24] Just as the "saying without a said" that Levinas sometimes invoked is always in fact accompanied by a said because one addresses the Other in language, so even what might be called "overlooking" someone's race, sex, or class thereby to see them in their singularity does not leave them deprived of all characteristics. The following passage from "The Rights of Man and the Rights of the Other," dating from 1985, shows Levinas attempting to negotiate what is for him a difficult problem:

> These rights of man . . . express the alterity or absolute of every person, the suspension of all *reference*: a violent tearing loose (*arrachement*) from the determining order of nature and the social structure in which each of us is obviously involved; an alterity of the *unique* and the incomparable, due to the belonging of each one to mankind (*au genre humain*), which,

> *ipso facto and paradoxically*, is annulled precisely to leave each man *the only one of his kind* (*unique dans son genre*).[25]

Levinas found himself forced to acknowledge that to relate to someone in his or her singularity through a certain dissolution of the particularity that would reduce that person to being a representative of a certain type, nevertheless still allows at least a passing reference of this singular person to the human genus. The question is whether this paradoxical structure, once allowed, could not also accommodate a passing reference to class and race.

Somewhat surprisingly given Levinas's personal history as a target of anti-Semitism, his account, at least in his philosophical as opposed to his confessional writings, bypasses the attachment to social identity that is often found on the part of the oppressed.[26] It ignores the fact that many people who have been discriminated against and persecuted want to be accepted, not just as a member of humanity, or for their singularity, but in the same terms under which they had previously been rejected. It is not enough to be "a man," "a woman," "a human being, nothing but a human being." Even if this were possible, it is not regarded as desirable. This is not only true of many Blacks, who choose to appropriate and transform the meaning of the labels assigned to them in the course of their oppression. Arendt also acknowledged this point on the basis of her experience of National Socialism: "If one is attacked as a Jew, one must defend oneself *as a Jew*. Not as a German, not as a world citizen, not as an upholder of the Rights of Man."[27] Similarly one can recall Benny Lévy's response to Sartre's *Anti-Semite and Jew* many years after first reading it. Sartre had led him to discover what he dreamt of discovering: "I am a man, not a Jew." However, Lévy subsequently recognized the price for doing so: he had embraced a form of self-denial.[28] He had sacrificed his identity in a way that, had it been sustained, would have been a victory for his oppressors, who would themselves still have seen him not in his humanity, but as a Jew.

Already in 1797 de Maistre wrote that "In my lifetime I have seen Frenchmen, Italians, Russians, etc.; thanks to Montesquieu, I even know that *one can be Persian*. But as for *man*, I declare that I have never in my life met him."[29] To see another as this or that, Black, East Asian, or White, male or female, young or old, to see someone as a representative of some class or group, is an irreducible aspect of social experience, even though the precise terms under which this takes place are culturally determined and the emphasis that is given to one of the terms in relation to the others can change historically with reference to the general context. Acknowledging that someone is of a certain race, sex, or class, does not necessarily reduce that person to being a representative of a type, a *persona*. It can also mean, among other things, recognizing and being sensitive to aspects of their experience that one might not have shared oneself but that one knows have touched them deeply. Only for the kind of people who, for example, preface a racist remark by declaring that some of there best friends are Black, could it make sense to say that they must "overlook" race to relate to someone. But they are precisely the kind of people most likely to make that same racist remark in front of their Black friends, precisely because they overlook race. The double bind that racism imposes on its targets lies in demanding assimilation while at the same time denying its possibility. Racism says, "Become like us," while always reasserting under its breath, "You can never become like us, because you are not one of us and we will not mistake you for one of us." The current proposal to move without delay to a society without racial designations has all the appearance of being, and perhaps sometimes is, a further example of Whites attempting to determine how, for example, African-Americans may present themselves in society. The phenomenological studies of Alfred Schutz are a helpful resource for understanding this kind of racism.[30]

In the course of his 1957 essay "Equality and the Meaning Structure of the World," Alfred Schutz offered an account of the impact of imposed typifications on groups.[31] Each group not only has a view of itself, it also has a view of other correlative groups with which it is in contact. Drawing on distinctions that he had already outlined in his classic 1932 study, *The Phenomenology of the Social World*, but which he now reformulated in the terminology of William Sumner, Schutz set out to describe how the meaning of the world as seen by an in-group or We-group relates to that of an Others-group or out-group.[32] Each group takes its own perspective for granted. It regards itself as the center of everything and rates everyone else in terms of their divergences from its own practices. Again borrowing from Sumner, Schutz called this perspective "ethnocentrism."[33] Furthermore, each group is inclined to feel itself misunderstood by the other groups, and the more misunderstood its members feel, the more they pull closer together in order to protect themselves from criticism. They are also liable to regard these misunderstandings as evidence of a hostility on the part of the other group, which vindicates their own initial antipathy and serves to fuel it. This has a serious impact on how the group understands itself, leading it, for example, to insist on ever more stringent forms of loyalty on the part of its members.[34]

The relevance of these considerations to the present inquiry is enhanced by the fact that Schutz went on to consider specifically the example of interaction between different races in the United States. Schutz considered race to be, in Max Scheler's terminology, a material factor or *Realfaktor*,[35] alongside such things as geopolitical structure, political power relationships, the conditions of economic production, and so on. However, it is immediately apparent from the context that Schutz did not thereby mean that race was a determining factor in the sense that it would be in a biologism, but rather that membership of a race, unlike membership of a voluntary group, locates one within "a preconstituted system of typifications, relevances, roles, positions, statues" which are not of one's own making but are handed down "as a social heritage."[36] One's race, like one's sex or the national group into which one is born, is, according to Schutz, an existential element of one's situation in the sense that it is something with which one has to come to terms. In a text contemporary with "Equality and the Social Meaning Structure," Schutz explained that the *Realfaktoren* belonged to "the world of everyday life taken for granted in the common-sense thinking of the actors on the social scene with which they have to come to terms."[37] Having already established that the view one group has of another group can, under certain conditions, serve to modify the way that second group comes to regard itself, Schutz introduced the question of the case where a group's world has come to be dominated by a perspective arising from another group that is hostile to it. According to Schutz, even though one cannot choose to which race one belongs, one should be free, among other things, to determine with what force one participates in group membership and what importance one gives to that identity.[38] He then proceeded to show how in the first half of the twentieth century African–Americans were denied that freedom.

Schutz took as his example the "separate but equal" doctrine formulated by the Supreme Court in *Plessy v. Ferguson*. Whatever its proponents claimed, the repercussions of the decision rendered were discriminatory:

> Even under the assumption that separation was not meant to involve an inferiority in the colored race, segregation is taken as an insult by the Negro and he becomes sensitive about it. His being treated as a type induces self-typification with an inverted sign. Even if he never intended to travel by sleeping car, the principled denial of its use becomes to him relevant in his own terms. He has a new problem to grapple with.[39]

Schutz argued that the imposition of a typification by one group on another correlative group is inevitable but not necessarily discriminatory.[40] Discrimination takes place only when the typification from outside is imposed in such a way as to become part of the experience of the afflicted individual. This may not coincide with what is ordinarily understood by discrimination, but the account does succeed in drawing attention to the fact that where one group is in a position to impose a typification on an individual as a member of another group, that individual becomes alienated from his or her own self-characterization and becomes a mere representative of the typified characteristics. Schutz added that such a person would be deprived of the right to the pursuit of happiness.[41] Schutz clearly wanted to draw on all the deep resonances that phrase has within the context of the United States, but it also shows the extent to which Schutz's analysis is governed by and to a certain extent limited to a specific context. In any case, in such circumstances the members of a minority group would not be content to seek equality with the dominant group in the form of assimilation, but would, Schutz noted, insist on being granted special rights to secure *real* equality, in addition to mere formal equality.[42]

In an attempt to explain what led African–Americans to demand special rights for themselves, Schutz appealed to Myrdal's account of how "the white man's rank order of discriminations" was the inverse of "the Negro's rank order." Myrdal's study of this difference in priorities between Whites and Blacks showed that Blacks were right to believe that even full realization of the principle of non-discrimination would secure them only formal equality with the dominant group and not real equality. Myrdal had observed that whereas Whites in the United States tended to focus on laws against intermarriage and sexual intercourse involving white women as the most important type of discrimination to correct, followed in importance by the demeaning social etiquette imposed on Blacks in their relation to Whites and by the legal barriers against interracial social intercourse, Blacks were more concerned with discrimination in economic matters such as securing land, credit, jobs, and public relief, with discrimination in the law courts and by the police next in the order of priority.[43] Schutz did not say what special rights Blacks were claiming, but clearly "compensatory or preferential treatment" of the kind Martin Luther King subsequently advocated would meet the description. In other words, Schutz showed how such a demand arises as a consequence of the form of racism to which Blacks are subjected in the United States.

Contemporary attempts to cast such demands as another form of racism are thereby exposed as a form of blindness to the concrete context, a form of blindness that serves to perpetuate White blindness to the Black gaze.

Schutz employed the example of life under segregation to highlight the way that European–Americans held a view of African–Americans that made itself felt in many aspects of the lives of African–Americans. The White stereotype of Blacks was, of course, contested by the meaning that African–Americans gave and continue to give to being African–American and it led to the inner conflict that W. E. B. Du Bois described as "double consciousness."[44] In *The Autobiography of an Ex-Colored Man*, James Weldon Johnson provided a description of this "sort of dual personality" and drew the inevitable conclusion: "I believe it to be a fact that the colored people of this country know and understand the white people better than the white people know and understand them."[45] European–Americans were largely oblivious to the way African–Americans saw them and, to a large extent, they still are. Schutz did not explore this asymmetry. Instead, he took his analysis in the direction of Sartre's account of the look.

A few years prior to the "Equality" essay, Schutz had criticized Sartre's description of the look as a site of conflict in which one is either the seer or the seen: it left no place for mutual interaction in freedom.[46] This is not the place to examine either Schutz's objections or the resources that Sartre subsequently developed for addressing this problem. Nor do I intend to determine the extent to which Schutz, having clearly shown how discriminatory practices arise, was able to conceive of a society without discrimination. One might think that because Schutz traced discrimination back to the inevitable discrepancy between the way a group looks at itself and the way it is seen by others, it was hard for him to explain the situation where discrimination did not arise, and when it did, how it might diminish, instead of grow. The problem was exacerbated in the case of groups organized in terms of race or sex as one's participation in those groups was not voluntary.[47] Schutz was, therefore, consistent when he conceded that "we had better courageously face the fact that prejudices are themselves elements of the interpretation of the social world and even one of the mainsprings that make it tick."[48] However, Schutz did recognize that when a minority group is satisfied with its relationship to the predominant group, that minority group is liable to see assimilation as the way forward.[49] When a group feels that its opportunities have been deliberately restricted by another group, an entirely different situation obtains. For the dominant group to insist upon assimilation as a precondition of economic empowerment, while at the same time excluding the possibility of assimilation from the outset, guarantees conflict. In other words, if the dominant group insists upon assimilation because it perceives a specific minority group as failing to conform to the standards it imposes, in all likelihood this is because it is operating with stereotypes that render it impossible for that group to meet the demand. The conditions that underlie the issuing of the demand make it impossible for the demand to be met: the demand to act White is addressed not to Whites but to those who are seen, for example, *as* Black. In the rare case in which Whites fail to act White, as in the case of young suburban Whites imitating the forms of dress associated with rap, they are not under the same pressure to conform: it is believed that they will outgrow it, because it is all an act. It is not real.

The invisibility of African–Americans in the public realm of appearances, as I have presented it in this essay, refers to the way European–Americans silence African–Americans, shield themselves from the gaze of African–Americans, so as to remain comfortable and uncontested in a White world that does not acknowledge itself as such. The invisibility of racial minorities arises from a refusal on the part of the majority to see them or, more precisely, to listen to them. My analysis does not deny that at various times and in various arenas European–Americans have had access to African–American perspectives on the world and on themselves. These have always been available; they have been the focus of attention from time to time, as at the time of the debate over the abolition of slavery and during the Civil Rights Movement, albeit often filtered through a White media. What is new is that Blacks, who have always contested the meaning of Blackness imposed on them, have forced this contestation into the public realm. Whites cannot avoid hearing it and cannot avoid seeing how it implicates them. They now find their own identity being challenged by the meaning Blacks impose on them. This is the context in which an increasing number of Whites declare that they would prefer to drop all talk of race. That they should make this proposal now is not surprising. It is too easy for academics and politicians to consider all talk of racial difference taboo in their own sphere, while at the same time race organizes society, as, for example, with residential apartheid. Racial identity will only cease to be salient when one can say of a newborn baby that its racial identity will have no significant impact on the kind of life he or she is likely to lead. But the conditions that would make it possible to say that cannot be brought about without a radical transformation of society of a kind that most Whites would not even contemplate.

To devote our efforts now to trying to determine how long it will be before we can get beyond the particularity of race seems hardly worthwhile, because even if it is sometimes possible for some people in some contexts to do so in some sense, even the minimal goal of a society in which people are not judged by the color of their skin is a long way off. Once it is recognized that in the present context it makes no sense to ask people suddenly to become literally color blind, as if one could ask them not to notice skin color or other physiognomic differences that have been given a meaning in contemporary society, attention can then pass to the construction and interaction of the various stereotypes. This is where the phenomenological studies of Schutz can be of assistance. The focus of this essay has not been the incoherence of the system of racial classification, nor the institutional segregation of American society that sustains the ignorance that fuels the racial stereotypes, but the imposition of the stereotypes and the conflicts that arise from them. However, if Schutz is correct, as I believe he is, White stereotypes of Blacks have an importance that, for example, White stereotypes of Japanese or Black stereotypes of Whites do not have, not because African–Americans are more sensitive than other ethnic groups, but because so many African–Americans remain economically disempowered. They recognize that these stereotypes seriously impact their lives both personally, for example, in terms of job promotions or loan approvals, and institutionally, for example, in terms of how those stereotypes work to determine where they live and thus what educational or job opportunities are available to them and their children. Consider, for example, the stereotypes of Jews or of the Irish that still operate in the United States. However unjust and unwarranted these typifications are, they tend not to have the impact they once had, because in contemporary North America the Jews and the Irish are not economically disempowered in the way African–Americans and some more recent immigrant groups are. When employers insist as a condition of employment that prospective employees have attained a level of assimilation that far exceeds what is necessary to do the work satisfactorily, one has a clear case in which issues of recognition and of economic justice cannot be kept separate.[50] Of course, the employers would probably insist that they were acting this way because their customers demanded it. It is the same kind of excuse used by White houseowners who do not want African–Americans living next door. They usually insist that they have no personal objection, but that they are worried about how the value of their house might suffer once the general perception of the neighborhood changes. These are some of the ways in which racism can permeate a society in which hardly anyone admits being a racist. An individual can proclaim the invisibility of racial minorities by insisting on the invisibility, the non-existence, of race, but this does not change anything, so long as one assumes that "everyone (all other Whites) except me" is operating with the stereotypes.

It is now possible to offer a provisional answer to my earlier question about what we know about the public realm of appearances given that those who are most visible for the dominant group can at the same time be rendered invisible within it. Treating African–Americans as invisible or, more precisely, rendering them invisible was, among other things, a mechanism by which European–Americans could protect themselves from encountering a point of view that conflicted with their own self-understanding. One can then better understand why European–Americans go to such lengths to avoid experiencing themselves as seen by African–Americans. That is a major part of why these two groups do not more often share the same schools, churches, clubs, factories, malls, playgrounds and, above all, the same housing districts. The invisibility of African–Americans, the suppression of their presence and thus of their gaze, has also been one of the ways Whites have secured their own disappearance as White. There are different kinds of racism operating by different logics but, according to, for example, the dominant logic of anti-Black racism within the United States, Whites do not thematize their identity, but disappear into the norm. This is the invisibility of the dominant group within the public realm of appearances. It sustains institutional racism by concealing it. Racial science often does not characterize the White race which, in Kant's formulation, "contains all impulses and talents in itself."[51] In such cases racial science proceeds by characterizing the particularity of the other races. Within such a system of thought, Whites set the standard. They represent the universality to which others are supposed to aspire, but from which they are excluded by virtue of the limitations of their race. Such prejudices lend themselves to a universalism that is not so much in opposition to racism as it is an instrument of racism. In this context, what it means to be human is contested and the statement "I AM A MAN" is anything but an underwriting of abstract humanism, because a certain model of humanity is covert within such a humanism. From this perspective, nothing is less surprising than the apparent contradiction between Enlightenment ideas about universal human equality and Enlightenment racism, so long as there is a dominant group that controls the look and thus the discourse of equality. In such a setting racism remains an irreducible component of the universalistic discourse, not its contrary, which is why we must always be suspicious of fine words and sentiments, as when people celebrate their color blindness by declaring race to be invisible.

On a personal note, I may not have been in the United States long enough to be called a European–American, but I have not forgotten that from the moment I arrived I was seen as White. Coming from England, I came from a context where, alongside class and gender, what mattered was being English. This was also, in a sense, a racial designation. In Europe in the nineteenth century, what today might be called national identities, ethnic identities and racial identities were understood as interrelated. In spite of my resistance to being designated simply as White, I was forced to recognize that this is how I appear in the United States. I do not ever expect to be comfortable with this label. But, however much I would like to imagine that I could disappear into being a singular human being and nothing more, in a polarized society I cannot deny my social identity.[52] Fortunately, I cannot, and certainly should not, be reduced to this social identity or any of my other social identities: like everyone else my singularity is mediated by several overlapping identities. To inherit a history is to assume the privileges, opportunities, and burdens that it brings, including certain responsibilities, among which is the responsibility to respond to how one is seen. Insofar as we fail to do so, it is we Whites who are trying to maintain our invisibility. But we will not be able to hide much longer.

Notes

1 For an account of the strike, see Joan Turner Beifuss, *At the River I Stand*, (Memphis: St. Lukes Press, 1990), esp. pp. 285–286 and 453.

2 James M. Washington, ed., *A Testament of Hope. The Essential Writings of Martin Luther King, Jr.*, (San Francisco: Harper and Row, 1986), p. 219.

3 Martin Luther King, Jr., *Why We Can't Wait*, (New York: Signet, 1964), p. 134.

4 Frantz Fanon, *Peau noire, masques blancs*, (Paris: Seuil, 1975), p. 91; trans. Charles Lam Markmann, *Black Skin, White Masks*, (New York: Grove, 1982), p. 113.

5 Olive Gilbert, *Narrative of Sojourner Truth*, (Oxford: Oxford University Press, 1991), p. 134. For a discussion of whether Sojourner Truth actually used the phrase, see Jeffrey Stewart's Introduction, pp. xxxiii–xxxiv.

6 See my paper, "Who Invented the Concept of Race?" (chapter 1, page 1, this volume)

7 The best example is, of course, Thomas Jefferson. See his "Notes on the State of Virginia," in Merill Peterson, ed., *Writings*, (New York: The Library of America, 1984), pp. 264–7. See also Paul Finkelman, "Jefferson and Slavery. 'Treason Against the Hopes of the World'," in Peter S. Onuf, ed., *Jeffersonian Legacies*, (Charlottesville: University Press of Virginia, 1993), pp. 181–221.

8 See, for example, Chas. Carroll, "*The Negro a Beast*", (1900), reprint edition (Salem, NH: Ayer, 1991).

9 I must emphasize at the outset that this paper is self-consciously one-sided insofar as it is a contribution to what Sartre called a "phenomenology of the oppressor." Jean-Paul Sartre, *Cahiers pour une morale*, (Paris: Gallimard, 1983), p. 579; trans. David Pellauer, *Notebooks for an Ethics*, (Chicago: University of Chicago Press, 1992), p. 561. Even though I have attempted to balance my observations by including testimony from those who have experienced discrimination, it is still inevitably one-sided with the identity – and the location – of the author clearly marked.

10 Hannah Arendt, *The Human Condition*, (Chicago: University of Chicago Press, 1958), p. 50. It is perhaps hard to see how Hannah Arendt's concept of the public realm of appearances can function as a definition of politics within the contemporary world, especially as a major part of Arendt's analysis in *The Human Condition* is an attempt to show that the distinctions that sustain the integrity of the public realm have become confused in the modern world. However, by borrowing her conception, it is still possible to clarify the relation of the ethical and the political, which is what is at issue here.

11 See Robert Bernasconi, "The Double Face of the Political and the Social: Hannah Arendt and America's Racial Divisions," *Research in Phenomenology*, 16, 1996, pp. 3–24.

12 This tendency is operative within contemporary attempts first to reduce racial difference to ethnic difference and then to deny that what used to be called races can successfully sustain an ethnic identity. See the writings of Anthony Appiah including "'But Would That Still be me?' Notes on Gender, 'Race,' Ethnicity, as Sources of 'Identity'," *The Journal of Philosophy*, 87 (10), October 1990, pp. 493–9. For an account of some of the unspoken assumptions underlying the historical development of this position, see Kamala Visweswaran "Race and the Culture of Anthropology," *American Anthropologist*, 100 (1), 1998, pp. 1–14.

13 Lorraine Hansberry, *Les Blancs: The Collected Last Plays*, ed. Robert Nemiroff, (New York: Random House, 1972), p. 122.

14 Ralph Ellison, *Invisible Man*, (New York: Vintage Books, 1989), p. 3.

15 bell hooks, *Killing Rage. Ending Racism*, (New York: Henry Holt, 1995), p. 35.

16 Jean-Paul Sartre, "Retour des Etats-Unis. Ce que j'ai appris du problème noir," *Le Figaro* 16 June 1945, p. 2; trans. T. Denean Sharpley-Whiting, "Return from the United States," in Lewis R. Gordon, ed., *Existence in Black*, (New York: Routledge, 1997), p. 84.

17 See Lewis R. Gordon, *Bad Faith and Antiblack Racism*, (New Jersey: Humanities Press, 1995), p. 102: "The white body is expected not to be looked at by black bodies. This is because the black body's situation of being-without-a-perspective cannot be maintained if blacks are able to unleash the Look." For an account of Sartre's application of his analysis of the look from *Being and Nothingness* to the struggle between the races, see Robert Bernasconi, "Sartre's Gaze Returned: The Transformation of the Phenomenology of Racism," *Graduate Faculty Philosophy Journal*, 18 (2) 1995, pp. 201–21.

18 See Richard H. Popkin, "The Philosophical Bases of Modern Racism," *The High Road to Pyrrhonism*, (San Diego: Austin Hill Press, 1980), pp. 79–80.

19 See, for example, Ludwig Ferdinand Claus, *Rasse und Seele. Ein Einführung in den Sinn der leiblichen Gestalt*, (Berlin: Büchergilde Gutenberg, 1939).

20 Nella Larsen, *Passing*, (New York: Alfred Knopf, 1929).

21 Emmanuel Levinas, "Paix et Proximité," in Jacques Rolland, ed., *Emmanuel Levinas. Les Cahiers de La nuit surveillée*, (Lagrasse: Verdier, 1984), p. 343; trans. Peter Atterton and Simon Critchley, "Peace and Proximity," in Adriaan Peperzak et al. eds., *Emmanuel Levinas: Basic Philosophical Writings*, (Bloomington: Indiana University Press, 1996), p. 166.

22 E. Levinas, *Éthique et infini*, (Paris: Fayard, 1982), p. 89; trans. R. Cohen, *Ethics and Infinity*, (Pittsburgh: Duquesne University Press, 1985), p. 85.

23 E. Levinas, "Enigma et phénomène," *En découvrant l'existence avec Husserl et Heidegger*, (Paris: Vrin, 1967), pp. 208–9; trans. A. Lingis, "Enigma and Phenomenon," *Basic Philosophical Writings*, p. 70.

24 E. Levinas, *Autrement qu'être ou au-delà de l'essence*, (The Hague: Martinus Nijhoff, 1974), pp. 47–9 and 58–65; trans. A. Lingis, *Otherwise than being or beyond essence*, (The Hague: Martinus Nijhoff, 1981), pp. 37–8 and 45–51.

25 Emmanuel Levinas, "Les droits de l'homme et les droits d'autrui," *Hors sujet*, (Saint Clement: Fata Morgana, 1987), p. 176; trans. Michael B. Smith, *Outside the Subject*, (Stanford: Stanford University Press, 1994), p. 117.

26 For a more sustained treatment of this aspect of Levinas's thought, see Robert Bernasconi, "Who is my neighbor? Who is the Other?" *Ethics and Responsibility in the Phenomenological Tradition*, (Pittsburgh: Simon Silverman Phenomenology Center, Duquesne University, 1992), pp. 1–31. I now regard as inadequate the attempt I made there to find further resources in Levinas to address racism. For a more detailed examination of the issues, see R. Bernasconi, "Wer ist der Dritte? Überkreuzung von Ethik und Politik bei Levinas," trans. Antje Kapust, *Der Anspruch des Anderen. Perspektiven phänomenologischer Ethik*, ed. by Bernhard Waldenfels and Iris Därmann, (Munich: Fink, 1998), pp. 87–110.

27 Hannah Arendt, "What remains? The Language remains," trans. Joan Stambaugh, *Essays in Understanding 1930–1954*, ed. Jerome Kohn, (New York: Harcourt Brace, 1994), p. 12. See also Hannah Arendt, "On Humanity in Dark Times: Thoughts about Lessing," in *Men in Dark Times*, (New York: Harcourt, Brace and World, 1968), pp. 17–18.

28 Benny Lévy, *L'espoir maintenant*, (Paris: Verdier, 1991), p. 72.

29 Joseph de Maistre, *Considérations sur la France*, eds. R. Johannet and F. Vermale, (Paris: Vrin, 1936), p. 81; trans. Richard A. Lebrun, *Considerations on France*, (Montreal: McGill-Queens University Press, 1974), p. 97.

30 The continuing relevance of Schutz's analyses of anonymity for the understanding of contemporary racism has already been demonstrated by Lewis Gordon. See his *Fanon and the Crisis of European Man*, (New York: Routledge, 1995), pp. 37–66 and "Existential Dynamics of Theorizing Black Invisibility," in Lewis R. Gordon, ed., *Existence in Black* (New York: Routledge, 1997), pp. 69–79.

31 Alfred Schutz, "Equality and the Meaning Structure of the Social World," *Collected Papers*, vol. 2, (The Hague: Martinus Nijhoff, 1964), pp. 226–73.

32 Ibid., p. 244. The distinction between the in-group or We-group and the Others-group or they-group was borrowed by Schutz from William Graham Sumner, *Folkways*, (Boston: Ginn, 1906), pp. 12–13. However, Schutz related it to a distinction, which he had already borrowed from Max Weber in 1932, between subjective meaning, which involves reference to a particular person, such a the producer of a product, and objective meaning, which is abstracted from and independent of particular persons. Alfred Schutz, *The Phenomenology of the Social World*, (London: Heinemann, 1972), pp. 132–6. In "Equality and the Meaning Structure of the Social World," Schutz modified his presentation of the distinction by acknowledging that "objective meaning" is relative to the observer or scientist who produced it. *Collected Papers*, vol. 2, p. 227.

33 Alfred Schutz, *Collected Papers*, vol. 2, p. 244. Cf. Sumner, *Folkways*, p. 13.

34 Alfred Schutz, *Collected Papers*, vol. 2, pp. 244–7.

35 Ibid., p. 249. Schutz adopted this term from Max Scheler. See the latter's *Probleme einer Soziologie des Wissens* in *Die Wissensformen und die Gesellschaft*, Gesammelte Werke 8, (Bern and Munich: Francke, 1960), pp. 20–3 and 44–51.

36 Alfred Schutz, *Collected Papers*, vol. 2, p. 252.

37 Alfred Schutz, "In search of the Middle Ground," *Collected Papers*, vol. 4, (Dordrecht: Kluwer, 1996), p. 149.

38 Alfred Schutz, *Collected Papers*, vol. 2, p. 254.

39 Ibid., p. 261.

40 Ibid., pp. 258–62.

41 Ibid., pp. 256–7. There is a further limitation that arises from the fact that Schutz had in effect defined discrimination not only in terms of an act or a motive, but also in terms of the power to impose a typification. This would seem to render the structures of discrimi-

nation ultimately inaccessible to phenomenological description, at least as Schutz practiced it, and call for the addition of other kinds of analysis. I am grateful to Kevin Thompson for pointing this out.

42 Ibid., pp. 265 and 267–8. Schutz presented "formal equality" as full equality before the law and full political equality, but suggested that where assimilation has not taken place "real equality" would be liable to entail special rights, such as the protection of one's national language in schools and before the courts.

43 Gunnar Myrdal, *An American Dilemma*, (New York: Harper, 1944), pp. 60–1.

44 W. E. B. Du Bois, *The Soul of Black Folk* in *Writings*, ed. Nathan Huggins, (New York: Library of America, 1986), pp. 363–5.

45 James Weldon Johnson, *The Autobiography of an Ex-Colored Man*, (New York: Penguin, 1990), pp. 14–15.

46 Alfred Schutz, "Sartre's Theory of the Alter Ego," *Collected Papers*, vol. 1, (The Hague: Martinus Nijhoff, 1967), p. 203.

47 Schutz, in his commentary on certain documents, issued by the United Nations appears to underwrite the suggestion that "each individual should be able to decide voluntarily whether or not he (sic) belongs to a specific minority." Alfred Schutz, *Collected Papers*, vol. 2, p. 266.

48 Ibid., p. 262.

49 Ibid., p. 265.

50 For the contemporary debate between the supporters of redistribution versus the upholders of recognition, see the essays by Nancy Fraser and Iris Young in Cynthia Willett, ed., *Theorizing Multiculturalism*, (Oxford: Blackwell, 1998).

51 I. Kant, *Vorlesungen über Anthropologie*, Gesammelte Schriften, vol. 25, pt. 2, (Berlin: de Gruyter, 1997), p. 1187.

52 For an explanation of this point, see Albert Memmi, *Portrait du colonisé*, (Paris: Gallimard, 1985); trans. H. Greenfield, *The Colonizer and the Colonized*, (Boston: Beacon Press, 1967).

INDEX